THE
BEATLES
A TO Z

Beatles pose with their pets, 1967. (*Henry Grossman/Transworld*)

THE BEATLES
A TO Z

BY

Goldie Friede, Robin Titone,
and Sue Weiner

Methuen, New York

Acknowledgments

A compilation of this scope could not have been written without researching other Beatle books. They are too numerous to mention here, but they and their authors are listed alphabetically (naturally!) within the text of this book. Magazine, newspaper, and fanzine articles, radio and television programs, and records served as research sources, as did eyewitness accounts and firsthand information.

Our special thanks to:

Christine Freeman—special assistant—for giving her time, insights, typing, and never-ending support and encouragement. Without her this book would be lacking quite a few pages! Karen Rose, the rock book expert at Rock Read, whose interest and concern helped turn this book into a reality; Nicholas Schaffner, whose Beatle expertise was an invaluable asset; and our appreciation to Fred Jordan, Barbara Lagowski, Sukey Howard, Scott Sack, Herb Michelman, Lou O'Neill Jr., Joe Pope/*Strawberry Fields Forever,* Jane Reino, and Etty for their help and support. We also wish to thank our parents who survived our Beatlemania.

Library of Congress Cataloging in Publication Data

Weiner, Sue.
The Beatles A–Z.

1. Beatles—Dictionaries, indexes, etc.   I. Friede, Goldie, joint author.   II. Titone, Robin, joint author.   III. Title.
ML421.B4W4   784.5′4′00922   80-16819
ISBN   0-416-00781-3   (pbk.)

Printed and bound in the United States of America by
Kingsport Press, Kingsport, Tennessee
Designed by David Rogers

First Edition

Published in the United States of America by
Methuen, Inc.
733 Third Avenue
New York, N.Y. 10017

To John, Paul, George, and Ringo who have given us all so much . . .

Contents

THE
BEATLES
A TO Z

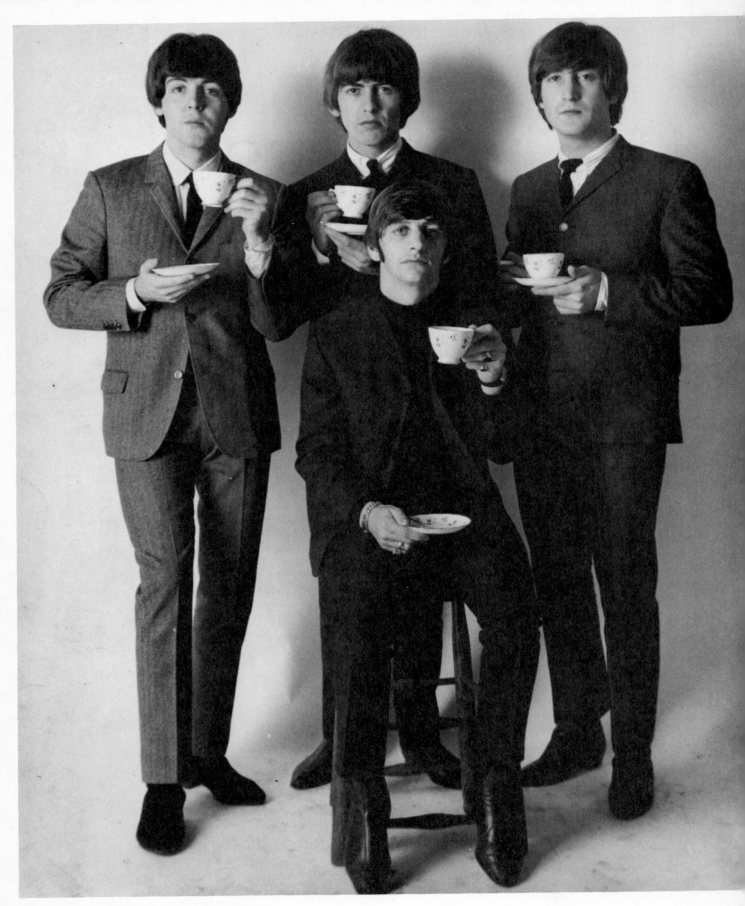

The Beatles, 1964. (*Keystone Press Agency*)

A

ABBEY ROAD
Artist: The Beatles
Producer: George Martin
Year first released: 1969
Record label: Apple
Tracks: 17

"Come Together"
"Something"
"Maxwell's Silver Hammer"
"Oh Darling"
"Octopus's Garden"
"I Want You"
"Here Comes the Sun"
"Because"
"You Never Give Me Your Money"
"Sun King"
"Mean Mr. Mustard"
"Polythene Pam"
"She Came In through the Bathroom Window"
"Golden Slumbers"
"Carry that Weight"
"The End"
"Her Majesty"

- This is the last album recorded by The Beatles as a group. John envisioned the album to be basic rock and roll, whereas Paul preferred a "rock symphony." The meshing of the two concepts resulted in a highly polished and skillfully produced recording encapsulating The Beatles' various styles throughout the previous years.
- ABBEY ROAD is the best-selling Beatles' album.
- The title is taken from a street in London where EMI Recording Studios is situated.
- The album won a Grammy Award.

Abbott, Pete
Recording engineer for The Beatles 1965 Hollywood Bowl Concert. He supplied the tapes for the album THE BEATLES AT THE HOLLYWOOD BOWL.

ABKCO
Allen Klein's management company which was affiliated with Apple Records, The Beatles' own record label, in 1969, after Klein became The Beatles' manager.

Able Label
Former European division of Ringo's record company, Ring O'Records. Able Label now serves as a production company.

ABRACADABRA
One of the tentative titles for the REVOLVER album.

Academy of Meditation
Maharishi Mahesh Yogi's Transcendental Meditation (TM) retreat in Shankaracharya Nagar in the Himalayas of India. The Beatles and their wives journeyed here to engage in a teacher-preparation course in meditation. They arrived at the Academy in February of 1968 and settled into ashrams (cottages) furnished with separate rooms for each member of the party. The camp included a large dining hall where breakfast was served early in the morning. Following the meal, all would gather in the lecture hall where the guru would conduct his seminars. Meditation and relaxation were all that was required for the rest of the day.

The Beatles spent most of their free time composing new songs, which later appeared on THE BEATLES album.

Though The Beatles' fervor for their new-found salvation could not be more sincere, the seeds of disenchantment were gradually being sown as the rigors of routine camp life started taking their toll. Ringo and his wife, Maureen, left the compound after only ten days, homesick for their children. Paul and Jane Asher were next to go, preferring to see the sights of India and travel on to Iran. John and George, along with their wives, held out for almost two months, but left suddenly, after becoming disillusioned with the Maharishi himself.

"Across the Universe"
Written by: Lennon/McCartney
Recorded by: The Beatles
Lead singer: John
Year first released: 1969
Record label: EMI's Starline (Britain); Apple (Britain and U.S.)
Album: NO ONE'S GONNA CHANGE OUR WORLD
        LET IT BE
        THE BEATLES 1967–1970
        THE BEATLES RARITIES
Performances: *Let It Be* movie

- The original recording was The Beatles' contribution to the World Wildlife Fund. The tempo and vocal arrangement differ from the later recording which appears on LET IT BE.
- David Bowie later recorded this song with John's guitar accompaniment.

Action for the Crippled Child
Charity for which John designed Christmas cards in 1966.

"Act Naturally"
Written by: Johnny Russell and Voni Morrison
Recorded by: The Beatles
Lead singer: Ringo
Year first released: 1965
Record label: Parlophone (Britain); Capitol (U.S.)

Album: HELP! (Britain)
"YESTERDAY" . . . AND TODAY
EP: YESTERDAY
Single: B side of "Yesterday" in U.S.
Performances: 1965 North American Tour (various cities)
"Ed Sullivan Show" (TV), 1965
1965 British Tour
"Cilla" TV show, 1965
"Ringo" TV show, 1978

Adler, Bill
Editor of the fan letters written to The Beatles which appear in the books *Dear Beatles* and *Love Letters to the Beatles*, both published in 1964.

Ad Lib, The
Exclusive London nightclub that The Beatles were members of in the mid-sixties.

Admiral Halsey
Character in the McCartney song "Uncle Albert/Admiral Halsey."

"After the Ball/Million Miles"
Written by: Paul McCartney
Recorded by: Wings
Lead singer: Paul
Year first released: 1979
Record label: Parlophone (Britain); Columbia (U.S.)
Album: BACK TO THE EGG
• Paul plays the concertina (squeeze box) on the second part of this song, "Million Miles."

"Again and Again and Again"
Written by: Denny Laine
Recorded by: Wings
Lead singer: Denny
Year first released: 1979
Record label: Parlophone (Britain); Columbia (U.S.)
Album: BACK TO THE EGG
Performances: 1979 Wings' British tour

"Ain't She Sweet"
Written by: Ager and Yellen
Recorded by: The Beatles
Lead singer: John
Year first released: 1964
Record label: Polydor (Britain); Atco (U.S.)
Album: THE BEATLES FIRST
THE EARLY YEARS
IN THE BEGINNING
Single: Britain and U.S.
• The Beatles recorded this song in 1961 in Hamburg, Germany, while backing singer Tony Sheridan.

"Ain't That a Shame"
Written by: Anton Domino and Dave Bartholemew
Recorded by: John
Lead singer: John
Year first released: 1975
Record label: Apple
Album: ROCK 'N' ROLL

"Ain't That Cute"
Song cowritten by George and Doris Troy. George produced Troy's recording of it in 1969.

"Aisumasen (I'm Sorry)"
Written by: John Lennon
Recorded by: John
Lead singer: John
Year first released: 1973
Record label: Apple
Album: MIND GAMES
• This was John's personal message to Yoko during their separation. "Aisumasen" is Japanese for "I'm sorry."

Akustik Studios
Recording studio in Hamburg, Germany, where The Beatles made their first studio recordings. They backed a member of Rory Storme and the Hurricanes on two numbers, "Summertime" and "Fever."

Albery Theatre
London theatre where Paul held auditions for a new Wings' drummer in 1974. Geoff Britton was hired out of the many eligibles.

Alchemical Wedding
Christmas party held at the Royal Albert Hall in London on December 18, 1968. John and Yoko sat on stage in a white bag for the event.

Aldo, Steve
Performer on the bill of The Beatles' 1965 British Tour.

Aldridge, Alan
Editor and contributing illustrator of the books *The Beatles Illustrated Lyrics, Volume I & II*. Aldridge designed the cover of George's WONDERWALL album and cover jacket for the British version of *The Beatles Authorized Biography*. Aldridge was also called upon to complete the design for The Beatles' Apple record label.

Alexander, David
Photographer who took the cover and inner sleeve photos of RINGO'S ROTOGRAVURE album.

Algernon
The mad scientist's assistant in the Beatles movie *Help!*, played by Roy Kinnear.

Alice Tully Hall
Concert hall located in New York's Lincoln Center. On January 10, 1972, Yoko, along with John's assistance, performed here. The performance had to be conducted from their seats in the audience, as they hadn't yet been granted U.S. work visas.

All about The Beatles
Book written by Edward DeBlasio and published by MacFadden-Bartell in 1964.

"All by Myself"
Written by: Richard Starkey and Vini Poncia
Recorded by: Ringo
Lead singer: Ringo
Year first released: 1975
Record label: Apple
Album: GOODNIGHT VIENNA

Allen, Dave
Performer on the same bill as The Beatles during their 1963 tour with Helen Shapiro.

Allison, Keith
American musician and 1960s Paul McCartney looka-like who in 1978 played guitar in Ringo's Roadside Attraction Band on the "Ringo" television special. He also cowrote two unreleased songs with Ringo, titled "All Right" and "It's Hard to Be Lovers."

"All I've Got to Do"
Written by: Lennon/McCartney
Recorded by: The Beatles
Lead singer: John
Year first released: 1963
Record label: Parlophone (Britain); Capitol (U.S.)
Album: WITH THE BEATLES
          MEET THE BEATLES

ALL MY LOVING (EP)
Artist: The Beatles
Producer: George Martin
Year first released: 1964
Record label: Parlophone
Tracks: 4
    "All My Loving"
    "Ask Me Why"
    "Money"
    "P.S. I Love You"
· British release

"All My Loving"
Written by: Lennon/McCartney
Recorded by: The Beatles
Lead singer: Paul

Year first released: 1963
Record label: Parlophone (Britain); Capitol (U.S.)
Album: WITH THE BEATLES
          MEET THE BEATLES
          THE BEATLES 1962–1966
          THE BEATLES AT THE HOLLYWOOD
              BOWL
EP: ALL MY LOVING
      4 BY THE BEATLES
Performances: Sunday Night at the London Palla-
                  dium, October 1963
                1964 Winter and Summer American
                  Tours
                "Ed Sullivan Show" (TV), 1964
                "Around the Beatles" TV show, 1964
                A Hard Day's Night movie (sound-
                  track)
· Paul thought of the lyrics to this song while shaving one morning. He was so excited, that he enthusiastically rushed downstairs to share his new song with the family he was living with at the time.

"All Right"
Unreleased song composed by Ringo and Keith Allison.

Allsop Place
London street located off Baker Street, where The Beatles and their "Magical Mystery Tour" bus began their two-week improvised journey for the filming of the movie *Magical Mystery Tour* in 1968. Paul, the film crew, and actors gathered at this point before embarking on the trip, and the other Beatles were picked up outside of London at Virginia Waters.

ALL THINGS MUST PASS
Artist: George Harrison
Producer: Phil Spector and George Harrison
Year first released: 1970
Record label: Apple
Tracks: 23
    "I'd Have You Anytime"
    "My Sweet Lord"
    "Wah-Wah"
    "Isn't It a Pity" (version one)
    "What Is Life"
    "If Not for You"
    "Behind that Locked Door"
    "Let It Down"
    "Run of the Mill"
    "Beware of Darkness"
    "Apple Scruffs"
    "Ballad of Sir Frankie Crisp (Let It Roll)"
    "Awaiting on You All"
    "All Things Must Pass"
    "I Dig Love"
    "Art of Dying"
    "Isn't It a Pity" (version two)

"Hear Me Lord"
"Out of the Blue"
"It's Johnny's Birthday"
"Plug Me In"
"I Remember Jeep"
"Thanks for the Pepperoni"
- This three-record package includes many songs written by George while he was still with The Beatles. Although George was never credited as being a major influence within The Beatles, on this album The Beatles' sound is more apparent than on any of the other Beatles' solo efforts.
- Despite the three-record price tag, ALL THINGS MUST PASS was George's most successful album.

"All Things Must Pass"
Written by: George Harrison
Recorded by: George
Lead singer: George
Year first released: 1970
Record label: Apple
Album: ALL THINGS MUST PASS
- This song was written in 1968 and slated for release on the LET IT BE album.
- George has stated that he was influenced by The Band when writing this song.

All This and WWII
1976 film consisting of actual footage from World War II set to the music of Lennon/McCartney, sung by various artists. A soundtrack album was released from this film.

"All Together Now"
Written by: Lennon/McCartney
Recorded by: The Beatles
Lead singer: Paul
Year first released: 1969
Record label: Apple
Album: YELLOW SUBMARINE
Performances: The Beatles introduce this song at the end of *Yellow Submarine*.

All Together Now
Discography of Beatle and Beatle-related records; written by Harry Castleman and Walter Podrazik. Published by Pierian Press in 1975, Ballantine Books in 1976.

All You Need Is Ears
Autobiography written by record producer George Martin and Jerome Hornsby, which includes several chapters pertaining to Martin's work with The Beatles. The book was published by St. Martin's Press in 1979.

"All You Need Is Love"
Written by: Lennon/McCartney
Recorded by: The Beatles
Lead singer: John
Year first released: 1967
Record label: Parlophone (Britain); Capitol (U.S.)
Album: MAGICAL MYSTERY TOUR
        YELLOW SUBMARINE
        THE BEATLES 1967–1970
Single: Britain and U.S.
- This song was written as The Beatles' message to the world for their live performance via satelite on the "Our World" television spectacular in 1967. The record was recorded during the live performance.

"All You Need Is Love"
British TV mini-series documentary on the history of rock music and The Beatles' contribution to it.

ALONG THE RED LEDGE
Hall and Oates album on which George plays guitar.

Alpha Band, The
Group on whose album SPARK IN THE DARK Ringo is featured on drums.

ALPHA OMEGA
A four-record set of Beatles' recordings released by Audio Tape, Inc. in 1972. This unauthorized release, which was quickly taken off the market, spurred Apple to produce THE BEATLES 1962–1966 and THE BEATLES 1967–1970.

A & M Records
American record company which distributed the records for George's Dark Horse record company from 1974–76. (See Dark Horse.)

A & M Studios
Los Angeles recording studio where George recorded his EXTRA TEXTURE album in 1975.

Americana Hotel
New York hotel where John and Paul held a press conference on May 13, 1968 to promote their newly formed record company, Apple. Two years prior to this, on August 22, 1966, two fans threatened to jump off the roof unless Paul, who was with the other Beatles across the street at the Warwick Hotel, agreed to meet them. The girls were brought down by the police before Paul could come to the rescue.

Anatomy of A Murder
Book Ringo was reading in the cafeteria scene, with Paul's grandfather, in the movie *A Hard Day's Night.*

Andersen, Oivind
Norwegian radio commentator who appears on the opening cut of the BACK TO THE EGG album.

"And I Love Her"
Written by: Lennon/McCartney
Recorded by: The Beatles
Lead singer: Paul
Year first released: 1964
Record label: Parlophone (Britain); United Artists and
                Capitol (U.S.)
Album: A HARD DAY'S NIGHT
            SOMETHING NEW
            THE BEATLES 1962–1966
            THE BEATLES RARITIES (U.S.)
            LOVE SONGS
EP: EXTRACTS FROM THE FILM A HARD
        DAY'S NIGHT
Single: U.S.
Performances: *A Hard Day's Night* movie
- This is one of Paul's first romantic ballads, written for his girlfriend, Jane Asher.
- John helped Paul write the middle eight bars of the song.
- THE BEATLES RARITIES contains a version with extra guitar riffs at the end.

Andrews, Nancy
American model who Ringo dated. She was named as correspondent in Ringo's wife Maureen's divorce suit against him in 1975. Nancy is credited with cowriting the song "Las Brisas" with Ringo, which appears on the album RINGO'S ROTOGRAVURE. She also took the photos for the cover and inner sleeve of his album BAD BOY.

"And the Sun Will Shine"
Paul Jones song in which Paul plays drums.

"And Your Bird Can Sing"
Written by: Lennon/McCartney
Recorded by: The Beatles
Lead singer: John
Year first released: 1966
Record label: Parlophone (Britain); Capitol (U.S.)
Album: REVOLVER (Britain)
            "YESTERDAY" . . . and TODAY

"Angela"
Written by: John Lennon and Yoko Ono
Recorded by: John and Yoko
Lead singer: John and Yoko
Year first released: 1972
Record label: Apple
Album: SOMETIME IN NEW YORK CITY
Performances: "The David Frost Show" (TV), 1972
                (U.S.)

- This song was written for Angela Davis, who was on trial for conspiring in the prison break of her boyfriend, George Jackson.

"Angel Baby"
This song was recorded by John and scheduled to be released on his ROCK 'N' ROLL album. The song did not appear on that album, although it is included on the bootleg album, ROOTS.

Angelus, Paul
Actor who dubbed in Ringo's voice in the *Yellow Submarine* movie.

"Anna"
Written by: Arthur Alexander
Recorded by: The Beatles
Lead singer: John
Year first released: 1963
Record label: Parlophone (Britain); Vee Jay and Capitol (U.S.)
Album: PLEASE PLEASE ME
            INTRODUCING THE BEATLES
            THE EARLY BEATLES
EP: THE BEATLES (NO. 1)
        THE BEATLES

"Annie"
Unreleased Beatles song which was recorded during the SGT. PEPPER sessions in 1967.

Annie
Theatrical musical production for which McCartney Productions Ltd. owns the music publishing rights. Paul and his family attended the New York and London performances of the play. Paul took out full-page ads in the Sunday *New York Times* and the *London Sunday Times* to congratulate the play on its success.

A.N. Other
Superstar rock group formed for one performance on the Rolling Stones TV extravaganza, "Rock and Roll Circus." The group consisted of John Lennon, Eric Clapton, Keith Richards, and Mitch Mitchell. The show was filmed on December 11, 1968, but was never aired.

"Another Day"
Written by: Paul and Linda McCartney
Recorded by: Paul and Linda
Lead singer: Paul
Year first released: 1971
Record label: Apple
Album: WINGS GREATEST
Single: Britain and U.S.
- This record was Paul's first solo single. The record caused a tremendous controversy due to the composing credit. Sir Lew Grade (ATV) owned the publish-

ing rights to all of Paul's and John's songs until 1976, and claimed that Paul had only given Linda songwriting credit to guarantee a share for himself of the songwriting royalties. Paul and Linda denied the allegation, but the McCartney/McCartney songwriting partnership was dissolved after the legal battle which ensued.

• John knocks this song in his song "How Do You Sleep?"

"Another Girl"
Written by: Lennon/McCartney
Recorded by: The Beatles
Lead singer: Paul
Year first released: 1965
Record label: Parlophone (Britain); Capitol (U.S.)
Album: HELP!
Performances: *Help!* movie

"Another Hard Day's Night"
Instrumental version of the Lennon/McCartney song "A Hard Day's Night." It appears on the American HELP! album, and is heard on the soundtrack of the movie *Help!* when The Beatles are in an Indian restaurant.

"Answer's at the End, The"
Written by: George Harrison
Recorded by: George
Lead singer: George
Year first released: 1975
Record label: Apple
Album: EXTRA TEXTURE

• This song was inspired by an inscription on the wall of George's Henley estate: "Scan not a friend with a microscopic glass, for you know his faults, now let his foibles pass."

Anthony, Les
John's personal chauffeur in the mid-sixties.

"Any Time at All"
Written by: Lennon/McCartney
Recorded by: The Beatles
Lead singer: John
Year first released: 1964
Record label: Parlophone (Britain); Capitol (U.S.)
Album: A HARD DAY'S NIGHT (Britain)
              SOMETHING NEW
              ROCK AND ROLL MUSIC
EP: EXTRACTS FROM THE ALBUM A HARD
         DAY'S NIGHT

Apple Corps Ltd.
Company established by The Beatles in 1967 to manage their partnership and to finance newcomers in the entertainment industry. The Beatles invested two million dollars into Apple's five divisions: records, films, electronics, retailing, and publishing. The Beatles, as presidents of the company, took an active role at its inception. Their concept of Apple was for it to be a "haven for the struggling artist," and The Beatles were determined to see their ideal realized within an open-door policy in an office run on trust and love. The majority of the executives were musicians and artists who could prove more sympathetic to the creative mind than suit-and-tie businessmen and who could ensure that the company would stay true to its "everyone gets a bite of the Apple" philosophy.

On December 7, 1967, Apple's first venture opened to the public. Ninety-four Baker Street was the site of the Apple Boutique. The designers, The Fool, worked on the premises, fashioning mod styles. John nicknamed the shop the "psychedelic Woolworth's."

In April of 1968, the first Apple headquarters was opened at 95 Wigmore Street in London. The original Apple executive lineup was as follows:

Presidents—John Lennon, Paul McCartney, George Harrison, and Richard Starkey
Managing Director—Neil Aspinall
A & R (Artists and Repertoire) Man for Apple Records and Chief In Charge of New Talent—Peter Asher
Assistant Managing Director—Malcolm Evans
Director of Public Relations—Derek Taylor
Electronics Expert—Alex Mardas
Manager of Films—Dennis O'Dell
Division Head of Records (dealing in overseas transactions)—Ron Kass
Consultant—Brian Lewis
Beatles' Personal Assistant/Director of Social Events—Peter Brown
Art Director—Jeremy Banks
Apple Films Assistant/Record Publicist—Tony Bramwell

On August 30, 1968 Apple's first recording, "Hey Jude"/"Revolution" was released. Apple's records were distributed by Capitol Records in America, Canada, and Mexico, while EMI Records distributed Apple Records to the rest of the world. Within one month, Apple sold over three million records. By 1969, the company had opened offices in Canada, France, West Germany, Switzerland, Italy, Sweden, the Netherlands, and America. The rapidly growing list of Apple artists soon included The Beatles, James Taylor, Mary Hopkin, Jackie Lomax, the Iveys (Badfinger), Doris Troy, White Trash, Billy Preston, the Modern Jazz Quartet, Radha Krishna Temple, and the Plastic Ono Band. In keeping with Apple's policy, artists' contracts were not mandatory. The company, with The Beatles as its political and musical leaders, was off to a flourishing start in its record division.

Meanwhile Apple's other divisions could not claim the same success. The Apple Boutique closed down after only eight months. Apple's electronics and publishing division had yet to get beyond the planning stages. The only other division holding its own was the film division, with its profits stemming from the production of The Beatles' movies.

By the middle of 1969 it became painfully apparent that Apple was running into financial trouble. Despite its high record sales, the company was taking a loss due to poor investments and misguided management. The Beatles soon learned of money being squandered on the lavish expenditures of their Apple staff, who were now residing in plush offices at 3 Saville Row. The lax and unbusinesslike setting led to a party atmosphere, with the participants getting all they could for free. Cars were bought on company expense accounts, office furniture could never be accounted for, and the food and liquor bills were exorbitant. Apple had become a haven for the shifless rather than for the creative, and had become a headache for its mentors, The Beatles.

After John and Paul each took turns running Apple, a decision was made to bring in experienced establishment advisors to sort out the Apple mess. Eastman and Eastman, a New York law firm, was brought in to salvage Apple's finances. The Eastmans were suggested to The Beatles by Paul's girlfriend at the time, Linda, who also happened to be Lee V. Eastman's daughter. Their official title was "financial advisors," yet it wasn't long before the Eastmans were comfortably settling in as managers of Apple. Just as everything seemed to be running smoothly, another New York advisor arrived on the scene.

Allen Klein, notorious rock manager, best known for his shrewd yet forthright manner, caught the eye of John Lennon. John introduced Klein as his personal choice for financial advisor, only a few weeks after the Eastmans were installed at Apple. George and Ringo were also swayed by Klein, and, with a vote of three-to-one, Allen Klein was put in charge of Apple. Paul alone stood loyal to his original choice of the Eastmans, refusing to let Klein represent him in any of The Beatles' business negotiations.

The Beatles had now become divided in their views on how to run their own partnership, and Apple had become a company riddled with dissension among its top executives as well as the struggling artists they employed. Allen Klein fired many of the useless personnel on the payroll and other employees quit, refusing to work under Klein's reign. Peter Asher, one of Apple's chief assets in the record production field, left the company, taking his fledgling discovery, James Taylor, with

him. Even Apple's highly respected director, Neil Aspinall, resigned due to the stifling atmosphere Apple's new management had created. Though it was true that Apple's books were finally being balanced, the core of the Apple philosophy had been eaten away. The Beatles' original enthusiasm had turned to disgust and disappointment. Paul, who had been Apple's most ardent supporter, left the company to pursue his own interests, abandoning Apple to the ruthless few who had taken control of *his* company—without his consent.

On August 4, 1970, the Apple press office closed down. Apple Corps Ltd.'s only function now was to collect Beatle royalties and deal with unfinished business. Six months later, on December 31, 1970, Paul began a high court action to dissolve all remaining connections between himself and Apple, which forced him to dissolve all connections between himself and the other three Beatles. Paul requested a receiver be appointed to collect debts accruing to the partnership. His claims of mismanaged monies by Allen Klein were opposed by the other Beatles. After months of court battles, on March 13, 1971, Paul won the first stage in dissolving The Beatles. A receiver for The Beatles' monies was appointed by the court. Though The Beatles still had contractual commitments to Apple up until 1976, they were able to fulfill their obligations with their individual recordings. The Beatles as a group had ceased to exist, and only the hollow shell of Apple stood to remind them of their past. Apple today is still in litigation, while it continues to collect Beatle royalties.

Applejacks, The
Group which recorded the Lennon/McCartney song "Like Dreamers Do."

"Apple Scruffs"
Written by: George Harrison
Recorded by: George
Lead singer: George
Year first released: 1970
Record label: Apple
Album: ALL THINGS MUST PASS
Single: B side of "What Is Life?" in U.S.
• Apple Scruffs was the affectionate name given the fans who stood vigil outside The Beatles' recording studios and Apple offices. Upon completion of the song, George invited them into the studio to hear his tribute to them.

Apple Studio
Recording studio built in the basement of the Apple headquarters at 3 Saville Row. The designer of the studio was Apple's ace electronics genius "Magic" Alex Mardas. The cost of the renovation was over $500,000. The Beatles recorded portions of their LET IT BE album here and are shown working in the studio in the

Let It Be movie. The studio was also used in several of The Beatles' solo ventures.

Apple Tailoring (Civil and Theatrical)
Apple franchise which opened on May 28, 1968 at 161 Kings Road in Chelsea, England. The shop supplied theatrical costumes. It closed within a year.

Apple to the Core
Book written by Peter McCabe and Robert D. Schonfeld; published by Pocket Books in 1972. This book is a technical account of the rise and fall of the Apple Empire.

APPROXIMATELY INFINITE UNIVERSE
Yoko Ono album which John coproduced. The cover is identical to John's MIND GAMES album, except his face is substituted by hers.

A & R Studios
Lagos, Nigeria recording studio where Paul recorded portions of his album BAND ON THE RUN. The studio was owned by ex-Cream member, Ginger Baker.

Arnold Grove (12)
George Harrison's birthplace and first home. It is located in Wavertree, Liverpool, England.

Arrowsmith, Clive
Photographer who took the sequence of facial photos which appear on the back cover of the album WINGS AT THE SPEED OF SOUND. He also took the group photo on WINGS GREATEST. Some of Arrowsmith's work also appears in *The Beatles Illustrated Lyrics.*

"Arrow through Me"
Written by: Paul McCartney
Recorded by: Wings
Lead singer: Paul
Year first released: 1979
Record Label: Parlophone (Britain); Columbia (U.S.)
Album: BACK TO THE EGG
Single: Britain and U.S.
Performances: Promo film clip/ "Back to the Egg" TV special, 1979
1979 Wings' British Tour
• There are no guitars played on this song; the sound is achieved through the use of a moog synthesizer and brass section.

"Art of Dying, The"
Written by: George Harrison
Recorded by: George
Lead singer: George
Year first released: 1970
Record label: Apple

Album: ALL THINGS MUST PASS
• This song was written in 1966, but George felt it was "too far out" to appear on a Beatles' album.

Arts Laboratory
Exhibition hall in London where John held his first art show in the summer of 1968. The exhibit featured John's sculpture, "Built Around," and many art pieces created by Yoko.

Arvi, M.V.
Luxury boat which The Beatles and their families used when they vacationed in Greece in July 1967. A year later, George rented the boat when he and his entire family returned to Greece.

Ascher, Kenny
Piano player appearing on John's MIND GAMES and WALLS AND BRIDGES albums.

Ascot Sound Studio
Recording studio John installed on his Ascot estate. He recorded several tracks of his IMAGINE album here.

Asher, Jane
British actress, born on April 5, 1946, who is best known for her true life role as Paul's former fiancée. Jane started acting professionally when she was only five years old and has been performing ever since, appearing in such stage and screen successes as *The Masque of the Red Death, Alfie, The Buttercup Chain, The Deep End, Henry the VIII, The Philanthropist, Romeo and Juliet,* and *Whose Life Is It Anyway?*

Jane and Paul met when she was covering a Beatles' concert as a teenage reporter for the *Radio Times* in 1963. Jane became Paul's constant companion, though, in order to avoid publicity, she tried to keep a low profile. A dedicated actress devoted to her craft, Jane did her best to maintain her accomplished career while under the constant scrutiny of press and public for her Beatle-girlfriend status. Though she desperately tried to keep her personal and professional lives separate, there was no respite from the public's only concern—whether she would become Mrs. McCartney. Despite the strain all this interference put on Jane, she refused to let the pressures destroy the love that she and Paul had attained.

Paul moved into Jane's family's home in London in 1963. He lived here for three years, and during that time, Jane introduced Paul to London's cultural offerings. Paul looked to Jane to help him in his quest for self-improvement. He began studying music seriously under the instruction of Jane's mother, a music professor, and tried his hand at learning to read and write music. His first written piece was presented to Jane for her to play on her classical guitar. Jane was the inspiration for most of Paul's love ballads.

In 1966, Paul and Jane moved from the Asher residence to Paul's new home in St. John's Wood, London. Jane helped him select the house and decorate the interior. Unlike the other Beatles, who had settled near each other in the suburbs, Paul elected to remain in London and pursue his interests with Jane. She also encouraged Paul to purchase a secluded farm in Scotland where they could escape from the rigors of public life. Though Paul and Jane had planned to marry on several occasions, they were hampered in their attempts by their commitments to their respective careers. Paul wanted Jane to give up acting full time to become a wife and mother. Jane was unwilling to stay home and end her career while her husband was engrossed with his Beatle activities. It was this impasse which was never reconciled. They became engaged to marry on December 25, 1967, but the relationship was to end approximately six months later. Jane remarked "I know it sounds corny, but we still see each other and love each other, but it hasn't worked out. Perhaps we'll be childhood sweethearts and meet again and get married when we're about seventy." Paul was never to comment publicly on the split.

Jane is now married to cartoonist Geralde Scafe and is the mother of their daughter, Kate, born in 1974.

Asher, Peter
Former member of the Peter and Gordon singing duo and brother of Jane Asher. Peter became a close friend of Paul and the other Beatles during the 1960s. Paul and John gave Peter several original compositions to record which launched Peter and Gordon's career.

In 1968 Peter was appointed A & R (Artists and Repertoire) man for Apple Records and was in charge of discovering and developing new talent. He remained with Apple for a year, before resigning along with his protégé, James Taylor.

Peter now resides in Los Angeles and manages and produces James Taylor and Linda Ronstadt. He is considered one of the world's top record producers.

Ashton, Gardner, and Dyke
Recording artists on whose album I'M THE SPIRITUAL BREADMAN George is featured on guitar.

"Ask Me Why"
Written by: Lennon/McCartney
Recorded by: The Beatles
Lead singer: John
Year first released: 1963
Record label: Parlophone (Britain); Vee Jay and Capitol (U.S.)
Albums: PLEASE PLEASE ME
INTRODUCING THE BEATLES
JOLLY WHAT! FRANK IFIELD ON STAGE
THE EARLY BEATLES
THE BEATLES LIVE AT THE STAR CLUB (Britain)
EP:ALL MY LOVING
THE BEATLES
Single:B side of "Please Please Me" in Britain
· Performed at the audition for Parlophone Records in 1962.

Aspinall, Neil
Beatles' head road manager, born on October 13, 1942 in Liverpool. Neil's job was to oversee that all went according to plan on The Beatles' tours. Neil was a schoolmate of George's and Paul's and a close friend of The Beatles' ex-drummer, Pete Best. He was studying to be an accountant when he began driving The Beatles to and from their local gigs in 1960, but he eventually gave up his studies to work full time for the group. In 1964 Neil wrote a syndicated monthly column, "Beatles and Me." He was highly regarded by The Beatles for his intellect and loyalty. In 1968, Neil was appointed as the director of Apple Corps Ltd. He also produced the *Let It Be* movie.

Neil is still working as The Beatles' representative in the ongoing negotiations concerning the dissolution of Apple.

Astaire, Fred
Dancer extraordinaire who made a cameo appearance in John's *Imagine* film. Paul dedicated his song, "You Gave Me the Answer," to Fred Astaire when he performed it during the Wings' 1975–76 World Tour.

As Time Goes By
Book written by Derek Taylor and published by Straight Arrow Press in 1973. The book deals in part with Taylor's involvement as press officer for The Beatles.

Astoria Theatre
Theatre in Finsbury Park, England where the Beatles played the three-week engagement of their 1963 Christmas shows, December 24–January 11, 1964.

Astor Towers
Hotel in Chicago where The Beatles held their first press conference of their 1966 American Tour. It was here that John publicly apologized to America for his controversial remarks on Christianity. (See Maureen Cleave.)

Atlantic Records
American record company which Ringo was contracted to from 1975 through 1978.

"Atlantis"
Donovan song on which Paul plays tambourine and sings background vocals.

"Attica State"
Written by: John Lennon and Yoko Ono
Recorded by: John and Yoko
Lead singer: John
Year first released: 1972
Record label: Apple
Album: SOMETIME IN NEW YORK CITY
Performances: John Sinclair Benefit in Ann Arbor, Michigan
     One to One Concert, 1972
     "The David Frost Show" (TV), (U.S.)
     "The Mike Douglas Show" (TV), (U.S.)

- This song was written following the killings of prisoners and prison guards at Attica State Prison in New York, when Rockefeller, who was then governor, sent in troops to stop the Attica uprising.
- In November of 1971 John performed at a benefit concert for Attica at New York's Apollo Theatre.

Attitudes
Group signed to Dark Horse Records in 1975. The group was comprised of Jim Keltner, Paul Stallworth, Danny Kortchmar, and David Foster. Ringo plays drums on their GOOD NEWS album.

ATV
Associated Television (ATV) is the British company which gained control of Northern Songs in 1969 after a dramatic power struggle with The Beatles for the publishing rights to their songs. ATV now owns the publishing rights to all Lennon/McCartney compositions. (See Northern Songs.)

"Au"
Song performed live by John, Yoko, and Frank Zappa and the Mothers of Invention at the Fillmore East in 1971. The composition is recorded live on the album SOMETIME IN NEW YORK CITY.

Auntie Gin
Character mentioned in the Wings' song, "Let 'Em In."

"Auntie Gin's Theme"
Working title of the song "I've Just Seen a Face." Paul's Aunt Gin was fond of this song, hence the temporary title. The George Martin Orchestra recorded an instrumental version of "I've Just Seen a Face" under this title.

Aunt Jessie
Ringo's fictitious aunt in the *Magical Mystery Tour* film.

Avenue Clinic
London hospital where two of Paul and Linda's children, Mary and James Louis, were born. Paul was in the delivery room for Mary's birth.

"Awaiting on You All"
Written by: George Harrison
Recorded by: George
Lead singer: George
Year first released: 1970
Record label: Apple
Album: ALL THINGS MUST PASS
   THE CONCERT FOR BANGLA DESH
Performances: The Concert for Bangla Desh, 1971

B

"Baby Don't Go"
Song John performed with Frank Zappa and the Mothers of Invention at the Fillmore East in 1971. This song was also a favorite with The Beatles in their early years.

"Baby Face"
Song recorded by Wings and the Tuxedo Brass Band while Paul and the group were visiting New Orleans in 1975. The session was filmed for the finale of the yet-to-be released film *The Sound of One Hand Clapping*.

"Baby It's You"
Written by: Hal David and Burt Bacharach
Recorded by: The Beatles
Lead singer: John
Year first released: 1963
Record label: Parlophone (Britain); Vee Jay and Capitol (U.S.)
Album: PLEASE PLEASE ME
INTRODUCING THE BEATLES
THE EARLY BEATLES

"Baby Jane I'm Sorry"
Unreleased Beatles' song recorded in 1965.

"Baby's Heartbeat"
Track which appears on the album UNFINISHED MUSIC NO. 2: LIFE WITH THE LIONS. The sound is the heartbeat of the child Yoko was carrying just prior to her miscarriage.

"Baby's in Black"
Written by: Lennon/McCartney
Recorded by: The Beatles
Lead singer: John and Paul
Year first released: 1964
Record label: Parlophone (Britain); Capitol (U.S.)
Album: BEATLES FOR SALE
BEATLES '65
EP: BEATLES FOR SALE (NO. 2)
Performances: 1964 Christmas shows
1965 North American Summer Tour
1965 European Summer Tour
1965 British December Tour
1966 Summer World Tour

"Baby's Request"
Written by: Paul McCartney
Recorded by: Wings
Lead singer: Paul
Year first released: 1979
Record label: Parlophone (Britain); Columbia (U.S.)
Album: BACK TO THE EGG

Single: B side of "Getting Closer" in Britain
• This sentimental "cocktail lounge" ballad was originally intended for the Mills Brothers to record.

"Baby You're a Rich Man"
Written by: Lennon/McCartney
Recorded by: The Beatles
Lead singer: John
Year first released: 1967
Record label: Parlophone (Britain); Capitol (U.S.)
Album: MAGICAL MYSTERY TOUR
Single: B side of "All You Need Is Love"
Performances: Heard on the soundtrack of *Yellow Submarine*
• Brian Jones plays the oboe on this song.
• In 1967, George serenaded hippies in Haight Ashbury, San Francisco, while he and Pattie strolled through Golden Gate Park singing this song.

Bach, Barbara
Actress who appears opposite Ringo in the movie *Caveman*. Since meeting on the set, they have been dating.

"Back in the USSR"
Written by: Lennon/McCartney
Recorded by: The Beatles
Lead singer: Paul
Year first released: 1968
Record label: Apple
Album: THE BEATLES
THE BEATLES 1967–1970
ROCK AND ROLL MUSIC
Single: Rereleased as a British single in 1976.
• The song's title originated from the "I'm Backing Britain" campaign which was enacted in England in 1968. The lyrics were intended to be "I'm Backing the USSR" but evolved into the present title.
• The song's sound is a deliberate mixture of Chuck Berry's "Back in the USA" set to the Beach Boys' music style.
• It was first written for model Twiggy to record on an album, but The Beatles decided to use the song themselves.
• John and George play bass on this song, while Paul plays lead guitar.

"Back Off Boogaloo"
Written by: Richard Starkey
Recorded by: Ringo
Lead singer: Ringo
Year first released: 1972
Record label: Apple
Album: BLAST FROM YOUR PAST
Single: Britain and U.S.

- Boogaloo was a name originally used by The Beatles as one of Paul's code names.
- The song was produced by George.

"Back Seat of My Car"
Written by: Paul McCartney
Recorded by: Paul
Lead singer: Paul
Year first released: 1971
Record label: Apple
Album: RAM
Single: Britain

BACK TO THE EGG
Artist: Wings
Producer: Paul McCartney and Chris Thomas
Year first released: 1979
Record label: Parlophone (Britain); Columbia (U.S.)
Tracks: 14
   "Reception"
   "Getting Closer"
   "We're Open Tonight"
   "Spin It On"
   "Again and Again and Again"
   "Old Siam, Sir"
   "Arrow through Me"
   "Rockestra Theme"
   "To You"
   "After the Ball"/"Million Miles"
   "Winter Rose"/"Love Awake"
   "The Broadcast"
   "So Glad to See You Here"
   "Baby's Request"
- Wings' first album for Columbia Records.
- Though Paul employed a number of renowned musicians to help out on the various tracks, the album did not fare as well as expected.

"Back to the Egg"
Thirty-minute promotional TV film consisting of "Baby's Request," "Getting Closer," "Old Siam, Sir," "Winter Rose"/"Love Awake," "Spin It On," "Arrow through Me," and "Good Night Tonight." The show was filmed and edited by Keef Productions.

"Backwards Traveller"
Written by: Paul McCartney
Recorded by: Wings
Lead singer: Paul
Year first released: 1978
Record label: Parlophone (Britain); Capitol (U.S.)
Album: LONDON TOWN

"Bad Boy"
Written by: Larry Williams
Recorded by: The Beatles
Lead singer: John
Year first released: 1965
Record label: Parlophone (Britain); Capitol (U.S.)
Album: A COLLECTION OF BEATLES OLDIES
   BEATLES VI
   ROCK AND ROLL MUSIC
   THE BEATLES RARITIES (Britain)

BAD BOY
Artist: Ringo
Producer: Vincent Poncia
Year first released: 1978
Record label: Polydor (Britain); Portrait (U.S.)
Tracks: 10
   "Who Needs a Heart"
   "Bad Boy"
   "Lipstick Traces (On a Cigarette)"
   "Heart on My Sleeve"
   "Where Did Our Love Go"
   "Hard Times"
   "Tonight"
   "Monkey See Monkey Do"
   "Old Time Relovin' "
   "A Man Like Me"
- Ringo's first album for Portrait Records.
- Parts of the album were performed on the "Ringo" TV special in 1978.

"Bad Boy"
Written by: L. Armstrong/A. Long
Recorded by: Ringo
Lead singer: Ringo
Year first released: 1978
Record label: Polydor (Britain); Portrait (U.S.)
Album: BAD BOY

Badfinger
Group signed to Apple Records in 1968, under the name The Iveys. The group, which later became Badfinger, consisted of Pete Ham, Joey Molland, Mike Gibbons, and Tom Evans. In 1969 Paul wrote and produced their song "Come and Get It," which they recorded for the soundtrack of the movie *The Magic Christian*.

Molland and Evans perform on John's song "I Don't Want to Be a Soldier," and the entire group is heard on George's albums ALL THINGS MUST PASS and THE CONCERT FOR BANGLA DESH (at which they appeared). In 1971 George coproduced their album STRAIGHT UP and their hit single "Day After Day." Badfinger recorded for Apple until 1973. In 1975 Pete Ham committed suicide and the rest of the group went their separate ways. Joey Molland and Tom Evans reformed as Badfinger in 1978.

"Badfinger Boogie"
Original title for "With a Little Help from My Friends."

"Badge"
Cream song written by George Harrison and Eric Clapton. George was indirectly responsible for the song's title when Eric misread a notation by George inserted in the lyrics for a "bridge" between verses. The music was also used by George as the middle section of his song "Here Comes the Sun." In 1971 George and Eric performed the song live at Eric's concert at the Rainbow Theatre.

"Bad to Me"
Lennon/McCartney song written for and recorded by Billy J. Kramer and the Dakotas in 1963.

Bagism
John and Yoko's concept of attaining peace through the elimination of discrimination. They demonstrated their concept at several public functions such as concerts, exhibitions, and TV shows by conducting their interviews from within big bags. "It's a concept. It doesn't matter who you are or what you're like—it's just what you say."

Bag One
Portfolio of John's erotic lithograph prints. (See London Arts Gallery.)

Bag Productions
Company set up by John and Yoko in 1969 to handle art and film ventures they did apart from The Beatles. John felt that in this way he might be able to salvage some of his material from "going down the Apple drain." In 1969 Bag Productions released seven of John and Yoko's films, *Smile, Two Virgins, Rape, Self-Portrait, Apothesis, Apothesis No. 2,* and *Imagine.*

Bain, Bob
Performer on the bill with The Beatles during their 1964 British Fall Tour.

Baker, Celia
Costume designer who helped design Wings' outfits for their 1975–76 World Tour.

Balasco, Ralph
Attorney who handled John and Yoko's custody case for Yoko's daughter, Kyoko, against Yoko's ex-husband Anthony Cox.

"Ballad of John and Yoko, The"
Written by: Lennon/McCartney
Recorded by: The Beatles
Lead singer: John
Year first released: 1969
Record label: Apple
Album: THE BEATLES AGAIN (HEY JUDE)
            THE BEATLES 1967–1970
Single: Britain and U.S.
Performances: Promo film clip

• This was the last Beatles' single recorded.
• John and Paul recorded the song alone in the studio in one day. Paul played drums, bass, and piano; John played guitar and sang lead.
• This song was banned because of the use of the word "Christ."

"Ballad of New York, The"
Song written by John, Yoko, and David Peel, which appears on David Peel's album THE POPE SMOKES DOPE.

"Ballad of Sir Frankie Crisp, The"
Written by: George Harrison
Recorded by: George
Lead singer: George
Year first released: 1970
Record label: Apple
Album: ALL THINGS MUST PASS
• Sir Frankie Crisp was the architect who designed George's castle in Henley.

Bambi, The
Cinema in Hamburg which served as The Beatles' sleeping quarters during their engagements in Germany in 1960. The theatre was allegedly set on fire by Paul and Pete Best, and they were jailed for one night and then deported. Paul later claimed that they were framed by a club owner who was taking revenge for a broken contract between himself and The Beatles.

Band, The
American group who came to prominence after backing Bob Dylan. The Band performed on the RINGO album after George arranged for them to play on the song he had written for Ringo, "Sunshine Life For Me (Sail Away Raymond)." For the Band's last concert at the Winterland in November, 1977, Ringo played drums on their performance of "I Shall Be Released" and on a thirty-minute jam. Ringo is seen in the film of the concert, *The Last Waltz,* and is on the soundtrack album.

"Band of Steel"
Song written by Ringo and recorded by Guthrie Thomas. Ringo helps on vocals on Thomas's recording.

BAND ON THE RUN
Artist: Paul McCartney and Wings
Producer: Paul McCartney
Year first released: 1973
Record label: Apple
Tracks: 9 (Britain); 10 (U.S.)
    "Band on the Run"
    "Jet"
    "Bluebird"
    "Mrs. Vanderbilt"
    "Let Me Roll It"

"Mamunia"
"No Words"
"Helen Wheels" (Only in U.S.)
"Picasso's Last Words"
"Nineteen Hundred and Eighty-five"
- Henry McCullough and Denny Seiwell left the band just prior to the scheduled recording of the album in Lagos, Nigeria, but despite Wings' personnel problems, the finished product was Wings' first great success. The album stayed at the top of the charts for three years.
- It was one of the first rock albums to be released in Russia.
- This is Paul's favorite Wings album, as he considers it a personal triumph of will in the face of adversity. He believes it was the success of this album which decided the fate of Wings.
- The album won a Grammy Award.

"Band on the Run"
Written by: Paul McCartney
Recorded by: Wings
Lead singer: Paul
Year first released: 1973
Record label: Apple
Album: BAND ON THE RUN
        WINGS OVER AMERICA
        WINGS GREATEST
Single: Britain and U.S.
Performances: Promo film clip on the photographing of the album cover was screened to the live music during Wings' 1975–76 World Tour.
        1979 Wings' British Tour
- Paul's favorite Wings song.

"Bangla Desh"
Written by: George Harrison
Recorded by: George
Lead singer: George
Year first released: 1971
Record label: Apple
Album: THE CONCERT FOR BANGLA DESH
        THE BEST OF GEORGE HARRISON
Single: Britain and U.S.
Performances: Concert for Bangla Desh, N.Y., 1971
        Promo film clip
- This song was written by George to gather support for the war-torn country of Bangla Desh, which also happened to be the homeland of his friend and teacher, Ravi Shankar.

"Bangla Dhun"
Piece performed by Ravi Shankar and his Indian orchestra at the Concert for Bangla Desh in 1971. The performance can be heard on the album THE CONCERT FOR BANGLA DESH.

Banks, Jeremy
Art director and partner of Derek Taylor in Apple's Press Office from 1968–69.

Bank Street
Location in New York's Greenwich Village where John and Yoko lived in a basement apartment from 1972–73. A photo of the apartment building appears on the album cover for SOMETIME IN NEW YORK CITY.

Baron Knights with Duke D'mond
Group on the bill of The Beatles' 1963 Christmas shows.

Barron, Bill
Captain of the Chinese junk that Paul, John, and the Apple executives rented while in New York in May of 1968. They held a business meeting on the boat as it sailed around Manhattan.

Barrow, Tony
Senior press officer for The Beatles. Barrow joined the Nems staff on May 1, 1963. He was hired by Brian Epstein to publicize the relatively unknown Beatles. To this effort, Barrow worked fervently making up flyers, circulars, and leaflets advertising all the group's engagements. Brian became aware of Tony Barrow through the column Barrow wrote for the *Liverpool Echo* under the name "Disker." Brian asked Barrow for advice on how to get The Beatles a recording contract, and Barrow helped arrange their audition with Decca Records. Although their first audition did not get them a contract, it wasn't long before Tony Barrow became the publicist for the world's most popular recording artists. Barrow handled the press releases pertaining to the group during the 1960s, and was responsible for many writing projects, including the editing of the MAGICAL MYSTERY TOUR booklet, which was included in the American album and in the British EP.

Bartlett, Orin
Former F.B.I. agent hired by Wings to head the security on the Wings over America Tour in 1976. Bartlett's main concern was to check out concert halls for bombs.

Baruch, Klaus
German hairdresser who was responsible for cutting John's hair for his role in the movie *How I Won the War*. The cutting took place in Germany on September 6, 1966 at 7:30 A.M.

Bassinini, Roberto
Ex-husband of Cynthia Lennon. Cynthia married the wealthy Italian hotel owner in 1970 and they were divorced three years later.

Battan, Peter
Actor who dubbed the voice for George in the movie *Yellow Submarine*.

Bayard Gallery
Art Gallery located in the Soho section of New York City. It was here that an exhibit of Linda McCartney's photos was on display from May 6 to June 1, 1978.

B. B. King
American blues artist on whose album, B. B. KING IN LONDON, Ringo plays drums.

Beach Boys, The
American group who popularized the "surf sound" during the 1960s. Paul, who feels their song "God Only Knows" is the best song ever written, produced The Beach Boys song "Vegetables" on their SMILEY SMILE album. Aside from professional collaborations, The Beatles and The Beach Boys were good friends,· joining together in many social activities, such as Mike Love and Bruce Johnston performing at The Beatles' party for *Magical Mystery Tour* in 1967. Love also attended the Academy of Meditation along with The Beatles in India in 1968.

The Beatles have openly credited the Beach Boys' style with influencing their writing of "Back in the USSR." In 1976 Paul and Linda attended The Beach Boys' concert in Anaheim, California, and they appear in the made-for-TV film of the event.

Beat Brothers, The (Beat Boys)
Name The Beatles used when recording with Tony Sheridan in Germany in 1961. The name was given them by the record producers because "The Beatles" alluded to a German vulgarity and was therefore an unsuitable title to record under.

Beatcomber
Pseudonym used by John when he wrote for Liverpool's music newspaper, *Mersey Beat,* in the early sixties. John dubbed himself with this alias as a take-off on the *Daily Express* newspaper's column "Beachcomber," which influenced his writings and drawings.

Beatle Book, The
Book published by Lancer in 1964, consisting of Beatle photographs taken by one-time Beatles photographer, Dezo Hoffman.

Beatlefan
National fund devised by John in 1966 to provide food and aid to famine-stricken countries. The organization never got past the planning stages.

Beatle Haircut
Bangs and hair covering the ears became the Beatles' most recognizable trademark as they started their climb to fame. This style, which was to revolutionize men's fashion, at first horrified parents of "clean-cut" teenagers in 1964.

The style came about when The Beatles were working in Germany in the early 1960s. Astrid Kirschner, the fiancée of then Beatle, Stu Sutcliffe, convinced Stu to brush his hair forward in the "French" style, as did many of her art student friends. After The Beatles stopped laughing at Stu, they too decided to give it a try. John was the last holdout, not wishing to abandon the "greasy look," but finally relented while visiting Paris with Paul a few months later.

Beatlemania
Term used to describe the state of the youth of the Western world during The Beatles' reign in the 1960s. This general hysteria was caused by the emotional excitement generated by having any contact with The Beatles or Beatle-related events. In 1977 *The National Lampoon* characterized Beatlemania as the "forgotten disease" and as far as can be seen it is still very prevalent in today's society.

Beatlemania
One of the original titles for the movie *A Hard Day's Night.* The title was rejected by The Beatles.

Beatlemania
Theatre production which attempted to produce a musical simulation of The Beatles. The musical opened on Broadway in 1977 for a limited engagement, but due to its huge success its run continued for three years. The producers, Leiber and Krebs, were sued by The Beatles in 1979 in protest over this unauthorized production.

Beatles, The

DEVELOPMENT

The Beatles began when Paul McCartney joined John Lennon's group, The Quarrymen, in June of 1955. George Harrison, another school friend, was soon inducted into the group and together with Stu Sutcliffe (bass guitar) and Peter Best (drums), The Beatles evolved. They played local clubs in Liverpool (under various names), but The Beatles' unique sound was not established until they began performing, night after night—for hours on end—in the seedy clubs of Hamburg, Germany in the early sixties. It was during these engagements that the group perfected their skill and style, as they were also given the opportunity to establish a stage presence and build a rapport with the demanding German audiences.

In 1961 Stu Sutcliffe left The Beatles. He remained in Hamburg to pursue his art studies while the others returned to Liverpool to reacquaint themselves with English audiences. Paul replaced Stu on bass, George remained on lead guitar, and John provided his talents on rhythm guitar and mouth organ. With the exception of drummer Ringo Starr, The Beatles' musical line-up was complete. The boys returned from Germany with something which set them apart from the other struggling Liverpool groups—"the Beatle haircut." Now with their long hair, leather jackets, and tight pants they looked as rebellious as their music sounded. Though John and Paul had begun composing early in The Beatles' career, the nucleus of The Beatles' stage act remained cover versions of their favorite rock 'n' roll and blues records. At this point in their career, John, Paul, and George shared equally on lead vocals during their performing sets.

On November 9, 1961, Brian Epstein, a local record shop owner, ventured into The Cavern club to see the group he'd been hearing so much about. He was immediately drawn to The Beatles, as their personalities on stage demonstrated a raw charm and unique musical style. Within one month, Epstein became The Beatles' manager. He encouraged the group to refine their act and polish up their appearance in order to obtain a more general appeal. He also arranged for The Beatles to audition for a major record company. In 1962 they cut a demonstration record for Decca Records, which was eventually rejected by the company. Brian took the rejected tapes to various record companies with no success, until he hit upon producer George Martin of EMI Records.

George Martin's assignment for EMI's Parlophone label was to discover new musical talent to help launch the label. Though The Beatles did not stun Martin with their talent, he did see promise in the group and signed them to record for Parlophone. Though everything was looking good for the Liverpool boys with the London-based record company, another problem was surfacing. The general consensus by The Beatles and mentors was that drummer Pete Best would have to go. Though reasons for Best's ouster have remained vague, Pete was out and Ringo Starr, another Liverpool drummer, was in—just in time for The Beatles' first recording session.

The Beatles' popularity was growing steadily throughout Britain, causing chaotic scenes wherever they performed. Their records were quickly climbing the charts and all systems were go, but there was still one horizon yet to conquer. In early 1964 The Beatles were scheduled to appear in the United States. Their first visit was sprung with an advance publicity budget of one million dollars. The media was saturated with pro-Beatles hype, even before the group was formally introduced to the nation. But once The Beatles were presented to the country, via the nationwide broadcast of the "Ed Sullivan Show" all hype aside, America fell in love with The Beatles. Beatlemania had now become a worldwide phenomenon, as they toured Europe, North America, Australia, Scandinavia, and Japan.

Their stage performance had been perfected after years on the road. John's squinting stare combined with his amusing dry wit perfectly balanced Paul's charming winks and smiles, which were calculated to send squeals throughout the audience. George, standing between the two, intense in his concentration on the guitar, and Ringo in the background, diligently keeping the steady drumbeat while shaking his head in time, completed The Beatles' picture. Everyone could claim a favorite Beatle, each with their individual talents contributing to the chemistry of the group's performance, yet when two or more Beatles joined their heads at the microphone to sing in harmony, the effect was electrifying.

MUSIC

The Beatles' music was composed everywhere—from hotel restaurants to backstage dressing rooms—as the Lennon/McCartney composing team flourished. They wrote together and apart, gathering ideas for songs from such diverse places as television commercials, advertisement posters, and newspaper articles, as well as their own personal experiences. Although the Lennon/McCartney credit was given to every song, it was not difficult to tell which Beatle composed the major part of each song. John's style was often raw, yet sensitive beneath the biting edge. He was reaching out to a higher level, using lyrics that had never been sung or even thought of in quite the same way before. Paul's soft ballads, either tenderly loving or painfully sad, exposed a man searching for an understanding in his own life. Together they perfectly complimented one another's songwriting styles, with each Lennon/McCartney composition a guaranteed chartbuster. Though The Beatles' music was predominantly composed by John and Paul, George Harrison too was showing songwriting ability. He contributed a few songs to The Beatles' repertoire, but being up against the Lennon/McCartney trademark limited his efforts to only one or two songs per album.

The Beatles were especially interested in utilizing and experimenting with sophisticated recording techniques in order to enhance their music. Over-dubbing, redubbing, backwards, forwards, orchestrated, synthesized, acoustic, or electrified; all methods of creating the desired effect on record were employed by The Beatles in the recording studio.

MOVIES

Not only did the public get to know The Beatles through their musical performances, but they were also entertained by the group in their feature films. *A Hard Day's Night,* filmed in 1964, was their first movie and this fictional-documentary musical chronicled The Beatles' life on the road. Their impact on the screen was almost as great as that on record. With their natural charm and exceptional looks, The Beatles' movie career was launched with great success. Of all the group, Ringo's

Beatles in Liverpool, 1963.
(*Rex Features*)

The Beatles, with George Martin and Brian Epstein,
receive a British Disc Award, 1964.
(*courtesy of Joe Pope/Strawberry Fields Forever.*)

The Beatles with Ed Sullivan, 1964. (*Retna*)

The Beatles perform on "The Ed Sullivan Show," 1964.
(*courtesy of Joe Pope/Strawberry Fields Forever.*)

The Beatles in concert, 1965.
(*David Redfern/Retna*)

The Beatles return to "The Ed Sullivan Show," 1965. (*courtesy of Vinnie Zuffante*)

Paul and John with friend, 1966.
(*Keystone Press Agency*)

The Beatles parodying themselves, 1967.
(*courtesy of Joe Pope/*
Strawberry Fields Forever.)

The Beatles and their wives are in attendance at
the Maharishi's London lecture, 1967. (*Popperfoto*)

George's 25th birthday celebration in India. (*Popperfoto*)

George and Ringo on the set of "A Hard Day's Night." (*courtesy of Joe Pope/ Strawberry Fields Forever.*)

Beatles and cast of "Magical Mystery Tour" take five from filming. (*Keystone Press Agency*)

hn, Peter Brown, Neill Aspinall, Derek Taylor, and Paul.
he formation of Apple, 1968. (*Transworld Features Syndicate*)

Ringo, Linda and Paul meet in New York.
(*Vinnie Zuffante*)

The Beatles "rooftop concert," January 30, 1969. (*Apple Records*)

performance showed the most natural acting ability, and he was featured in The Beatles' second movie *Help!* Though *Help!* was filmed with a bigger budget and was the group's first color movie, The Beatles felt that the fantasy plot was not as stimulating or clever as that of *A Hard Day's Night.* Their movie career was halted, while The Beatles preferred to wait until an appropriate script was submitted.

In 1967 The Beatles created and produced a one-hour, made-for-television movie in which they starred. The movie, *Magical Mystery Tour,* was produced as an elaborate home movie with the cast and crew never exactly knowing what would be happening next. They hired a coach to travel the countryside with themselves and crew on board. The script was improvised as they went about their mystery tour to the soundtrack of The Beatles' music. The movie was not favorably reviewed in the press and was proclaimed The Beatles' "first official failure."

By 1969, The Beatles had still not fulfilled their three-movie contract to United Artists. In order to comply with the agreement, The Beatles allowed themselves to be filmed while working in the recording studio. This resulted in the feature film *Let It Be.*

BEATLEMANIA

The Beatles' phenomenal success was in high gear by 1964. They had become the leaders of a generation as the teenage population of the Western world looked to The Beatles to set the standards in music, fashion, and social attitudes. Their songs consistently topped the music charts, as their record sales soared. On October 26, 1965, The Beatles were invested by the Queen as Members of the British Empire (MBE) for their service to Britain's export industry. The Beatles had become a public commodity, as the eyes of the world watched, analyzed, and evaluated their every move.

During the height of their career The Beatles remained each others' closest friends. In Ringo's words they were "siamese quads," each instinctually attuned to the other's needs and wants. The many years spent working together since adolescence had culminated in a bizarre whirlwind of fame with the four boys at the eye of the storm. This common bond separated The Beatles from loved ones and friends alike. Together they faced the pressures and inconsistencies of superstardom, relying on each other to help keep themselves rooted in reality.

By the end of 1966 The Beatles decided to forego touring and instead concentrate on their musical progression in the recording studio. It was during this period that The Beatles resolved to pursue separate interests. John tried his hand at acting; George furthered his religious studies; Paul composed a movie score; and Ringo cameoed in various films.

They began to search for a means of achieving an inner tranquility to go along with their financial freedom. It was a time for introspection and self-awareness, as The Beatles' songs reflected the mood of a generation. The summer of 1967 was launched to the theme of "All You Need Is Love" as the alienated flower children ran to the tune of "She's Leaving Home."

THE BREAKUP

Apple Corps Limited was established by The Beatles in 1968. The company's primary function was to manage The Beatles (Brian Epstein had died the previous year) as well as to discover and represent new talent. The Beatles took an active role as Apple's presidents and worked enthusiastically on its development.

The Beatles were experiencing many personal changes during this time. John had begun a serious relationship apart from The Beatles with his new love, Yoko Ono. His musical interest had veered toward the avant-garde, preferring his musical creations with Yoko to The Beatles' more "conventional" sound. Paul, on the other hand, had experienced a personal upset with the dissolution of his long-time engagement to Jane Asher. The Beatles had become ever more important to Paul as he directed all of his energies into his music. By this time, George's confidence had grown enough to demand equal time for his talents in the recording studio. Even Ringo had threatened to quit the group several times due to the atmosphere of tension and pressure.

Despite their personal and musical differences, they managed to work out their problems until the final blow to The Beatles' unit came with the conflict over who should preside as manager of the group. Apple had become a mess of squandered monies and unhappy artists. It was apparent that someone was needed to straighten out the books or the company would soon go under. Paul elected to entrust his company's business dealings to his soon-to-be in-laws, New York attorneys Lee and John Eastman. John, and later George and Ringo, preferred the guidance of another from New York, music manager Allen Klein.

The power struggle soon spilled over into the courts with The Beatles pitted against one another in their quest to attain their individual preference regarding money management. Paul sued the other Beatles along with Allen Klein in order to insure representation by his own choice of agents, the Eastmans. On April 10, 1970 The Beatles officially broke up.

TODAY

In 1964 The Beatles predicted their run would probably last no longer than five years. It so happens that The Beatles last album was recorded in 1969. Though the group had stopped recording and performing together as a unit, their recording contract did not expire for another seven years. All of their solo records up until 1976 were bound together financially due to this previous commitment and each member shared in any losses or gains. Despite the success of The Beatles as solo artists, the public still clamored for the group's reunion. Each Beatle, since the split, has taken turns either denying or encouraging the possibilities of a reunion.

"If Yoko and Linda did it (caused the split) they deserve the credit." John, 1971

"At times I wish we were together, and at times not." George, 1971

"How can The Beatles ever get together again if George won't play with Paul?" Ringo, 1974

"I'm sure if we ever did anything it would be in 1976 when the contract runs out." John, 1974

"It's a probably not, with the possibility of a maybe." Paul, 1976

"No reunion. If we're getting together we'll tell you." Ringo, 1976

"I suppose if The Beatles, all the other three, were really wild keen to do it and it looked like a real great thing to go and do, then there's a real slim chance I'd kind of say, yeah o.k." Paul, 1979

The Beatles have not yet reunited in any official capacity. Though a reunion has seemed imminent at times, due mostly to overzealous promoters talking through their hats, The Beatles have remained content to carry on with their individual pursuits. Paul has evolved into a major recording artist of the seventies; George and Ringo continue to perform and record on their own; John has elected to retire from the entertainment field for the time being and devote himself to his family. Though a decade has passed since The Beatles performed together, their mass appeal as a group has never dwindled. Beatles revivals continue to flourish as millions of fans press on to keep The Beatles' memory alive.

On May 20, 1979, Paul, Ringo and George reunited in a social capacity for a spontaneous concert performed at a party given by Eric and Pattie Clapton. Since that ray of hope, another rumor of gigantic proportions was spurred on when the United Nations became involved in a promoter's drive to get The Beatles together to raise money for the Cambodian refugees.

Though The Beatles have not succumbed to the public pressure to reinstate the group, there seems to be no letup in the fans' optimism concerning a reunion. One thing is for certain, as long as there are Beatles, there will always be the possibility of seeing them together once more.

BEATLES, THE

Artist: The Beatles
Producer: George Martin
Year first released: 1968
Record label: Apple
Tracks: 30

"Back in the USSR"
"Dear Prudence"
"Glass Onion"
"Ob-la-di, Ob-la-da"
"Wild Honey Pie"
"The Continuing Story of Bungalow Bill"
"While My Guitar Gently Weeps"
"Happiness Is a Warm Gun"
"Martha My Dear"
"I'm So Tired"
"Blackbird"
"Piggies"
"Rocky Raccoon"
"Don't Pass Me By"
"Why Don't We Do It in the Road"
"I Will"
"Julia"
"Birthday"
"Yer Blues"
"Mother Nature's Son"
"Everybody's Got Something to Hide except for Me and My Monkey"
"Sexy Sadie"
"Helter Skelter"
"Long Long Long"
"Revolution 1"
"Honey Pie"
"Savoy Truffle"
"Cry Baby Cry"
"Revolution 9"
"Good Night"

- The first Beatles album to be released on Apple Records.
- The Beatles' first double album. They decided to record a double-record package in order to fulfill their contract to EMI as soon as possible. The majority of songs were written while The Beatles were studying meditation in India.
- Ringo quit for two weeks during the recording of this album, due to a row with Paul.
- John called this album "Son of SGT. PEPPER."
- In The Beatles' most musically versatile package, their distinct individual styles can be heard, as very little collaboration went on within the group on any of the songs.
- The album's plain white cover was chosen to contrast with the ornate SGT. PEPPER cover released the previous year. The original album cover for THE BEATLES was set to be a drawing of the group in a

fantasy setting, but it was scrapped when they decided the connection was too similar to that of YELLOW SUBMARINE.

BEATLES, THE (EP)
Artist: The Beatles
Producer: George Martin
Year first released: 1964
Record label: Vee Jay
Tracks: 4
    "Misery"
    "A Taste of Honey"
    "Ask Me Why"
    "Anna"
- U.S. release.

Beatles, The
Biography published in 1968 by Signet Press; authored by Anthony Scaduto.

Beatles, The
Children's book published in 1974 by Creative Education; written by Patricia Pirmington.

BEATLES AGAIN, THE (HEY JUDE)
Artist: The Beatles
Producer: George Martin
Year first released: 1970
Record label: Apple
Tracks: 10
    "Can't Buy Me Love"
    "I Should Have Known Better"
    "Paperback Writer"
    "Rain"
    "Lady Madonna"
    "Revolution"
    "Hey Jude"
    "Old Brown Shoe"
    "Don't Let Me Down"
    "The Ballad of John and Yoko"
- U.S. release, which consists of the A and B sides of some of The Beatles' hit singles.
- The album was released in Britain in 1979.
- The album is also referred to as the "HEY JUDE album" due to the printing on the binding of the album cover.

Beatles Again, The
Book published in 1978 by Pierian Press. The book's authors are Harry Castleman and Walter Podrazik. It is "Part Two" of *All Together Now*.

Beatles: An Illustrated Record, The
Discography published in 1975 by Harmony Books. Updated editions published in 1978 and 1980. Authored by Roy Carr and Tony Tyler.

Beatles around the World, The
Movie released in 1978 consisting of film clips and newsreels of The Beatles throughout their career.

Beatles: A Study in Drugs, Sex, and Revolution, The
Book written by David Noebel; published in 1968 by the Christian Crusade. It condemns The Beatles as a destructive influence on society.

BEATLES AT THE HOLLYWOOD BOWL, THE
Artist: The Beatles
Producer: George Martin
Year first released: 1977
Record label: Parlophone (Britain); Capitol (U.S.)
Tracks: 13
    "Twist and Shout"
    "She's a Woman"
    "Dizzy Miss Lizzie"
    "Ticket to Ride"
    "Can't Buy Me Love"
    "Things We Said Today"
    "Roll Over Beethoven"
    "Boys"
    "A Hard Day's Night"
    "Help!"
    "All My Loving"
    "She Loves You"
    "Long Tall Sally"
- Live recordings from The Beatles' performances at Los Angeles' Hollywood Bowl on August 23, 1964 and August 30, 1965.
- George Martin remixed all of the tapes for this album.
- Though The Beatles were against releasing the album due to the fair sound quality, the company was free to release the material after The Beatles' contract had expired.

Beatles: The Authorized Biography, The
Biography published in 1968 by William Heindmann Ltd. in Britain and by McGraw-Hill in America. The book was written by Hunter Davies, who researched the work with the full cooperation of The Beatles. McGraw-Hill paid $150,000 for the publishing rights, claiming this was the biggest advance on royalties ever made by the company for a single book until that time. The book was on the best seller list in November of 1968. It was reprinted with a new intro and postscript in 1978. The American and British editions are slightly different, with the British edition containing a few additional pages.

Beatles Book, The
Essays on The Beatles published in 1968 by Cowles; edited by Edward E. Davis.

Beatles Book Monthly
British magazine booklet devoted to The Beatles. The magazine was first issued in August 1963 and published monthly until December of 1969. It contained photos, interviews, and updates. The editor, Johnny Dean, reissued *Beatles Book Monthly* in 1976 under the title *The Beatles Book Appreciation Society Magazine*. It contains the original book plus updated information.

"Beatles Cartoon, The"
Thirty-nine episode cartoon series produced by Al Brodax for King Features, made for American television in 1965. The Beatles reluctantly agreed to the series, though none of their voices were lent to those of the animated figures of the group. The series was not shown in England, due to The Beatles' dissatisfaction with the quality of the show.

BEATLES CHRISTMAS ALBUM, THE
Compilation of all the Christmas messages The Beatles recorded for their fan club members from 1963–69. This album was the last gift The Beatles gave their American fans. It was never sold commercially.

BEATLES FEATURING TONY SHERIDAN IN THE BEGINNING, THE
American album released on Polydor in 1970. The album contains material taken from the early sixties when The Beatles performed as back-up band for singer Tony Sheridan in Hamburg, Germany.

BEATLES' FIRST, THE
British album released in 1964 on Polydor Records. The album includes songs which The Beatles recorded in Hamburg, Germany backing singer Tony Sheridan.

Beatles Forever, The
Book written by Nicholas Schaffner; published by Cameron Press/Stackpole Books, in 1978 (McGraw-Hill—paperback).

BEATLES FOR SALE
Artist: The Beatles
Producer: George Martin
Year first released: 1964
Record label: Parlophone
Tracks: 14
  "No Reply"
  "I'm a Loser"
  "Baby's in Black"
  "Rock and Roll Music"
  "I'll Follow the Sun"
  "Mr. Moonlight"
  "Kansas City"
  "Eight Days a Week"

  "Words of Love"
  "Honey Don't"
  "Every Little Thing"
  "I Don't Want to Spoil the Party"
  "What You're Doing"
  "Everybody's Trying to Be My Baby"
• British release.

BEATLES FOR SALE (EP)
Artist: The Beatles
Producer: George Martin
Year first released: 1965
Record label: Parlophone
Tracks: 4
  "No Reply"
  "I'm a Loser"
  "Rock and Roll Music"
  "Eight Days a Week"
• British release.

BEATLES FOR SALE (NO. 2) (EP)
Artist: The Beatles
Producer: George Martin
Year first released: 1965
Record label: Parlophone
Tracks: 4
  "I'll Follow the Sun"
  "Baby's in Black"
  "Words of Love"
  "I Don't Want to Spoil the Party"
• British release.

Beatles Get Back, The
Booklet which was originally included in the LET IT BE album package (except in U.S.). The authors are Jonathan Cott and David Dalton, with photos by Ethan Russell. The book contains dialogue and movie stills during rehearsals.

BEATLES' HITS, THE (EP)
Artist: The Beatles
Producer: George Martin
Year first released: 1963
Record label: Parlophone
Tracks: 4
  "From Me to You"
  "Thank You Girl"
  "Please Please Me"
  "Love Me Do"
• British release.

Beatles Illustrated Lyrics (I and II), The
Two volumes edited by Alan Aldridge. First published in 1969, second published in 1971, both by Delacorte Press. The books contain the works of contemporary artists illustrating and interpreting The Beatles' song lyrics. In 1975, the two volumes were published as a paperback without the illustrations.

Beatles in Their Own Words
Book of Beatle quotes compiled by Miles; published by Music Sales in England in 1978.

BEATLES LIVE AT THE STAR CLUB IN HAMBURG, GERMANY 1962, THE
Artist: The Beatles
Producer: Larry Grossberg, Larry Halpern, and Mitchell Margo
Year first released: 1977
Record label: Lingasong
Tracks: 26

BRITAIN

"I Saw Her Standing There"
"Roll Over Beethoven"
"Hippy Hippy Shake"
"Sweet Little Sixteen"
"Lend Me Your Comb"
"Your Feet's Too Big"
"Twist and Shout"
"Mr. Moonlight"
"A Taste of Honey"
"Besame Mucho"
"Reminiscing"
"Kansas City"
"Nothin' Shakin' "
"To Know Her Is to Love Her"
"Little Queenie"
"Falling In Love Again"
"Ask Me Why"
"Be-Bop-A-Lula"
"Hallelujah, I Love Her So"
"Red Sails in the Sunset"
"Everybody's Trying to Be My Baby"
"Matchbox"
"I'm Talking About You"
"Shimmy Shake"
"Long Tall Sally"
"I Remember You"

U.S.

"Roll Over Beethoven"
"Hippy Hippy Shake"
"Sweet Little Sixteen"
"Lend Me Your Comb"
"Your Feet's Too Big"
"Mr. Moonlight"
"A Taste Of Honey"
"Besame Mucho"
"Kansas City"
"Nothin' Shakin' "
"To Know Her Is to Love Her"
"Little Queenie"
"Falling In Love Again"
"Be-Bop-A-Lula"
"Hallelujah, I Love Her So"

"Red Sails in the Sunset"
"Everybody's Trying to Be My Baby"
"Matchbox"
"I'm Talking About You"
"Shimmy Shake"
"Long Tall Sally"
"I Remember You"
"I'm Gonna Sit Right Down and Cry"
"Where Have You Been All My Life"
"Till There Was You"
"Sheila"

- This two-record set was put out by one-time Beatles' agent Allan Williams. The tapes, recorded by King-Size Taylor and Paul Murphy during The Beatles performance at The Star Club, cost the producers $85,-000 to improve the sound quality.
- These tapes were offered to Brian Epstein when he became The Beatles' manager, but due to poor sound quality he rejected the suggestion that he pay a substantial amount for the tapes.
- The Beatles were against the release of the album, but their move to stop its production fell through.

BEATLES MILLION SELLERS, THE (EP)
Artist: The Beatles
Producer: George Martin
Year first released: 1965
Record label: Parlophone
Tracks: 4
   "She Loves You"
   "I Want to Hold Your Hand"
   "Can't Buy Me Love"
   "I Feel Fine"
- British release.

BEATLES 1962–1966, THE
Artist: The Beatles
Producer: George Martin
Year first released: 1973
Record label: Apple
Tracks: 26
   "Love Me Do"
   "Please Please Me"
   "From Me to You"
   "She Loves You"
   "I Want to Hold Your Hand"
   "All My Loving"
   "Can't Buy Me Love"
   "A Hard Day's Night"
   "And I Love Her"
   "Eight Days a Week"
   "I Feel Fine"
   "Ticket to Ride"
   "Yesterday"
   "Help!"
   "You've Got to Hide Your Love Away"
   "We Can Work It Out"

"Day Tripper"
"Drive My Car"
"Norwegian Wood"
"Nowhere Man"
"Michelle"
"In My Life"
"Girl"
"Paperback Writer"
"Eleanor Rigby"
"Yellow Submarine"
• Two-record compilation of Beatles hits.

BEATLES 1967–1970, THE
Artist: The Beatles
Producer: George Martin
Year first released: 1973
Record label: Apple
Tracks: 28
    "Strawberry Fields Forever"
    "Penny Lane"
    "Sgt. Pepper's Lonely Hearts Club Band"
    "With a Little Help from My Friends"
    "Lucy in the Sky with Diamonds"
    "A Day in the Life"
    "All You Need Is Love"
    "I Am the Walrus"
    "Hello Goodbye"
    "The Fool on the Hill"
    "Magical Mystery Tour"
    "Lady Madonna"
    "Back In the USSR"
    "While My Guitar Gently Weeps"
    "Hey Jude"
    "Revolution"
    "Ob-la-di Ob-la-da"
    "Get Back"
    "Don't Let Me Down"
    "The Ballad of John and Yoko"
    "Old Brown Shoe"
    "Here Comes the Sun"
    "Come Together"
    "Something"
    "Octopus's Garden"
    "Let It Be"
    "Across the Universe"
    "The Long and Winding Road"
• Two-record set consisting of a compilation of Beatles'
  hits.

BEATLES (NO. 1), THE (EP)
Artist: The Beatles
Producer: George Martin
Year first released: 1963
Record label: Parlophone
Tracks: 4
    "I Saw Her Standing There"

"Misery"
"Anna"
"Chains"
• British release.

BEATLES RARITIES, THE
Artist: The Beatles
Producer: George Martin
Year first released: 1979
Record label: Parlophone
Tracks: 17
    "Across the Universe"
    "Yes It Is"
    "This Boy"
    "The Inner Light"
    "I'll Get You"
    "Thank You Girl"
    "I Want to Hold Your Hand" ("Komm, Gib Mir
        Deine Hand"—second pressing)
    "You Know My Name (Look Up the Number)"
    "She Loves You" ("Sie Liebt Dich"—second press-
        ing)
    "Rain"
    "She's a Woman"
    "Matchbox"
    "I Call Your Name"
    "Bad Boy"
    "Slow Down"
    "I'm Down"
    "Long Tall Sally"
• The songs contained on this album are "rare" due to
  the different mixes, which are not heard on any of the
  previous releases of the same songs.
• The album was originally included in the BEATLES
  COMPLETE, a set of British albums released by
  Capitol Records in the U.S. Sold in Britain as a single
  record.

BEATLES RARITIES, THE
Artist: The Beatles
Producer: George Martin
Year first released: 1980
Record label: Capitol
Tracks: 15
    "Love Me Do"
    "Misery"
    "There's a Place"
    "Sie Liebt Dich"
    "And I Love Her"
    "Help!"
    "I'm Only Sleeping"
    "I Am the Walrus"
    "Penny Lane"
    "Helter Skelter"
    "Don't Pass Me By"
    "The Inner Light"
    "Across the Universe"

"You Know My Name (Look Up the Number)"
"Sgt. Pepper's Inner Groove"
- Album cover contains the notorious "butcher block" photo which was pulled from the cover of "YESTERDAY"... AND TODAY in 1966, when a public protest was raised over the gory pose.
- U.S. release.

BEATLES SECOND ALBUM, THE
Artist: The Beatles
Producer: George Martin
Year first released: 1964
Record label: Capitol
Tracks: 11
    "Roll Over Beethoven"
    "Thank You Girl"
    "You Really Got a Hold on Me"
    "Devil in Her Heart"
    "Money"
    "You Can't Do That"
    "Long Tall Sally"
    "I Call Your Name"
    "Please Mr. Postman"
    "I'll Get You"
    "She Loves You"
- U.S. release.
- This album consists of more songs written by other artists than any other American album by The Beatles.

BEATLES VI
Artist: The Beatles
Producer: George Martin
Year first released: 1965
Record label: Capitol
Tracks: 11
    "Kansas City"
    "Eight Days a Week"
    "You Like Me Too Much"
    "Bad Boy"
    "I Don't Want to Spoil the Party"
    "Words of Love"
    "What You're Doing"
    "Yes It Is"
    "Dizzy Miss Lizzie"
    "Tell Me What You See"
    "Every Little Thing"
- U.S. release.

BEATLES '65
Artist: The Beatles
Producer: George Martin
Year first released: 1964
Record label: Capitol
Tracks: 11
    "No Reply"
    "I'm a Loser"

    "Baby's in Black"
    "Rock and Roll Music"
    "I'll Follow the Sun"
    "Mr. Moonlight"
    "Honey Don't"
    "I'll Be Back"
    "She's a Woman"
    "I Feel Fine"
    "Everybody's Trying to Be My Baby"
- U.S. release.

BEATLES' STORY, THE
Two-record documentary of The Beatles' early career; includes interviews and snatches of songs. Released on Capitol Records in America in 1964.

BEATLES TAPES FROM THE DAVID WIGG INTERVIEWS, THE
Two-record set released on Polydor Records in Britain in 1977. Each side is a separate interview between Wigg and each Beatle, conducted between December 1968 and December 1973. Ringo and George lost their bid to have the record stopped before it was released.

Beatles, the Fabulous Story of John, Paul, George, and Ringo, The
Book written by Robert Burt and Jeremy Pascall; published by Octopus Press in 1975.

Beatles: The Real Story, The
Book written by Julius Fast; published by Putnam in 1968.

Beatles Trivia Quiz Book, The
Book written by Helen Rosenbaum; published by Signet in 1978.

Beatles up to Date, The
Book published by Cancer in 1964.

BEATLES WITH TONY SHERIDAN AND THEIR GUESTS, THE
Album released on MGM Records in 1964. The Beatles appear on four songs: "My Bonnie," "Cry For a Shadow," "The Saints," and "Why."

Beatles: Words without Music, The
Book of Beatle quotes compiled by Rick Friedman; published by Grosset and Dunlap in 1968.

Beatles—Yesterday... Today... Tomorrow, The
Book written by Rochelle Larkin; published by Scholastic Books in 1974.

Beatmakers, The
A group comprised of The Beatles and Gerry and the Pacemakers. They joined together for a one-night per-

formance at Litherland Town Hall in Liverpool in 1961. George played lead guitar, John was on piano, and Paul played rhythm guitar.

BEAUCOUPS OF BLUES
Artist: Ringo
Producer: Pete Drake
Year first released: 1970
Record label: Apple
Tracks: 11
> "Beaucoups of Blues"
> "Love Don't Last Long"
> "Fastest Growing Heartache in the West"
> "Without Her"
> "Woman of the Night"
> "I'd Be Talking All the Time"
> "$15 Draw"
> "Wine, Women, and Loud Happy Song"
> "Loser's Lounge"
> "Waiting"
> "Silent Homecoming"

- Ringo recorded this country-western flavored album in Nashville, Tennessee.
- This was the first album by any of The Beatles to be recorded outside of Great Britain.
- The album was reissued in 1976 with a different cover.

"Beaucoups of Blues"
Written by: Buzz Rabin
Recorded by: Ringo
Lead singer: Ringo
Year first released: 1970
Record label: Apple
Album: BEAUCOUPS OF BLUES
Single: U.S.

"Beautiful Dreamer"
The Beatles performed this song on the "Saturday Club" radio show in January of 1963.

"Beautiful Girl"
Written by: George Harrison
Recorded by: George
Lead singer: George
Year first released: 1976
Record label: Dark Horse
Album: 33⅓

"Be-Bop-a-Lula"
Written by: Gene Vincent and Tex Davis
Recorded by: John
Lead singer: John
Year first released: 1975
Record label: Apple
Album: ROCK 'N' ROLL
THE BEATLES LIVE AT THE STAR CLUB

- Live version by The Beatles with lead singer Horst Obber (a waiter).
- One of the first songs Paul played for John when they met in June 1955.

"Because"
Written by: Lennon/McCartney
Recorded by: The Beatles
Lead singer: John
Year first released: 1969
Record label: Apple
Album: ABBEY ROAD
- John wrote all the lyrics for this song.
- George feels this contains the best Beatle harmonies of any of their songs.
- A piece of this music was first heard on John and Yoko's THE WEDDING ALBUM.

Bed-in For Peace
In 1969 John and Yoko held a series of press conferences from their honeymoon suite in order to promote world peace. They decided to use the publicity which followed their every move in a positive and constructive way. Their first bed-in took place in Amsterdam's Hilton Hotel and another was held soon afterward in Montreal's Queen Elizabeth Hotel. Segments of these conferences are included in THE WEDDING ALBUM.

"Beef Jerky"
Written by: John Lennon
Recorded by: John
Lead singer: None (Instrumental)
Year first released: 1974
Record label: Apple
Album: WALLS AND BRIDGES
Single: B side of "Whatever Gets You thru the Night" (U.S.)

"Be Here Now"
Written by: George Harrison
Recorded by: George
Lead singer: George
Year first released: 1973
Record label: Apple
Album: LIVING IN THE MATERIAL WORLD

"Behind that Locked Door"
Written by: George Harrison
Recorded by: George
Lead singer: George
Year first released: 1970
Record label: Apple
Album: ALL THINGS MUST PASS
- George sang this song to Bob Dylan to demonstrate his new composition when he visited with Dylan on the Isle Of Wight in 1969.

Behind The Beatles Songs
Book written by Philip Cowan; published by Polytantrid Press in 1978.

Behm, Marc
Coauthor of the story and screenplay for The Beatles' second movie *Help!*

"Being for the Benefit of Mr. Kite"
Written by: Lennon/McCartney
Recorded by: The Beatles
Lead singer: John
Year first released: 1967
Record label: Parlophone (Britain); Capitol (U.S.)
Album: SGT. PEPPER'S LONELY HEARTS CLUB
BAND
· John's inspiration for this song was an old circus poster.

"Be My Baby"
Song recorded by John and released on the bootleg album ROOTS.

Bendry, Peter
John's personal assistant during the early seventies.

Bennett, Peter
Promotion chief who worked for The Beatles' advisor Allen Klein. Bennett was in charge of promotion at Klein's company ABKCO. In 1977 he and Klein were sued for selling unauthorized copies of Beatles albums and not declaring the profits. Bennett later became a witness for the prosecution as he testified against Klein.

Benson, Ray
Film editor for *Magical Mystery Tour*.

Beresford, Elizabeth
Sixteen-year-old fan who, in 1967, was invited by Paul into his house for a "friendly chat and a cup of tea." A few days later, English newspapers were full of Elizabeth's account of her time with Paul, complete with a demand from the girl's mother for Paul to make an honest woman of her little girl. Paul explained that nothing improper went on, and he was just trying to give the girl a lucky break in meeting with her idol. The issue was not pursued by the Beresfords, but Paul has since refrained from inviting young fans in for tea.

Bernstein, Sid
New York concert promoter who booked The Beatles for their first concert in the U.S. at New York's Carnegie Hall on February 12, 1964. The Beatles were paid $6,500 for the two shows. Bernstein later promoted The Beatles performances at Shea Stadium in 1965 and 1966. In recent years Sid Bernstein has made many offers to The Beatles to play together again for a more substantial amount of money than his original offer in 1964. In the fall of 1979 Bernstein took out a full-page ad in *The New York Times* requesting a Beatles reunion in the name of charity.

Berry, Chuck
American rock 'n' roll innovator who was a strong influence on The Beatles during their formative years. They recorded two Berry songs "Rock and Roll Music" and "Roll Over Beethoven." John also recorded two Berry compositions which are included on his ROCK 'N' ROLL album: "You Can't Catch Me" and "Sweet Little Sixteen." In 1972 John specifically requested Chuck Berry as a guest on the "Mike Douglas Show" during the week that he and Yoko cohosted the show. John and Chuck performed together despite John's nervousness about performing with one of his "idols."

Berry, Mike
Performer on the bill with The Beatles during their 1963 tours of Britain and Sweden.

"Besame Mucho"
Song written by Consuelo Velasquez and Selig Shaftel which The Beatles perform on the album THE BEATLES LIVE AT THE STAR CLUB. This song was also part of the group's repertoire for their audition for Decca and Parlophone Records. In the movie *Let It Be* Paul gives a stirring rendition of the song to the other Beatles' accompaniment and amusement.

Best, Peter
Original drummer for The Beatles. Best worked with the group from 1960–62. He was abruptly fired from The Beatles just after they signed their first recording contract. The reasons for Pete's sudden departure have remained sketchy to this day, but despite his popularity with The Beatles' fans, he was never very close with the other Beatles. Though story has it that it was the advice of record producer George Martin that Best should be replaced by a better drummer, it seems that it was the personality conflict within the group which was the deciding factor. Pete went on to form another group and, in 1964, tried to cash in on The Beatles name with his album BEST OF THE BEATLES. The album did not confuse enough people to amount to many sales and his group eventually disbanded. In 1968 Best won a libel suit against The Beatles over some disparaging remarks made by Ringo in a 1965 *Playboy* magazine interview. In 1979 Best worked as an advisor on the production of the TV movie biography of The Beatles, "The Birth of The Beatles."

"Best Friends"
Song performed by Wings during their 1972 tour of Europe. The song was never released.

BEST OF DELANEY AND BONNIE, THE
Album on which George performs.

BEST OF GEORGE HARRISON, THE
Artist: George Harrison
Producer: George Martin, Phil Spector, and George
Year first released: 1976
Record label: Parlophone (Britain); Capitol (U.S.)
Tracks: 13
>   "Something"
>   "If I Needed Someone"
>   "Here Comes the Sun"
>   "Taxman"
>   "Think for Yourself"
>   "For You Blue"
>   "While My Guitar Gently Weeps"
>   "My Sweet Lord"
>   "Give Me Love"
>   "You"
>   "Bangla Desh"
>   "Dark Horse"
>   "What Is Life"

• Side one of this album contains George's hits while still a Beatle, the second side is the best of George's solo works. George was annoyed with the release of this album because he felt it did not concentrate on his solo efforts as did John's album SHAVED FISH and Ringo's album BLAST FROM YOUR PAST.

BEST OF LEON
Leon Russell album on which Ringo performs.

Betty
Character in the Wings song "C Moon."

"Beware My Love"
Written by: Paul McCartney
Recorded by: Wings
Lead singer: Paul
Year first released: 1976
Record label: Parlophone (Britain); Capitol (U.S.)
Album: WINGS AT THE SPEED OF SOUND
              WINGS OVER AMERICA
Single: B side of "Let 'Em In"
Performances: 1975–76 Wings' World Tour.

"Beware Of Darkness"
Written by: George Harrison
Recorded by: George
Lead singer: George
Year first released: 1970
Record label: Apple
Album: ALL THINGS MUST PASS
              THE CONCERT FOR BANGLA DESH
Performances: The Concert for Bangla Desh
• George composed this song while still with The Beatles, but felt the underlying religious philosophy did not go along with The Beatles' style.

Bhaktivedanta Manor
Mansion in England which George bought for the members of the Radha Krishna Temple in 1970.

Bicknell, Alf
The Beatles official chauffeur in the mid-sixties.

"Big Barn Bed"
Written by: Paul McCartney
Recorded by: Wings
Lead singer: Paul
Year first released: 1973
Record label: Apple
Album: RED ROSE SPEEDWAY
Performances: 1973 Wings' British Tour
                      "James Paul McCartney" TV special
• This tune first appeared as the intro to the song "Back Seat of My Car" on RAM.

Bill Black Combo
Group on the bill with The Beatles on their 1964 North American Summer Tour.

Bill Elliot and the Elastic Oz Band
Group which recorded John and Yoko's composition "God Save Us" in 1971. The single was produced by John, Yoko, Mal Evans, and Phil Spector.

Billy J. Kramer and the Dakotas
Liverpool group which was managed by Brian Epstein in the early sixties. The group recorded several Lennon/McCartney songs including "Bad To Me," "From a Window," "Do You Want to Know a Secret," "I'll Keep You Satisfied," and "I'll Be on My Way." Billy J. Kramer and the Dakotas performed on the bill with The Beatles on their 1963 British Summer/Fall Tour and appeared in The Beatles first Christmas shows in December 1963.

"Bip Bop"
Written by: Paul and Linda McCartney
Recorded by: Wings
Lead singer: Paul
Year first released: 1971
Record label: Apple
Album: WILD LIFE
Performances: Wings' 1972 European Tour
• Paul says that this song was inspired by his baby daughter, Mary, who babbled this expression.

"Birthday"
Written by: Lennon/McCartney
Recorded by: The Beatles
Lead singer: John and Paul
Year first released: 1968
Record label: Apple
Album: THE BEATLES
              ROCK AND ROLL MUSIC

- This song was written in India for Pattie Harrison and another TM follower who were both celebrating their birthdays during their stay with the Maharishi.
- Pattie and Yoko help sing background vocals.

Birth of The Beatles, The
Feature film produced for television in 1979. The film dramatization chronicles the group's formation and rise to fame. Pete Best was a special consultant to Dick Clark, the producer. The Beatles sued for forty million dollars to prevent the airing of the movie but to no avail.

"Bit More of You"
Written by: George Harrison
Recorded by: George
Lead singer: George
Year first released: 1975
Record label: Apple
Album: EXTRA TEXTURE
- Reprise of the song "You."

"Bitter End, The"
Part of an instrumental medley with "You Can't Do That" which appears on the HELP! album in the U.S. and is heard in the movie soundtrack. The music accompanies the scene in which an attempt is made to steal Ringo's ring from his finger while he is asleep.

Black, Cilla
Born Priscilla White. Cilla worked as a singer at The Cavern and became a close friend of The Beatles. Cilla, also managed by Brian Epstein, appeared in The Beatles 1963 Christmas Shows and went on to record the Lennon/McCartney compositions "Love of the Loved," "It's for You," and "Step Inside Love." She became a television personality with her own show in Britain, on which Ringo guest starred in 1968. Just before air time, the other three Beatles sent Ringo a telegram: "Big Brothers are watching and wishing you well. Love from all your Big Brothers."

"Blackbird"
Written by: Lennon/McCartney
Recorded by: The Beatles
Lead singer: Paul
Year first released: 1968
Record label: Apple
Album: THE BEATLES
            WINGS OVER AMERICA
Performances: 1975–76 Wings' World Tour
- Paul wrote this song as an analogy of the black power struggle in America. He was inspired while reading a newspaper account of the race riots during the summer of 1968.

Blackboard Jungle, The
Movie released in the mid-fifties which first presented the rock 'n' roll classic "Rock Around the Clock." The Beatles credit this movie as one of the enticements that lured them into the world of rock. John showed up at the movie ready to riot in the seats after reading of the tumultuous reception given the film by England's youth. He was extremely disappointed to have encountered a tame crowd who just watched the movie. Paul and George were both not old enough at the time to pass the age requirements of the theatre, so they wore fake mustaches in order to gain admission.

Black Dyke Mills Brass Band
One of England's top brass bands. They recorded Paul's composition "Thingumybob" for the theme song of a TV comedy program of the same name. The band was signed to Apple Records, and they also recorded an instrumental version of "Yellow Submarine." In 1979 the Black Dyke Mills Brass Band appeared with Wings on the album BACK TO THE EGG.

Blacker's
Liverpool firm for which George worked as an apprentice electrician in the late fifties.

Blair, Lionel
Dancer in the movie A Hard Day's Night. The Beatles originally danced under Blair's guidance in a sequence of the film that was edited from the final version.

Blair, Lorne
Director of two unreleased films produced by Ringo with music by George. Both films included footage of Blair's trips through Indonesia.

Blake, Peter
Codesigner (along with Jan Haworth) of the album cover for SGT. PEPPER'S LONELY HEARTS CLUB BAND.

BLAST FROM YOUR PAST
Artist: Ringo Starr
Producer: Ringo Starr, George Harrison, Richard Perry, and Peter Drake
Year first released: 1975
Record label: Apple
Tracks: 10
    "You're Sixteen"
    "No No Song"
    "It Don't Come Easy"
    "Photograph"
    "Back Off Boogaloo"
    "Only You (And You Alone)"
    "Beaucoups Of Blues"

"Oh My My"
"Early 1970"
"I'm the Greatest"
- Ringo's greatest hits album.

Blessing, Adam
Editor of the 1964 book of photos *Out of the Mouths of The Beatles.*

"Bless You"
Written by: John Lennon
Recorded by: John
Lead singer: John
Year first released: 1974
Record label: Apple
Album: WALLS AND BRIDGES
- John feels this is the best track on the album.

Blindman
Movie released in 1971 starring Ringo Starr. This spaghetti western was distributed by ABKCO, directed by Ferdinando Baldi, produced by Saul Swimmer. Mal Evans and Allen Klein gave cameo performances in the film.

"Blindman"
Written by: Richard Starkey
Recorded by: Ringo
Lead singer: Ringo
Year first released: 1972
Record label: Apple
Single: B side of "Back Off Boogaloo"
- Title song for the movie *Blindman.*

Bloodvessel, Buster
Character who falls in love with Ringo's Aunt Jessie in the movie *Magical Mystery Tour.*

"Blow Away"
Written by: George Harrison
Recorded by: George
Lead singer: George
Year first released: 1979
Record label: Dark Horse
Album: GEORGE HARRISON
Single: Britain and U.S.
Performances: Promo film clip

"Blowin' in the Wind"
Bob Dylan classic, which he performed at The Concert for Bangla Desh and is included on the album.

Bloxham, Jeff
Photographer for the cover of the album GEORGE HARRISON.

Blue Angel
Liverpool club owned by Alan Williams in the late fifties and early sixties. In 1959, Williams held auditions here for British promoter Larry Parnes, who was looking for a band to back one of his singers. The Beatles performed for Parnes and he was pleased with their ability but suggested the bass player (Stu Sutcliffe) be replaced. The Beatles refused under those conditions, so lost the position. Later in the year the group auditioned here again and this time Parnes accepted The Beatles as they were and booked them on their first tour, backing singer Johnny Gentle in Scotland. In 1961 the Blue Angel was the site of the first meeting between Brian Epstein and Ringo.

"Bluebird"
Written by: Paul McCartney
Recorded by: Wings
Lead singer: Paul
Year first released: 1973
Record label: Apple
Album: BAND ON THE RUN
            WINGS OVER AMERICA
Performances: "James Paul McCartney" TV Special,
                1973
                1975–76 Wings' World Tour
- Paul and Linda first presented this song on a live New York radio interview in 1971.

"Blue Jay Way"
Written by: George Harrison
Recorded by: The Beatles
Lead singer: George
Year first released: 1967
Record label: Parlophone (Britain); Capitol (U.S.)
Album: MAGICAL MYSTERY TOUR
EP: MAGICAL MYSTERY TOUR
Performances: *Magical Mystery Tour* movie.
- This song was written while George was visiting Los Angeles and residing in the Hollywood Hills on Blue Jay Way. He composed the song while waiting for friend Derek Taylor to find his way to the house.

Blue Meanies
Miserable characters who occupied Pepperland, abolishing all music and love until they were finally overtaken and shown the way in *Yellow Submarine.*

"Blue Moon of Kentucky"
Song performed by Wings during their 1972 University Tour and Wings over Europe Tour. During its performance a moon would be projected on the backdrop of the stage. The song was never released on record.

"Blue Suede Shoes"
Song written by Carl Perkins and performed by John and the Plastic Ono Band at the Toronto Rock 'n' Roll

Revival Concert in 1969. The song was recorded and appears on the album LIVE PEACE IN TORONTO.

"Blue Turning Grey Over You"
Written by: Andy Razaf/Fats Waller
Recorded by: Ringo
Lead singer: Ringo
Year first released: 1970
Record label: Apple
Album: SENTIMENTAL JOURNEY

Bluthnell, John
Actor who played one of the thugs who break into The Beatles' home in the movie *Help!* The Beatles were impressed with the high-neck collars worn by Bluthnell and had their tailor copy the style for themselves.

Blythdale Children's Hospital
Hospital in New York which received the money collected by the Warwick Hotel when the hotel sold the Beatles' bed sheets from their stays in 1965 and 1966.

Bobby
He lives with Betty in the song "C Moon."

BOBBY KEYS
Album on which George and Ringo perform.

"Bo Didley"
Song performed by Paul with the Crickets on stage at London's Hammersmith Odeon during Buddy Holly Week, 1979.

Body Count
Book written by Fran Schwartz; published by Straight Arrow in 1972. One of the chapters in the book deals with the relationship the author had with Paul in the summer of 1968.

"Boil Oil"
Song written by Paul in 1978 but never released.

Bolan, Marc
Late British pop star who starred in Ringo's movie production *Born To Boogie* in 1972. Ringo photographed the cover for Bolan's THE SLIDER album, and Marc Bolan appears on the album RINGO.

Bolyard, Captain H.B.
Skipper of the Happy Days yacht on which Paul, Jane, Ringo, and Maureen holidayed in the Virgin Islands in 1964. Because none of the couples were married at the time, Captain Bolyard and his wife were dubbed chaperones in order to relieve the public's mind.

Bonham, John
Member of Led Zeppelin who appears on the album BACK TO THE EGG. Bonham joined Wings on stage at the concert for Kampuchea as part of the rockestra.

"Bony Maronie"
Written by: Larry Williams
Recorded by: John
Lead singer: John
Year first released: 1975
Record label: Apple
Album: ROCK 'N' ROLL

Bonzo Dog Doo Dah Band
Satirical musical group who performed with the stripper in the movie *Magical Mystery Tour*. The Bonzos also performed live at The Beatles' party to celebrate the movie's release and were joined on stage by other performers, such as The Beach Boys and John's singing dad, Fred. Paul later produced their song "I'm the Urban Spaceman" under the pseudonym Apollo C. Vermouth.

Boob, Jeremy Hilary
The "nowhere man" who appears in the animated movie, *Yellow Submarine.*

Boreham, D.A.
Registrar who married Ringo and Maureen on February 11, 1965.

"Born In a Prison"
Written by: Yoko Ono
Recorded by: Yoko and John
Lead singer: Yoko
Year first released: 1972
Record label: Apple
Album: SOMETIME IN NEW YORK CITY
Performances: One to One Concert, 1972

Born to Boogie
Film starring Marc Bolan and T Rex; directed by Ringo Starr. The film was shot on March 18, 1972 at a T Rex performance at England's Wembley Stadium. A new generation of fans on hand for the performance screamed and cheered for their hero, Bolan, as cameraman Ringo went virtually unnoticed.

Bowie, David
Musician with whom John cowrote the song "Fame" in 1975. Bowie recorded the song and John helped out on background vocals.

Boyd, Patricia Ann
Maiden name of George's ex-wife, Pattie. (See Pattie Clapton.)

"Boys"
Written by: Luther Dixon and Wes Farrell
Recorded by: The Beatles
Lead singer: Ringo

Year first released: 1963
Record label: Parlophone (Britain); Vee Jay and Capitol (U.S.)
Album: PLEASE PLEASE ME
       INTRODUCING THE BEATLES
       THE EARLY BEATLES
       ROCK AND ROLL MUSIC
       THE BEATLES AT THE HOLLYWOOD
         BOWL
Single: U.S.
Performances: 1964 North American Summer Tour
       "Shindig" TV show, 1965

Boys from Liverpool: John, Paul, George, Ringo, The
Book for young teens written by Nicholas Schaffner; published by Methuen, Inc. in 1980.

Brainsby, Tony
Publicist for Wings.

Brambell, Wilfred
Actor who played the part of Paul's grandfather in *A Hard Day's Night*. Brambell first met The Beatles when they were appearing on the same bill at the Royal Variety Performance in November 1963.

Bramwell, Tony
Ex-head of Apple's production department. Bramwell had formerly worked for Brian Epstein at Nems Enterprises. In 1968 Bramwell accompanied Paul to Los Angeles for an Apple promotional visit.

Brandon, Steve
Assistant engineer for the album RINGO'S ROTOGRAVURE.

Bratley, John
Artist who painted three portraits of Paul, which were on exhibit at the Zwemmer Gallery in England in 1967. Each portrait was priced at £350.

Braun, Michael
Author of the book *Love Me Do*. Braun traveled with The Beatles to Paris and America in 1964.

Brautigan, Richard
Author/poet who was signed to Zapple, a division of Apple Records, in 1969. He recorded the album LISTENING TO RICHARD BRAUTIGAN.

Bravo, Lizzie
Teenage fan who in 1969 was invited into The Beatles' recording session to sing on their record "Across the Universe." Lizzie was one of two girls who, while waiting outside the studio, was asked in to add female harmonies to the recording, which appears on the albums NO ONE'S GONNA CHANGE OUR WORLD and THE BEATLES RARITIES.

Bresner, Bernard
Police bodyguard who was assigned to protect The Beatles when they vacationed in Miami Beach in 1964. Bresner and his family hosted a homemade dinner for The Beatles which was widely covered by the press.

Brickey Builders
Construction firm in which Ringo invested in 1966. The company built a large portion of Ringo's Weybridge home. It went out of business in 1967.

"Bridge over the River Suite"
Written by: Paul and Linda McCartney
Recorded by: The Country Hams
Lead singer: None (Instrumental)
Year first released: 1974
Record label: EMI (Britain); Capitol (U.S.)
Single: B side of "Walking in the Park with Eloise"
• Paul, Linda, and their Nashville friends recorded this one under the name Country Hams.

Bridges, Digby
Architect who designed the dome which stands in the garden of Paul's London home. The soundproof fourteen feet high, thirty feet wide structure, stands on a concrete sun lounge with a moving platform. Paul purchased the dome for $30,000 in October of 1967. The dome was orginally used as a cathedral for meditation.

Bright Tunes
Publishing company which sued George for plagiarizing their song "He's So Fine" in his composition "My Sweet Lord." Although a court later ruled that George's song was unintentionally similar in melody to that of the Bright song, the publishing company was awarded $50,000 in the suit.

In his recording "This Song" George parodies his troubles with Bright Tunes.

"Bring It On Home to Me"/"Send Me Some Lovin' "
Written by: Sam Cooke
Recorded by: John
Lead singer: John
Year first released: 1975
Record label: Apple
Album: ROCK 'N' ROLL

"Bring on the Lucie (Freda Peeple)"
Written by: John Lennon
Recorded by: John
Lead singer: John
Year first released: 1973
Record label: Apple
Album: MIND GAMES

Brinsley Schwarz
British group which performed as the opening act for Wings during their 1973 British Tour. One of their songs "Run Rudolf Run" was recorded live during the Wings' tour.

Britton, Geoff
Former drummer for Wings who replaced Denny Seiwell in 1974. He was with the group for their recordings of "Junior's Farm" and VENUS AND MARS. During this time, Paul directed a film on Britton, a karate expert, while he was at a championship meet.

In 1975 Britton left Wings for a short period to return to England on personal business while they were recording in Nashville. When he rejoined the group in Nashville, he was informed that another drummer, Joe English, would be replacing him in Wings.

"Broadcast, The"
Track on the album BACK TO THE EGG consisting of Paul's accompaniment to the work of Ian Hay ("The Sport of Kings") and John Galsworthy ("The Little Man"). The prose is recited by Mr. Margary, the owner of Lympne Castle, where Wings were recording at the time.

Brodax, Al
Producer of "The Beatles Cartoon" series for television in 1965. Brodax also worked on the movie *Yellow Submarine*. Brodax was not as impressed with the real-life Beatles; he found Ringo "a drunken clod" and Paul "a conceited wise guy."

"Broken Arrow"
Buffalo Springfield song which begins with the audience roar taken from The Beatles concert at the Hollywood Bowl in 1966.

Brolly, Brian
Former manager of Paul's McCartney Productions Ltd. He worked for Paul from 1974 until 1978.

Bromberg, David
Singer/composer who cowrote the song "The Holdup" with George. George's publishing company, Harrisongs, owns the copyright to the song which appears on Bromberg's album DAVID BROMBERG. In 1971 Bromberg appeared on the "David Frost Show" along with George, who helped out on vocals when they performed the song. Bromberg also performs on the albums RINGO and RINGO THE 4TH.

Bron, Eleanor
Actress who played the part of Ahme in The Beatles' movie *Help!* Coincidentally, her father, a music publisher, once employed The Beatles' music publisher Dick James.

Brook Brothers
Group on the bill with The Beatles on their 1963 British Winter Tour.

Brooker, Gary
Member of Procol Harum who appears on George's album ALL THINGS MUST PASS and Paul's album BACK TO THE EGG.

Brookes, Diane
Head of McCartney Productions' New York office when it first opened in 1971.

Brooks, Elkie
Singer on the bill with The Beatles at their 1964 Christmas shows.

BROTHER
Lon and Derek Van Eaton album produced by George, on which Ringo plays drums.

Brother John
Character in Paul's song "Let 'Em In."

Brother Michael
Another of the relatives who visits Paul in his song "Let 'Em In."

Brower, John
Canadian promoter who handled John and Yoko's dealings in Canada in 1969. He organized the Toronto Rock 'n' Roll Revival Concert, to which he invited John to perform. John subsequently formed the Plastic Ono Band to back him at the event. Brower also arranged for John and Yoko's meeting with Canada's Prime Minister Trudeau.

Brown, Ken
One-time guitarist with The Quarrymen in 1959. Brown first played with George in a group called the Les Stewart Quartet until they both left to join John and Paul's group. Brown soon quit the Quarrymen after a row over money. The other members refused to pay him after a performance they gave which Brown didn't attend.

Brown, Peter
Personal assistant to The Beatles after the death of Brian Epstein in 1967. Brown was first hired by Epstein in 1960 to manage his record shop, Nems. By 1962 Peter Brown was working for Nems Enterprises and soon became Epstein's personal assistant. It was Brown who had the unfortunate task of informing The Beatles of Epstein's death. Peter Brown was appointed as Apple's social coordinator in 1968 and is mentioned in John's song "The Ballad Of John and Yoko." He was on twenty-

four-hour alert for any Beatle emergency, with a hot line to which only the four Beatles knew the number. Today Brown works for the Robert Stigwood Organization.

Brown, Tara
Late heir to the Guinness fortune. Brown was a friend of The Beatles and was killed in a motor accident, which The Beatles make a reference to in the song "A Day In the Life."

Bruce, Jack
Musician on whose album, SONGS FOR A TAILOR, George plays guitar.

Bruckner, Tim
Designer of the front and back covers of the album RINGO.

Brute Force
Group signed to Apple Records whose only release for the label was the record "King Of Fun."

Bryan, Michael
Illustrator of the cover of John's album SHAVED FISH.

Bryce, Leslie
Photographer for the *Beatles Book Monthly* magazine who worked with The Beatles from 1963 to 1969. The Beatles, being interested in photography themselves, learned much about the technical aspects of the camera from Bryce. Bryce felt The Beatles were very good subjects, who loved off-the-cuff pictures best.

Brydor Cars
1964 Liverpool car dealership set up by Brian Epstein and Terry Doran. The Beatles were among their customers, but the business folded after only a short time in operation.

Bryman Estates Ltd.
Landlord of an apartment leased to Ringo on Montague Square in Marylebone, London. It was in this apartment, which John and Yoko were temporarily subletting, that the Lennons were busted for possession of marijuana on October 18, 1968. In February 1969 Bryman Estates Ltd. sued Ringo, claiming he had violated his lease by letting John and Yoko live there and also stated that the premises could not be used in an "illegal or immoral" manner. The case was settled in a private hearing on February 28, 1969.

"B Side of C Side"
B side of the "Seaside Woman" single by Suzy and the Red Stripes (alias Wings). Jimmy McCulloch, Denny Laine, Dave Lutton, and Paul and Linda appear on the record, which Paul produced. Linda wrote this song in Africa while the band was recording BAND ON THE RUN.

Budo Kan Hall
Arena in Japan where the Beatles performed from June 30 to July 2, 1966. A controversy arose when followers of Budo, a martial art, protested against The Beatles playing in this sacred arena. They felt only martial arts should be performed here. Security for the concerts was very tight and the engagement was completed peacefully. The shows were filmed for posterity. In January 1980 Wings was scheduled to perform a series of concerts here, but they were cancelled due to Paul's marijuana bust. Only 37 percent of the ticket holders asked for a refund, while the others preferred to hold on to their tickets for souvenirs.

"Built Around"
Title of John's first sculpture exhibit. The piece, which was displayed in the Arts Laboratory Hall in London in June of 1968, required observers to add anything they wanted to it.

Bumblers, The
Group consisting of Frank Sinatra, Sammy Davis, Jr., Bing Crosby, and Dean Martin. In 1964 they recorded a record parodying The Beatles.

Burke, John
Author of the book *A Hard Day's Night* based on Alun Owen's screenplay.

Burman's Theatrical Agency
Company which created the costumes worn by The Beatles on the SGT. PEPPER album. The Beatles chose the material and design.

Burt, Robert
Coauthor of the book *The Beatles: The Fabulous Story of John, Paul, George, and Ringo.*

Bush, Mel
British tour promoter who handled Wings' 1975 tour.

Butlins Holiday Camp
Holiday resort in England, catering to working-class vacationers, where all The Beatles played prior to their becoming famous. When they were young teenagers, Paul and his brother Michael performed here while on holiday with their parents. In 1968, Ringo compared the Maharishi's Indian retreat to Butlins.

"Bye Bye Blackbird"
Written by: Mort Dixon and Ray Henderson
Recorded by: Ringo

Lead singer: Ringo
Year first released: 1970
Record label: Apple
Album: SENTIMENTAL JOURNEY
• Maurice Gibb arranged this song.

"Bye Bye Love"
Written by: Felice Bryant and Boudleaux Bryant
Recorded by: George
Lead singer: George
Year first released: 1974

Record label: Apple
Album: DARK HORSE
• George adds some lyrics to this song, converting it into a satrical piece about the affair between his wife Pattie and Eric (Clapper) Clapton. George credits Pattie and Eric with helping out on this song.
• During the rehearsal for the "Saturday Night Live" TV show, in November of 1976, George and Paul Simon sang this song. Their rendition was cut from the aired show.

C

Cadillacs, The
Early fifties Liverpool group in which Ringo played drums. This was the first group with which Ringo performed.

"Cafe on the Left Bank"
Written by: Paul McCartney
Recorded by: Wings
Lead singer: Paul
Year first released: 1978
Record label: Parlophone (Britain); Capitol (U.S.)
Album: LONDON TOWN

Cafe Royale
Reception hall on Regent Street in London where Wings held a party for the completion of their British tour on May 27, 1973. Paul performed on stage during the festivities, alternating between piano, drums, and lead guitar. Elton John was among the guests who also performed.

Paul was honored here by the readers of the London *Daily Mirror,* which presented him with an award for the Outstanding Musical Personality of 1979 on February 26, 1980.

Caleb
Astrologer employed by Apple, in 1968, to chart horoscopes for The Beatles and make I Ching predictions.

"Call Me"
Written by: Richard Starkey
Recorded by: Ringo
Lead singer: Ringo
Year first released: 1974
Record label: Apple
Album: GOODNIGHT VIENNA
Single: B side of "Only You"

"Call Me Back Again"
Written by: Paul McCartney
Recorded by: Wings
Lead singer: Paul
Year first released: 1975
Record label: Parlophone (Britain); Capitol (U.S.)
Album: VENUS AND MARS
　　　　　 WINGS OVER AMERICA
Performances: 1975–76 Wings' World Tour

"Cambridge 1969"
John and Yoko performed at Cambridge, England at Lady Mitchell Hall on March 2, 1969. The performance was recorded and appears on the album UNFINISHED MUSIC NO. 2: LIFE WITH THE LIONS. George played guitar during the concert.

Campbeltown
Scottish town where Paul's farm is located.

Campbeltown Pipe Band
Twenty-one bagpipe players who perform on Wings' "Mull of Kintyre." The band also appears in the promo film clip for the song filmed in Scotland in 1977. When the song became such a huge success throughout Great Britain, Paul found himself being criticized in the press for paying the band, whose sound so greatly contributed to the record, union-scale rates while he reaped the profits. To rectify the situation Paul awarded a £200 bonus to each member of the band.

Can-Base Studios
Recording studios located in Canada, where Ringo worked on his BAD BOY album.

Candlestick Park
San Francisco stadium where The Beatles gave their last live performance before an audience on August 29, 1966. Approximately twenty-five thousand people attended the concert, which completed the group's North American Summer Tour.

Candy
Movie in which Ringo costarred. The film, released in 1968, was produced by Robert Haggles and directed by Christian Marquand for Cinerama Releasing Corp. This was Ringo's first feature film apart from The Beatles. For his part as a Mexican gardener Ringo's hair was dyed jet black.

Candy
Character portrayed by Ringo in the 1972 movie *Blindman.*

Cannibal and the Headhunters
Group that performed on the bill with The Beatles on their 1965 North American tour.

"Can She Do It Like She Dances"
Written by: Steve Duboff and Gerry Robinson
Recorded by: Ringo
Lead singer: Ringo
Year first released: 1977
Record label: Polydor (Britain); Atlantic (U.S.)
Album: RINGO THE 4TH

"Can't Buy Me Love"
Written by: Lennon/McCartney
Recorded by: The Beatles
Lead singer: Paul
Year first released: 1964

Record label: Parlophone (Britain); United Artists and
              Capitol (U.S.)
Album: A HARD DAY'S NIGHT
       A COLLECTION OF BEATLES OLDIES
       THE BEATLES 1962–1966
       THE BEATLES AGAIN
       THE BEATLES AT THE HOLLYWOOD
         BOWL
EP: THE BEATLES MILLION SELLERS
Single: Britain and U.S.
Performances: Soundtrack to *A Hard Day's Night*
              1964 North American Summer Tour
              1964 Christmas Shows
              "Around The Beatles" TV show, 1964
              1964 Australian Tour
              1965 European Summer Tour
              1965 North American Summer Tour
- This song was written in Miami, Florida during The
  Beatles' first visit to America in 1964. It was recorded
  on George's twenty-first birthday.

"Can't Stop Thinking About You"
Written by: George Harrison
Recorded by: George
Lead singer: George
Year first released: 1975
Record label: Apple
Album: EXTRA TEXTURE

Capitol Records
American record company which is the U.S. affiliate of
EMI Records in Europe. The Beatles' records were distributed in the U.S. on the Capitol label from 1964 to
1968. When The Beatles formed their own record company, Apple, Capitol handled its U.S. distribution. In
1976 Paul signed with Capitol Records for the U.S. distribution of his records. When the two-year contract expired, Paul did not re-sign with the company.

Caravelles, The
Group on the bill with The Beatles for their first tour of
America, in 1964.

Cargill, Patrick
British actor who played the role of the "famous" Scotland Yard inspector in the movie *Help!*

Carlinsky, Dan
Coauthor of the book *The Compleat Beatles Quiz Book.*

Carnegie Hall
New York concert hall where The Beatles performed
two shows on February 12, 1964, during their first visit
to America. The concerts were promoted by Sid Bernstein and Theatre Three Productions. Tickets, ranging
from $1.65 to $5.50 in price, were sold out within six

hours. Fifty additional seats were placed on the stage to
accommodate the dignitaries and fans who met the requirements of being over age thirty.

Carney, Art
Comedy actor who portrayed Ognir Rrats's drunken father in the 1978 TV special "Ringo."

"Carol"
Chuck Berry song which The Beatles performed on the
"Pop Go The Beatles" radio show in July, 1963.

Carr, Roy
Coauthor of the book *The Beatles Illustrated Record.*

Carrog
Welsh village which was the location of Paul's brother
Michael's wedding in June 1968. Paul and Jane attended
the ceremony, with Paul serving as best man.

"Carry that Weight"
Written by: Lennon/McCartney
Recorded by: The Beatles
Lead singer: John, Paul, and George
Year first released: 1969
Record label: Apple
Album: ABBEY ROAD
- Paul felt this song reflected his feelings on the burden
  he carried in trying to hold The Beatles together dur-
  ing this year of musical and personal conflicts.

Carson, Jan
Stripper in the film *Magical Mystery Tour.*

Casbah, The
Liverpool club which was located in the cellar of ex-
Beatle Pete Best's home in West Darby. Paul, George,
John, and John's girlfriend, Cynthia, helped decorate
the club for its opening in August, 1958. The Quarrymen
performed here with Pete Best sitting in on drums. In
December of 1961 The Beatles were at the Casbah when
they signed their contract with manager Brian Epstein.

Casey, Howie
Liverpool musician who first worked with The Beatles
during their struggling days in Liverpool and Hamburg.
Casey later appeared on the Wings albums BAND ON
THE RUN and BACK TO THE EGG. In 1975 Casey
played in the brass section on Wings' worldwide tour,
and he joined the band again on their 1979 British Tour.

"Casket, The"
Song written by Paul and Roger McGough for the
MCGEAR album. Paul performs on the recording.

Cass and the Cassanovas
Early sixties Liverpool group which was indirectly responsible for The Beatles' first Hamburg performance.

In August 1960, The Beatles were asked to replace the Cassanovas at the Indra Club when the group canceled their booking.

Castell, Paul
Artist who photographed the apple used as the logo for Apple Records.

Castleman, Harry
Coauthor of the books *All Together Now* and *The Beatles Again*.

Castro, Bernard
President of the Castro Convertible Company when, on February 14, 1964, he hosted The Beatles aboard his yacht in Miami, Florida. The group took advantage of the privacy to rest and relax before returning to their hectic schedule.

Caswell-Massey
Cosmetic firm which was employed by Paul to create a specially designed scent for himself. Paul's bill came to $2,000.

"Catcall"
Originally titled "Cat's Walk," this instrumental was written by Paul and performed by The Beatles in 1961. The song was later recorded by the Chris Barber Band, in 1967, with Paul joining in on the "cat calls."

Cato, Bob
Photographer who took the cover photo of the British release of THE BEST OF GEORGE HARRISON. Cato also designed the cover for the album 33 1/3.

Caveman
United Artists movie release, starring Ringo, which began production in February 1980.

Cavendish Avenue
Street in London's St. John's Wood section where Paul and family live. Paul purchased the house on April 14, 1965 for £40,000, after it had been brought to his attention by Jane Asher. Paul moved into the house in 1966. The nineteenth-century villa-style home had four floors and sixteen rooms, including a basement with servant's quarters. Paul has his own music room on the top floor. On August 3, 1968, Paul's home was designated for preservation by the Westminster City Council, due to its architectural style. In 1979 the house was renovated for a reported cost of approximately two million dollars.

Cavendish, Leslie
Hairdresser who was employed by The Beatles to style their hair during the mid-sixties. Cavendish was first introduced to Paul by his girlfriend, Jane, because she felt his hair should be styled properly. He layered Paul's locks and soon the other Beatles followed suit. In 1968 The Beatles financed an exclusive men's hair salon on Kings Road which was managed by Cavendish.

Cavern, The
Liverpool basement club which was the "in" spot during the early sixties. The Cavern, located at 10 Matthew Street, was owned by Ray McFall. The Beatles first played here on March 21, 1961 after their return from Germany. They soon became the house band and developed a large and loyal following. Brian Epstein first saw The Beatles perform here on November 9, 1961. From 1961 to 1963 The Beatles played The Cavern 292 times. They were paid £5 for their first performance in 1961 and by August 3, 1963 their salary had increased to £300. The Cavern was torn down in June of 1973 to make way for a railway station. A new Cavern, called Eric's, was built across the street.

Cavett, Dick
American TV talk show host who interviewed John and Yoko on his program in 1971 and again in 1972. Cavett also played host to George on his show in 1971. In 1972 Dick Cavett cameoed in John and Yoko's *Imagine* film. He also was a character witness on John's behalf during the immigration hearings.

Caxton Hall
London Registry office where Ringo and Maureen were married on Februrary 11, 1965. John, George, and Brian Epstein attended the wedding.

Cellarful of Noise, A
Book written by Brian Epstein; published by Doubleday in 1964. The book was Brian's account of his early years managing The Beatles as well as other Nems artists.

Century Plaza Hotel
Los Angeles hotel where Capitol Records held a convention in June, 1968. Paul attended the conference as a surprise guest and he previewed a promotional film of Apple Records. The film included The Beatles working in their Apple offices and in the recording studio. Mary Hopkin, Apple's newest artist, was also featured in the film.

"Chains"
Written by: Jerry Goffin and Carole King
Recorded by: The Beatles
Lead singer: George
Year first released: 1963
Record label: Parlophone (Britain); Vee Jay and Capitol (U.S.)
Album: PLEASE PLEASE ME
            INTRODUCING THE BEATLES
            THE EARLY BEATLES
EP: THE BEATLES (NO. 1)

Chambers, John
Liverpool City Council member who, in 1977, originated a proposal to have Liverpool erect a statue in honor of The Beatles, but the proposal was rejected by the Council by a vote of 10 to 8. The Beatles themselves stated they did not care to be immortalized in this fashion, but the decision was later reversed, with the understanding that Liverpool would not foot the £30,000 bill.

Chapman, Norman
Temporary drummer with The Beatles while they were performing at Liverpool's Jacaranda club in 1960. The Beatles, in need of a drummer, had first heard Chapman drumming while passing his apartment building and they called through the street until he came to his window. His Beatle career was cut short when he was drafted into the National Service.

Chappell Studios
London recording studio where The Beatles recorded some of their songs for the album MAGICAL MYSTERY TOUR.

Charles, Thomas
Disc jockey for Alabama radio station WAQY who, in 1966, led the campaign to "Ban The Beatles" after John's controversial remarks on religion. Charles' aim was to present the group with the remains of their burnt-up records when they arrived in America for their summer tour.

"Chase, The"
Instrumental written by Ken Thorne for the soundtrack of *Help!* The recording appears on the U.S. album HELP!

Chelsea Town Hall
Theatre in London where Apple held a press reception for the release of the record "Give Peace a Chance" on July 3, 1969. Ringo and Maureen attended the reception in place of John and Yoko, who were hospitalized after a car accident in Scotland.

Cherokee Studios
Los Angeles recording studio where Ringo recorded RINGO'S ROTOGRAVURE.

Cherry Vanilla
Punk rock star who was sent to John's house by Ringo as a present for his thirty-sixth birthday. For the occasion she recited her own unique version of *Romeo and Juliet*.

Cheswick House
English estate on which The Beatles filmed their promotional films for "Paperback Writer" and "Rain."

Chiffons, The
Group that appeared on the bill with The Beatles for their 1964 American Tour.

"Children Children"
Written by: Paul McCartney and Denny Laine
Recorded by: Wings
Lead singer: Denny Laine
Year first released: 1978
Record label: Parlophone (Britain); Capitol (U.S.)
Album: LONDON TOWN
· Only song on this album to feature Denny as lead singer.

Chris Barber Band, The
Jazz group that recorded the Paul McCartney composition "Catcall" in 1967. Chris Barber, an old friend from The Cavern days, appeared on the bill with The Beatles at the Royal Albert Hall in 1963.

Christie, John
Performer who recorded "4th Of July," a song written by Paul and Linda McCartney.

Chuck
Imaginary grandchild Paul sings about in the song "When I'm Sixty-Four."

Churchyard, Steve
Engineer on the album LONDON TOWN.

Cicala, Roy
Engineer who worked on John's albums: SOMETIME IN NEW YORK CITY, IMAGINE, MIND GAMES, WALLS AND BRIDGES, and ROCK 'N' ROLL. Cicala also cowrote an unreleased song with John entitled "Incantation."

Cicalo, Hank
Assistant engineer for the album 33 1/3.

"Circles"
Unreleased Harrison composition written during The Beatles days and later intended for release on the album GEORGE HARRISON.

Civil Defense Fund of Ireland
Organization which received the proceeds from John's recording "Luck of the Irish."

Clang
Eastern cult leader portrayed by Leo McKern in the movie *Help!*

Clapton, Eric
Guitarist who worked in such supergroups as the Yardbirds, Cream, Blind Faith, and Derek and the Domi-

noes. In the late sixties Clapton became a close friend of George's. He became the first rock musician to perform on a Beatles record when George invited him to play lead guitar on "While My Guitar Gently Weeps." It was in Eric Clapton's garden that George composed "Here Comes the Sun." In 1969 Clapton was asked by John to play in his Plastic Ono Supergroup Band at the Toronto Rock 'n' Roll Revival Concert. John was so intent on having Clapton in the band that he rescheduled his plane flight to Canada to coincide with Eric's availability.

Clapton has worked on several of The Beatles' solo projects, including LIVE PEACE IN TORONTO, ALL THINGS MUST PASS, DARK HORSE, GEORGE HARRISON, RINGO'S ROTOGRAVURE (on which Ringo performs Clapton's composition "This Be Called a Song") and BACK TO THE EGG. Eric was a participant in George's Concert for Bangla Desh.

In 1970 Eric Clapton composed LAYLA, a lament about his unrequited love for, he later admitted, George's wife, Pattie.

In 1974, after George and Pattie formally separated, Pattie moved in with Eric and the two continued to remain friendly with George. On March 27, 1979 Eric and Pattie married, and two months later celebrated with a party attended by three Beatles. It was at this occasion that George, Paul, and Ringo sang and performed on stage together for the first time in a decade.

Clapton, Pattie Harrison

Born on March 17, 1944; ex-wife of George Harrison. Pattie was working as one of London's top models when she was hired by director Richard Lester to play a small part in The Beatles' first movie *A Hard Day's Night*. George and Pattie first met on the set of that movie in 1964. Though George was immediately attracted to the blue-eyed blonde with the upper-class manner, Pattie had at first spurned his attempts to become better acquainted, since at the time she was engaged to another man. Eventually George's determination in pursuing Pattie won out and the two started dating. Pattie moved into George's Esher home in 1965. During this time, aside from her modeling work, she began writing a feature column, "Pattie's Letter from London," about the English rock scene, which appeared in the U.S. magazine *16*.

On January 21, 1966 Pattie and George were married, with Paul the only Beatle present at the ceremony. The couple honeymooned in Barbados, as the photographers snapped away at the lovely and loving couple romping along the beach. After marriage Pattie went into semiretirement, not wishing to capitalize on and/or be exploited by her new Beatle-wife status. She became involved with the study of Indian culture, an interest which she and George cultivated with many trips to India and

deep religious study. It was Pattie who first became aware of the Maharishi Mahesh Yogi and his instruction in Transcendental Meditation, to which she introduced George and the other Beatles. Along with her religious interests, Pattie was still very much involved in the fashion world. She discovered a group called Fool, which was soon signed to Apple to design clothes and run the Apple Boutique. Pattie has inspired many of George's most romantic compositions, including "Something," "For You Blue," and "It's All Too Much." Their mod marriage typified the swinging London pop scene and their common interests and pursuits seemed to make for an ideal union, but it was their obsessive interest in religious studies that began to work against their relationship. George began devoting most of his time and energies toward his goal of spiritual enlightment, which left Pattie feeling alienated and alone. In an attempt to instill jealousy in her husband, Pattie began a relationship with his close friend, Eric Clapton. She left Clapton when she and George reconciled, but the marriage was not to last much longer. They were separated in 1974, and Pattie went back to Eric Clapton. George and Pattie remained friendly after divorcing in 1977 and George attended the wedding reception held for Eric and Pattie in 1979.

"Clarabella"

Song The Beatles performed on "Pop Go The Beatles" in July 1963.

Clarke, Tony

Engineer at EMI studios in London who worked with Paul on his albums WILD LIFE and WINGS AT THE SPEED OF SOUND. Paul mentions Tony's name at the beginning of his song "Mumbo."

Cleave, Maureen

British journalist who was the first to give The Beatles national coverage in her article for the *London Evening Standard* in February 1963. Ms. Cleave became noted for her interview with John in 1966, when he stated, in another of her articles for the *London Evening Standard,* that Christianity was on the wane. "We're [The Beatles] more popular than Jesus now. I don't know which will go first . . . rock 'n' roll or Christianity." The statement had gone unnoticed in Britain, but when it appeared in a U.S. publication, *Datebook* magazine, it caused a heated controversy throughout America. It especially caused a hostile reaction among the southern "Bible-belt" states, initiating anti-Beatles rallies and record burnings. The comment caused such havoc, that The Beatles' upcoming tour of America was put into jeopardy. Manager Brian Epstein had to fly to America from his sick bed to assure the public that the statement was taken out of context and was said out of concern on John's part rather than to boast about The Beatles' popularity. When The Beatles did arrive for their tour, John publicly apologized for any damage done and reiterated his position that he deplored the fact that religion, in his view, seemed to be declining.

Cliff Bennett and the Rebel Rousers
Group on the bill with The Beatles for their 1966 tour of Germany and Japan.

Cliff, Edgar
Paul's favorite history teacher. He tried to persuade Paul to pursue a career in teaching.

Clive, John
Actor who dubbed in the voice of John in the animated movie *Yellow Submarine*.

Club Sandwich
Newsletter published by the official Wings Fun Club, sponsored by MPL. Paul and Linda thought up the name for the paper, for which Linda is the staff photographer.

"C Moon"
Written by: Paul McCartney
Recorded by: Wings
Lead singer: Paul
Year first released: 1972
Record label: Apple
Single: B side of "Hi Hi Hi"
Performances: 1973 British Tour
1975 British Tour
"James Paul McCartney" TV special, 1973
- One of Paul's first reggae attempts. The phrase "C Moon" is meant to be the opposite of the expression L7, which is a term meaning "square."
- The song is a commentary on the generation gap and has Paul's children singing along on the chorus.
- On the record all of Wings members, except Linda, play instruments other than their own. Paul is on piano, Denny is on bass, Henry plays drums, and Denny Seiwell is on trumpet.
- When performed in concert, this song was played in medley with "Little Woman Love."

Coburn, James
Actor whose picture appears on the album cover of BAND ON THE RUN.

"Cold Turkey"
Written by: John Lennon
Recorded by: John Lennon and the Plastic Ono Band
Lead singer: John
Year first released: 1969
Record label: Apple

Album: LIVE PEACE IN TORONTO
SOMETIME IN NEW YORK CITY
SHAVED FISH
Single: Britain and U.S.
Performances: Promo film clip
Toronto Rock 'n' Roll Revival Concert, September 1969
Lyceum Ballroom, December 1969
One to One Concert, August 1972
- Since Paul would not play on this recording, John decided it was as good a time as any to release the record without the Lennon/McCartney songwriting credit.
- The single version is a studio cut; the album versions (except SHAVED FISH) are live performances.
- Eric Clapton is featured on guitar.

Coleman, Syd
Manager of Aidmore and Beechwood, EMI's publishing outlet in 1962. Coleman heard the audition tapes which The Beatles had originally recorded for Decca Records, and he agreed to have someone at EMI Records listen to them.

COLLECTION OF BEATLES OLDIES, A
Artist: The Beatles
Producer: George Martin
Year first released: 1966
Record label: Parlophone
Tracks: 16
"She Loves You"
"From Me to You"
"We Can Work It Out"
"Help!"
"Michelle"
"Yesterday"
"I Feel Fine"
"Yellow Submarine"
"Can't Buy Me Love"
"Bad Boy"
"Day Tripper"
"A Hard Day's Night"
"Ticket to Ride"
"Paperback Writer"
"Eleanor Rigby"
"I Want to Hold Your Hand"
- British release.

"Colliding Circles"
Unreleased song written by John and recorded by The Beatles during the sessions for SGT. PEPPER.

Collingham, Anne
Secretary of the Official Beatles Fan Club in England, which folded in 1972.

Columbia Recording Studios
New York recording studio where Paul recorded RAM in 1970.

Columbia Records
U.S. record company to which Paul and Ringo are currently under contract. Ringo signed with the Portrait division of Columbia in 1978. In 1979, when Paul signed with Columbia, he became the highest paid recording artist in the industry, with a salary of two million dollars per album, plus 22 percent of the royalties.

"Come and Get It"
Badfinger song written and produced by Paul in 1969 for the soundtrack of *The Magic Christian*. The record was released on Apple.

"Come Go With Me"
Song which John was singing at the village fete when Paul first met him on June 15, 1955.

"Come On, Come In"
Original title for "Everybody's Got Something to Hide except Me and My Monkey."

"Come Together"
Written by: Lennon/McCartney
Recorded by: The Beatles
Lead singer: John
Year first released: 1969
Record label: Apple
Album: ABBEY ROAD
Single: B side of "Something"
Performances: One to One Concert, August 1972
• John was sued for stealing the opening melody and first two lines of the lyrics to this song from an early Chuck Berry recording. A settlement was made, and John agreed to record two Chuck Berry songs in the future. He fulfilled his commitment when he released his ROCK 'N' ROLL album in 1975 with the songs "You Can't Catch Me" and "Sweet Little Sixteen" included on it.

COMING OUT
Manhattan Transfer album on which Ringo plays drums.

"Coming Up"
Song performed by Wings on their 1979 British concert tour and intended for release by Paul in 1980.

"Commonwealth"
Unreleased Beatles song recorded during the LET IT BE sessions.

Communism, Hypnotism, and The Beatles
An anti-Beatles booklet by Reverend David A. Noebel and published by the Christian Crusade in 1965.

Compleat Beatles Quiz Book, The
Book by Edwin Goodgold and Dan Carlinsky; published by Warner Books.

Concert for Bangla Desh, The
A benefit concert organized by George and Ravi Shankar to aid the United Nations Children's Fund (UNICEF) for the relief of refugee children of Bangla Desh. This monumental event came about when Shankar asked George to help aid the people of his ravaged homeland. On August 1, 1971, George assembled Ravi Shankar (and his orchestra), Ringo, Eric Clapton, Bob Dylan, Leon Russell, Billy Preston, Klaus Voorman, Badfinger, and various others "from around the world" to give two concerts at New York's Madison Square Garden.

All of The Beatles were invited to participate in this event but, except for Ringo, they declined. John had initially accepted the invitation, but when he realized Yoko wasn't welcome, he withdrew from the line-up. Paul refused from the onset, stating it wasn't the right time for a Beatles reunion.

This first American post-Beatles concert became one of the most significant musical events of the decade. On August 12, 1971, a check for $243,418.50 was sent to the United Nations Relief Fund from the monies raised at the two shows.

Film
The concerts were filmed and distributed by Twentieth-Century Fox in 1972. George took a personal interest in the film, splicing together the best footage of both shows. He also produced it in conjunction with Allen Klein. The movie was directed by Saul Swimmer.

On March 22, 1972, the movie previewed in New York at the DeMille Theatre with John, Yoko, Jerry Rubin, and Nino Tempo in attendance. They all sat in the balcony and John, in good spirits, cheered and applauded the movie, but left the theatre in the middle of Dylan's segment. The movie officially opened in New York the following day.

THE CONCERT FOR BANGLA DESH
Artist: George Harrison (and friends)
Producer: George and Phil Spector
Year first released: 1971
Record label: Apple
Tracks: 17
   "Bangla Dhun"
   "Wah Wah"
   "My Sweet Lord"

"Awaiting On You All"
"That's the Way God Planned It"
"It Don't Come Easy"
"Beware of Darkness"
"While My Guitar Gently Weeps"
"Jumping Jack Flash/Youngblood"
"Here Comes the Sun"
"A Hard Rain's Gonna Fall"
"It Takes Alot to Laugh/It Takes a Train to Cry"
"Blowin' in the Wind"
"Mr. Tambourine Man"
"Just like a Woman"
"Something"
"Bangla Desh"
- This three-record boxed package included a booklet of photographs from the concerts.
- George was upset about the high price of the album, but had no control over the matter.
- The album won a Grammy Award.

The proceeds from the record, the film, and the concerts raised over fifteen million dollars, most of which never made it to Bangla Desh. It was tied up in legal hassles with other artist's record companies, along with accusations of wrongdoings by George's business manager, Allen Klein. George, being upset with the delay, even offered to deliver the money himself.

To this day, some of the money still has not been turned over to Bangla Desh.

On June 5, 1972, UNICEF bestowed the "Child Is the Father of the Man" award to George and Ravi Shankar for their contributions to the Children's Fund.

Connolly, Billy
Performer on the bill with Wings for the concert for Kampuchea on December 29, 1979.

Conservative Club
Liverpool site of the first performance John and Paul gave together as The Quarrymen in 1956.

Conteh, John
Boxing champion who appears on the album cover of BAND ON THE RUN.

Contemporary Art Society
British organization which John and Cynthia joined in 1966.

"Continuing Story of Bungalow Bill, The"
Written by: Lennon/McCartney
Recorded by: The Beatles
Lead singer: John
Year first released: 1968
Record label: Apple
Album: THE BEATLES
- Yoko and Maureen are among the chorus singers.

"Coochy-Coochy"
Written by: Richard Starkey
Recorded by: Ringo
Lead singer: Ringo
Year first released: 1970
Record label: Apple
Single: B side of "Beaucoups of Blues" in U.S.
- Originally 28 minutes long.

"Cook Of the House"
Written by: Paul McCartney
Recorded by: Wings
Lead singer: Linda
Year first released: 1976
Record label: Parlophone (Britain); Capitol (U.S.)
Album: WINGS AT THE SPEED OF SOUND
Single: B side of "Silly Love Songs"
Performances: 1979 Wings' British Tour
- Only Wings song on which Linda sings lead.
- The first few lines were taken directly from a commercial plaque.
- All of the events in the song were actually happening in their kitchen at the time Paul wrote the song.
- The sizzling sound at the record's end is that of a meal being cooked on the stove.

"Cookin' "
Written by: John Lennon
Recorded by: Ringo
Lead singer: Ringo
Year first released: 1976
Record label: Polydor (Britain); Atlantic (U.S.)
Album: RINGO'S ROTOGRAVURE
- John and Yoko visited Ringo in the studio in Los Angeles to help out on the song.

Cooper, Michael
Photographer of the cover of the album SGT. PEPPER'S LONELY HEARTS CLUB BAND.

Cooper, Ray
Percussionist who performed on the albums GEORGE HARRISON and BACK TO THE EGG. Cooper joined Wings on stage at the benefit concert for Kampuchea on December 29, 1979.

Copely, Peter
Actor who portrayed the jeweler in the movie *Help!*

Corbitt, Bill
Beatles' chauffeur who went on to work as John's personal chauffeur in 1964.

Cordet, Louise
Singer who toured with The Beatles on their 1963 British Tour.

Costello, Elvis
Performer on the bill with Wings at the Charity concert for Kampuchea on December 29, 1979.

Cott, Jonathan
Coauthor of the booklet *The Beatles Get Back,* which was packaged with the LET IT BE album everywhere but in the U.S. The book is now out of print and has become a collector's item.

"Country Dreamer"
Written by: Paul McCartney
Recorded by: Wings
Lead singer: Paul
Year first released: 1973
Record label: Apple
Single: B side of "Helen Wheels"

Country Hams, The
Group consisting of Wings (Paul, Linda, and Denny), plus Nashville musicians: Chet Atkins, Floyd Kramer, Vasser Clements, and Bobby Thompson. This impromptu group recorded the instrumental "Walking in the Park with Eloise" and "Bridge over the River Suite" in Nashville in 1974.

Corvello, Joe
Photographer who took the photos on the album THE BEATLES SECOND ALBUM, as well as many of the Beatle bubble gum card pictures.

Coventry Cathedral
London church where John and Yoko planted "potted acorns for peace" in the front yard. The church council was upset by the couple's action and protested the planting. A few days later the acorns mysteriously disappeared.

Cowan, Philip
Author of the book *Behind The Beatles' Songs.*

"Cowboy Museum"
Written by: George Harrison
Recorded by: George
Lead singer: None (Instrumental)
Year first released: 1968
Record label: Apple
Album: WONDERWALL

Cox, Anthony
Ex-husband of Yoko Ono. Cox, an American filmmaker, was involved in a much publicized custody battle with Yoko over their daughter, Kyoko, during the early seventies. Cox refused to obey a court order and relinquish custody of Kyoko and give her to John and Yoko. He went into hiding with Kyoko as John and Yoko desperately tried to locate the child. This search for Yoko's daughter was a major reason given the U.S. Immigration Department as to why it was imperative that John be allowed to remain in the country during that time. Kyoko remained with Cox.

Cox, Kyoko
Daughter of Yoko Ono, born in 1963.

Cox, Maureen
Maiden name of Ringo's ex-wife, Maureen.

"Crackerbox Palace"
Written by: George Harrison
Recorded by: George
Lead singer: George
Year first released: 1976
Record label: Dark Horse
Album: 33⅓
Single: U.S.
Performances: Promo film clip
• George originally got the name from the home of comedian Lord Buckley.
• The sign outside George's Henley estate reads "Welcome To Crackerbox Palace."

Crawford, Ian
Singer on the bill with The Beatles on their 1963 British Tour.

Crickets, The
Buddy Holly's back-up band in the 1950s. The Beatles were great fans of Buddy Holly and the Crickets. Late Beatle Stu Sutcliffe suggested the group name themselves "Beetles," in the same vein as Crickets; John later changed the spelling to Beatles. In 1977, Paul arranged for the appearance of the original Crickets, Jerry Allison, Sonny Curtis, and Joe Maudlin, to perform in honor of Buddy Holly at the Buddy Holly Week celebration; the group played together for the first time in seventeen years.

"Crippled Inside"
Written by: John Lennon
Recorded by: John
Lead singer: John
Year first released: 1971
Record label: Apple
Album: IMAGINE
Performances: Promo film clip in *Imagine* movie
• Another in the genre of "get Paul" songs. John stated his justification was due to the fact that Paul had attacked him in his song "3 Legs."

Crisp, Sir Frankie
Architect who designed the castle in which George lives. George titled his song "The Ballad of Sir Frankie Crisp" after Crisp.

Crittle, John
Clothing designer who designed the costumes for the Apple Tailoring Shop in London in 1968. On May 22, 1968, the day before the shop's official opening, a fashion show was staged previewing Crittle's designs. George, Pattie, John, and Yoko were among the celebrities in attendance.

Cropper, Steve
Musician who plays guitar on the albums RINGO and GOODNIGHT VIENNA.

CROSSROADS
Larry Hosford album on which George plays guitar and sings background vocals.

"Crossroads Theme"
Written by: Tony Hatch
Recorded by: Wings
Lead singer: Instrumental
Year first released: 1975
Record label: Parlophone (Britain); Capitol (U.S.)
Album: VENUS AND MARS
- "Crossroads" is a popular British television soap opera. Paul used its theme song and rearranged the music to record on the album. Though he was criticized for recording the song for a rock 'n' roll album, Paul felt the mood of the music was in keeping with the album's theme.
- Paul's version later replaced the television theme song.

Crowder, Alan
Management executive of McCartney Productions. Crowder is in charge of marketing and organizing Wings' ventures.

Cruikshank, Robin
British designer who decorated the Apple offices and was then hired by Ringo to design the interior of his home according to Ringo's conceptual blueprints. In 1970 Ringo and Cruikshank formed a partnership called ROR (Ringo or Robin) which custom designs contemporary furniture.

"Cry Baby Cry"
Written by: Lennon/McCartney
Recorded by: The Beatles
Lead singer: John
Year first released: 1968
Record label: Apple
Album: THE BEATLES
- John got the idea for this one from television commercials. The original verse was "make your mother buy."

"Cry for a Shadow"
Written by: Harrison/Lennon
Recorded by: The Beatles and Tony Sheridan
Lead singer: Instrumental
Record label: Polydor
Album: THE BEATLES FIRST
        IN THE BEGINNING
- Original title for this song was "Beatle Bop."
- The only song John and George ever composed together.

"Cryin' "
Written by: Richard Starkey and Vini Poncia
Recorded by: Ringo
Lead singer: Ringo
Year first released: 1976
Record label: Polydor (Britain); Atlantic (U.S.)
Album: RINGO'S ROTOGRAVURE
Single: B side of "A Dose of Rock and Roll"

"Crying, Waiting, Hoping"
Song performed by The Beatles at their Decca Records audition in 1962.

"Cufflink"
Written by: Paul McCartney
Recorded by: Wings
Lead singer: Instrumental
Year first released: 1978
Record label: Parlophone (Britain); Capitol (U.S.)
Album: LONDON TOWN

Cummins, Jeff
Artist of the inner cover painting of the WINGS OVER AMERICA album.

Curzon Terrace
House located in Benedict Canyon, Los Angeles, where The Beatles stayed during the west coast dates of their 1966 American Tour. John and George had their first experience with LSD here.

Cutler, Ivor
Actor/poet who played the role of Buster Bloodvessel in the film *Magical Mystery Tour*. When The Beatles considered opening the Apple School for their children and children of Apple employees, Cutler was to be appointed headmaster.

Cyrkle, The
Nems artists who were managed by Brian Epstein's American partner, Nathan Weiss. John suggested the group's name. The Cyrkle appeared on the bill with The Beatles on their 1966 North American Tour.

D

Daily Howl

Dovedale Primary School newspaper for which John was a contributing editor at age nine. It was in this publication that John first publicly displayed his poetry and sketches. After his graduation, John continued to write *Daily Howl*-type material, which he later used in his two books, *In His Own Write* and *A Spaniard in the Works*.

Dakota, The

Luxury apartment building where John and Yoko reside on New York's upper west side. The twelve-room duplex, which was originally owned by the late actor Robert Ryan, was purchased by the Lennons in 1973. John has since bought several apartments within the building, including a basement flat which doubles as a recording studio.

Dalton, David

Coauthor of *The Beatles Get Back* booklet, which was included in the LET IT BE album package in all countries but the U.S.

Daltrey, Roger

Lead singer of The Who. In 1975 Daltrey starred in *Lisztomania,* in which Ringo cameoed as the Pope. Daltrey recorded Paul's composition "Giddy," which is included on his album ONE OF THE BOYS.

Dan

Villainous character in the song "Rocky Raccoon."

"Dance the Do"

Mike McGear song cowritten and produced by Paul.

Danher, Bert

Paul's cousin, who contributes to the *Wings Fun Club* newsletter. Bert's specialty is the crossword puzzle.

DARK HORSE

Artist: George Harrison
Producer: George
Year first released: 1974
Record label: Apple
Tracks: 9
    "Hari's on Tour (Express)"
    "Simply Shady"
    "So Sad"
    "Bye Bye Love"
    "Maya Love"
    "Ding Dong; Ding Dong"
    "Dark Horse"
    "Far East Man"
    "It Is He (Jai Sri Krishna)"

- The album was released to coincide with George's first solo tour. George rush-released the album before embarking on his twenty-seven-city tour of America and Canada. Due to a rush to meet his deadline, George was forced to record the songs while fighting a losing battle with laryngitis.
- The album received mixed reviews, with much of the criticism stemming from the poor condition of George's voice at the time of recording.
- Ringo plays drums on some cuts on the album.
- The cover photos were taken by George's assistant Terry Doran.

"Dark Horse"

Written by: George Harrison
Recorded by: George
Lead singer: George
Year first released: 1974
Record label: Apple
Album: DARK HORSE
       THE BEST OF GEORGE HARRISON
Single: Britain and U.S.
Performances: 1974 Dark Horse Tour
          Rehearsal for "Saturday Night Live"
          TV show (not aired)

- George wrote this song to coincide with the opening of his new record company, Dark Horse.
- The phrase Dark Horse is a Liverpool expression meaning an outcast; George felt it was an appropriate title for his company.

Dark Horse Records

George's record company established in May of 1974. Dark Horse originated as George's answer to The Beatles' ill-fated Apple company, which he felt failed due to a lack of proper organization. George's concept was for Dark Horse to cater to the talents of artists, allowing them the creativity that established companies might neglect. The company's logo design was discovered by George while in India. He noticed a can of paint with a white horse on the label. George commissioned a designer to darken the horse's color and position it to coincide with the direction of a revolving record on a turntable.

At its inception, Dark Horse was distributed by A & M Records. Because of George's prior commitment to Apple Records he was forced to wait to record for his label until his contract with Apple ran out in 1976. The original list of artists releasing records on Dark Horse were Ravi Shankar, Splinter, Jiva, and Attitudes.

Dark Horse's association with A & M lasted two years and ended in litigation. They sued George, claiming he was late in delivering the first album he was to record for them, 33⅓. After the lawsuit was settled, George took his album to Warner Brothers, where a deal was then made to have the company distribute the

Dark Horse label. 33⅓ was released on Dark Horse in November of 1976.

"Dark Sweet Lady"
Written by: George Harrison
Recorded by: George
Lead singer: George
Year first released: 1979
Record label: Dark Horse
Album: GEORGE HARRISON
• Inspired by wife Olivia.

Darktown Skifflers
British group in which Ringo played drums in 1958.

Datebook
1960s magazine for teens which introduced *Beatles Book Monthly* (the British publication dedicated to The Beatles) to the American audience, with its excerpts on pink paper. It was in *Datebook* where John's controversial statements on Christianity first appeared in the U.S. Art Unger, the magazine's editor, became a close friend of The Beatles and obtained many exclusive interviews.

Dave Clark Five, The
British pop group that rivaled The Beatles for the top group position for a brief period in 1964.

Davies, Hugh
Recording engineer who supplied the tapes for the 1964 concert portion of the album THE BEATLES AT THE HOLLYWOOD BOWL.

Davies, Hunter
Author of *The Beatles: The Authorized Biography* published in 1968. Davies first contacted Paul in 1966 about his idea for a Beatles' biography, and Paul consented to get The Beatles' full cooperation for the venture. The original manuscript had to be cut from two volumes. Davies admitted that pending The Beatles' approval, he had to rewrite and alter much of the material to suit their tastes. Paul, he felt, was the most difficult to interview; George required the most revisions, due to his changing philosophies, and John and Ringo were the most open and easy going. Davies became a close friend of The Beatles through his work, and in 1969, hosted Paul and Linda for two weeks at his home in Malta. Davies, who is currently the editor of the *Sunday Times Magazine,* has written The Beatles' obits for *The London Times* obituary file.

Davis, Jessie Ed
Guitarist who performed at the Bangla Desh Concert in 1971. He released George's composition "Sue Me, Sue You Blues" prior to George's recording. Davis appears on the albums THE CONCERT FOR BANGLA DESH, EXTRA TEXTURE, WALLS AND BRIDGES, GOODNIGHT VIENNA, and RINGO'S ROTOGRAVURE.

Davis, Rodney
One of the original members of The Quarrymen.

"Day in the Life, A"
Written by: Lennon/McCartney
Recorded by: The Beatles
Lead singer: John
Year first released: 1967
Record label: Parlophone (Britain); Capitol (U.S.)
Album: SGT. PEPPER'S LONELY HEARTS CLUB
         BAND
         THE BEATLES 1967–1970
Single: Rereleased in America in 1978 as the B side of
         "Sgt. Pepper's Lonely Hearts Club Band"/
         "With A Little Help From My Friends"
Performances: Promo film clip
• The Beatles hired forty-two musicians from the London Philharmonic Orchestra to play simultaneously in different keys to achieve the desired effect in the climactic interludes.
• On this song The Beatles used the melotron (an electronic keyboard with programmed taped sounds) for the first time. It has since become standard recording equipment.
• "A Day in the Life" was originally two separate songs, which John and Paul combined. Paul wrote the middle verse.
• The BBC banned this masterpiece of social commentary, because they felt it might be drug-oriented.
• The last note of the song lingers for 43½ seconds, with the final inaudible sound intended only for Paul's dog, Martha's, ears.

Day in the Life, A
Book written by Tom Schultheiss; published by Pierian Press in 1979.

"Day the World Gets Round, The"
Written by: George Harrison
Recorded by: George
Lead singer: George
Year first released: 1973
Record label: Apple
Album: LIVING IN THE MATERIAL WORLD

"Daytime Nightime Suffering"
Written by: Paul McCartney
Recorded by: Wings
Lead singer: Paul
Year first released: 1979
Record label: Parlophone (Britain); Columbia (U.S.)
Single: B side of "Goodnight Tonight"
• During a break in the chorus a child's cry can be heard.

"Day Tripper"
Written by: Lennon/McCartney
Recorded by: The Beatles
Lead singer: Paul
Year first released: 1965
Record label: Parlphone (Britain); Capitol (U.S.)
Album: A COLLECTION OF BEATLES OLDIES
         "YESTERDAY" . . . AND TODAY
         THE BEATLES 1962–1966
Single: Double A side with "We Can Work It Out"
Performances: Promo film clip
                1965 British Winter Tour
                1966 Summer World Tour
                "The Music of Lennon and McCart-
                   ney" TV show, 1965

Dean, Johnny
Editor of *Beatles Book Monthly*.

Dear Beatles
Book edited by Bill Adler and published by Grosset and
Dunlap in 1964. The book contains various fan letters to
The Beatles.

"Dear Boy"
Written by: Paul and Linda McCartney
Recorded by: Paul
Lead singer: Paul
Year first released: 1971
Record label: Apple
Album: RAM

"Dear Friend"
Written by: Paul and Linda McCartney
Recorded by: Wings
Lead singer: Paul
Year first released: 1971
Record label: Apple
Album: WILD LIFE
• Paul's response to John's "How Do You Sleep?"

"Dear One"
Written by: George Harrison
Recorded by: George
Lead singer: George
Year first released: 1976
Record label: Dark Horse
Album: 33⅓

"Dear Prudence"
Written by: Lennon/McCartney
Recorded by: The Beatles
Lead singer: John
Year first released: 1968
Record label: Apple
Album: THE BEATLES

• This song was written in India for actress Mia Farrow's sister, Prudence, who spent most of her time
meditating in her room.

Death of Variety
London club which Paul and Linda intended to finance
in 1975. The deal was never finalized.

Deauville Hotel
Miami, Florida, hotel where The Beatles filmed their
February 16, 1964, segment of the "Ed Sullivan Show."
While vacationing here they also attended the nightclub
performances of Don Rickles, Myron Cohen, and Carol
Lawrence.

DeBlasio, Edward
Author of the book *All about The Beatles*.

Decca Records
British record company which turned down The Beatles
for a recording contract in 1962. Decca sent executive
Mike Smith to Liverpool to see The Beatles, and he then
set up an audition in a West Hampstead, London, studio.
They performed "September in the Rain," "To Know
Her Is to Love Her," "Memphis," "Love of the Loved,"
"Like Dreamers Do," "Hello Little Girl," "Sheik of
Araby," "Please Mr. Postman," "Besame Mucho,"
"Money," "Three Cool Cats," "Till There Was You,"
"Red Sails in the Sunset," "Searchin'," "Crying, Wait-
ing, Hoping," and "Take Good Care Of My Baby."
Decca felt The Beatles weren't right for the times.

Dee, Simon
British journalist and television commentator who interviewed Jane Asher on his program "Dee Time" in
July 1968. It was on this show that Jane announced her
engagement to Paul was "broken."

"Deep Blue"
Written by: George Harrison
Recorded by: George
Lead singer: George
Year first released: 1971
Record label: Apple
Single: B side of "Bangla Desh"
• In this song George expresses his feelings of helpless-
ness during his mother's incurable illness.

Delaney and Bonnie
American rock band which, with George, recorded an
album that was never released. George performed with
the group on some of their British tour dates in 1969.
He played from behind the amps so as not to attract
too much attention. Their show was recorded for the
album DELANEY AND BONNIE ON TOUR. On December 15, 1969, Delaney and Bonnie joined John on

stage at their Lyceum Ballroom concert. Their album ACCEPT NO SUBSTITUTES was released on Apple.

Delaware County, New York
Location of John's 150-acre dairy farm purchased in 1978.

"Deliver Your Children"
Written by: Paul McCartney and Denny Laine
Recorded by: Wings
Lead singer: Denny
Year first released: 1978
Record label: Parlophone (Britain); Capitol (U.S.)
Album: LONDON TOWN
Single: B side of "I've Had Enough"

Delmonte Lodge
Country club hotel in Monterey where Ringo, Maureen, George, and Pattie stayed during a trip they took to California in June of 1968.

de Miquita, Señor Bueno
British commissioner of oathes who, on April 22, 1969, officiated at the ceremony for the changing of John's middle name from Winston to Ono. The ceremony took place on Apple's rooftop at 3 Saville Row.

de Paul, Lynsey
British singer/songwriter whom Ringo dated in 1976. Ringo also plays drums on her album.

Derek and the Dominoes
Eric Clapton's band, which he formed in 1970. George plays guitar on their song "Tell the Truth."

Derry Wilke and the Seniors
Liverpool group which paved the way for The Beatles' first engagement in Hamburg, Germany. The Seniors' successful enagagements at the Indra club prompted the management to book The Beatles as well as many other Liverpool performers.

DeShannon, Jackie
American performer on the bill of the Beatles 1964 U.S. summer tour. Jackie was terrified to go out and sing in front of the Beatlemaniacs, who only wanted The Beatles, but Paul's encouraging words helped give her the confidence to go on stage.

deStyl, Stu
Stage name used by Stu Sutcliffe on The Beatles' 1960 Scottish Tour, when the group called themselves The Silver Beatles.

DeSwaan, Sylvia
Photographer of the black-and-white poster included in the album VENUS AND MARS.

"Devil in Her Heart"
Written by: Richard B. Drapkin
Recorded by: The Beatles
Lead singer: George
Year first released: 1963
Record label: Parlophone (Britain); Capitol (U.S.)
Album: WITH THE BEATLES
                THE BEATLES' SECOND ALBUM

"Devil Woman"
Written by: Richard Starkey and Vini Poncia
Recorded by: Ringo
Lead singer: Ringo
Year first released: 1973
Record label: Apple
Album: RINGO
Single: B side of "You're Sixteen"

Dexter, Dave
Assistant producer of the American albums BEATLES '65 and HELP!

Dice
The dalmation who was photographed with The Beatles in New York's Central Park in 1964. These photos of The Beatles with the dog were first used on the Beatle bubblegum cards.

Dickinson, Angie
Actress who appeared as a policewoman in the 1978 television special "Ringo."

Dietrich, Marlene
German actress who appeared on the bill with The Beatles at the Royal Variety Show on November 4, 1963.

diFranco, Philip
Editor of the book *A Hard Day's Night.*

"Dig It"
Written by: Lennon/McCartney/Harrison/Starr
Recorded by: The Beatles
Lead singer: John
Year first released: 1970
Record label: Apple
Album: LET IT BE
• During the performance in the movie John rattles off an improvised litany of celebrated institutions and personalities, accompanied by an impromptu musical backing.
• The song was edited for the album version.

DiLello, Richard
American author of the book *The Longest Cocktail Party.* DiLello was assistant to Derek Taylor at Apple's press office from 1968 to 1969. The book is his account of his times with Apple and The Beatles.

Diltz, Henry
Photographer of several of the photos included in the album LONDON TOWN.

"Ding Dong; Ding Dong"
Written by: George Harrison
Recorded by: George
Lead singer: George
Year first released: 1974
Record label: Apple
Album: DARK HORSE
Single: Britain and U.S.
Performances: Promo film clip
· George's optimistic New Year's resolution. His satirical chronology of The Beatle years is depicted in his promo film clip, which also allows the public a teaser look at a "nude" George!

Dingle
Area in Liverpool where Ringo was born and raised.

Dingle Vale Secondary Modern
School in Liverpool where Ringo attended classes from age eleven up until his mid-teens, when he left school due to an illness.

Dixon, Jeanne
Clairvoyant who allegedly predicted that The Beatles would be involved in an air crash during their 1964 American concert tour. This report led to much worry and concern on the part of The Beatles and their families. Though Dixon denied having made the prediction, the plane The Beatles had chartered without incident did crash two years later, killing all on board.

"Dizzy Miss Lizzie"
Written by: Larry Williams
Recorded by: The Beatles
Lead singer: John
Year first released: 1965
Record label: Parlophone (Britain); Capitol (U.S.)
Album: BEATLES VI
        HELP! (Britain)
        LIVE PEACE IN TORONTO
        ROCK AND ROLL MUSIC
        THE BEATLES AT THE HOLLYWOOD
        BOWL
Performances: 1965 North American Summer Tour
        1965 British Tour
        Toronto Rock 'n' Roll Revival Concert, 1969 (John and the Plastic Ono Band)

DOLL'S HOUSE, A
Intended title for the album THE BEATLES. The idea was dropped after The Beatles discovered the title was already an Ibsen play. The premise was to be a musical score about a girl and the different people visiting her house of pleasure.

Donovan
British musician on whose songs "Mellow Yellow" and "Atlantis" Paul sings background vocals.

"Don't Bother Me"
Written by: George Harrison
Recorded by: The Beatles
Lead singer: George
Year first released: 1963
Record label: Parlophone (Britain); Capitol (U.S.)
Album: WITH THE BEATLES
        MEET THE BEATLES
· George's first original composition.
· Written while George was sick in bed during The Beatles tour of Britain in 1963.

"Don't Dig No Pakistanis"
Unreleased song recorded during the LET IT BE sessions. Paul improvised the lyrics to the tune of "Get Back." He had originally conceived "Get Back" to be a political statement.

"Don't Ever Change"
Song The Beatles performed in the early 1960s.

"Don't Let It Bring You Down"
Written by: Paul McCartney and Denny Laine
Recorded by: Wings
Lead singer: Paul
Year first released: 1978
Record label: Parlophone (Britain); Capitol (U.S.)
Album: LONDON TOWN

"Don't Let Me Down"
Written by: Lennon/McCartney
Recorded by: The Beatles
Lead singer: John
Year first released: 1970
Record label: Apple
Album: THE BEATLES AGAIN
        THE BEATLES 1967–1970
Single: B side of "Get Back"
Performances: *Let It Be* movie
· The movie and single version differ due to the change in producers. George Martin produced the single, Phil Spector the album.
· Another composition dedicated to Yoko.

"Don't Let Me Wait Too Long"
Written by: George Harrison
Recorded by: George
Lead singer: George

Year first released: 1973
Record label: Apple
Album: LIVING IN THE MATERIAL WORLD
• This song was written about the fans who wait outside the recording studio. After completion of the record George invited his fans inside to hear the recording.

"Don't Pass Me By"
Written by: Richard Starkey
Recorded by: The Beatles
Lead singer: Ringo
Year first released: 1968
Record label: Apple
Album: THE BEATLES
THE BEATLES RARITIES (U.S.)
• This is the first song that Ringo composed on his own.

"Don't Worry Kyoko (Mummy's Only Looking for Her Hand In the Snow)"
Yoko composition dedicated to her daugher, Kyoko. It appears as the B side of John's "Cold Turkey" single and was performed live by the Plastic Ono Band at the Toronto Rock 'n' Roll Revival Concert (LIVE PEACE IN TORONTO) and the Lyceum Ballroom Concert (SOMETIME IN NEW YORK CITY).

"Don't You Remember When"
Vera Lynn song, written by Lynsey de Paul, on which Ringo plays tambourine.

"Don't You Rock Me, Daddy"
One of the first songs George and Paul learned to play together while practicing guitar chords in 1955.

Dooley, Arthur
Sculptor who created the statues of The Beatles erected on the wall of the new Cavern Club in Liverpool. The statue is of a Madonna holding three babies, with the fourth baby flying away. A plaque underneath is inscribed: "Four lads that shook the world." The statue, unveiled in April 1974, was produced by funds raised by the people of Liverpool and fans throughout Britain. Dooley intended the statue to be symbolic as the Madonna represents the Merseyside and the babies are The Beatles; the flying baby is Paul leaving The Beatles.

Doran, Terry
Personal assistant to The Beatles, who later became George's assistant. Doran originally worked as Brian Epstein's associate at Nems. He became friends with all The Beatles and is the inspiration behind the line in "She's Leaving Home" about the man from the motor trade. (Doran worked as a car salesman before working with The Beatles.) When The Beatles formed Apple, Doran was appointed head of Apple's publishing division, but did various jobs at Apple before becoming personal assistant to George.

In 1978 Terry Doran promoted "The Concert of the Century," project Interspeak, benefit for the preservation of whales. The concert, which was rumored to headline George Harrison among others, never materialized.

Dorchester Hotel
London hotel where The Beatles held two private dinner parties to celebrate the premieres of their feature movies *A Hard Day's Night* and *Help!* The Dorchester was also the site of a literary luncheon sponsored by Foyle's bookshop in honor of John on April 23, 1964.

DORIS TROY
Album on which George and Ringo appear.

Dornish
Island off the coast of Ireland which John and Yoko purchased in 1970.

Dorsey, Tony
Trombone player who performed with Wings on their albums VENUS AND MARS, WINGS AT THE SPEED OF SOUND, WINGS OVER AMERICA, and BACK TO THE EGG. Dorsey toured with the band on their 1975–76 World Tour and Wings' 1979 British Tour, for which he wrote the arrangements for the brass section. When Paul was looking for a drummer in 1975, it was Dorsey who suggested drummer Joe English.

"Dose of Rock 'n' Roll, A"
Written by: Carl Grossman
Recorded by: Ringo
Lead singer: Ringo
Year first released: 1976
Record label: Polydor (Britain); Atlantic (U.S.)
Album: RINGO'S ROTOGRAVURE
Single: Britain and U.S.
Performances: Promo film clip

"Do the Oz"
Written by: John Lennon and Yoko Ono
Recorded by: John Lennon and the Elastic Oz Band
Lead singer: John
Year first released: 1971
Record label: Apple
Single: B side of "God Save Us"
Performances: John Sinclair Benefit, 1972
• John recorded this song to help raise funds for the defense of the editor of *Oz* magazine, who was on trial for obscenity, in 1971.

Douglas, Jack
Coengineer of John's albums IMAGINE and SOMETIME IN NEW YORK CITY.

Douglas, Mike

American talk show host whose television program was cohosted by John and Yoko during the week of February 21–25, 1972. Douglas claimed that John and Yoko were two of the most difficult guests he ever worked with, due to their specific demands as to who should appear along with them on the show. Some of their choices for guests included Chuck Berry, Jerry Rubin, George Carlin, Bobby Seale, The Chambers Brothers, and Ralph Nader. John also performed with the Elephant's Memory Band for the first time in public. In 1978, Ringo guested on the "Mike Douglas Show" to plug his "Ringo" television special, in which Douglas also cameoed.

Dovedale Primary

School in Liverpool where John and George were enrolled. This was the first school they both attended.

"Down and Out"

Written by: Richard Starkey
Recorded by: Ringo
Lead singer: Ringo
Year first released: 1973
Record label: Apple
Album: RINGO
Single: B side of "Photograph"

"Do You Like Me Just a Little Bit?"

Song performed on the "Cilla" television show by Ringo and Cilla Black. Paul's father suggested they do the song.

"Do You Want to Dance"

Written by: Bobby Freeman
Recorded by: John
Lead singer: John
Year first released: 1975
Record label: Apple
Album: ROCK 'N' ROLL

"Do You Want to Know a Secret"

Written by: Lennon/McCartney
Recorded by: The Beatles
Lead singer: George
Year first released: 1963
Record label: Parlophone (Britain); Vee Jay and Capitol (U.S.)
Album: PLEASE PLEASE ME
        INTRODUCING THE BEATLES
        THE EARLY BEATLES
EP: TWIST AND SHOUT
Single: U.S.
- Billy J. Kramer had a big hit with this song in England.
- John came up with the idea for the song from the song "Wishing Well" heard in the Disney movie *Snow White and the Seven Dwarfs*.

Drake, Peter

Producer of Ringo's album BEAUCOUPS OF BLUES. It was while Drake was working with George on ALL THINGS MUST PASS that he suggested to Ringo that he record a country-western album. Drake again worked with George on his album LIVING IN THE MATERIAL WORLD.

Drake's Drum

Race horse which Paul bought for £1,200 and presented to his father for his sixty-second birthday. The horse came in second place in its first race for the McCartney owners, and Paul was on hand to root him in.

Dr. Dream

Pseudonym John uses on his song "#9 Dream."

"Dream"

Written by: Johnny Mercer
Recorded by: Ringo
Lead singer: Ringo
Year first released: 1970
Record label: Apple
Album: SENTIMENTAL JOURNEY

"Dream Baby"

Roy Orbison song which The Beatles performed on the British radio program "Here We Go" in 1962.

"Drilling a Hole/Guru Vandana"

Written by: George Harrison
Recorded by: George
Lead singer: None (Instrumental)
Year first released: 1968
Record label: Apple
Album: WONDERWALL

"Drive My Car"

Written by: Lennon/McCartney
Recorded by: The Beatles
Lead singer: Paul
Year first released: 1966
Record label: Parlophone (Britain); Capitol (U.S.)
Album: RUBBER SOUL (Britain)
        "YESTERDAY" . . . AND TODAY
        ROCK AND ROLL MUSIC
        THE BEATLES 1962–1966
EP: NOWHERE MAN

Dr. John

Rock musician who joined John in 1974 for a jam session on stage at L.A.'s Troubadour Club. In 1975, at St. Bernard's Civic Center Auditorium in New Orleans, Paul was thrown off the stage at a Dr. John concert when he was mistaken for a fan. Paul was in costume as a clown and was not recognized by the security guards.

Dr. John appears on the albums WALLS AND BRIDGES, GOODNIGHT VIENNA, and RINGO'S ROTOGRAVURE. Ringo acted as MC for Dr. John's live album recording HOLLYWOOD BE THY NAME, and Ringo also appears on his album I GOT RIZZUM.

"Drowning in the Sea of Love"
Written by: Kenny Gamble and Leon Huff
Recorded by: Ringo
Lead singer: Ringo
Year first released: 1977
Record label: Polydor (Britain); Atlantic (U.S.)
Album: RINGO THE 4TH
Single: U.S.
Performances: Promo film clip
• Extended version promoted as a disco record was also released.

"Dr. Robert"
Written by: Lennon/McCartney
Recorded by: The Beatles
Lead singer: John
Year first released: 1966
Record label: Parlophone (Britain); Capitol (U.S.)
Album: REVOLVER (Britain)
        "YESTERDAY" . . . AND TODAY
• Beatles dedication to a doctor who prescribed drugs to expand the mind. . . .

Dr. Winston and Booker Table and the Maitre D's
John's pseudonym on the song "Beef Jerky."

Duffy Square
Broadway location in New York where John, Yoko, and thousands of demonstrators gathered on May 20, 1972, to protest America's involvement in the Vietnam War. John spoke to the crowd and joined the marchers in a chorus of "Give Peace a Chance."

DUIT ON MONDEI
Harry Nilsson album on which Ringo plays drums and helps out with vocals. This saying is also seen on the album cover of the RINGO album.

Dunbar, John
Co-owner of the bookshop–art gallery Indica. It was through his partnership with Peter Asher that Dunbar (ex-husband of Marianne Faithfull) became associated with The Beatles. In 1966 it was John Dunbar who introduced John to Yoko while Yoko was staging an exhibit in his art gallery.

Dunning, George
Director of the move *Yellow Submarine.*

Dykins, Mr.
Name of John's mother's boyfriend whom she lived with after her separation from John's father. "Twitchy" (as John referred to him) was the father of John's half-sisters, Julia and Jacqueline.

Dylan, Bob
American singer/composer who became one of the biggest influences of the sixties generation. He first met The Beatles in 1964, through New York newspaper columnist Al Aronowitz. On this occasion, Dylan is credited with introducing The Beatles to their first experience with marijuana. Dylan's profound social commentaries also inspired the group to aspire to more meaningful lyrics in their songs. John credits Dylan with the lyrical inspiration and musical style for "You've Got to Hide Your Love Away." Dylan was later mentioned in John's compositions "Yer Blues" and "God."

George became a close friend of Dylan and they holidayed together with their families on several occasions. In November of 1968 George visited Dylan at his Woodstock home in New York while Dylan was recuperating from injuries after a motorcycle accident.

Dylan played George his song "If Not for You" and offered it to George, who later recorded it for his album ALL THINGS MUST PASS. On the same album Harrison and Dylan collaborated on the song "I'd Have You Anytime." Dylan's friendship and encouragement was a tremendous source of strength to George when he was feeling stifled and dissatisfied in his association with The Beatles. In 1969, George, Pattie, Ringo, and Maureen were Bob Dylan's guests at his Isle of Wight performance.

In 1971 Dylan made a rare concert appearance at George's Concert for Bangla Desh. He performed five songs which were recorded for the album and movie releases. The movie *The Concert for Bangla Desh* was co-edited by Dylan.

E

EARLY BEATLES, THE
Artist: The Beatles
Producer: George Martin
Year first released: 1965
Record label: Capitol
Tracks: 11
"Love Me Do"
"Twist and Shout"
"Anna"
"Chains"
"Boys"
"Ask Me Why"
"Please Please Me"
"P.S. I Love You"
"Baby It's You"
"A Taste of Honey"
"Do You Want to Know a Secret"
• An American release, which Capitol released after buying the rights to these songs from Vee Jay Records.

"Early 1970"
Written by: Richard Starkey
Recorded by: Ringo
Lead singer: Ringo
Year first released: 1971
Record label: Apple
Album: BLAST FROM YOUR PAST
Single: B side of "It Don't Come Easy"
• Ringo's sentimental commentary on the breakup of The Beatles.
• George helps out on guitar and background vocals.

EARLY YEARS, THE
Album released in Britain in 1971. It consisted of material recorded by The Beatles in Germany in 1961, while backing singer Tony Sheridan.

Eastman and Eastman
New York law firm headed by Linda Eastman McCartney's father, Lee V. Eastman, and her brother, John Eastman, which represents Paul in all his business dealings.

In early 1969, Linda suggested to Paul that Eastman and Eastman sort out The Beatles' financial difficulties with their Apple company. Paul contacted Eastman, and the firm became the legal advisors and acting managers of Apple on February 4, 1969. They headed Apple for only one month, until another manger, Allen Klein, was brought in by John to handle his personal finances. John, together with Ringo and George, voted for Klein to replace the Eastmans as Apple's manager, with Paul alone casting the dissenting vote in favor of his original choice of Eastman and Eastman. Klein and the other Beatles agreed to keep the Eastmans on as legal advisors, but it was made clear that Klein would be in charge. The Eastmans resented playing second fiddle to Klein and advised an already wary Paul not to sign Klein on as his manager. Paul opted to remain with the Eastmans and refused Klein's representation. This irreconcilable split in The Beatles' management became the main stumbling block in the group's ability to remain a cohesive unit.

Under the advice of Eastman and Eastman, Paul sued The Beatles in order to be free of his Apple ties. He was then able to continue as a free agent with his own choice of management. Eastman and Eastman continued to represent Paul in all of his business ventures, and, as of today, are credited with securing for Paul and Wings the biggest record deal in the industry's history. John Eastman is presently a director of Apple and is Paul's representative in the company. McCartney Productions Ltd.'s U.S. base is in the New York offices of Eastman and Eastman.

Eastman, Linda
Maiden name of Paul's wife, Linda.

"Easy Beat"
BBC radio series on which The Beatles performed four times from 1963 through 1964.

"Easy for Me"
Written by: Harry Nilsson
Recorded by: Ringo
Lead singer: Ringo
Year first released: 1974
Record label: Apple
Album: GOODNIGHT VIENNA

"Eat at Home"
Written by: Paul and Linda McCartney
Recorded by: Paul
Lead singer: Paul
Year first released: 1971
Record label: Apple
Album: RAM
Performances: Wings Over Europe tour
• John's favorite song on Paul's album.

Eckhorn, Peter
Manager of Hamburg's Top Ten club, where The Beatles performed in 1960 and 1961.

Eddie Clayton Skiffle Group
One of the first groups Ringo played drums in.

Edgewater Hotel
Seattle, Washington, hotel where The Beatles stayed during their 1964 U.S. Tour. The Beatles destroyed their bedsheets by pouring a concoction of milk, liquor, and orange juice on them. This extreme tactic was taken by the group in order to foil the plan that they uncovered in which the hotel staff was preparing to sell The Beatles' sheets.

Edison, Maxwell
Murderous medical student who is the fictional hero of the song "Maxwell's Silver Hammer."

Edmunds, Dave
Musician who joined Wings on stage at the Hammersmith Odeon to perform at the charity concert for Kampuchea on December 29, 1979.

Edward H. Morris Music
Music publishing company purchased by McCartney Productions Ltd. in 1976. With this purchase MPL acquired the rights to the Buddy Holly music catalogue.

Eight Arms to Hold You
Original title for the movie _Help!_ The first pressing of the single "Help!" and "Ticket to Ride" contains the label caption: "From the United Artists Screenplay, _Eight Arms to Hold You._"

"Eight Days a Week"
Written by: Lennon/McCartney
Recorded by: The Beatles
Lead singer: John
Year first released: 1964
Record label: Parlophone (Britain); Capitol (U.S.)
Album: BEATLES FOR SALE
            THE BEATLES VI
            THE BEATLES 1962–1966
EP: BEATLES FOR SALE
Single: U.S.
Performances: Promo film clip.

"1882"
Unreleased song performed by Wings on their 1972 Wings Over Europe Tour.

Elastic Oz Band
Name John dubbed his Plastic Ono Band during the recording of the single, "God Save Us"/"Do the Oz" in 1971.

"Eleanor Rigby"
Written by: Lennon/McCartney
Recorded by: The Beatles
Lead singer: Paul
Year first released: 1966
Record label: Parlophone (Britain); Capitol (U.S.)
Album: REVOLVER
            A COLLECTION OF BEATLES OLDIES
            THE BEATLES 1962–1966
Single: Britain and U.S.
• Paul felt that though this follow-up to "Yesterday" was more complex in lyrics and music, his voice was inferior, and therefore left the song with less appeal.
• The intended title for the song was "Daisy Hawkins," a name Paul observed on a shop sign in Bristol, England.
• The "father" referred to in the lyrics was originally called McCartney, but Paul decided to change the name at the last minute so as not to raise any misconceptions about his personal life and at the same time provide a more universal theme.
• None of The Beatles play instruments on the song.
• The song won a Grammy Award.

Electronic Music Industry
See EMI.

ELECTRONIC SOUND
Artist: George Harrison
Producer: George
Year first released: 1969
Record label: Zapple
Tracks: 2
      "Under the Mersey Wall"
      "No Time or Space"
• The sound is George playing the moog synthesizer.
• George drew the cover design.

Elephant's Memory Band
New York group that backed John and Yoko during the early seventies. The band, consisting of Stan Bronstein, Richard Frank, Jr., Gary Van Seyoc, Adam Ippolito, Wayne Gabriel, and John LaBosca, first worked with John in 1971. They appeared on stage with John and Yoko at the One to One benefit concert at Madison Square Garden to help perform the songs from John's album SOMETIME IN NEW YORK CITY, on which they also backed John. In 1972 John and Yoko produced their album ELEPHANT'S MEMORY for Apple Records.

Elite Recording Studio
Recording studio located in the Bahamas where Ringo recorded part of his BAD BOY album in 1978.

Elliot, Bill
British musician who sang lead on John's "God Save Us" single in 1971. He later became a member of the group Splinter, which was signed to George's Dark Horse Records.

Ellis, Geoffrey
Personal assistant to The Beatles and Brian Epstein since Nems' inception in 1962. After Epstein's death in 1967, Ellis was appointed one of Nems' managing directors.

Ellis, Robert
Photographer whose photos appear on the album covers for RED ROSE SPEEDWAY, WINGS AT THE SPEED OF SOUND, and WINGS OVER AMERICA. Ellis also is responsible for the poster photo included in the album WINGS AT THE SPEED OF SOUND.

Elstead, Surrey
Town where Ringo made his home in 1968. He purchased the house from actor Peter Sellers. Ringo soon realized that commuting from the sixteenth-century mansion to London, forty miles away, proved too difficult, so he sold the house in 1969. The next buyer was musician Stephen Stills.

Elstree Studios
Location in London where Paul and Wings rehearsed for their 1975–76 World Tour. A preview of the show was performed here to an audience of one hundred people including Ringo, Victor Spinetti, Elton John, Twiggy, and members of the Wings Fun Club.

El Toro
One of the yachts used by Wings during the recording of the album LONDON TOWN, while the group visited the Virgin Islands.

Emanual
Mexican gardener portrayed by Ringo in the movie *Candy*.

Emerick, Geoff
Assistant to producer George Martin who worked on most of The Beatles recordings. Emerick was awarded a Grammy for his work on SGT. PEPPER'S LONELY HEARTS CLUB BAND. In recent years he has worked on Paul's albums BAND ON THE RUN (for which he received a Grammy), VENUS AND MARS, and LONDON TOWN. Emerick also helped mix the tapes for THE BEATLES AT THE HOLLYWOOD BOWL.

Emerine, Larry
Assistant engineer and photographer of the inner sleeve photo for the album, GOODNIGHT VIENNA.

EMI
Electrical and Musical Industries; the largest recording company in the world when The Beatles were signed to record for them in 1962.

The Beatles had sent a copy of their audition tape to several companies and were rejected by each one, including EMI. When The Beatles' manager, Brian Epstein, met personally with EMI producer, George Martin, he played him the demonstration tapes and Martin found the sound to his liking. He auditioned the group for Parlophone Records (a division of EMI) on June 6, 1962, and The Beatles were signed to record for the label. Their contract called for the group to record for Parlophone in England and Capitol (EMI's United States affiliate) in America. The Beatles' first recording session for Parlophone was at EMI studios on Abbey Road on Sept. 11, 1962.

In those early years The Beatles were only paid a couple of cents royalties per recording, which was the standard agreement in those days. In 1967 a new contract was drawn up between The Beatles, under Brian Epstein's management, and EMI. The deal required the group to record for EMI for nine more years and record at least seventy songs. In return The Beatles would receive ten percent of the album's wholesale price and seventeen percent of the American sales.

By 1969 The Beatles had become disenchanted with what they felt were too little profits coming from their own recordings.

Now, under the management of Allen Klein, their contract with EMI was renegotiated. Klein claimed The Beatles had misunderstood their original contract, thinking that since they had already recorded seventy songs for the company, their obligation had been fulfilled. In a desperate attempt on the part of EMI to hold on to their biggest money-makers, EMI agreed to revise the contract, guaranteeing The Beatles greater control over their product and a huge increase in royalties. This unprecedented deal for a recording artist suited the group enough to keep them recording for the label, though record prices across the board were increased due to The Beatles new profit margin.

In 1976 The Beatles contract with EMI expired. Paul is the only Beatle who continues to record for EMI.

EMI Studios, Abbey Road
Recording studio located in the St. John's Wood section of London. The Beatles first auditioned for Parlophone Records here in 1962 using studio #3. EMI Studio has since become the base in which the bulk of The Beatles material was recorded, usually in studio #2.

The studio has continued to be a favorite of Paul's, who books the facilities on a regular basis. On one occasion in 1979, when Paul found he was unable to use the studio for a recording session, he decided to build a duplicate portable studio to be utilized when EMI's studio #2 is not at his disposal.

Emperor's Gate
First London flat John and Cynthia lived in. It was located in the Kensington section of London.

Empire Ballroom
Dance hall located in Leicester Square, London, which was the site of a party given by Paul to promote the Wings album WILD LIFE on November 8, 1971. Paul handwrote all the invitations to the costumed gala, which was headlined by an old-fashioned dance band.

Empire Theatre
Hall in Liverpool where The Beatles auditioned, under the name Johnny and the Moondogs, for the Caroll Levis "Discoveries" television show in 1959. In 1963 The Beatles staged their Christmas shows here, and ten years later Paul and Wings performed at the Empire. The Empire is also the theatre in which Paul attended his first pop concert at age twelve. Eric Delaney's Band were the entertainers on the bill.

Empty Hand
Thirty-two-minute documentary of ex-Wings member Geoff Britton winning a karate championship in 1974. Paul produced the film and provided the percussion background to the soundtrack. The film was released in 1977.

ENCOURAGING WORDS
Billy Preston album which George coproduced with Preston.

"End, The"
Written by: Lennon/McCartney
Recorded by: The Beatles
Lead singer: Paul
Year first released: 1969
Record label: Apple
Album: ABBEY ROAD
- John, Paul, and George all share on the alternating lead guitar solos.
- Appropriately titled, The Beatles gave this song as their final message to the world.

English, Joe
Former drummer with Wings. English, an American session musician, became a member of the band in 1975 after the departure of Geoff Britton. He was introduced to Paul by Tony Dorsey, arranger of the brass section on the album VENUS AND MARS. English worked on Wings' albums VENUS AND MARS, WINGS AT THE SPEED OF SOUND, and LONDON TOWN. He also accompanied Wings on their 1975–76 World Tour and is on the album WINGS OVER AMERICA. English left the band in 1977 to pursue his own interests in America.

English Ritchie
Pseudonym used by Ringo on the Stephen Stills album STILLS.

Eppy
Nickname used by The Beatles for their manager Brian Epstein.

Epsom Registry Office
Registry office in Surrey, England, where George married Pattie Boyd on January 21, 1966. Paul was the only Beatle to attend the ceremony.

Epstein, Brian
September 19, 1935–August 27, 1967

The Beatles' manager from 1961 up until his death in 1967.

Brian Epstein was born in Liverpool to a prominent family who owned a small furniture store in the area. The first son of Harry and Queenie Epstein, Brian was trained in the family philosophy of working hard in order to succeed in business and in life. As Brian grew older it became apparent to his family that their son was not interested in attaining his parents' goals. Though Brian was unquestionably sensitive and highly intelligent, his interest in schoolwork was minimal and he did not do well scholastically. He found himself in a perpetual state of instability and he preferred the shelter of his room to the company of friends.

After leaving school, Brian rejected his father's request to partake in the family business, and instead chose to try his hand at various artistic professions from designing clothes to acting. It wasn't long before Brian became bored and discontented in each of his endeavors. After a disastrous stint in the British Army, for which he received a discharge due to mental incapacity, Brian returned home and reluctantly settled into his parents' business. He went to work as a salesman in the record department of his father's Nems store. Though Brian did not relish the job, he tackled the post with the enthusiasm and professionalism characteristic of Brian in any new pursuit. Under Brian's management Nems became the most reputable record shop in Liverpool.

It was during a day's work at Nems that Brian was informed about the German recording made by a Liverpool group called The Beatles. Sparked by the numerous inquiries about the recording (which he hadn't stocked) and the general interest in the group among his customers (which, unknown to him, included The Beatles), Brian decided to find out more about The Beatles. On November 9, 1961, Brian went to The Cavern Club to observe a Beatles performance and see for himself what all the fuss was about. He was immediately drawn to the magnetism of the group's personality and the professionalism in their music. After returning to the club several times, Brian approached the group with a management proposition. The Beatles, who were impressed with Brian's middle-class manner and sophistication, accepted the offer with no hesitation. In December of the same year, John, Paul, George, and Peter Best signed a contract to have Brian Epstein manage The Beatles. Ironically, Brian's signature never appeared on the document, which entitled him to a whopping 25 percent commission fee on all of The Beatles' future earnings.

Brian's main concern in life now was "his Beatles," and he was determined to see that they succeeded. He had finally found a way to satisfy his own penchant for artistic creativity as he helped mold and guide the career of The Beatles. His first priority was to secure a recording contract for the group, and he worked diligently toward this goal, going from one record company to another with The Beatles' demonstration tapes. After much disappointment and rejection Brian hit upon EMI record producer George Martin, who agreed to audition The Beatles on May 9, 1962. The audition was held in June, but three months later there was still no word from the company. Brian became so incensed with the delay in EMI's decision that he decided to help move things along by threatening to cancel EMI record orders from his shop unless The Beatles were signed. A short time later The Beatles were offered a recording contract with EMI's Parlophone label.

Though The Beatles' musical talent was indisputable, Brian realized their dress and stage presence left much to be desired. In order to gain mass acceptance with the general public, The Beatles would have to tone down the tough boys' image and become more genteel in dress and manner. The leather and jeans were replaced with Pierre Cardin suits; the hair remained long but styled and always clean and combed. The Beatles were also encouraged by Brian to coordinate their act into a professional performance complete with dramatic final bow, a far cry from their usual stance of eating and roughhousing during shows. Brian treated The Beatles with the admiration and respect usually reserved for superstars, long before anyone outside of Liverpool even heard of the group. His faith in The Beatles was tremendous. He was confident of their imminent success and he demanded that his group be treated accordingly by all club owners and promoters. His flair for public relations and creative management was a great asset in promoting The Beatles, but Brian's main concern for the boys always stemmed from his genuine love for them as friends. His paternal attitude toward the group was foremost when it came to looking after them and keeping them happy at all costs. As a result of his all-consuming concern for The Beatles, Brian was sometimes accused by his other Nems clients of being neglectful of their careers.

By 1967, at the age of thirty-two, Brian had built a multi-million-dollar empire and headed one of the biggest talent agencies in the world. But once again frustration and discontentment started to overshadow the good fortune in his life.

The Beatles had by this time grown independent, and Brian's services as manager were becoming obsolete. Brian found himself spending more and more time apart from the group, as their social circles rarely mingled. He became bored and lonely, relying on drugs and liquor to help soothe the pain caused by his imagined uselessness.

On August 27, 1967, Brian Epstein died of what was later ruled as an accidental overdose of drugs and alcohol. At the time of his death Brian's estimated worth was over five million dollars. The Beatles were never again to agree on a manager for the group.

Epstein, Clive

Brother of Brian Epstein; Clive became head of Nems, Brian's management company, after Brian's death in 1967. In 1968 Clive Epstein sold his shares in the company to Triumph Investment Trust Bank of England. (See Nems.)

Escorts, The

Group on the bill with The Beatles for their last appearance at The Cavern on August 3, 1963. Paul later produced their single, "From Head To Toe"/"Night Time."

Eubanks, Bob

Los Angeles TV/radio personality who promoted The Beatles' Hollywood Bowl Concert in 1964. Eubanks hired The Beatles' PR man Derek Taylor in 1964.

Evans, Malcolm
May 27, 1935–January 4, 1975

Beatles' road manager and general assistant.

Mal was working as a bouncer at Liverpool's Cavern Club in 1961 when he first became friendly with The Beatles. After The Beatles had signed with Brian Epstein, Mal started working exclusively for the group, lugging equipment from one gig to the next. When The Beatles began touring the world, Mal became chief roadie responsible for setting up the instruments on stage and overseeing the transference of all The Beatles' equipment. On their off-hours Mal doubled as personal bodyguard for each member of the group and often accompanied them on private holidays.

Mal was regarded by The Beatles as one of their closest friends and a loyal employee. In 1968 he was appointed Assistant General Manager of their Apple company. He was also an integral part of The Beatles' recording sessions, furnishing everything from refreshments to occasional help with song lyrics. He cameoed in three of The Beatles' movies, *Help!*, *Magical Mystery Tour,* and *Let It Be.* Mal also had a bit part in Ringo's solo movie, *Blindman.*

After The Beatles split up, Mal spent his time managing and producing Apple artists, Badfinger. He is credited with cowriting the Ringo song "You and Me (Babe)" along with George Harrison. In 1974 Mal Evans began work on a book about his life with The Beatles. He was still working on this project when he was shot by the Los Angeles Police Department while they were trying to prevent his own suicide attempt with a rifle in 1975. He allegedly turned the gun on the officers in his confusion, and they shot and killed him in their defense.

Evans, Shirley
Accordionist in the movie *Magical Mystery Tour.*

Everett, Kenny
British disc jockey who helped edit The Beatles' Christmas recordings for the fan club members. In 1968 Everett recorded the promo advertisements for their new company, Apple.

Everson Museum of Art
Museum in Syracuse, New York, where Yoko held her art exhibition "This Is Not Here" on October 9, 1971. Among the guests who attended the opening were John, Allen Klein, Ringo and Maureen, and Phil Spector.

"Everybody's Got Something to Hide except Me and My Monkey"
Written by: Lennon/McCartney
Recorded by: The Beatles
Lead singer: John
Year first released: 1968
Record label: Apple
Album: THE BEATLES

"Everybody's Trying to Be My Baby"
Written by: Carl Perkins
Recorded by: The Beatles
Lead singer: George
Year first released: 1964
Record label: Parlophone (Britain); Capitol (U.S.)
Album: BEATLES FOR SALE
        BEATLES '65
        ROCK AND ROLL MUSIC
        THE BEATLES LIVE AT THE STAR
           CLUB
EP: 4 BY THE BEATLES
Performances: Christmas shows 1964
                1965 European Summer Tour
                1965 North American Summer Tour.
· George chose this Perkins composition for obvious reasons.

"Every Little Thing"
Written by: Lennon/McCartney
Recorded by: The Beatles
Lead singer: John and Paul
Year first released: 1964
Record label: Parlophone (Britain); Capitol (U.S.)
Album: BEATLES FOR SALE
        BEATLES VI
        LOVE SONGS

Everyman Theatre
Liverpool theatre which premiered the play, *John, Paul, George, Ringo and Bert* in 1974. The production ran for six weeks before moving to London.

"Every Night"
Written by: Paul McCartney
Recorded by: Paul
Lead singer: Paul
Year first released: 1970
Record label: Apple
Album: McCARTNEY
Performances: 1979 Wings' British Tour

Exciters, The
Group on tour with The Beatles on their 1964 North American Summer Tour.

EXTRACTS FROM THE ALBUM A HARD DAY'S NIGHT (EP)
Artist: The Beatles
Producer: George Martin
Year first released: 1964
Record label: Parlophone
Tracks: 4
     "Any Time at All"
     "I'll Cry Instead"
     "Things We Said Today"
     "When I Get Home"
· This EP was released in Britain as the follow-up to EXTRACTS FROM THE FILM A HARD DAY'S NIGHT.

EXTRACTS FROM THE FILM A HARD DAY'S NIGHT (EP)
Artist: The Beatles
Producer: George Martin
Year first released: 1964
Record label: Parlophone
Tracks: 4
     "I Should Have Known Better"
     "If I Fell"
     "Tell Me Why"
     "And I Love Her"
· British EP.

66

EXTRA TEXTURE (READ ALL ABOUT IT)
Artist: George Harrison
Producer: George
Year first released: 1975
Record label: Apple
Tracks: 10
   "You"
   "The Answer's at the End"
   "This Guitar (Can't Keep From Crying)"
   "Oo-Baby (You Know That I Love You)"
   "World of Stone"
   "A Bit More of You"
   "Can't Stop Thinking about You"
   "Tired of Midnight Blue"
   "Grey Cloudy Lies"
   "His Name Is Legs (Ladies and Gentleman)"
- This was the last album recorded by a Beatle to be released on Apple Records.
- George came up with the album's title while playing a word game with a fellow musician.

F

Fab Four
Affectionate term coined by the media in 1964 to describe The Beatles. The term was also used by close friends and associates and even The Beatles themselves from time to time.

Fab Magazine
British teen publication which, in 1964, supplied the vital information on The Beatles' physical statistics and characteristics for the first (Beatles) effigies to be exhibited at Madame Tussaud's Wax Museum.

Facts About a Pop Group: Featuring Wings
Book written by David Gelly and published by G. Whizzard Publications (Britain) and Harmony Books (U.S.). The American version is titled *Facts About a Rock Group: Featuring Wings*. Paul supplies the introduction.

Fair Carol
Yacht chartered by Paul and family while visiting the Virgin Islands in 1977. Paul arranged for a recording studio to be equipped on the vessel for the recording of LONDON TOWN.

Faith, Adam
Musician on whose album I SURVIVE Paul appears.

Faithfull, Marianne
Singer/actress who appeared with The Beatles on the 1965 television special "The Music of Lennon and McCartney." Paul and Marianne shared the spotlight singing "Yesterday."

"Falling in Love Again"
Paul sings lead on The Beatles' rendition of this 1930s ballad. The song appears on THE BEATLES LIVE AT THE STAR CLUB. It was later released as a single in Britain.

Fallwell, Jr., Marshall
Photographer whose photos appear on the cover of Ringo's album, BEAUCOUPS OF BLUES.

"Fame"
Song written by John Lennon, David Bowie, and Luther Andross and recorded by David Bowie in 1975. John helps out on vocals on the record.

Family Way, The
Movie for which Paul composed the soundtrack, with the help of producer George Martin, in 1967. A movie soundtrack album was released by London Records.

68

"Famous Groupies"
Written by: Paul McCartney
Recorded by: Wings
Lead singer: Paul
Year first released: 1978
Record label: Parlophone (Britain); Capitol (U.S.)
Album: LONDON TOWN

Fan Clubs
There were and are thousands of unauthorized Beatles fan clubs throughout the world. They've come in all forms; dedicated to the group (together and individually), as well as to their family members.

The Official Beatles Fan Club was established in Liverpool in 1961. As The Beatles' popularity grew, the club expanded to include all of Britain and eventually included chapters in various parts of the world. The Beatles worked very closely with their fan club, contributing time and material exclusively for its members. Every Christmas from 1963 to 1969 The Beatles recorded special messages for their club members, which were distributed on record through the club. These special recordings were not sold commercially.

The Official Beatles Fan Club was dissolved in 1972.

"Fantasy Sequence/Glass Box"
Written by: George Harrison
Recorded by: George
Lead singer: None (Instrumental)
Year first released: 1968
Record label: Apple
Album: WONDERWALL

"Far East Man"
Written by: George Harrison
Recorded by: George
Lead singer: George
Year first released: 1974
Record label: Apple
Album: DARK HORSE
• George dedicates this song to Frank Sinatra.

Farrow, Mia
Actress who studied Transcendental Meditation in India with The Beatles. John stated that an alleged pass made by the guru, Maharishi Mahesh Yogi, toward Mia Farrow was one of the factors that contributed to The Beatles' disillusionment with him.

Fascher, Horst
Manager of The Star Club in Germany, where The Beatles performed in 1962.

Fast, Julius
Author of the book *The Beatles: The Real Story*.

"Faster"
Written by: George Harrison
Recorded by: George
Lead singer: George
Year first released: 1979
Record label: Dark Horse
Album: GEORGE HARRISON
Single: Released in Britain
Performances: Promo film clip
- George wrote this song for his pals on the Formula One racing circuit, after promising them he'd write them a song.
- The title is the same as a book written by racer Jackie Stewart.
- The royalties from the British single were donated to the Cancer Foundation chapter established in memory of Swedish racing driver Gunnar Nilsson.

"Fastest Growing Heartache in the West"
Written by: Larry Kingston and Fred Dycus
Recorded by: Ringo
Lead singer: Ringo
Year first released: 1970
Record label: Apple
Album: BEAUCOUPS OF BLUES

Fataar, Rikki
Musician who portrayed Stig O'Hara in the television film *The Rutles*.

Faulkner Street
Liverpool street on which John and Cynthia first lived as husband and wife in 1962. The flat was given to them by Brian Epstein.

Fawcett, Anthony
Author of the book *One Day at a Time*. Fawcett was employed as John and Yoko's personal assistant in 1969 and worked for the couple until 1971.

Federal Bureau of Radiological Health
American government agency which investigated Wings' 1976 U.S. concerts in order to determine whether the laser beams used in the light show were hazardous to the audience's eyesight.

FEELING THE SPACE
Yoko Ono album on which John appears.

Fein, Hal
American business partner in Bert Kaempfert Productions in 1961. Fein claims to have been the original discoverer of The Beatles by bringing Kaempfert's attention to the group when they were performing in Germany in 1961. It was Fein's alleged coaxing which resulted in The Beatles' German recording contract backing singer Tony Sheridan.

Feinstein, Barry
Photographer/designer for the albums ALL THINGS MUST PASS, THE CONCERT FOR BANGLA DESH, and RINGO.

"Fever"
Song performed by The Beatles at their first recording session in Germany in 1960. They backed a singer from a rival band, Rory Storme and the Hurricanes.

Fieldsteel, Ira
New York judge who, on March 23, 1973, ruled that John Lennon would have to voluntarily leave his residence in the United States within sixty days or face deportation. The action stemmed from a case made against John by the U.S. Immigration and Naturalization Bureau after he was deemed an undesirable candidate for residency in the U.S. John's previous conviction in England, four years earlier, for possessing a small amount of cannabis, was the main reason cited by the court for his criminal status. John had technically overstayed his visitor's visa to the U.S. and was, therefore, subject to deportation. John appealed the decision to the Board of Immigration Appeals in Washington. His wife, Yoko, a U.S. citizen, was not subject to deportation, and was determined to stay in the country due to a court battle she was involved in concerning custody of her daughter from a previous marriage. The Lennons were being forced to choose between separating or giving up Yoko's daughter and returning to England together. They chose to stay and fight it out in the courts. During the next two years it was discovered that the persecution of John Lennon had stemmed from a Washington conspiracy to oust John from the country due to his disagreement with the U.S. government's politics.

After much public outcry and the support of the press, politicians, and artists alike, Judge Fieldsteel's original decision was overturned by the Court of Appeals in 1975. On July 27, 1976, John was awarded his permanent residency card by Judge Ira Fieldsteel. The "Green Card," number al7-597-321, was John's ticket to live in peace in the United States and to travel abroad worry-free.

"$15 Draw"
Written by: Sorrels Pickard
Recorded by: Ringo
Lead singer: Ringo
Year first released: 1970
Record label: Apple
Album: BEAUCOUPS OF BLUES

Fillmore East
New York City concert hall where John and Yoko made an unannounced appearance, joining Frank Zappa and the Mothers of Invention on stage in 1971. A recording

of the event appears on John's SOMETIME IN NEW YORK CITY album.

It was also at this theatre that the fledging photographer Linda Eastman became known as the "house photographer" during the late sixties.

Findley, Chuck
Musician who performed in the horn section at George's 1971 Concert for Bangla Desh and on his 1974 Dark Horse Tour of North America. Findley also worked on the albums DARK HORSE, GOODNIGHT VIENNA, RINGO, and EXTRA TEXTURE.

Finley, Charles
Baseball club owner who, in 1964, persuaded Brian Epstein to add a performance to The Beatles' tour itinerary and appear at his Kansas City ballpark. He paid them $150,000, the highest sum ever offered a stage act at that time.

Finer, Morris
One of the lawyers who represented John, George, Ringo, and Apple Corps Limited when Paul sued them in 1971.

Fisher, Carrie
Actress who played the girlfriend of Ognir Rrats in the 1978 "Ringo" television special.

Fisher, John
Chauffeur who worked for Nems Enterprises in New York. Fisher was given the assignment of chauffeuring John and Paul in May of 1968, while they were in New York to promote Apple Corps Limited.

"Fixing a Hole"
Written by: Lennon/McCartney
Recorded by: The Beatles
Lead singer: Paul
Year first released: 1967
Record label: Parlophone (Britain); Capitol (U.S.)
Album: SGT. PEPPER'S LONELY HEARTS CLUB BAND
• Mal Evans, The Beatles' assistant, claimed to have cowritten this song. Although he was not given formal credit, he was paid for his contribution.

Flack, Roberta
Singer who performed on the bill, with John and Yoko, of the 1972 One to One concert.

Fleetwood, Jenny Boyd
Younger sister of Pattie Harrison Clapton. Jenny, being very close to her sister, often accompanied her when she and George and the other Beatles and wives vacationed in places like Wales, Greece, and India. Jenny was employed by The Beatles to work in their Apple Boutique in 1969. She was twice married to Mick Fleetwood of Fleetwood Mac, but they have since divorced.

Flux Fiddlers
Group John credits on his IMAGINE album.

FLY
Yoko album which John produced in 1971.

"Flying"
Written by: Lennon/McCartney/Harrison/Starkey
Recorded by: The Beatles
Lead singer: None (Instrumental)
Year first released: 1967
Record label: Parlophone (Britain); Capitol (U.S.)
Album: MAGICAL MYSTERY TOUR (U.S.)
EP: MAGICAL MYSTERY TOUR
Performances: Soundtrack to the film, *Magical Mystery Tour*
• The only recorded song which was written by all four Beatles.

Flying Cow
Name of the bar in Ringo's Weybridge home.

Fool, The
Mod artists who operated and designed clothes for the Apple Boutique. The Fool, Simon, Marijke, Josje, and Barry was first brought to the attention of The Beatles by Pattie Harrison.

"Fool on the Hill, The"
Written by: Lennon/McCartney
Recorded by: The Beatles
Lead singer: Paul
Year first released: 1967
Record label: Parlophone (Britain); Capitol (U.S.)
Album: MAGICAL MYSTERY TOUR
          THE BEATLES 1967–1970
EP: MAGICAL MYSTERY TOUR
Performances: *Magical Mystery Tour* movie
                1979 Wings' British Tour
• Paul plays flute and recorder on this autobiographical song.

Foote, Dr.
Mad scientist in The Beatles' movie *Help!*, played by British actor Victor Spinetti.

FOOTPRINT
Gary Wright album on which George plays guitar.

Ford, Jack
Son of United States former President, Gerald Ford. Jack Ford arranged a meeting between his father and

George, on December 13, 1974, during George's North American Dark Horse Tour. Ravi Shankar, Billy Preston, Jim Keltner, and George's father were included at the meeting with the President.

Ford, Robben
Lead guitarist, along with George, during the 1974 Dark Horse Tour. Ford also appears on the DARK HORSE album.

"For No One"
Written by: Lennon/McCartney
Recorded by: The Beatles
Lead singer: Paul
Year first released: 1966
Record label: Parlophone (Britain); Capitol (U.S.)
Album: REVOLVER
         LOVE SONGS
• John claims this is one of his favorite Beatle songs.

Forthlin Road, 20
Address of Paul's home in Liverpool where he lived from 1955 until he moved to London in 1964.

"For You Blue"
Written by: George Harrison
Recorded by: The Beatles
Lead singer: George
Year first released: 1970
Record label: Apple
Album: LET IT BE
         THE BEST OF GEORGE HARRISON
Single: B side of "The Long and Winding Road"
Performances: *Let It Be* movie
                1974 Dark Horse Tour
• John plays slide guitar on this song.

Foster, David
Original member of Dark Horse recording artists, Attitudes. Forster later worked on the albums EXTRA TEXTURE, 33⅓, GOODNIGHT VIENNA, and RINGO THE 4TH.

FOUR BY THE BEATLES
Two Beatle EP's were issued in the U.S. under this title. The first was released by Capitol in 1964 with the songs "Roll Over Beethoven," "All My Loving," "This Boy," and "Please Mr. Postman" on it. The second EP (4 BY THE BEATLES) was released by Capitol in 1965 containing the songs "Honey Don't," "I'm a Loser," "Mr. Moonlight," and "Everybody's Trying to Be My Baby."

Fourmost, The
British group originally managed by Brian Epstein. The Fourmost appeared on the bill with The Beatles at their 1963 British Christmas shows. The group recorded the Lennon/McCartney composition "Hello Little Girl" in 1964 and in 1969 Paul produced their record "Rossetta."

"4th of July, The"
John Christie recording which was composed by Paul and Linda in 1974.

Foyle's
London bookshop which, on April 23, 1964, sponsored a literary luncheon attended by John and Cynthia in honor of John's first book, *John Lennon: In His Own Write*. In 1970 John and Yoko appeared here to autograph copies of Yoko's book, *Grapefruit*.

F.P.S.H.O.T.
Abbreviation for Friar Park Studio Henley-on-Thames. This recording studio, located in George's home, is where George recorded the albums DARK HORSE, 33⅓, and GEORGE HARRISON.

Frampton, Peter
British recording artist on whose album WIND OF CHANGE Ringo plays drums. Frampton appears on RINGO'S ROTOGRAVURE album.

France, The SS
Luxury ocean liner on which Paul and family traveled from England to New York in October 1970 to record the RAM album. George was on board The France in September 1971 while traveling from London to New York to edit the film of the Bangla Desh concert.

Franques, Pablo
Character in the song "Being For the Benefit of Mr. Kite."

Freddie and the Dreamers
Group on the bill with the Beatles for their 1964 Christmas shows.

Freeman, Robert
Photographer whose photos appear on the covers of the albums WITH THE BEATLES, MEET THE BEATLES, A HARD DAY'S NIGHT, HELP!, and RUBBER SOUL. Also on the EP's ALL MY LOVING and LONG TALL SALLY.

FREEZE FRAME
Godley and Creme album on which Paul performs.

Freud, Clement
Member of British Parliament whose photo appears on the BAND ON THE RUN album cover.

Friar Park
George's forty-acre estate in Henley-on-Thames, England. The thirty-room castle was built as a monastery

in the late 1800s and was purchased by George in 1970 for $300,000. The photos for the albums ALL THINGS MUST PASS, LIVING IN THE MATERIAL WORLD, DARK HORSE, and 33⅓ were taken on the estate, which includes several guest cottages and a man-made lake on its grounds.

Friede, Goldie
Coauthor of the book *The Beatles A to Z.*

Friedman, Kinky
American musician on whose album LASSO FROM EL PASO Ringo plays drums and is heard as the voice of Jesus in his song "Men's Room, L.A."

"From a Window"
Lennon/McCartney composition that was recorded by Billy J. Kramer and the Dakotas in 1964.

"From Head to Toe"
Song Paul produced for The Escorts.

"From Me to You"
Written by: Lennon/McCartney
Recorded by: The Beatles
Lead singer: John
Year first released: 1963
Record label: Parlophone (Britain); Vee Jay and Capitol (U.S.)
Album: JOLLY WHAT! THE BEATLES AND FRANK IFIELD ON STAGE
A COLLECTION OF BEATLES OLDIES
THE BEATLES 1962–1966
EP: THE BEATLES' HITS
Single: B side of "Please Please Me"
Performances: Royal Variety Performance, November 4, 1963

"Ed Sullivan Show" (TV), February 1964
"Around The Beatles" TV special
• John and Paul wrote this song on the bus during the 1963 Helen Shapiro tour of Britain.
• The title was taken from a newspaper column called "From Us to You."
• The British single has a different harmonica opening than any other version.

"From Me to You Fantasy"
Instrumental which appears on the American release of the HELP! album. It is performed by the George Martin Orchestra.

FROM THEM TO US
Title of The Beatles Christmas album distributed through their British Fan Club. The album is a compilation of all the specially recorded Christmas messages done by The Beatles for their fans from 1963 through 1969.

"From Us to You"
British radio series, starring The Beatles, which consisted of five two-hour programs. For the series, broadcast from December 1963 to June 1965, The Beatles changed the lyrics in the title of their song "From Me to You" to that of the program's title.

Frost, David
British talk show host who interviewed The Beatles on television frequently from 1964 to 1976. A close friend of The Beatles, Frost also hosted television specials about them in 1975 and 1977. The Beatles performed "Hey Jude" live and previewed their promo film clip for "Revolution" on his British TV show in 1968.

G

Gambaccini, Paul
Author of the book *Paul McCartney: In His Own Words*. Gambaccini interviewed Paul for *Rolling Stone* in 1975, and with the fifty thousand unused words compiled this book.

Gambier Terrace
Liverpool flat shared by John and Stuart Sutcliffe in early 1960. The sparsely furnished apartment was supposedly equipped with a coffin in which John sometimes slept.

Ganga Publishing B.V.
George Harrison's music publishing company.

Gardner, Nelson
Virginian farmer who in 1979 sold John two hundred dairy cows for his farm in New York State.

Garner, Frank
The Beatles' first road manager. Garner originally worked at Liverpool's Casbah Club when he began assisting The Beatles by lugging their equipment to and from gigs; he was later replaced by Neil Aspinall.

Gary, Len
One of the original members of The Quarrymen.

"Gave It All Up"
Written by: Richard Starkey and Vini Poncia
Recorded by: Ringo
Lead singer: Ringo
Year first released: 1977
Record label: Polydor (Britain); Atlantic (U.S.)
Album: RINGO THE 4TH

Gelly, David
Author of the book *Facts about a Pop Group Featuring Wings*.

Gentle, Johnny
British singer whom The Beatles backed on their first tour, in Scotland in 1960. The group, which consisted of John, Paul, George, Stu Sutcliffe, and Tommy Moore on drums, was paid $200 a week.

George V
Hotel in Paris where The Beatles stayed in January, 1964. It was during this stay that they celebrated their first number one record on the U.S. charts: "I Want to Hold Your Hand." In 1976 Paul was barred from the hotel after his children redecorated the wallpaper in one of the rooms with felt-tipped markers.

GEORGE HARRISON
Artist: George Harrison
Producer: George Harrison and Russ Titelman
Year first released: 1979
Record label: Dark Horse
Tracks: 10
   "Love Comes to Everyone"
   "Not Guilty"
   "Here Comes the Moon"
   "Soft-Hearted Hana"
   "Blow Away"
   "Faster"
   "Dark Sweet Lady"
   "Your Love Is Forever"
   "Soft Touch"
   "If You Believe"

George Harrison Yesterday & Today
Book written by Ross Michaels; published by Flash Books in 1977.

George Martin Orchestra
Orchestra conducted by The Beatles' producer, George Martin. They performed on the albums A HARD DAY'S NIGHT (U.S.) and YELLOW SUBMARINE. The George Martin Orchestra also performs on Paul's composition "Live and Let Die."

George O'Hara Smith Singers
Credit given for the background vocals on George's album ALL THINGS MUST PASS. The voices are actually George overdubbed several times.

Georgeson, Hari
Pseudonym used by George on Billy Preston's album IT'S MY PLEASURE.

Gerrard, Hillary
Former Apple employee who is presently one of the directors of Apple Corp. Ltd., representing Ringo in his business dealings. Gerrard is also Ringo's personal assistant.

Gerry and the Pacemakers
Liverpool group that was managed by Brian Epstein in the early sixties. Gerry and the Pacemakers performed on The Beatles' 1963 British Tour and appeared in The Beatles' 1963 Christmas shows. The group's first hit record "How Do You Do It" was given to them by George Martin after The Beatles rejected it.

GET BACK
Original title of the album LET IT BE. (See LET IT BE.)

"Get Back"
Written by: Lennon/McCartney
Recorded by: The Beatles
Lead singer: Paul
Year first released: 1969
Record label: Apple
Album: LET IT BE
           THE BEATLES 1967–1970
           ROCK AND ROLL MUSIC
Single: Britain and U.S.
Performances: *Let It Be* movie
- The original production of the song, produced by George Martin, is heard on the single and the albums THE BEATLES 1967–1970 and ROCK AND ROLL MUSIC. The LET IT BE version was produced by Phil Spector.
- Paul ad-libs an extra verse during The Beatles' performance in the *Let It Be* film.
- The song was first intended as a political statement mocking Britain's anti-immigrant proponents.

"Get on the Right Thing"
Written by: Paul McCartney
Recorded by: Wings
Lead singer: Paul
Year first released: 1973
Record label: Apple
Album: RED ROSE SPEEDWAY

"Getting Better"
Written by: Lennon/McCartney
Recorded by: The Beatles
Lead singer: Paul
Year first released: 1967
Record label: Parlophone (Britain); Capitol (U.S.)
Album: SGT. PEPPER'S LONELY HEARTS CLUB BAND
- Paul's account of his changing attitudes.
- The phrase "getting better" came from drummer Jimmy Nichol when he was substituting for Ringo during The Beatles' engagement in Australia in 1964. When asked how he thought things were going, Nichol would always reply, "It's getting better."

"Getting Closer"
Written by: Paul McCartney
Recorded by: Wings
Lead singer: Paul
Year first released: 1979
Record label: Parlophone (Britain); Columbia (U.S.)
Album: BACK TO THE EGG
Single: Britain and U.S.
Performances: 1979 Wings' British Tour
                 Promo film clip "Back to the Egg" TV special, 1979

Ghurkin, Reverend Fred
Pseudonym used by John on his album WALLS AND BRIDGES.

Ghurkin, Reverend Thumbs
Pseudonym John uses on his song "Old Dirt Road."

Gibbs, Russ
Program director of radio station WKNR in Michigan when, in 1969, he brought the "Paul Is Dead" rumor to the airwaves for the first time in the U.S. The rumor was to mushroom into worldwide speculation that Paul McCartney had been dead for three years and had been replaced by a lookalike carrying on his role in The Beatles. The theory was fueled by what seemed to be an inordinate amount of clues, which were laced throughout The Beatles' recordings, indicating Paul's death.

Gibson, Bob
Artist who illustrated the booklet included in the MAGICAL MYSTERY TOUR album.

"Giddy"
Song written by Paul which appears on Roger Daltrey's ONE OF THE BOYS album.

Gilmore, Voyle
Producer of THE BEATLES AT THE HOLLYWOOD BOWL.

Gilmour, Dave
Member of Pink Floyd who plays guitar in the rockestra on the album BACK TO THE EGG.

"Girl"
Written by: Lennon/McCartney
Recorded by: The Beatles
Lead singer: John
Year first released: 1965
Record label: Parlophone (Britain); Capitol (U.S.)
Album: RUBBER SOUL
           THE BEATLES 1962–1966
           LOVE SONGS

"Girlfriend"
Written by: Paul McCartney
Recorded by: Wings
Lead singer: Paul
Year first released: 1978
Record label: Parlophone (Britain); Capitol (U.S.)
Album: LONDON TOWN
- Paul wrote this song with the intention of giving it to Michael Jackson to record. Jackson recorded it in 1979.

"Girls' School"
Written by: Paul McCartney
Recorded by: Wings
Lead singer: Paul
Year first released: 1977
Record label: Parlophone (Britain); Capitol (U.S.)
Single: A side and later B side of "Mull of Kintyre"
· Paul got the idea for this song from ads for porno movies in the newspaper.
· The original title was "Love School."

Girl Who Sang with The Beatles, The
Award-winning short story written by Robert Henenway; published by Knopf in 1970 in the book *The Girl Who Sang with The Beatles and Other Stories*.

"Give Ireland Back to the Irish"
Written by: Paul and Linda McCartney
Recorded by: Wings
Lead singer: Paul
Year first released: 1972
Record label: Apple
Single: Britain and U.S.
Performances: 1972 Wings' European Tour
· The B side of the record is an instrumental version of this song.
· Paul wrote this song in protest of the British occupation of Northern Ireland after the "Bloody Sunday" incident.
· The song was banned by the BBC.

"Give Me Back My Dynamite"
Song cowritten by George and Doris Troy for her album DORIS TROY.

"Give Me Love"
Written by: George Harrison
Recorded by: George
Lead singer: George
Year first released: 1973
Record label: Apple
Album: LIVING IN THE MATERIAL WORLD
            THE BEST OF GEORGE HARRISON
Single: Britain and U.S.
Performances: 1974 Dark Horse Tour

"Give Me Some Truth"
Written by: John Lennon
Recorded by: John
Lead singer: John
Year first released: 1971
Record label: Apple
Album: IMAGINE
· The song was written during The Beatles' stay in India in 1968.
· The Beatles rehearsed this song during the LET IT BE sessions.
· George plays lead guitar on the recording.

"Give Peace a Chance"
Written by: Lennon/McCartney
Recorded by: John Lennon/Plastic Ono Band
Lead singer: John
Year first released: 1969
Record label: Apple
Album: LIVE PEACE IN TORONTO
            SHAVED FISH
Single: Britain and U.S.
Performances: Toronto Rock 'n' Roll Revival Concert, 1969
            Peace demonstration in New York, May 1972
            One to One Concert, 1972, Promo film clip
· The song was recorded live from the Queen Elizabeth Hotel in Montreal during John and Yoko's honeymoon bed-in for peace. Some of the vocalists on hand for the chorus were Allen Ginsberg, Timothy Leary, Tommy Smothers, Derek Taylor, a rabbi, a priest, and the Canadian Chapter of the Radha Krishna Temple.
· "Give Peace a Chance" became the anthem of the peace marchers of the Vietnam antiwar movement.

"Givin' Grease a Ride"
Song cowritten by Paul and his brother, Michael, which appears on Mike's album MCGEAR. Paul performs on the record.

"Glad All Over"
Song The Beatles performed in the early 1960s.

Glasgow, Betty
Hairdresser who styled The Beatles' hair for their movies *A Hard Day's Night* and *Help!* Their hair was washed every three days and trimmed once a week.

"Glasses"
Written by: Paul McCartney
Recorded by: Paul
Lead singer: None (Instrumental)
Year first released: 1970
Record label: Apple
Album: McCARTNEY
· Paul plays glasses on this song, which is heard in medley with "Hot As Sun."

"Glass Onion"
Written by: Lennon/McCartney
Recorded by: The Beatles
Lead singer: John
Year first released: 1968
Record label: Apple
Album: THE BEATLES
· The lyrics contain mention of five previous Beatle releases: "Lady Madonna," "Fixing a Hole," "Straw-

berry Fields Forever," "Fool on the Hill," and "I Am the Walrus."
- John stated that he wrote the line about Paul claiming he's the walrus out of guilt for neglecting his friendship with Paul after he had met Yoko.

"God"
Written by: John Lennon
Recorded by: John Lennon and the Plastic Ono Band
Lead singer: John
Year first released: 1970
Record label: Apple
Album: JOHN LENNON/PLASTIC ONO BAND
- John's musical emancipation proclamation separating himself from a litany of myths in which he once believed—including The Beatles.
- John claims he wrote the song as a reaction to George's belief in religion.

"God Save Us"
Written by: John Lennon and Yoko Ono
Recorded by: The Elastic Oz Band (including John and Yoko)
Lead singer: Bill Elliot
Year first released: 1971
Record label: Apple
Single: Britain and U.S.
Performances: 1971 Benefit for John Sinclair Concert
- This song was written for the *Oz* magazine obscenity trial defense fund. The profits were used to help the underground magazine pay court costs.

"Going Down On Love"
Written by: John Lennon
Recorded by: John
Lead singer: John
Year first released: 1974
Record label: Apple
Album: WALLS AND BRIDGES

Golden Gate Hotel
Hotel located in Scotland. Paul and Jane spent time here in 1968 while awaiting the repair of their car after it broke down on the way to their farm in Campbeltown.

Golden Gate Park
Park in San Francisco's Haight-Ashbury district where George and Pattie visited on August 8, 1967. George strolled through the park serenading the crowds on a borrowed guitar. He later admitted that he was very disappointed by the hippies' seemingly wasted lifestyle.

"Golden Slumbers"
Written by: Lennon/McCartney
Recorded by: The Beatles
Lead singer: Paul
Year first released: 1969

Record label: Apple
Album: ABBEY ROAD
- This track was the last song The Beatles ever recorded together. The recording took place on July 31, 1969.
- Paul had taken the lyrics (written by Thomas Dekker) from his stepsister's music book. Since Paul couldn't read the music to accompany himself on the piano, he improvised his own version. The words are from a 400-year-old poem.

Goldman, Peter
Swedish television producer who in 1967 filmed The Beatles' promo films for "Penny Lane" and "Strawberry Fields Forever."

Goldsmith, Harvey
Concert promoter who promoted Wings' 1979 British Tour and the ill-fated tour of Japan.

Golspie Hospital
Hospital located in Scotland where John, Yoko, and their children, Julian and Kyoko, were taken after a car crash on July 1, 1969. John, who was driving, received twenty stitches in his chin and Yoko was treated for a concussion and a fractured back. The children were treated for minor injuries. They were released on July 6.

"Go Now"
Written by: Larry Bank and Milton Bennet
Recorded by: Wings
Lead singer: Denny Laine
Year first released: 1976
Record label: Parlophone (Britain); Capitol (U.S.)
Album: WINGS OVER AMERICA
Performances: 1973 Wings' British Tour
                1976 Wings' Los Angeles Concerts
                1979 Wings' British Tour

"Goodbye"
Lennon/McCartney song recorded by Apple artist Mary Hopkin. Paul produced the single and also performs on the record and its promo film clip.

"Good Day Sunshine"
Written by: Lennon/McCartney
Recorded by: The Beatles
Lead singer: Paul
Year first released: 1966
Record label: Parlophone (Britain); Capitol (U.S.)
Album: REVOLVER

Goode, Jack
British producer of The Beatles' one-hour television special "Around The Beatles" in 1964. Goode later secured a Beatles performance taped in Britain in 1965 for his American TV music series "Shindig."

Goodgold, Edwin
Coauthor of *The Compleat Beatles Quiz Book.*

"Good Morning, Good Morning"
Written by: Lennon/McCartney
Recorded by: The Beatles
Lead singer: John
Year first released: 1967
Record label: Parlophone (Britain); Capitol (U.S.)
Album: SGT. PEPPER'S LONELY HEARTS CLUB
            BAND
· John got the title from a cereal commercial on television.

Good News
Brand of candy which inspired George to compose "Savoy Truffle." All of the candies in the song lyrics were listed on the top of the candy box.

"Goodnight"
Written by: Lennon/McCartney
Recorded by: The Beatles
Lead singer: Ringo
Year first released: 1968
Record label: Apple
Album: THE BEATLES
· John wrote this song specifically for Ringo to sing.

"Goodnight Tonight"
Written by: Paul McCartney
Recorded by: Wings
Lead singer: Paul
Year first released: 1979
Record label: Parlophone (Britain); Columbia (U.S.)
Single: Britain and U.S.
Performances: Promo film clip
                1979 Wings' British Tour
· Paul's first record for Columbia; a contribution to the disco craze.
· An extended disco version was released, which is different from the ordinary single.

GOODNIGHT VIENNA
Artist: Ringo Starr
Producer: Richard Perry
Year first released: 1974
Record label: Apple
Tracks: 11
    "Goodnight Vienna"
    "Occapella"
    "Oo-Wee"
    "Husbands and Wives"
    "Snookeroo"
    "All by Myself"
    "Call Me"
    "No No Song"

    "Only You"
    "Easy for Me"
    "Goodnight Vienna Reprise"

"Goodnight Vienna"
Written by: John Lennon
Recorded by: Ringo
Lead singer: Ringo
Year first released: 1974
Record label: Apple
Album: GOODNIGHT VIENNA
Single: U.S.
· Song title was derived from a Liverpool slang expression meaning "get me out of here."
· John sings and plays guitar on this track.

Goon Show Scripts, The
Book by Spike Milligan which John favorably reviewed for the *New York Times Book Review* Section on September 30, 1973. The recordings of the scripts were favorites of John's since childhood and, ironically, were produced by George Martin.

"Gonna Get My Baby Back"
Song written by George, Ringo, Stephen Stills, and Doris Troy. It appears on the album DORIS TROY.

Gordon, Dr.
Physician who treated George's virus when The Beatles arrived in New York for their American debut in 1964.

Gordon, Jim
Drummer who worked on the albums ALL THINGS MUST PASS, LIVING IN THE MATERIAL WORLD, EXTRA TEXTURE, IMAGINE, and SOMETIME IN NEW YORK CITY.

"Gotta Sing, Gotta Dance"
Song written by Paul which was originally intended for Twiggy to perform on a television special that never materialized. The song was never released, but Paul performed the song in a dance number on his own television special "James Paul McCartney" in 1973.

"Got to Get You Into My Life"
Written by: Lennon/McCartney
Recorded by: The Beatles
Lead singer: Paul
Year first released: 1966
Record label: Parlophone (Britain); Capitol (U.S.)
Album: REVOLVER
          THE BEATLES 1962–1966
          ROCK AND ROLL MUSIC
Single: Reissued as a U.S. single in 1976
Performances: 1979 Wings' British Tour

Grade, Sir Lew
Head of Britain's Associated Television (ATV) when the company gained control of the publishing rights to The Beatles' songs in 1969. (See Northern Songs.) In 1973 Lew Grade produced the television special "James Paul McCartney." When John appeared on a televison salute to Sir Lew Grade in 1975, he and his band performed costumed in two-face masks, a sardonic reference to John's feelings on Sir Lew's character.

Graham, Bill
Rock concert promoter and owner of the now defunct Fillmores East and West. Graham promoted George's Dark Horse Tour of North America in 1974 and the Wings Over America Tour in 1976.

Grammy Awards
Award presented to artists by the American National Academy of Recording Arts and Sciences. The Beatles, as a group, received a total of eleven Grammys:
1964—Best New Artist and Best Vocal performance by a group.
1966—Song of the Year—"Michelle"
    Best Contemporary Vocal Performance—"Eleanor Rigby"
    Best Sleeve Design—REVOLVER
1967—Best Album—SGT. PEPPER'S LONELY HEARTS CLUB BAND
    Best Contemporary Album—SGT. PEPPER'S LONELY HEARTS CLUB BAND
    Best Album Cover—SGT. PEPPER'S LONELY HEARTS CLUB BAND
    Best Engineered Album—SGT. PEPPER'S LONELY HEARTS CLUB BAND
1969—Best Engineered Recording—ABBEY ROAD
1970—Best Original Movie Score—LET IT BE
1971—Best Arrangement Accompanying Vocalists—Paul McCartney—"Uncle Albert/Admiral Halsey"
1972—Best Album—George Harrison—THE CONCERT FOR BANGLA DESH
1973—Best Arrangement Accompanying Vocalists—Paul McCartney and Wings—"Live and Let Die"
1974—Best Engineered Recording—BAND ON THE RUN
1975—Hall of Fame—Beatles bestowed with this special award
1979—Best Instrumental Recording—Wings—"Rockestra"

Grand, Youngman
Character portrayed by Ringo in the movie *The Magic Christian*.

Grant, Erkey
Performer on the bill with The Beatles on their 1963 British Tour.

Grant, Julie
Performer on the bill with The Beatles on their 1962 British Tour.

Grapefruit
First recording artists signed to Apple in January of 1967. Their name was suggested by John. The Beatles welcomed the new band to their company with a promotional party attended by such rock luminaries as Brian Jones and Donovan. The group consisted of George Alexander, John Perry, Peter Sweetenham, and Geoff Sweetenham. Since the company had not yet gotten off the ground, a record was never released up to the time the band left the label in 1968, though Paul did produce a promo film clip for the band.

Grapefruit
Book written by Yoko Ono; published by Wanternaum Press in 1964. The book, which consists of poems, concepts, and drawings, was reissued by Simon and Schuster in 1970 with the addition of a two-line introduction by John.

Graves, Elsie Starkey
Mother of Ringo Starr. Mrs. Graves raised Ringo alone after she divorced her husband in 1943. She worked as a barmaid to support the family, and in 1953 she married Harry Graves. Mr. and Mrs. Graves were the last of The Beatles' parents to stay in their old section of Liverpool, even though their son could well afford to relocate the family. Mrs. Graves finally relented so as not to insult her son's generosity, and they moved to a more prominent section of Liverpool.

Graves, Harry
Stepfather of Ringo Starr. Mr. Graves married Ringo's mother in 1953.

Gray, Anthony
Sculptor who created The Beatles in bronze, which was on exhibit at the Chenil Gallery in Chelsea, London.

"Greasy Legs/Ski-ing and Gat Kirivani/Dream Scene"
Written by: George Harrison
Recorded by: George
Lead singer: Instrumental
Year first released: 1968
Record label: Apple
Album: WONDERWALL

Greeland, Tim
Recording engineer for the albums RAM and RED ROSE SPEEDWAY.

Green Street
Site of The Beatles' first London flat in 1963.

Gregory, Mr.
Contractor hired by Ringo in 1967 to landscape gardens surrounding his house. Though his original price was £2,500, Gregory asked for £8,000 more before the job was finished. Ringo refused to pay the extra cost and was sued by Gregory. Ringo countersued and the matter was brought to the courts.

"Grey Cloudy Lies"
Written by: George Harrison
Recorded by: George
Lead singer: George
Year first released: 1975
Record label: Apple
Album: EXTRA TEXTURE

Griffiths, Eric
One of the original members of The Quarrymen.

Gripweed, Private
Character portrayed by John in his 1966 solo acting debut in the movie *How I Won the War*.

Gross, Michael
Artist who designed the sleeve for the album SOMETIME IN NEW YORK CITY.

Grossberg, Larry
Producer of the album THE BEATLES LIVE AT THE STAR CLUB.

Grosse Freiheit
Street in Hamburg, Germany, where The Beatles appeared nightly during engagements at the Indra, Kaiserkeller, and the Star Club in 1960–62.

Grossman, Henry
Official Beatles' photographer from 1965 to 1968. He also took the photographs for the DARK HORSE and EXTRA TEXTURE albums.

Groszmann, Carl
Artist signed to Ring O'Records.

Grove, Martin A.
Author of the book *Paul McCartney: Beatle with Wings*.

Growing Up with The Beatles
Book written by Ron Schaumberg; published by Pyramid Books in 1976.

Gruen, Bob
Photographer who often worked with John after he moved to New York. Gruen's photos appear on the WALLS AND BRIDGES album.

Guinness Book of World Records
In April 1964 The Beatles were entered in the Guinness Book for holding the first five positions on the singles charts and the first two album positions all at the same time.

In 1979 Paul was awarded a rhodium-plated disc for his record-breaking achievements in songwriting and record sales. He had forty-three songs that were over one million sellers, sixty gold discs, and sold more records worldwide than any other artist.

Guyler, Derryck
Actor who played the role of the police chief in *A Hard Day's Night*.

"Gypsies in Flight"
Written by: Richard Starkey and Vini Poncia
Recorded by: Ringo
Lead singer: Ringo
Year first released: 1977
Record label: Polydor (Britain); Atlantic (U.S.)
Album: RINGO THE 4TH

H

H., George
Alias used by George for his guitar work on Billy Preston's album I WROTE A SIMPLE SONG.

Hague, Jonathan
British artist who attended Liverpool Art College with John in 1958. Ten years later, John and Paul sponsored Hague's first art exhibition at a London gallery.

Hahn, Lew
Engineer on RINGO'S ROTOGRAVURE album.

Haigh, Kenneth
Actor who played Simon the advertising executive in *A Hard Day's Night*.

Haight Ashbury Free Medical Clinic
San Francisco clinic to which George donated $66,000 in proceeds from his 1974 San Francisco concert.

Hall & Oates
Recording artists on whose album, ALONG THE RED LEDGE, George plays guitar.

"Hallelujah, I Love You So"
Ray Charles composition which The Beatles performed At The Star Club in Hamburg, Germany. On the album THE BEATLES LIVE AT THE STAR CLUB, Horst Obber, a waiter, sings lead.

Halsey, John
Actor/musician who portrayed the character of Barry Wom in the Rutles TV special.

Hamburg
Port city in Germany. The Beatles—John, Paul, George, Pete Best, and Stu Sutcliffe—performed here at various times between 1960 and 1962 at such clubs as the Indra, Kaiserkeller, Top Ten, and Star Club. It was in Hamburg that John, Paul, George, and Ringo first played together, when Ringo sat in on drums for Pete Best. The Beatles credit Hamburg and the grueling hours of work they put in here as the basis for their sound in later years.

Hammel, John
Roadie who maintained the instruments for the 1975–76 Wings Tour.

Hammersmith Odeon
Theatre in London where The Beatles held their Christmas Shows in 1964. Paul performed here with Wings in 1973 and 1979.

Hamp, Johnny
Television producer who booked The Beatles on their first TV appearance, "People and Places," shown in northern England in 1962. A tape of The Beatles performing the song "Some Other Guy" at the Cavern Club was aired on this show.

Hands Across the Water
Book of photos, taken by Hipgnosis, of Wings' 1976 American Tour; published by Reed Books in 1978.

"Hands of Love"
Written by: Paul McCartney
Recorded by: Wings
Lead singer: Paul
Year first released: 1973
Record label: Apple
Album: RED ROSE SPEEDWAY

Hanley, Tommy
Photographer of the back cover of Ringo's album RINGO'S ROTOGRAVURE. The photo is of the graffiti-covered door of the abandoned Apple building on Saville Row.

Hanover, Marc
Photographer of the sleeve photo on RINGO'S ROTOGRAVURE album.

Hanson, Colin
One of the original members of The Quarrymen.

Hanson, Wendy
Brian Epstein's personal assistant during the Beatle years.

"Happiness Is a Warm Gun"
Written by: Lennon/McCartney
Recorded by: The Beatles
Lead singer: John
Year first released: 1968
Record label: Apple
Album: THE BEATLES
- Due to its ambiguous sexual symbolism, this song was banned by the BBC.
- John got the idea for the song from an ad in an American gun magazine.
- It is Paul's favorite song on the album.

Happy Days
Yacht on which Paul, Jane, Ringo, and Maureen sailed while on holiday in the Virgin Islands in 1964. Paul composed the song, "Things We Said Today" on board.

"Happy Xmas (War Is Over)"
Written by: John Lennon and Yoko Ono
Recorded by: John and the Plastic Ono Band

Lead singer: John
Year first released: 1971
Record label: Apple
Album: SHAVED FISH
Single: Britain and U.S.
- John and Yoko whisper the names of their children, Julian and Kyoko, at the beginning of the song.
- Ads for peace with the slogan "War Is Over" were taken out in the *New York Times* and on billboards in large cities around the world two years before the record was released.

Hard Day's Night, A
First feature film starring The Beatles; released through United Artists in 1964. Directed by Richard Lester; produced by Walter Shenson; written by Alun Owen. This ninety-minute, black-and-white musical is a semifictional account of "a day in the life" of The Beatles, and includes eight songs written specifically for the film.

Shooting began on March 2, 1964, with The Beatles arriving on the set each morning at 8:30 A.M. and leaving at 6:00 P.M. The film was completed two months later, and premiered on July 6, 1964, at the London Pavilion, with Princess Margaret and other members of the Royal Family in attendance. *A Hard Day's Night* received unanimously favorable reviews and was nominated for two Academy Awards.

Film notes:
- Title of the film was first mentioned in a line from John's short story "Sad Michael," which appears in his first book, *In His Own Write*.
- British Railways rescheduled its train routes in order to coincide with the filming of the train segment.
- The train compartment scene, where The Beatles perform "I Should Have Known Better," was filmed in a van, with crew members rocking the vehicle to simulate a train in motion.
- The field scene was filmed at Gatwick Airport. Due to a hangover, Paul was absent from some of the filming of that scene.
- A complete scene involving Paul and a young Shakespearian actress was filmed, but cut from the final print because of Paul's self-conscious performance.
- George met his first wife, Pattie, who had a bit part in the film, on the set.
- A copy of John's *In His Own Write* can be seen in the background of a dressing room scene.
- Ringo's nervousness concerning his first solo acting sequence caused him to have a few too many before filming began—hence the relaxed, natural performance given during his scene on the banks of the Thames River with a young boy.
- All four Beatles were unable to control their laughter in the scene involving the partially clad hotel waiter who was hiding in their closet, and the scene had to be shot numerous times.

HARD DAY'S NIGHT, A
Artist: The Beatles
Producer: George Martin
Year first released: 1964
Record label: Parlophone (Britain); United Artists (U.S.)
Tracks: 13 (Britain); 12 (U.S.)

Britain

"A Hard Day's Night"
"I Should Have Known Better"
"If I Fell"
"I'm Happy Just to Dance With You"
"And I Love Her"
"Tell Me Why"
"Can't Buy Me Love"
"Any Time At All"
"I'll Cry Instead"
"Things We Said Today"
"When I Get Home"
"You Can't Do That"
"I'll Be Back"

U.S.

"A Hard Day's Night" (instrumental and vocal versions)
"Tell Me Why"
"I'll Cry Instead"
"I Should Have Known Better"
"I'm Happy Just To Dance with You" (instrumental and vocal versions)
"And I Love Her" (instrumental and vocal versions)
"If I Fell"
"Ringo's Theme"
"Can't Buy Me Love"
- Each song on the album was recorded in one day because The Beatles were pressed for time.
- The George Martin Orchestra performs the instrumentals on the American album.

"Hard Day's Night, A"
Written by: Lennon/McCartney
Recorded by: The Beatles
Lead singer: John
Year first released: 1964
Record label: Parlophone (Britain); United Artists and Capitol (U.S.)
Album: A HARD DAY'S NIGHT
A COLLECTION OF BEATLES OLDIES
THE BEATLES 1962–1966
THE BEATLES AT THE HOLLYWOOD BOWL
Single: Britain and U.S.
Performances: *A Hard Day's Night* movie
1964 North American Summer Tour
1964 Christmas Shows, London

1965 European Summer Tour
1965 North American Summer Tour
- This was the first time John and Paul were required to compose a song around a specific title.

Hard Day's Night, A
Book written by John Burke, based on Alun Owen's screenplay; published by Dell in 1964.

Hard Day's Night, A
Book of complete dialogue, including deleted material and still photos from the movie. Edited by Philip di Franco; published by Chelsea House in 1977.

"Hard Rain's Gonna Fall, A"
Song performed by Bob Dylan at the Concert for Bangla Desh, and included on the concert album, THE CONCERT FOR BANGLA DESH.

Hard Rock Cafe
Restaurant in London where Wings held an unannounced benefit concert for Release, a drug abuse program. The concert was held on March 18, 1973, ten days after Paul was sentenced in Scotland for possession of marijuana.

"Hard Times"
Written by: Peter Skellern
Recorded by: Ringo
Lead singer: Ringo
Year first released: 1978
Record label: Polydor (Britain): Portrait (U.S.)
Album: BAD BOY
Performances: "Ringo" TV special, 1978

HARD TIMES
Peter Skellern album on which George plays guitar.

Hargrave, Lynn
President of The Beatles U.S.A. Fan Club in 1964.

Harisein, Jai Raj
Pseudonym George uses on the SPLINTER album.

"Hari's on Tour (Express)"
Written by: George Harrison
Recorded by: George
Lead singer: None (Instrumenatal)
Year first released: 1974
Record label: Apple
Album: DARK HORSE
Single: B side of "Dark Horse" (Britain)
        B side of "Ding Dong; Ding Dong" (U.S.)
Performances: 1974 Dark Horse Tour
- George opened his concert with this number.

Harlem Community Choir
Children's chorus which sings on John's "Happy Xmas (War Is Over)" single. Their photo appears on the record sleeve.

Harold Lloyd Estate
Mansion located in California's Benedict Canyon where a gala for Wings was held on June 24, 1976, to celebrate the completion of the band's first American tour. The party cost over $75,000, and all of the guests were instructed to wear white. The Nelson Riddle Orchestra performed.

Harper, Roy
English rock performer for whose album Paul did a promotional spot. Paul appears on his ONE OF THOSE DAYS IN ENGLAND album.

Harrigan, Clint
Writer responsible for the liner notes on the Wings' WILD LIFE album.

Harris, Rolf
Performer who appeared on the bill at The Beatles 1963 Christmas shows.

Harrison, Carl
Stage name George used during The Silver Beatles' 1960 Tour of Scotland.

Harrison, Dhani
First son born to George and Olivia Harrison on August 1, 1978. Dhani was born in Windsor, England, and his name is Hindu for "wealthy person."

Harrison, George
Born in Liverpool on February 25, 1943, George was the fourth and last child born to Harold and Louise Harrison. He was raised in a close-knit family, where self-expression was highly regarded. At an early age George exhibited an independent nature and a nonconformist attitude. He refused to adhere to the age-old dress codes set forth by his school and flaunted his defiance by attiring himself in tight blue jeans to complement his long hair. Though George's mother understood her son's need to realize his own identity, she and her husband would not condone his disrespectful attitude toward authority. George soon learned to tone down his rebellion, but his dissatisfaction with formal education left him an apathetic student.

While George was attending the Liverpool Institute in 1955, he became friendly with schoolmate Paul McCartney, who shared his budding interest in music. The two boys would practice their guitar playing during their free time at school and in each other's homes. George spent endless hours dedicated to perfecting his

REGISTRATION DISTRICT _Liverpool South_

1943 BIRTH in the Sub-district of _Wavertree_ in the _County Borough of Liverpool_

Columns	1	2	3	4	5	6	7	8	9	10
No.	When and where born	Name, if any	Sex	Name, and surname of father	Name, surname, and maiden surname of mother	Occupation of father	Signature, description, and residence of informant	When registered	Signature of registrar	Name entered after registration
357	Twenty-fifth February 1943 12 Arnold Grove U D	George	Boy	Harold Hargreaves Harrison	Louise Harrison formerly French	Inspector of Mains Drive	H.H. Harrison father 12 Arnold Grove Liverpool 15	Twenty sixth February 1943	H. Thorne Registrar	

CERTIFIED to be a true copy of an entry in the certified copy of a Register of Births in the District above mentioned.
Given at the GENERAL REGISTER OFFICE, SOMERSET HOUSE, LONDON, under the Seal of the said Office, the 17th day of July 1968.

*See note overleaf

BX 524348

George's birth certificate.

George with Beatle paraphenalia, 1964.
(*LFI/Retna*)

With first wife, Pattie, at press reception following their wedding, 1966. (*Pictorial Parade*)

George, 1968—complete with Dundreary whiskers. (*Keystone Press Agency*)

George in concert with friend and teacher Ravi Shankar. (*Pattie O'Neil*)

George at Kinfawn, 1967. (*Sylvia Purbs*)

With Mal Evans, arriving at EMI, 1969. (*Carol Siegel*)

George performs with Bob Dylan at the
Concert for Bangla Desh, August 1, 1971.
(*Keystone Photo Agency*)

During Dark Horse tour, 1974.
(*Robin Titone*)

George's Crackerbox Palace,
Henley-on-Thames.
(*Robin Titone*)

En route to the taping of "Saturday Night Live," November 1976.
(*Robin Titone*)

In his BMW, London, 1977.
(*Goldie Friede*)

George with friend, Michael Palin of Monty Python,
New York, 1979. (*Robin Titone*)

George and family: wife, Olivia, son, Dhani,
April 1979. (*Transworld Features Syndicate.*)

playing. His determination was such that he often kept on at the instrument until his fingers bled. He soon became so proficient at his craft that Paul felt his presence in his band, would be welcome, and he brought George to see the group's leader, John Lennon. Though John at first was hesitant in admitting George, three years his junior, he could not deny George's extraordinary musical skill, which overrode any reservations he had. In 1956 George met The Quarrymen and was later appointed the group's lead guitarist. Being the youngest member of the group, George assumed a role of acquiescence to the others. This precarious position caused George to strive to maintain a musical supremacy which would secure his place in the band.

George was very involved in the progression of The Beatles and was as major a vocalist as John and Paul during their early years. It wasn't until the Lennon/McCartney composing team was established that George began taking a back seat in the recording studio and on stage. Though he did write some songs, his confidence was quickly diminished as the world focused its attention solely on John and Paul's efforts. This resulted in a number of unrecorded songs written throughout the years which were rejected by The Beatles for one reason or another. George was a serious musician who worked diligently to perfect his playing. His intense concentration was apparent even during the group's performances. There were occasions when George had to make a conscious effort on stage so as not to appear solemn compared to the wild antics of the other members of the group.

By 1966 George had openly expressed his dissatisfaction with performing before an audience. He had grown tired of touring because he felt The Beatles' musical progression was halted during their engagements on the road. George's main concern was music, and he never fully enjoyed the celebrity status he acquired along with his success.

When The Beatles stopped touring, in order to concentrate on their work in the recording studio, George took the time to begin familiarizing himself with the music of the East. His interest in Indian music had originally been sparked during The Beatles' filming of the movie *Help!*, which dealt loosely with Eastern culture. It wasn't long before George's commitment to the music and religious culture of India prompted him to try to incorporate the sounds of East and West through The Beatles' music. He began instructions on the sitar and became fast friends with his tutor, Ravi Shankar. His enthusiasm about his newfound awareness in religious culture, which accompanied his musical pursuits, soon spread to the other Beatles, who also began to investigate Eastern philosophy as a means to spiritual enlightenment.

George married model Pattie Boyd in 1966. They had met two years earlier on the set of The Beatles' first movie, *A Hard Day's Night,* in which she had a bit part. Together, George and Pattie pursued their interest in religion, traveling regularly to India, which had by now become their second home. In 1967 George and Pattie became involved with the teachings of another Indian, the guru Maharishi Mahesh Yogi. George believed that the Maharishi's method of attaining inner tranquility through transcendental meditation would help him discover an identity apart from his world renown as a Beatle. He became so enthusiastic about the guru's teachings that once again he influenced The Beatles to learn the art. With his growing self-confidence, George began recording more songs which appeared on The Beatles' albums. It was during this time that the conflict in egos began to take their toll on the group as personal as well as musical conflicts arose. Now, with George demanding just time in the studio, the group was torn by competitive jealousies as each member strived to record their own material. When The Beatles eventually split up and went their separate ways, George released his first solo album ALL THINGS MUST PASS. The album consisted of many of the songs which George had written as a Beatle. The album received critical acclaim and was a great commercial success.

In 1971 George produced and starred in the "Concert of the Decade"—The Concert for Bangla Desh. He arranged for the music industry's top recording artists to come together and perform in order to raise money to aid the people of the war-torn country of Bangla Desh.

The following years did not prove as promising for George's career. His subsequent albums only attained mild success as the public became bored by George's preoccupation with religious themes in his music. In 1974 George embarked on a twenty-seven city tour of North America to launch his new record label, Dark Horse. The concert tour was beset by troubles, due to the poor notices George was receiving along the way. Most of the criticism stemmed from the harsh quality of George's voice, due to a severe case of laryngitis. Another problem George had to cope with was the unwillingness of his audience to accept the music of Ravi Shankar and his Indian orchestra, who also performed on the bill. Even George's renditions of his own recordings were not met with approval, since he rearranged many of the songs looked upon by his fans as classics which should not be tampered with. George carried on with the tour and, though he experienced financial success, he was glad when it was over and has since been reluctant to return to the stage and the circuslike atmosphere which accompanies life on the road. After the completion of the tour George's confidence was cracked but not shattered; he went on recording and released several albums, which achieved moderate success. In

1977 George's marriage to Pattie ended in divorce after an eleven-year childless union.

George married his companion of five years, a former Dark Horse secretary, Olivia Arias, after their son, Dhani, was born in 1978. In 1979 George broke a three-year musical silence by releasing the album GEORGE HARRISON. This album again gained George critical acclaim and became a best seller.

George has just completed his autobiography, titled *I Me Mine,* and when he isn't working he can be found as a spectator on the Grand Prix circuit.

Harrison, George
Reporter on the *Liverpool Echo* newspaper who helped The Beatles in their early days by supplying newspaper coverage of their concerts. He later accompanied them on many of their foreign tours.

Harrison, Harold
George's father. Mr. Harrison worked as a Liverpool bus driver when George was growing up, and it had always been George's dream to be rich enough to buy his father his own bus. After his wife's death in 1970, Mr. Harrison became even closer to George, moving onto the grounds of George's estate. In 1974, he accompanied George and his entourage when they were presented to President Ford during George's Dark Horse Tour. Early in May 1978 George reportedly had a vision in a dream of his father bidding him farewell, and the next day Mr. Harrison died at home.

Harrison, Harold
George's eldest brother.

Harrison, Louise French
George's mother. Mrs. Harrison was the only Beatle parent to give her son constant support in his musical endeavors. Once The Beatles gained success, she faithfully answered all her fan mail and even appeared on television to talk about The Beatles. Mrs. Harrison died of cancer in 1970.

Harrison, Louise
Maiden name of George's only sister. (See Louise Kane.)

Harrison, Olivia Arias
Born in 1948; wife of George Harrison and mother of their son, Dhani. Olivia and George met in 1974 when Olivia was working as a secretary for Dark Horse Records in Los Angeles. After numerous business conversations over the phone, George was inspired to have a friend "check out" Olivia as a future prospect for himself. George moved to Los Angeles to be with Olivia and soon brought her back to live with him in his castle in

Henley, England. They planned to marry in May, 1978, but, due to the death of George's father, the wedding was postponed. They were married on September 7, a month after the birth of their son.

Harrison, Patricia Boyd
George's first wife. (See Pattie Clapton.)

Harrison, Peter
George's older brother.

Harrisongs, Ltd.
George's former music publishing company.

Harry, Bill
Editor of *Mersey Beat,* Liverpool's entertainment newspaper. Harry saw The Beatles' potential from their early days at The Cavern, and his support and publicity helped promote their career. In 1978, Harry edited *The Mersey Beat: The Beginnings of The Beatles,* a compilation of the articles on The Beatles which were first printed in his newspaper.

Harrysong, George
Name George uses on Nilsson's SON OF SCHMILSSON album.

Haslam, Michael
Artist who appeared on the bill with The Beatles on their 1964 British Fall Tour and their Christmas show of the same year.

Haslem Terrace
Los Angeles home in which Ringo resided in the mid-seventies.

Hatfield, Bobby
Singer who was a member of the Righteous Brothers. Ringo plays drums on his song, "Oo-Wee Baby, I Love You."

"Have I Told You Lately That I Love You"
Written by: Scott Wiseman
Recorded by: Ringo
Lead singer: Ringo
Year first released: 1970
Record label: Apple
Album: SENTIMENTAL JOURNEY

"Haven't We Met Somewhere Before"
Song written by Paul McCartney which was originally intended for the soundtrack of the movie *Heaven Can Wait.* Although it was never used there, it appeared as the opening number in the Ramones' movie, *Rock 'n' Roll High School.*

"Have You Got Problems"
Song cowritten by Paul and his brother, Michael McGear, which appears on the McGEAR album.

Hawkins, Daisy
Working title for the song "Eleanor Rigby." Paul originally intended the character Eleanor Rigby to be named Daisy Hawkins, after he saw the name in a shop window in Bristol, England.

Hawkins, Ronnie
Singer on whose Toronto farm John and Yoko spent several days in December of 1969. They had arrived to make plans for the Toronto Peace Festival, which never materialized, and to discuss peace with Prime Minister Trudeau. It was here that John signed his three hundred lithographs before they were put on exhibition.

Haworth, Jan
Codesigner, with Peter Blake, of the SGT. PEPPER'S LONELY HEARTS CLUB BAND album cover. The cover, costing £25,000, was the most expensive cover design up to this time.

Haworth, Jill
British actress Paul met while The Beatles were in New York in February 1964. Ms. Haworth seemingly took the relationship more seriously than Paul had intended when she announced their engagement to the newspapers and then followed The Beatles to Miami Beach. Paul denied the engagement.

Haylings Island
Location of the supermarket which was purchased by The Beatles and managed by their old friend Pete Shotton, an original member of The Quarrymen.

"Hear Me Lord"
Written by: George Harrison
Recorded by: George
Lead singer: George
Year first released: 1970
Record label: Apple
Album: ALL THINGS MUST PASS
Performances: Concert for Bangla Desh (Only at the matinee performance.)

HEAR THE BEATLES TELL ALL
Interview album released on Vee Jay Records in the U.S. in 1965.

"Heart of the Country"
Written by: Paul and Linda McCartney
Recorded by: Paul
Lead singer: Paul
Year first released: 1971
Record label: Apple
Album: RAM
Single: B side of "Back Seat of My Car" (Britain)
Performances: "James Paul McCartney" TV special

"Heart on My Sleeve"
Written by: B. Gallager and G. Lyle
Recorded by: Ringo
Lead singer: Ringo
Year first released: 1978
Record label: Polydor (Britain); Portrait (U.S.)
Album: BAD BOY
Performances: "Ringo" TV special, 1978

"Heart That You Broke"
Country western ballad recorded by Wings in Nashville in 1974.

"Heather"
Song Paul wrote in 1968 for his daughter Heather, which was never released.

Hebb, Bobby
Singer who toured with The Beatles on their 1966 North American Summer Tour.

"Helen Wheels"
Written by: Paul McCartney
Recorded by: Wings
Lead singer: Paul
Year first released: 1973
Record label: Apple
Album: BAND ON THE RUN (U.S.)
Single: Britain and U.S.
Performances: Promo film clip
• Title refers to Paul's Land Rover.

"Hello Goodbye"
Written by: Lennon/McCartney
Recorded by: The Beatles
Lead singer: Paul
Year first released: 1967
Record label: Parlophone (Britain); Capitol (U.S.)
Album: MAGICAL MYSTERY TOUR
          THE BEATLES 1967–1970
Single: Britain and U.S.
Performances: Promo film clip
• The film clip was banned by the BBC when Paul showed that he was lip synching, an action that went against the British musician's union rules.

"Hello Little Girl"
Song written by Paul and John during their school days. Never formally recorded by The Beatles, it was performed during their Decca and Parlophone auditions in 1962. The Fourmost, a Liverpool group managed by Brian Epstein, later had a hit with this song.

Help!

Second feature film starring The Beatles; released through United Artists in 1965. Directed by Richard Lester; produced by Walter Shenson; written by Marc Behm and Charles Wood. Filmed February to April 1965.

The *Help!* script cast The Beatles as themselves, as in *A Hard Day's Night;* though the first was a black-and-white semidocumentary, *Help!* exploded in a colorful surrealism of fantasy adventure filmed against the scenic backdrops of England, Austria, and the Bahamas. Seven new compositions were recorded for the soundtrack, as The Beatles are chased from country to country by a fanatical Eastern cult and a mad British scientist intent on gaining possession of a sacred ring worn by Ringo. The film premiered at the London Pavilion on July 29, 1965. All reviews were favorable, but less so than those of *A Hard Day's Night.* The Beatles admitted they enjoyed filming *Help!,* but preferred *A Hard Day's Night* in the finished product.

Film notes:

- After initial filming at Twickenham Studios, England, the first location scenes were filmed in the Bahamas. Since the movie was shot out of sequence, and with this location the last shown in the film, The Beatles had to guard against tanning and burning so as not to look out of place in earlier film shots.
- The armed soldiers who appeared in the movie to protect The Beatles on the Salisbury Plain were actually supplied by the War Office of England.
- The skiing sequence filmed during the song, "Ticket to Ride," included spontaneous antics, as The Beatles were amateur skiiers prone to accidents.
- During the shooting of the softball scene in the Bahamas, Ringo was actually hurt by the bomb that exploded on the field. He was overcome by the smoke, and tried to alert the crew to stop filming, but his efforts went unnoticed and the cameras kept rolling.
- George first became interested in the sitar during the filming of this movie, which dealt loosely with aspects of Eastern culture.
- Paul used to serenade the film crew by playing Bach selections on the organ shown in The Beatles' fictional home.
- John gives his books a plug in two different scenes. He recites a verse of "I Sat Belonely" from his *In His Own Write* and holds up a copy of *A Spaniard in the Works* in his bedroom.
- The movie won first prize in the Rio de Janeiro Film Festival in 1965.

HELP!
Artist: The Beatles
Producer: George Martin
Year first released: 1965
Record label: Parlophone (Britain); Capitol (U.S.)
Tracks: 14 (Britain); 12 (U.S.)

Britain

"Help!"
"The Night Before"
"You've Got to Hide Your Love Away"
"I Need You"
"Another Girl"
"You're Gonna Lose That Girl"
"Ticket to Ride"
"Act Naturally"
"It's Only Love"
"You Like Me Too Much"
"Tell Me What You See"
"I've Just Seen a Face"
"Yesterday"
"Dizzy Miss Lizzie"

U.S.

"James Bond Theme"/"Help!"
"The Night Before"
"From Me to You Fantasy"
"You've Got to Hide Your Love Away"
"I Need You"
"In the Tyrol"
"Another Girl"
"Another Hard Day's Night"
"Ticket to Ride"
"The Bitter End"/"You Can't Do That"
"You're Gonna Lose That Girl"
"The Chase"

"Help!"
Written by: Lennon/McCartney
Recorded by: The Beatles
Lead singer: John
Year first released: 1965
Record label: Parlophone (Britain); Capitol (U.S.)
Album: HELP!
    A COLLECTION OF BEATLES OLDIES
    THE BEATLES 1962–1966
    THE BEATLES AT THE HOLLYWOOD
      BOWL
    THE BEATLES RARITIES (U.S.)
Single: Britain and U.S.
Performances: *Help!* movie
    1965 North American Tour
    "Ed Sullivan Show" (TV), September
    1965
    1965 British Winter Tour
- A lyric is different on the single record in contrast to the album version.
- THE BEATLES RARITIES track has a different vocal arrangement.

Help!
Paperback novelization of the movie script. Written by Al Hine; published by Dell in 1965.

Help! The Beatles
Hardcover book containing pictures and dialogue from the movie; published by Random House in 1965.

Helping Hand Marathon
Benefit given by radio station WFIL in Philadelphia, Pennsylvania, on May 17–18, 1974, in support of the station. John donated his time to play DJ and mingle with prospective contributors in order to help the cause.

"Helter Skelter"
Written by: Lennon/McCartney
Recorded by: The Beatles
Lead singer: Paul
Year first released: 1968
Record label: Apple
Album: THE BEATLES
   ROCK AND ROLL MUSIC
   THE BEATLES RARITIES (U.S.)
Single: Rereleased as the B side of "Got to Get You into My Life" in 1976
• This sexy rocker was erroneously taken by Charles Manson to be violence-oriented and reportedly inspired him to commit the Tate murders in 1969.
• This song was originally twenty-five minutes long (but twenty-one and a half minutes were cut from the final version), hence Ringo's blistered fingers.
• THE BEATLES RARITIES contains a mono version of this song.

Hemenway, Robert
Author of the Pulitzer prize winning short story, *The Girl Who Sang with The Beatles.*

Henderson, Pete
Engineer on the albums WINGS AT THE SPEED OF SOUND and LONDON TOWN.

Hendersons, The
Performers who dance and sing for the benefit of "Mr. Kite."

Henry Hansbacher and Co.
Beatles' bank advisors during the Apple years.

"Henry's Blues"
Song featuring Henry McCullough performed during Wings' 1972 European Tour, but never released.

Henry the Horse
Waltzing horse in the song "Being for the Benefit of Mr. Kite."

Hensley, Tom
Pianist on the albums RINGO and GOODNIGHT VIENNA.

Hentschel, David
First artist signed to Ring O'Records in 1974. He recorded the RINGO album on a synthesizer for his own album, STA*RTLING MUSIC.

"Here Comes the Moon"
Written by: George Harrison
Recorded by: George
Lead singer: George
Year first released: 1979
Record label: Dark Horse
Album: GEORGE HARRISON
• George wrote this song while under the influence of LSD for the first time after a ten-year abstinence.

"Here Comes the Sun"
Written by: George Harrison
Recorded by: The Beatles
Lead singer: George
Year first released: 1969
Record label: Apple
Album: ABBEY ROAD
   THE CONCERT FOR BANGLA DESH
   THE BEATLES 1967–1970
   THE BEST OF GEORGE HARRISON
Performances: The Concert for Bangla Desh, 1971
     "Saturday Night Live" TV show, with Paul Simon, November 1976
• This song was written in Eric Clapton's garden on one of the first sunny days toward winter's end. George played hookey from The Beatles' recording session to enjoy the warm day and escape from the pressures at work.
• The middle section has the same refrain as "Badge," the song George cowrote with Eric Clapton for Cream.
• George felt this song was similar in structure to the song, "If I Needed Someone."

"Here, There and Everywhere"
Written by: Lennon/McCartney
Recorded by: The Beatles
Lead singer: Paul
Year first released: 1966
Record label: Parlophone (Britain); Capitol (U.S.)
Album: REVOLVER
   LOVE SONGS
• Love song inspired by the Beach Boys song "God Only Knows."
• Paul feels that this is the song of his that comes closest to perfection.

"Here We Go"
British radio series on which The Beatles performed five times, from 1962 to 1963. For the first two shows Pete Best was still a member of the group.

"Here We Go Again"
Song which was written by John and Phil Spector during the sessions for ROCK 'N' ROLL, and never released.

"Her Majesty"
Written by: Lennon/McCartney
Recorded by: The Beatles
Lead singer: Paul
Year first released: 1969
Record label: Apple
Album: ABBEY ROAD
· This acoustic ditty was added by Paul as an afterthought so as not to end The Beatles' last album on the saccharine lyrics of "The End."

Herschberg, Lee
Coengineer on the GEORGE HARRISON album.

"Hey Baby"
Written by: Bruce Hannel and Margaret Cobb
Recorded by: Ringo
Lead singer: Ringo
Year first released: 1976
Record label: Polydor (Britain); Atlantic (U.S.)
Album: RINGO'S ROTOGRAVURE
Single: Britain and U.S.
Performances: Promo film clip

"Hey, Bulldog"
Written by: Lennon/McCartney
Recorded by: The Beatles
Lead singer: John
Year first released: 1969
Record label: Apple
Album: YELLOW SUBMARINE
          ROCK AND ROLL MUSIC
Performances: *Yellow Submarine* movie (European version only)
· This was the last song recorded before The Beatles left for India in 1968. It was recorded spontaneously on the same day they filmed their "Lady Madonna" promo film clip. Since EMI studio time had already been booked for the filming, they decided to get their money's worth by recording this song as well.
· First time Yoko was ever in the recording studio with John.

"Hey Diddle"
Unreleased Wings song, which was written in 1974.

HEY JUDE
Alternate name for THE BEATLES AGAIN album. (See THE BEATLES AGAIN.)

"Hey Jude"
Written by: Lennon/McCartney
Recorded by: The Beatles
Lead singer: Paul
Year first released: 1968
Record label: Apple
Album: THE BEATLES AGAIN
          THE BEATLES 1967–1970
Single: Britain and U.S.
Performances: "David Frost Show" (TV), Britain, September 1968 (live)
                "Smothers Brothers Show" (TV), U.S., October 1968 (film clip)
· The Beatles' first Apple single. Clocking in at seven minutes and eleven seconds, "Hey Jude" was the first 45 r.p.m. record running over five minutes to receive extensive commercial airplay.
· Though many interpretations have been made, Paul says the material is autobiographical and that the name "Jude" was inspired by John's son, Julian.
· Paul was influenced by the Drifters' song, "Save the Last Dance for Me" when he first started writing this song.
· The single received the Ivor Novello Award for the highest certified record sales in Britain in 1968.
· "Hey Jude" is frequently cited as the most popular Beatles song.

High Park Farm
Paul's 183-acre farm located in Campbeltown, Scotland. Purchased in 1966, Paul often retreats here, where his duties include shearing sheep, plowing, and carpentry.

In December of 1972, when police discovered cannabis plants on the grounds of High Park Farm, Paul was arrested and charged with cultivating and possessing marijuana. On March 8, 1973, Paul had to pay a £100 fine for cultivating the weed, but the charge of possession was dropped. Paul claimed he wasn't guilty and that a fan had sent him the seeds, which he had planted innocently.

"Hi Hi Hi"
Written by: Paul and Linda McCartney
Recorded by: Wings
Lead singer: Paul
Year first released: 1972
Record label: Apple
Album: WINGS OVER AMERICA
          WINGS' GREATEST
Single: Britain and U.S.

Performances: "James Paul McCartney" TV special
(British version only)
1972 Wings Over Europe Tour
1973 Wings' British Tour
1975–76 Wings' World Tour
• Banned by the BBC for sexual references.

Hilton Hotel
London hotel where The Beatles attended a lecture given by the Maharishi Mahesh Yogi on August 24, 1968. It was here that The Beatles were invited to join the Transcendental Meditation movement.

Hine, Al
Author of the novel version of *Help!,* based on the screenplay.

Hines, Brian
Denny Laine's given name.

Hines, Rebecca
Paul's secretary, arrested along with him, Linda, and Denny Seiwell in Sweden in 1972 for possession of drugs.

Hipgnosis
Team of designers, Aubrey Powell and George Hardy, who designed the record packages for the albums VENUS AND MARS, WINGS AT THE SPEED OF SOUND, WINGS OVER AMERICA, LONDON TOWN, and BACK TO THE EGG. They also designed the PERCY THRILLINGTON album for McCartney Productions Ltd. In 1978, *Hands Across the Water,* a book of their photographs of Wings' 1976 concert tour, was published.

Hippopotamus
New York nightclub where George held a party to celebrate his 1974 Dark Horse tour. The party was held on December 20, 1974, and the guests included such luminaries as John and Yoko, Alice Cooper, and Maureen Starkey.

"Hippy Hippy Shake"
Song The Beatles sang in the early days, which appears on THE BEATLES LIVE AT THE STAR CLUB, with Paul singing lead. When The Beatles performed this song for their Decca audition, George sang lead.

"His Name Is Legs (Ladies and Gentlemen)"
Written by: George Harrison
Recorded by: George
Lead singer: George
Year first released: 1975
Record label: Apple
Album: EXTRA TEXTURE
• Inspired by Legs Larry Smith, who also appears on the track.

H. Hunt and Sons
Engineering firm where Ringo worked as an electrical apprentice in his teen years.

H.M.V. Record Shop
Record store in London where, in 1962, Brian Epstein brought The Beatles' demo tapes to have them converted into record discs for auditions with record companies. The engineer pressing the record was so impressed with The Beatles' sound that he phoned a publisher friend, Syd Coleman, who put The Beatles in touch with George Martin at EMI Records.

Hockney, David
Artist whose work appears in *The Beatles Illustrated Lyrics.* His painting "The Chair" was displayed on stage during the 1975–76 Wings' World Tour.

Hodge, Chris
Apple recording artist who released two singles, "We're on Our Way" and "Goodbye Sweet Lorraine," while with the label.

Hoffman, Dezo
One of the first professional photographers hired to work with the Beatles. Hoffman's photographs appear in *The Beatles Book* and *The Beatles,* published only in Japan. His photos also appear on THE BEATLES TAPES album.

"Hold Me Tight"
Written by: Lennon/McCartney
Recorded by: The Beatles
Lead singer: Paul
Year first released: 1963
Record label: Parlophone (Britain); Capitol (U.S.)
Album: WITH THE BEATLES
MEET THE BEATLES

"Hold Me Tight"
Written by: Paul McCartney
Recorded by: Wings
Lead singer: Paul
Year first released: 1973
Record label: Apple
Album: RED ROSE SPEEDWAY
• First part of a four-song medley which ends the RED ROSE SPEEDWAY album.

"Hold On"
Written by: John Lennon
Recorded by: John Lennon/Plastic Ono Band
Lead singer: John
Year first released: 1970
Record label: Apple
Album: JOHN LENNON PLASTIC ONO BAND
• John's pep talk to himself and Yoko.

"Hold On (Have You Seen My Baby)"
Written by: Randy Newman
Recorded by: Ringo
Lead singer: Ringo
Year first released: 1973
Record label: Apple
Album: RINGO

"Holdup, The"
Song cowritten by George and David Bromberg which appears on the DAVID BROMBERG album. George and Bromberg performed it on the "Dick Cavett Show" in 1972.

Holloway, Brenda
Perfomer on the bill with The Beatles on their 1965 North American Summer Tour.

Holly, Buddy
Late singer/composer who headed the group Buddy Holly and the Crickets. The Beatles credit Holly as a major influence on their music, and have recorded two of his rock classics: "Words of Love" and "Crying, Waiting, Hoping" (the latter never released). In 1974 John recorded his song "Peggy Sue." Buddy Holly was killed in a plane crash in 1959. In 1976 Paul won the rights to Holly's music publishing catalog, outbidding various buyers, including George. In September of 1976, Paul launched "Buddy Holly Week" (to become an annual event) to commemorate Holly's birthday and to promote Holly's material. Norman Petty, Holly's producer, presented Paul with a gift of the cufflinks Holly was wearing at the time of his death.

HOLLY DAYS
Denny Laine album recorded at Paul's Rude Studio in Scotland. Paul arranged, produced, and appears on the album. Photographs of Paul and Denny can be seen on the album's inner cover and the back cover of the album.

Holly, Steve
Wings drummer who replaced Joe English in 1978. Holly, who previously worked with Kiki Dee and Elton John, was referred to Paul by Denny Laine.

"Homeward Bound"
Simon and Garfunkel classic which George and Paul Simon performed on the American TV show, "Saturday Night Live" in November of 1976.

"Honey Don't"
Written by: Carl Perkins
Recorded by: The Beatles
Lead singer: Ringo
Year first released: 1964

Record label: Parlophone (Britain); Capitol (U.S.)
Album: BEATLES FOR SALE
BEATLES '65
EP: 4 BY THE BEATLES
Performances: 1964 Christmas Shows
1965 European Summer Tour

"Honey Pie"
Written by: Lennon/McCartney
Recorded by: The Beatles
Lead singer: Paul
Year first released: 1968
Record label: Apple
Album: THE BEATLES

Honeys, The
Group appearing on the bill with The Beatles on the 1963 tour with Helen Shapiro.

Hope Street Registry Office, The
Bureau in Liverpool which issued John and Cynthia a marriage license for their wedding in 1962.

Hopkin, Mary
Welsh singer who was signed to Apple Records in 1968. Mary was discovered on an amateur hour TV show, "Opportunity Knocks," by model Twiggy, who informed Paul of Mary's talent. Paul watched the show the next week, and invited Mary to London to record for Apple Records. Her first song, "Those Were the Days," was one of Apple's first releases and her album POST-CARD was produced by Paul. Her greatest hits album, THOSE WERE THE DAYS, contains five songs produced by Paul. Her second single, "Goodbye," was written by Lennon/McCartney and produced by Paul.

Hopkins, Nicky
British keyboard player who appears on George's albums: ALL THINGS MUST PASS, LIVING IN THE MATERIAL WORLD, DARK HORSE, and EXTRA TEXTURE; on John's albums: IMAGINE, SOMETIME IN NEW YORK CITY, and WALLS AND BRIDGES; and on Ringo's albums: RINGO and GOODNIGHT VIENNA. George plays guitar on Hopkins's THE TIN MAN WAS A DREAMER album.

Horn, Ian
One of Wings' roadies.

Horn, Jim
Horn player who performed at the Concert for Bangla Desh and on George's 1974 Dark Horse Tour. He is heard on the albums THE CONCERT FOR BANGLA DESH, LIVING IN THE MATERIAL WORLD, EXTRA TEXTURE, and DARK HORSE.

Hornsby, Jerome
Coauthor of the book *All You Need Is Love*.

Hosford, Larry
Artist on whose album, CROSSWORDS, George sings background vocals and plays guitar.

"Hot As Sun"
Written by: Paul McCartney
Recorded by: Paul
Lead singer: None (Instrumental)
Year first released: 1970
Record label: Apple
Album: McCARTNEY
Performance: 1979 Wings' British tour

Hot Chocolate Band, The
Group that had a short-term contract with Apple Records, releasing only one record, a reggae version of John's "Give Peace a Chance." In 1974 Paul hired the band to perform on the boat he rented to sail on the Mississippi River in New Orleans.

HOT HITS AND COLD CUTS
Album intended for release, consisting of Wings' greatest hits and unreleased material.

Hot Spot
Liverpool club where The Beatles occasionally performed in their early days.

"Hound Dog"
Elvis's hit which John performed at the One to One Benefit Concert in August 1972. During the song, John shouted out, "I love you, Elvis."

House, Jack
Author of *The Beatles Quiz Book*.

"How?"
Written by: John Lennon
Recorded by: John
Lead singer: John
Year first released: 1971
Record label: Apple
Album: IMAGINE
Performances: *Imagine* film

Howard, Frankie
British comedian who was originally cast in The Beatles' movie, *Help!*, but whose sequence was cut from the film. Howard hosted a TV variety show in 1969 on which Paul guested and introduced his Apple protégée, Mary Hopkin. In 1978, Frankie Howard played Mean Mr. Mustard in the *Sgt. Pepper* movie.

Howard, Steve
Member of the horn section, playing trumpet and flugelhorn, on the 1975–76 Wings' World Tour. He also appears on the album BACK TO THE EGG and as a member of the rockestra performing at the benefit concert for Kampuchea in December of 1979.

"How Do You Do It"
1963 Gerry & the Pacemakers hit, which was first recorded by The Beatles. The Beatles were not satisfied with the song, and therefore, their version was never released.

"How Do You Sleep?"
Written by: John Lennon
Recorded by: John
Lead singer: John
Year first released: 1971
Record label: Apple
Album: IMAGINE
- John's scathing attack on Paul and his music. John claimed Paul had subtly criticized him and Yoko on his album RAM, and therefore this was justifiable retaliation. Two of the bitterest lines in the song were contributed by Allen Klein. George plays guitar on this song.

- "If you can't fight with your best friend, who can you fight with?" John, 1972.

Howe, Elias
Inventor of the Singer sewing machine, to whom The Beatles dedicated their second movie, *Help!*

Howes, Arthur
British concert promoter who booked The Beatles in Britain from 1964 to 1966.

How I Won the War
1967 movie in which John made his solo acting debut. Released through United Artists; produced and directed by Richard Lester; written by Patrick Ryan, and screenplay by Charles Wood. In this antiwar satire, John plays a WW II soldier who is killed at the end of the film. For his role as Private Gripweed, John was required to cut his hair short and wear spectacles. After filming, John decided to continue to wear his glasses in his real-life role. (Previously he had worn contact lenses.) The film premiered at the London Pavilion on October 18, 1967, with The Beatles and wives in attendance. The movie and John received good reviews.

Howlin' Wolf
Performer on whose album THE LONDON HOWLIN' WOLF SESSIONS Ringo plays drums.

"How the Web Was Woven"
Jackie Lomax song which George produced.

Hughes, Geoffrey
Actor who dubbed Paul's voice in the *Yellow Submarine* movie.

Hughes, Graham
Photographer of the picture poster included in the LONDON TOWN album and on the cover of the "Mull of Kintyre" single.

"Hunting Scene"
Cut on the soundtrack album of *The Magic Christian* movie on which Ringo's voice is heard.

"Husbands and Wives"
Written by: Roger Miller
Recorded by: Ringo

Lead singer: Ringo
Year first released: 1974
Record label: Apple
Album: GOODNIGHT VIENNA
· Song about marital incompatibility. Ringo's choice to record this song was appropriately timed, since he had recently separated from his wife, Maureen.

"Hush-a-bye, Hush-a-bye"
Track that appears on John and Yoko's UNFINISHED MUSIC NO. 1: TWO VIRGINS album.

Hutchinson, Johnny
Drummer who performed with John, Paul, George, and Stu Sutcliffe when they auditioned for Larry Parnes in 1959.

I

Iachimore, Ian
Imaginary character about whom Paul composed the song "Paperback Writer." Paul wrote the lyrics in a letter format and signed the letter "Ian Iachimore," after realizing the name was similar to his own name played backwards on a tape loop.

I Am Also a You
Book written by Jay Thompson for which John wrote the introduction.

"I Am the Walrus"
Written by: Lennon/McCartney
Recorded by: The Beatles
Lead singer: John
Year first released: 1967
Record label: Parlophone (Britain); Capitol (U.S.)
Album: MAGICAL MYSTERY TOUR
      THE BEATLES 1967–1970
      THE BEATLES RARITIES (U.S.)
EP: MAGICAL MYSTERY TOUR
Single: B side of "Hello Goodbye"
Performance: *Magical Mystery Tour* movie
- The U.S. and British releases have different timing sequences in the musical intros. The version that appears on THE BEATLES RARITIES is a combination of the British and American versions.
- The chant at the record's end is The Beatles repeating "everybody's got one."
- The final stanza of the song includes a radio broadcast of *King Lear* recorded from a BBC program. John taped the voices from the radio though it was only years later that he realized which play it was.
- John deliberately strung together random thoughts and phrases in order to indulge the fancy of those who sought to find profound meaning in the lyrics.
- The music was originally inspired by the sound of a police siren passing John's home.

"I Am Your Singer"
Written by: Paul and Linda McCartney
Recorded by: Wings
Lead singer: Paul and Linda
Year first released: 1971
Record label: Apple
Album: WILD LIFE
Performances: 1972 Wings Over Europe Tour
- When Paul and Linda played this song on the radio in New York, in 1971, they dedicated it to their fathers.

Ian and the Kilburns
Name of the rock group sketched on the inner sleeve of the Wings album WINGS AT THE SPEED OF SOUND.

"I Call Your Name"
Written by: Lennon/McCartney
Recorded by: The Beatles
Lead singer: John
Year first released: 1964
Record label: Parlophone (Britain); Capitol (U.S.)
Album: THE BEATLES SECOND ALBUM
      ROCK AND ROLL MUSIC
      THE BEATLES RARITIES (Britain)
EP: LONG TALL SALLY
- John wrote the music for this song when he was sixteen years old.

Ichiwanagi, Toshi
Yoko Ono's first husband. Yoko married Ichiwanagi, a Japanese musician, in America in 1957, and they were divorced five years later.

"I'd Be Talking All the Time"
Written by: Chuck Howard and Larry Kingston
Recorded by: Ringo
Lead singer: Ringo
Year first released: 1970
Record label: Apple
Album: BEAUCOUPS OF BLUES

"I'd Have You Anytime"
Written by: George Harrison and Bob Dylan
Recorded by: George
Lead singer: George
Year first released: 1970
Record label: Apple
Album: ALL THINGS MUST PASS
- This song was written while George was visiting Bob Dylan at his home in Woodstock, New York, in November of 1968.

"I Dig a Pony"
Written by: Lennon/McCartney
Recorded by: The Beatles
Lead singer: John
Year first released: 1970
Record label: Apple
Album: LET IT BE
Performances: Rooftop sequence in the movie *Let It Be*

"I Dig Love"
Written by: George Harrison
Recorded by: George
Lead singer: George
Year first released: 1970
Record label: Apple
Album: ALL THINGS MUST PASS

Idle, Eric
Comedy writer who performs in the comedy group Monty Python's Flying Circus. Idle, George's close friend, directed the promo film clips for "True Love" and "Crackerbox Palace" in 1976. In 1978 Idle appeared as Dirk McQuikly in a film spoofing The Beatles, *All You Need Is Cash,* which he cowrote for television. The program starred The Rutles, who also recorded an album of their Beatle parodies.

"I Do Like to Be beside the Seaside"
Song which was performed by The Beatles on the television special "Blackpool Night Out" in 1965. All the group shared lead vocals.

"I Don't Care Anymore"
Written by: George Harrison
Recorded by: George
Lead singer: George
Year first released: 1974
Record label: Apple
Single: B side of "Dark Horse" in U.S.
           B side of "Ding Dong; Ding Dong" in Britain
· This song never appeared on an album.

"I Don't Want to Be a Soldier, Mama, I Don't Want to Die"
Written by: John Lennon
Recorded by: John
Lead singer: John
Year first released: 1971
Record label: Apple
Album: IMAGINE
· George plays slide guitar on this track.

"I Don't Want to See You Again"
Peter and Gordon song composed by Lennon/McCartney.

"I Don't Want to Smile"
Unreleased Denny Laine song recorded by Wings.

"I Don't Want to Spoil the Party"
Written by: Lennon/McCartney
Recorded by: The Beatles
Lead singer: John
Year first released: 1964
Record label: Parlophone (Britain); Capitol (U.S.)
Album: BEATLES FOR SALE
           BEATLES VI
EP: BEATLES FOR SALE (NO. 2)
Single: B side of "Eight Days a Week"

"I Feel Fine"
Written by: Lennon/McCartney
Recorded by: The Beatles
Lead singer: John
Year first released: 1964
Record label: Parlophone (Britain); Capitol (U.S.)
Album: BEATLES '65
           A COLLECTION OF BEATLES OLDIES
           THE BEATLES 1962–1966
EP: THE BEATLES MILLION SELLERS
Single: Britain and U.S.
Performances: 1964 Beatles' Christmas Shows
                    1965 European Summer Tour
                    1965 North American Tour
                    "Ed Sullivan Show" (TV), September
                    1965
                    1965 British Tour
                    1966 Summer World Tour
· The Beatles used feedback for the first time on this record. Though the amplifier buzz was accidental, they liked the effect and decided to keep it in the recording.

Ifield, Frank
British performer who headlined the bill on which The Beatles performed in 1962. This was The Beatles' first British concert outside of their home town of Liverpool and their reception was lukewarm, with Ifield's audience interested only in the star. An album of the concert was recorded.

"If I Fell"
Written by: Lennon/McCartney
Recorded by: The Beatles
Lead singer: John
Year first released: 1964
Record label: Parlophone (Britain); United Artists and
                  Capitol (U.S.)
Album: A HARD DAY'S NIGHT
           SOMETHING NEW
           LOVE SONGS
EP: EXCERPTS FROM THE FILM A HARD
      DAY'S NIGHT
Single: Britain; B side of "And I Love Her" in the U.S.
Performances: *A Hard Day's Night* movie
                    1964 North American Summer Tour

"If I Needed Someone"
Written by: George Harrison
Recorded by: The Beatles
Lead singer: George
Year first released: 1966
Record label: Parlophone (Britain); Capitol (U.S.)
Album: RUBBER SOUL (Britain)
           "YESTERDAY" . . . AND TODAY
           THE BEST OF GEORGE HARRISON
Performances: 1965 British Tour
                    1966 World Tour

"If Not for You"
Written by: Bob Dylan
Recorded by: George
Lead singer: George
Year first released: 1970
Record label: Apple
Album: ALL THINGS MUST PASS
• This song was written in 1968. George had first heard it when he was visiting Bob Dylan in upstate New York while Dylan was still composing the song.

"I Found Out"
Written by: John Lennon
Recorded by: John
Lead singer: John
Year first released: 1970
Record label: Apple
Album: JOHN LENNON/PLASTIC ONO BAND

"If You Believe"
Written by: George Harrison and Gary Wright
Recorded by: George
Lead singer: George
Year first released: 1979
Record label: Dark Horse
Album: GEORGE HARRISON
• This song was first scheduled as a single, but was scratched at the last moment.

"If You Love Me, Baby"
Song The Beatles recorded with Tony Sheridan in Hamburg in 1961. It is the B side of the British single "Ain't She Sweet" and appears on the album THE BEATLES FIRST.

"If You've Got Troubles"
Song written by Paul in 1965, but which was never released.

"I Got To Find My Baby"
Chuck Berry song performed by The Beatles on the British radio shows "Pop Go The Beatles" and "Saturday Club" in 1963.

"I Know (I Know)"
Written by: John Lennon
Recorded by: John
Lead singer: John
Year first released: 1973
Record label: Apple
Album: MIND GAMES

"I Lie Around"
Written by: Paul McCartney
Recorded by: Wings

Lead singer: Denny Laine
Year first released: 1973
Record label: Apple
Single: B side of "Live and Let Die"
• Only Wings single on which Paul didn't sing lead.

"I'll Be Back"
Written by: Lennon/McCartney
Recorded by: The Beatles
Lead singer: John
Year first released: 1964
Record label: Parlophone (Britain); Capitol (U.S.)
Album: A HARD DAY'S NIGHT (Britain)
        BEATLES '65
        LOVE SONGS

"I'll Be on My Way"
Early Lennon/McCartney composition which was recorded by Billy J. Kramer and the Dakotas.

"I'll Cry Instead"
Written by: Lennon/McCartney
Recorded by: The Beatles
Lead singer: John
Year first released: 1964
Record label: Parlophone (Britain); United Artists and Capitol (U.S.)
Album: A HARD DAY'S NIGHT (U.S.)
        SOMETHING NEW
EP: EXTRACTS FROM THE ALBUM A HARD DAY'S NIGHT
Single: U.S.
• This song was excluded from the movie, but was left on the album soundtrack.
• An extra verse is included in the version on the U.S. A HARD DAY'S NIGHT.

"I'll Follow the Sun"
Written by: Lennon/McCartney
Recorded by: The Beatles
Lead singer: Paul
Year first released: 1964
Record label: Parlophone (Britain); Capitol (U.S.)
Album: BEATLES FOR SALE
        BEATLES '65
        LOVE SONGS
EP: BEATLES FOR SALE (NO. 2)

"I'll Get You"
Written by: Lennon/McCartney
Recorded by: The Beatles
Lead singer: John
Year first released: 1963
Record label: Parlophone (Britain); Swan, Capitol (U.S.)
Album: THE BEATLES SECOND ALBUM
        THE BEATLES RARITIES (Britain)

Single: B side of "She Loves You"
B side of "Sie Liebt Dich" in U.S.

"I'll Keep You Satisfied"
Billy J. Kramer and the Dakotas song written by Lennon/McCartney.

"I'll Still Love You"
Written by: George Harrison
Recorded by: Ringo
Lead singer: Ringo
Year first released: 1976
Record label: Polydor (Britain); Atlantic (U.S.)
Album: RINGO'S ROTOGRAVURE
Performance: Promo film clip

"I Lost My Little Girl"
Paul wrote this song in 1956, but it was never released. This was the first original composition he ever played for John.

"I'm a Fool to Care"
Written by: Ted Daffan
Recorded by: Ringo
Lead singer: Ringo
Year first released: 1970
Record label: Apple
Album: SENTIMENTAL JOURNEY
• This song was arranged by Klaus Voorman.

IMAGINE
Artist: John Lennon
Producer: John
Year first released: 1971
Record label: Apple
Tracks: 10
    "Imagine"
    "Crippled Inside"
    "Jealous Guy"
    "It's So Hard"
    "I Don't Want to Be a Soldier Mama, I Don't Want
      to Die"
    "Give Me Some Truth"
    "Oh My Love"
    "How Do You Sleep?"
    "How?"
    "Oh, Yoko"
• This album was recorded at John's home recording studio on his Ascot estate, Tittenhurst Park.
• The album differed from John's previous solo work with the emphasis being on melody and orchestration as opposed to his more basic productions.
• John claimed he purposely sugarcoated the album's contents in order to reach a more general audience.
• Much of the package is laced through with hostile barbs directed at Paul. Aside from the most obvious

musical attack in "How Do You Sleep?," the package included a picture postcard photo of John mocking Paul's RAM album cover. This photo, of John and a pig, was deleted from later pressings.

"Imagine"
Written by: John Lennon
Recorded by: John
Lead singer: John
Year first released: 1971
Record label: Apple
Album: IMAGINE
          SHAVED FISH
Single: U.S. (1971) and Britain (1975)
Performances: Promo film clip
           One to One Concert, 1972
           "Jerry Lewis Labor Day Telethon"
             (U.S.), 1972
           "The Mike Douglas Show" (TV),
             (U.S.), 1972
           "Salute to Lew Grade" TV special,
             1975
• This song became the theme song for the One to One charity foundation.

Imagine
Promotional film that was made for the IMAGINE album; produced and directed by John and Yoko for Joko productions. Some forty thousand feet of film were shot of John and Yoko engaged in various activities, accompanied by the album's music. Cameo appearances were made by George Harrison, Fred Astaire, Dick Cavett, and Andy Warhol.

"I'm a Loser"
Written by: Lennon/McCartney
Recorded by: The Beatles
Lead singer: John
Year first released: 1964
Record label: Parlophone (Britain); Capitol (U.S.)
Album: BEATLES FOR SALE
          BEATLES '65
EP: BEATLES FOR SALE
    4 BY THE BEATLES
Performances: 1964 Beatles' Christmas Shows
           1965 European Tour
           "Shindig" TV show, January 1965
• John feels that this is one of his best early efforts.

"I'm Carrying"
Written by: Paul McCartney
Recorded by: Wings
Lead singer: Paul
Year first released: 1978
Record label: Parlophone (Britain); Capitol (U.S.)
Album: LONDON TOWN
• Paul still "carrying a torch" for an ex-love.
• George's favorite cut on the album.

"I'm Down"
Written by: Lennon/McCartney
Recorded by: The Beatles
Lead singer: Paul
Year first released: 1965
Record label: Parlophone (Britain); Capitol (U.S.)
Album: ROCK AND ROLL MUSIC
           THE BEATLES RARITIES (Britain)
Single: B side of "Help!"
Performances: 1965 World Tour
                 1966 World Tour
                 "Ed Sullivan Show" (TV), September
                 1965
- The Beatles closed many concert shows with this song.

"I Me Mine"
Written by: George Harrison
Recorded by: The Beatles
Lead singer: George
Year first released: 1970
Record label: Apple
Album: LET IT BE
Performances: *Let It Be* movie
- George performs this song in the film as he previews his new composition to Ringo with only an acoustic guitar for accompaniment. Later, The Beatles (sans John, who is waltzing with Yoko) perform the song.

I Me Mine
Title of George's autobiography; published by Genesis in 1980. A limited collectors' edition was printed, complete with leather-bound cover and each individually autographed by George. The book includes George's personal anecdotes regarding the Beatle years and reproductions of his original compositions.

"I'm Going to Sit Right Down and Cry"
Song which The Beatles performed in the early days. It appears on the U.S. version of THE BEATLES LIVE AT THE STAR CLUB.

"I'm Happy Just to Dance with You"
Written by: Lennon/McCartney
Recorded by: The Beatles
Lead singer: George
Year first released: 1964
Record label: Parlophone (Britain); United Artists and
                 Capitol (U.S.)
Album: A HARD DAY'S NIGHT
           SOMETHING NEW
Single: B side of "I'll Cry Instead" in U.S.
Performances: *A Hard Day's Night* movie

"I'm in Love"
Foremost song written by Lennon/McCartney.

"I'm Looking through You"
Written by: Lennon/McCartney
Recorded by: The Beatles
Lead singer: Paul
Year first released: 1965
Record label: Parlophone (Britain); Capitol (U.S.)
Album: RUBBER SOUL
- U.S. stereo version begins with two false guitar intros.
- The song was written during a separation between Paul and his girlfriend, Jane.

"I'm Only Sleeping"
Written by: Lennon/McCartney
Recorded by: The Beatles
Lead singer: John
Year first released: 1966
Record label: Parlophone (Britain); Capitol (U.S.)
Album: REVOLVER (Britain)
           "YESTERDAY" . . . AND TODAY
           THE BEATLES RARITIES (U.S.)

"I'm So Tired"
Written by: Lennon/McCartney
Recorded by: The Beatles
Lead singer: John
Year first released: 1968
Record label: Apple
Album: THE BEATLES
- This song was finished in one take on John's twenty-eighth birthday.
- John wrote this song during a stressful period in his life when he had to decide whether or not to leave his wife to pursue a life with Yoko.

"I'm Talking about You"
Chuck Berry song which The Beatles perform on the album THE BEATLES LIVE AT THE STAR CLUB.

"I'm the Greatest"
Written by: John Lennon
Recorded by: Ringo
Lead singer: Ringo
Year first released: 1973
Record label: Apple
Album: RINGO
           BLAST FROM YOUR PAST
Performances: "Ringo" TV special, 1978
- John's biographical tribute to Ringo.
- George and John are heard on this track.

"Incantation"
Unreleased song written by John Lennon and Ray Cicala in 1974.

IN CONCERT 1972
Live album by Ravi Shankar and Ali Akba Khan, which George coproduced with Phil McDonald and Zakir Hussein.

"India"
Unreleased song written by George and recorded by The Beatles during the sessions for SGT. PEPPER.

Indica Gallery
London bookshop owned by Peter Asher, Miles, and John Dunbar in the mid-sixties. The store specialized in works on music and contemporary literature. Paul personally designed the shop's wrapping paper, which he presented as a gift for its opening.

In November of 1966 an art exhibit by Yoko Ono was held at the Indica. It was at this exhibit where John first met Yoko.

Indra Club, The
Nightclub which The Beatles were booked into on their first trip to Germany in August 1960. They performed here for two months until the club closed because of neighbors' complaints about the noise.

"I Need You"
Written by: George Harrison
Recorded by: The Beatles
Lead singer: George
Year first released: 1965
Record label: Parlophone (Britain); Capitol (U.S.)
Album: HELP!
     LOVE SONGS
Performances: *Help!* movie
· George wrote this song while away from Pattie during the filming of *Help!* on location in the Bahamas.

In His Own Write
First book written by John Lennon; published by Jonathan Cape (Britain) and Simon and Schuster (U.S.) in 1964.

The book, consisting of short stories, poetry, and sketchings, is John's absurd yet biting commentary on British life. Much of the material was gathered from John's early writings at school, which John styled after his favorites, Lewis Carroll and James Thurber.

Paul helped with the book's title and wrote the introduction. The book was critically acclaimed; *The New York Times* called it "inspired nonsense." John felt the book was his way of expressing himself apart from music and The Beatles.

In His Own Write
One-act play based on John's two books. The production was adapted for the theatre by John, Adrienne Kennedy, and Victor Spinetti (who also directed the production). The play, performed by the National Theatre Company, officially opened on June 18, 1968 at the Old Vic Theatre in London. Yoko's attendance with John at the opening night performance started the press's speculation about their relationship.

"In My Life"
Written by: Lennon/McCartney
Recorded by: The Beatles
Lead singer: John
Year first released: 1965
Record label: Parlophone (Britain); Capitol (U.S.)
Album: RUBBER SOUL
     THE BEATLES 1962–1966
     LOVE SONGS
Performances: George's 1974 Dark Horse Tour
· One of John's personal favorites.
· Though one of George's favorite Lennon/McCartney compositions, when he rearranged the music and lyrics for his rendition in concert, he received much public criticism for tampering with a classic.

"Inner Light, The"
Written by: George Harrison
Recorded by: The Beatles
Lead singer: George
Year first released: 1968
Record label: Parlophone (Britain); Capitol (U.S.)
Album: THE BEATLES RARITIES
Single: B side of "Lady Madonna"
· George recorded this song with various Indian musicians, and none of the other Beatles appear on the record.
· The lyrics were borrowed from a Japanese poem by Roshi.

Innes, Neil
Comedian who portrayed Ron Nasty in the television spoof starring The Rutles, for which he also composed the music. Innes, originally a member of The Bonzo Dog Band, appeared in the *Magical Mystery Tour* film as one of the back-up singers in the strip club scene. He later joined the musical/comedy team of Grimms (of which Mike McGear was a member) and then went on to become a member of Monty Python's Flying Circus.

Inn on the Park
Hotel in London where John and Yoko resided in 1970 while their home in Tittenhurst was being renovated.

"Instant Karma"
Written by: John Lennon
Recorded by: John and the Plastic Ono Band
Lead singer: John
Year first released: 1970
Record label: Apple
Album: SHAVED FISH
Single: Britain and U.S.
Performances: One to One Concert, August 1972
     Promo film clip
· John wrote and recorded this song in one day.
· George is heard on the record, along with a chorus of people John picked out of a crowd in a nightclub,

after John decided he wanted more voices in the background. George conducted and directed the chorus.

International Times
Underground British newspaper to which John donated £1,000 to aid in its struggle to survive during the late 1960s.

IN THE BEGINNING
See THE BEATLES FEATURING TONY SHERIDAN IN THE BEGINNING.

"In the Tyrol"
Instrumental piece which appears on the American HELP! release and is included in the soundtrack of the film during the ski scene when The Beatles appear as part of the Austrian marching band. This piece was composed by Wagner as an introduction to his Overture to Act III of *Lohengrin*.

INTRODUCING THE BEATLES
Artist: The Beatles
Producer: George Martin
Year first released: 1963
Record label: Vee Jay
Tracks: 12
    "I Saw Her Standing There"
    "Misery"
    "Anna"
    "Chains"
    "Boys"
    "Love Me Do" (original album)
    "Ask Me Why" (second pressing)
    "P.S. I Love You" (original album)
    "Please Please Me" (second pressing)
    "Baby It's You"
    "Do You Want to Know a Secret"
    "A Taste of Honey"
    "There's a Place"
    "Twist and Shout"
· First Beatles album released in America.
· Due to Capitol's control of copyrights to "Love Me Do" and "P.S. I Love You," Vee Jay was forced to replace these two songs on future pressings of the album.

"Intuition"
Written by: John Lennon
Recorded by: John
Lead singer: John
Year first released: 1973
Record label: Apple
Album: MIND GAMES

104

Invisible Strings
Music credited on SOMETIME IN NEW YORK CITY album.

"I Remember Jeep"
Instrumental written by George, which appears on the "Apple Jam" part of the album ALL THINGS MUST PASS.

"I Remember You"
Song performed by The Beatles, which appears on the album THE BEATLES LIVE AT THE STAR CLUB.

"I Saw Her Standing There"
Written by: Lennon/McCartney
Recorded by: The Beatles
Lead singer: Paul
Year first released: 1963
Record label: Parlophone (Britain); Vee Jay and Capitol (U.S.)
Album: PLEASE PLEASE ME
    INTRODUCING THE BEATLES
    MEET THE BEATLES
    ROCK AND ROLL MUSIC
    THE BEATLES LIVE AT THE STAR CLUB
EP: THE BEATLES (NO. 1)
Single: B side of "I Want to Hold Your Hand" (U.S.)
Performances: 1964 U.S. Tour (February)
    "Ed Sullivan Show" (TV) February 1964
    1964 North American Tour
· This song was written early in The Beatles' career and was a favorite of their fans in Liverpool and Germany.
· In 1974 John joined Elton John on stage at Madison Square Garden and performed the song in concert. John introduced the song to the audience as "a song written by an old fiancée of mine called Paul."
· Elton John released the recorded performance in 1975.

"I Should Have Known Better"
Written by: Lennon/McCartney
Recorded by: The Beatles
Lead singer: John
Year first released: 1964
Record label: Parlophone (Britain); United Artists and Capitol (U.S.)
Album: A HARD DAY'S NIGHT
    THE BEATLES AGAIN
EP: EXTRACTS FROM THE FILM A HARD DAY'S NIGHT
Single: B side of "A Hard Day's Night" (U.S.)
    B side of "Yesterday" rereleased in 1976 (Britain)

Performances: Train sequence in the movie *A Hard Day's Night*
· The instrumental version is heard only on the U.S. album soundtrack.

"I Should Like to Live up a Tree"
Unreleased Ringo song recorded during the LET IT BE album sessions.

"Isn't It a Pity"
Written by: George Harrison
Recorded by: George
Lead singer: George
Year first released: 1970
Record label: Apple
Album: ALL THINGS MUST PASS
Single: B side of "My Sweet Lord"
· Two different versions of the song appear on the album with musical changes in tempo and length.
· The longer version includes an end verse which is similar to the repetitious ending of "Hey Jude."

"Isolation"
Written by: John Lennon
Recorded by: John Lennon/Plastic Ono Band
Lead singer: John
Year first released: 1970
Record label: Apple
Album: JOHN LENNON/PLASTIC ONO BAND

"IS THIS WHAT YOU WANT?"
Jackie Lomax album produced by George, who along with Ringo also plays on the album.

I SURVIVE
Adam Faith album on which Paul sings and plays the synthesizer.

"It Don't Come Easy"
Written by: Richard Starkey
Recorded by: Ringo
Lead singer: Ringo
Year first released: 1971
Record label: Apple
Album: THE CONCERT FOR BANGLA DESH
        BLAST FROM YOUR PAST
Single: U.S. and Britain
Performances: Concert for Bangla Desh, 1971
· Ringo's first solo single release.
· George produced and performs on the record.
· The concert album includes Ringo's live version, complete with all the forgotten lyrics.

"It Is He (Jai Sri Krishna)"
Written by: George Harrison
Recorded by: George

Lead singer: George
Year first released: 1974
Record label: Apple
Album: DARK HORSE

"It's All Too Much"
Written by: George Harrison
Recorded by: The Beatles
Lead singer: George
Year first released: 1969
Record label: Apple
Album: YELLOW SUBMARINE
· The song is heard on the *Yellow Submarine* movie soundtrack, with an additional verse which is not included on the record.
· George refers to his wife, Pattie, in the line with the description of long blond hair and eyes of blue. These lyrics were taken from the Mersey's hit song "Sorrow."

"It's for You"
Lennon/McCartney composition recorded by Cilla Black.

"It's Hard to Be Lovers"
Song cowritten by Ringo and Keith Allison, which has never been released.

"It's Johnny's Birthday"
Song which appears on the Apple Jam record of George's ALL THINGS MUST PASS album. George wrote this song in honor of John's thirtieth birthday.

IT'S LIKE YOU NEVER LEFT
Dave Mason album on which George plays guitar.

IT'S MY PLEASURE
Billy Preston album on which George plays guitar.

"It's No Secret"
Written by: Richard Starkey/Vini Poncia
Recorded by: Ringo
Lead singer: Ringo
Year first released: 1977
Record label: Polydor (Britain); Atlantic (U.S.)
Album: RINGO THE 4TH

"It's Only Love"
Written by: Lennon/McCartney
Recorded by: The Beatles
Lead singer: John
Year first released: 1965
Record label: Parlophone (Britain); Capitol (U.S.)
Album: HELP! (Britain)
        RUBBER SOUL (U.S.)
        LOVE SONGS
ED: YESTERDAY

"It's So Easy"
Buddy Holly song which John, Paul, and George performed (as Johnny and the Moondogs) on the Caroll Levis "Discoveries" TV show in 1959. In 1979 Paul joined the Crickets on stage at London's Hammersmith Odeon for a rendition of this song.

"It's So Hard"
Written by: John Lennon
Recorded by: John
Lead singer: John
Year first released: 1971
Record label: Apple
Album: IMAGINE
Single: B side of "Imagine" in U.S.
Performances: One to One Concert, August 1972
　　　　　　　　"The Mike Douglas Show" (TV),
　　　　　　　　(U.S.), 1972

"It's What You Value"
Written by: George Harrison
Recorded by: George
Lead singer: George
Year first released: 1976
Record label: Dark Horse
Album: 33⅓
Single: Britain

"It Takes Alot to Laugh/It Takes a Train to Cry"
Bob Dylan song which he performed at the Concert for Bangla Desh in 1971.

"It Won't Be Long"
Written by: Lennon/McCartney
Recorded by: The Beatles
Lead singer: John
Year first released: 1963
Record label: Parlophone (Britain); Capitol (U.S.)
Album: WITH THE BEATLES
　　　　MEET THE BEATLES

"I've Got a Feeling"
Written by: Lennon/McCartney
Recorded by: The Beatles
Lead singer: John and Paul
Year first released: 1970
Record label: Apple
Album: LET IT BE
Performances: *Let It Be* film

I'VE GOT MY OWN ALBUM TO DO
Ron Wood album on which George and Paul appear.

"I've Had Enough"
Written by: Paul McCartney
Recorded by: Wings
Lead singer: Paul

Year first released: 1978
Record label: Parlophone (Britain); Capitol (U.S.)
Album: LONDON TOWN
Single: Britain and U.S.
Performances: 1979 Wings' British Tour
　　　　　　　　Promo film clip
· The song was recorded on a boat in the Virgin Islands.

"I've Just Seen a Face"
Written by: Lennon/McCartney
Recorded by: The Beatles
Lead singer: Paul
Year first released: 1965
Record label: Parlophone (Britain); Capitol (U.S.)
Album: HELP! (Britain)
　　　　RUBBER SOUL (U.S.)
　　　　WINGS OVER AMERICA
Performances: 1975–76 Wings' World Tour

Iveys, The
Original name of Apple recording artists, Badfinger.

Ivor Novello Awards
Awards presented by the British music industry. The Beatles received ten awards from 1964 through 1969.
  1. Most outstanding contribution to music (1964)
  2. "She Loves You" (1964)
  3. "I Want to Hold Your Hand" (1964)
  4. "All My Loving" (1964)
  5. "We Can Work It Out" (1966)
  6. "Yesterday" (1966)
  7. "Help!" (1966)
  8. "Michelle" (1967)
  9. "Yellow Submarine" (1967)
  10. "Hey Jude" (1969)

"I Wanna Be Your Man"
Written by: Lennon/McCartney
Recorded by: The Beatles
Lead singer: Ringo
Year first released: 1963
Record label: Parlophone (Britain); Capitol (U.S.)
Album: WITH THE BEATLES
　　　　MEET THE BEATLES
Performances: 1964 U.S. Tour (February)
　　　　　　　　"Big Night Out" TV show, 1964
　　　　　　　　1965 European Summer Tour
　　　　　　　　1965 North American Tour (alternate
　　　　　　　　　shows)
　　　　　　　　1966 Summer Tour
· John and Paul wrote this composition in ten minutes to give to the Rolling Stones, who had their first hit record with the song.

"I Want to Hold Your Hand"
Written by: Lennon/McCartney
Recorded by: The Beatles
Lead singer: John
Year first released: 1963
Record label: Parlophone (Britain); Capitol (U.S.)
Album: MEET THE BEATLES
        A COLLECTION OF BEATLES OLDIES
        THE BEATLES 1962–1966
        THE BEATLES RARITIES
EP: THE BEATLES MILLION SELLERS
Single: Britain and U.S.
Performances: "Sunday Night at the London Palla-
        dium," October 1963
        "Ed Sullivan Show" (TV), February
        1964
        1964 U.S. Tour (February)
        1964 North American Tour
        "Around The Beatles" TV show, 1964
- This song was written by John and Paul while loung-ing in the basement den of Jane Asher's home.
- The Beatles first #1 record in America.

"I Want to Tell You"
Written by: George Harrison
Recorded by: The Beatles
Lead singer: George
Year first released: 1966
Record label: Parlophone (Britain); Capitol (U.S.)
Album: REVOLVER

"I Want You (She's So Heavy)"
Written by: Lennon/McCartney
Recorded by: The Beatles
Lead singer: John
Year first released: 1969
Record label: Apple
Album: ABBEY ROAD
- John plays lead guitar on this song.

"I Will"
Written by: Lennon/McCartney
Recorded by: The Beatles
Lead singer: Paul
Year first released: 1968
Record label: Apple
Album: THE BEATLES
        LOVE SONGS

"I Wouldn't Have You Any Other Way"
Written by: Chuck Howard
Recorded by: Ringo
Lead singer: Ringo
Year first released: 1970
Record label: Apple
Album: BEAUCOUPS OF BLUES

"I Would Only Smile"
Wings' song which was performed on their 1972 Wings over Europe Tour, but the song was never released on record.

I WROTE A SIMPLE SONG
Billy Preston album on which George plays guitar.

J

Jacaranda, The
Liverpool club where The Beatles frequently performed in the early sixties. The "Jac," owned by Allan Williams, was originally a wine cellar of a small house which was converted into a music club complete with dance floor. The Beatles helped design the interior of the club by painting murals on the walls.

Jackson, Mr.
Name on Ringo's hospital room door at the University College Hospital where he was treated for a tonsil infection in 1964.

Jagger, Mick
Lead singer of the Rolling Stones. Mick, though a professional rival, has been a friend of The Beatles since the early days of 1963.

In 1971, Paul and Ringo, with respective families, flew to St. Tropez, France, to attend Mick's wedding. Though Paul and Ringo flew from London on the same flight they remained apart throughout the journey.

James, Carrol
Washington disc jockey who was the first to play a Beatles record on American radio.

James, Dick
Music publisher of The Beatles' songs from 1962 through 1968. James first became interested in The Beatles after his friend, producer George Martin, informed him of their talents. In November of 1962, when Brian Epstein presented James with The Beatles' recording of "Please Please Me," James was very confident about The Beatles' future prospects and proposed that The Beatles become his clients. Brian had set forth one stipulation—James would have to arrange for The Beatles to get national exposure. James subsequently booked the group on the nationwide television program "Thank Your Lucky Stars," thereby securing the publishing rights to their songs.

In 1964 The Beatles formed their own publishing company, Northern Songs Ltd., and James was appointed head of the corporation. The following year, when the company went on the open market, James became a major stockholder, owning 37 percent of the company's shares. In 1969, unbeknownst to The Beatles, James sold his shares of Northern Songs to Associated Television (ATV). This action caused The Beatles to eventually lose total control of the publishing rights to their own songs. (See Northern Songs Ltd.) The Beatles felt that James's action was a stab in the back.

James, Frederick
Chief interviewer for *The Beatles Book Monthly* magazine from 1963 through 1969.

"James Bond Theme, The"
Monty Norman composition of which a sixteen-second segment is heard on the *HELP!* soundtrack. The music is also included on the U.S. album version of the song "Help!"

"James Paul McCartney"
Sixty-minute television special starring Paul and Wings; produced by Hemien/Smith for ATV. The hour consisted of Paul and Wings performing in concert plus comedy and homey sequences, including a family singalong in Liverpool and an elaborate Busby Berkley-style dance scene. Paul was given complete artistic control over the program's structure. The show also featured Paul performing a Beatles' song ("Yesterday") publicly for the first time since the breakup.

The show was aired first in the U.S. on April 16, 1973. The British broadcast was shown a month later (May 10) and differed from the U.S. show only in musical content. The U.S. version included the song "Long Tall Sally," whereas the British version omitted this number and included "Hi Hi Hi" instead.

Paul admitted a few years later that he felt the show was a little disjointed, but in general he was pleased with the results.

JAMES TAYLOR
First and only album by James Taylor to be released on Apple Records. Paul plays bass on one cut.

"Jamrag"
Live jam session recorded at the performance at the Fillmore East by John, Yoko, and Frank Zappa and the Mothers of Invention on June 6, 1971. This song appears on the album SOMETIME IN NEW YORK CITY.

Jan Baum and Iris Silverman Gallery
Los Angeles art gallery where Linda McCartney held a photo exhibit from December 17, 1977 through January 28, 1978.

Janov, Arthur
American psychologist and writer of the book *Primal Therapy: The Cure for Neurosis*. In 1970 John and Yoko read his book and then enrolled in his therapy program in London. After a month's therapy in England, John and Yoko flew to Los Angeles and were indoctrinated into Janov's four-month program of reliving repressed pain. It was during this time that John composed much of the emotion-packed material which later appeared on his first solo album, JOHN LENNON/PLASTIC ONO BAND.

"Japanese Tears"
Song Denny Laine composed after Paul's 1980 Tokyo drug bust.

Jasper, Tony
British rock journalist who authored the book *Paul McCartney and Wings.*

"Jealous Guy"
Written by: John Lennon
Recorded by: John
Lead singer: John
Year first released: 1971
Record label: Apple
Album: IMAGINE
• Yoko inspired and helped write this song.

Jelly babies
English counterpart of the American jelly beans. These candies became the symbol of Beatle adulation as fans deluged the group with their favorite sweets while they performed on stage. The Beatles soon found this practice to be so annoying that they were forced to retract a previous statement citing jelly babies as their favorite candy.

"Jerry Lewis Labor Day Telethon"
Television benefit held annually to raise money for Muscular Dystrophy. John and Yoko appeared on this program with the Elephant's Memory Band in 1972. They performed "Imagine," "Now or Never," and "Give Peace a Chance." In 1979 Ringo performed on the program with Bill Wyman, Todd Rundgren, Doug Kershaw, and Kiki Dee. Among the numbers they performed were "Money," "Twist and Shout," and "Jumpin' Jack Flash." Ringo also stayed on hand to take pledges from viewers. Paul donated his film clip "Getting Closer" to be aired on the telethon the same year.

"Jessie's Dream"
Instrumental song written by The Beatles and performed on the soundtrack of the movie *Magical Mystery Tour.*

"Jet"
Written by: Paul McCartney
Recorded by: Paul
Lead singer: Paul
Year first released: 1973
Record label: Apple
Album: BAND ON THE RUN
　　　　 WINGS OVER AMERICA
　　　　 WINGS GREATEST
Single: Britain and U.S.
Performances: 1975–76 Wings' World Tour
• One of Paul's most lyrically complex tunes. Though he seems to to be referring to a broken love affair with

a highly independent woman (suffragette), Paul claims the song is about his puppy, Jet.

Jim Mac's Jazz Band
Nineteen twenties jazz band which was led by Paul's father, Jim.

Jimmy Scott and his Obla Di Obla Da Band
Calypso band from which Paul took the title for his song "Ob-la-di, Ob-la-da."

Jimmy Westons
New York restaurant in which a party was given by George for the performers on the bill at the Concert for Bangla Desh on August 1, 1971.

Jiva
Dark Horse artists who recorded one album, JIVA, during their one-year affiliation with the record label.

Joan
Quizzical character who is murdered by Maxwell Edison in the song "Maxwell's Silver Hammer." Joan is also the name of George's maid, whom he sings about in his song "The Ballad of Sir Frankie Crisp."

JOHN DAWSON WINTER III
Johnny Winter album on which John's composition "Rock and Roll People" appears.

John, Elton
British composer/musician who first worked as an errand boy for The Beatles' music publisher Dick James before becoming famous in his own right.

On November 28, 1974, Elton John was joined on stage by John at his New York concert at Madison Square Garden, and they performed three numbers together: "Whatever Gets You Thru the Night," "Lucy In the Sky With Diamonds," and "I Saw Her Standing There." The appearance by John had been promised to Elton when John made a deal to come on stage with him if his song "Whatever Gets You Thru the Night" became number one on the charts. On the evening of the concert John and Yoko were reconciled backstage after a year-long separation.

Elton John appears on John's song "Whatever Gets You Thru the Night." The live version of "I Saw Her Standing There" was released as the B side to Elton's single "Philadelphia Freedom."

Elton John and Bernie Taupin wrote "Snookeroo" especially for Ringo to record.

"John, John ((Let's Hope For Peace)"
Yoko's song which was performed at the Toronto Rock 'n' Roll Revival Concert and appears on the album

PLASTIC ONO BAND/LIVE PEACE IN TORONTO.

JOHN LENNON/PLASTIC ONO BAND
Artist: John Lennon
Producer: John, Yoko, and Phil Spector
Year first released: 1970
Record label: Apple
Tracks: 11
    "Mother"
    "Hold On"
    "I Found Out"
    "Working Class Hero"
    "Isolation"
    "Remember"
    "Love"
    "Well Well Well"
    "Look At Me"
    "God"
    "My Mummy's Dead"
- John's first and most artistically acclaimed album since the breakup of The Beatles.
- The album was recorded in England as a result of the primal scream therapy program John and Yoko were enrolled in. The album's "painfully" honest and autobiographical material initiated more personal songwriting techniques among other artists.
- The album was censored in some countries because of the explicit language.

John Lennon Story, The
Book written by George Tremlett; published by Futura Publications Ltd.

John, Paul, George, Ringo, and Bert
Play written by William Russell which was based on The Beatles' career from their Cavern days up until their breakup. The character Bert was the fictional Beatle who was booted out before the group became famous. Bert narrates the story and also portrays the universal fan who watches as The Beatles develop and progress.

The play originally opened at the Everyman Theatre in Liverpool and was later brought to London by Robert Stigwood. The London production opened at the Lyric Theatre on August 15, 1974.

The only Beatle to see the play was George, who left during the intermission. Paul read the script and felt it falsely portrayed him as the villain and therefore denied Stigwood the film rights. Coincidentally, Mike McGear, Paul's brother, felt the play was worthwhile.

George made the producers pull "Here Comes the Sun" from the production and it was replaced with "Good Day Sunshine."

110

"John Sinclair"
Written by: John Lennon
Recorded by: John and the Elephant's Memory Band
Lead singer: John
Year first released: 1972
Record label: Apple
Album: SOMETIME IN NEW YORK CITY
Performances: Benefit for John Sinclair in Ann Arbor, Michigan, December 1971
    "The David Frost Show" (TV), (U.S.), January 1972
- John wrote this song in protest of the incarceration of John Sinclair, who was sentenced to ten years in prison for the possession of marijuana.
- John plays slide guitar.

Johnny and the Moondogs
Name the Beatles performed under for their first TV appearance on the Caroll Levis "Discoveries" TV show in 1959. The Moondogs sang "It's So Easy" and "Think It Over."

"Johnny B. Goode"
Chuck Berry composition which John sang with Berry on "The Mike Douglas Show" (TV) on February 23, 1972.

Johns, Glyn
EMI recording engineer who worked closely with The Beatles on several of their recordings. Glyn Johns also worked on the Wings' album RED ROSE SPEEDWAY.

Johnson, Kendall
Photographer who took the photos for George's LIVING IN THE MATERIAL WORLD album.

Jo Jo
Character in the song "Get Back."

Joko
Production company set up by John and Yoko in 1969.

Jolly Jimmy Johnson
The courier on the bus in *Magical Mystery Tour*, portrayed by British actor Derek Royale.

JOLLY WHAT! THE BEATLES AND FRANK IFIELD ON STAGE
Artist: The Beatles/Frank Ifield
Producer: George Martin
Year first released: 1964
Record label: Vee Jay
Tracks: 4 Beatle cuts
    "Please Please Me"
    "From Me To You"

"Ask Me Why"
"Thank You Girl"
• U.S. release.

Jones, Alan
Art designer of the album cover for RED ROSE SPEEDWAY.

Jones, Brian
Late member of the Rolling Stones who played saxophone on The Beatles records "Baby You're a Rich Man" and "You Know My Name (Look Up the Number)."

Jones, Desmond and Molly
Fictional characters who take turns singing with the band in the song "Ob-la-di, Ob-la-da."

Jones, John Paul
Member of the group Led Zeppelin who appears on the album BACK TO THE EGG. On December 29, 1979 Jones performed with Wings as part of the rockestra at the charity concert for Kampuchea.

Jones, Paul
Musician on whose recording "And the Sun Will Shine" Paul plays drums.

Jones, Pauline
Nineteen-year-old student who married John's fifty-four-year-old dad in 1967. The couple presented John with a half brother.

Jones, Raymond
Young man credited with bringing The Beatles to the attention of Brian Epstein in 1961. He reportedly asked to purchase a record at Epstein's shop which was recorded by a new "German" group called The Beatles.

Jones, Trevor
Head road manager for Wings. Jones has worked on all of Wings' tours.

Joseph Williams Primary School
Located in Liverpool; second school Paul attended.

Jotta Herra
Dutch group that recorded Paul's composition "Penina."

Juber, Laurence
Wings' guitarist who replaced Jimmy McCulloch in the summer of 1978. Juber had previously worked as a session musician and was brought to Paul's attention by mutual friend, Wings' member Denny Laine. His only meeting with Paul prior to his playing with the band was in a recording studio men's room.

"Julia"
Written by: Lennon/McCartney
Recorded by: The Beatles
Lead singer: John
Year first released: 1968
Record label: Apple
Album: THE BEATLES
Single: Rereleased as the B side of "Ob-la-di, Ob-la-da" in 1976 in the U.S.
• John's ode to his late mother.

Julie
Name of the seal that appears in the film and photo jacket for the Wings' song "Junior's Farm."

"Jumpin' Jack Flash"/"Youngblood"
Medley performed by Leon Russell at the Concert for Bangla Desh in 1971. The song also appears on the album from the concert.

Jumping Jack Productions Ltd.
English firm which coproduced the Wings Over Europe Tour with McCartney Productions Ltd.

Juniper
Antique shop located on London's Kings Road, where, in 1967, Pattie Harrison and her sister Jenny ran a small business. The shop was soon to close due to Pattie's other commitments.

"Junior's Farm"
Written by: Paul McCartney
Recorded by: Wings
Lead singer: Paul
Year first released: 1974
Record label: Apple
Album: WINGS GREATEST
Single: First released as A side of "Sally G" but was later switched to B side.
Performances: Promo film clip
• Written during the McCartneys' visit to Nashville and their stay on Junior Putnam's farm in 1974.

"Junk"
Written by: Paul McCartney
Recorded by: Paul
Lead singer: Paul
Year first released: 1970
Record label: Apple
Album: McCARTNEY
Performances: 1972 Wings Over Europe Tour
• Paul wrote this song in 1968 while in India with The Beatles.
• Its original title was "Jubilee."
• The Beatles recorded a version of this song intended for ABBEY ROAD but it was not released commercially.

- An instrumental version of this song is included on the album McCARTNEY.

Junkin, John
Actor who played the part of Shake, The Beatles' assistant road manager, in *A Hard Day's Night*.

"Just a Dream"
Written by: Richard Starkey and Vini Poncia
Recorded by: Ringo
Lead singer: Ringo
Year first released: 1977
Record label: Polydor (Britain); Atlantic (U.S.)
Single: B side of "Wings" in U.S. and B side of "Drowning in the Sea of Love" in Britain and U.S.

"Just Because"
Written by: Lloyd Price
Recorded by: John
Lead singer: John
Year first released: 1975
Record label: Apple
Album: ROCK 'N' ROLL

"Just Fun"
Unreleased song composed by John and Paul in 1960.

"Just Like a Woman"
Bob Dylan song which he performed at the Concert for Bangla Desh in 1971. George accompanied Dylan on guitar along with vocal harmonies. The song appears on the album release of the concert.

K

Kaempfert, Bert
German composer/arranger who produced The Beatles' first recording in 1961. The Beatles were brought to Kaempfert's attention while they were playing an engagement in Hamburg's Top Ten Club. They were signed to his production company to back singer Tony Sheridan under the name The Beat Brothers. Their recordings together included "My Bonnie," "The Saints," and "Cry For a Shadow" (an original composition by Lennon and Harrison).

In 1962, Bert Kaempfert released The Beatles from their contract, at the request of their new manager, Brian Epstein, because he felt it was unfeasible to manage a British group while he was based in Germany.

Kaili
Eastern god to whom Ringo is sacrificial bait in the movie *Help!*

Kaiserkeller, The
Hamburg club, owned by Bruno Koschmider, where The Beatles performed from October through December 1960. It was here that they intentionally broke the performing stage during one of their wild numbers in hopes that it would force management to provide a new set. Their plan backfired when no stage was installed, and they were required to do the remaining shows from the floor.

Kampuchea
Cambodian refugee camp which was the subject of a series of charity concerts held in London during the week of December 26–29, 1979. Wings headlined the final concert.

Kane, Louise Harrison Caldwell
Sister of George Harrison who moved to the United States prior to her brother's fame. When the American public became aware of The Beatles, Louise Caldwell (married name at that time) was sought after for any information concerning her brother and his group. In 1965, an album, ALL ABOUT THE BEATLES, containing an interview with Louise Harrison Caldwell, was released.

George's first trip to America occurred before his tour with The Beatles, when he came to visit his sister in Illinois in September 1963.

"Kansas City"
Written by: Jerry Leiber and Mike Stoller
Recorded by: The Beatles
Lead singer: Paul
Year first released: 1964
Record label: Parlophone (Britain); Capitol (U.S.)
Album: BEATLES FOR SALE
BEATLES VI
THE BEATLES LIVE AT THE STAR
CLUB
ROCK AND ROLL MUSIC
Single: B side of "Boys" in U.S.
Performances: "Shindig" TV show, January 1965
• The Beatles styled their rendition of this song after Little Richard's version, using the combination of the original "Kansas City" in medley with Richard's "Hey Hey Hey Hey."

Kaptain Kundalini
Pseudonym used by John on his song "What You Got."

"Karate Chaos"
Unreleased Wings song recorded during the VENUS AND MARS album sessions in 1974. The song was inspired by ex-Wings member Geoff Britton's expertise in the martial arts.

Karolny, Laslo
Temperamental movie director role played by Ringo in the 1977 film, *Sextette*.

Kass, Ron
Former head of Apple Records, in charge of international negotiations. In 1968 Kass accompanied Paul to Los Angeles for an Apple promotional campaign and organized the establishment of a California-based Apple office.

Kass's position at Apple was terminated in 1969 when Allen Klein was hired to manage The Beatles.

Kaufman, Murray (the K)
New York disc jockey who, in 1964, accompanied The Beatles on their first American tour. Throughout their touring years, The Beatles were impressed with Murray's seemingly "hip" style and they welcomed him as part of their entourage. Murray the K quickly bestowed the title of the "fifth Beatle" upon himself, until Brian Epstein threatened him with a lawsuit if he continued the gimmick.

In 1966 George contributed the introduction to Murray the K's book *Murray the K Tells It Like It Is, Baby*. In 1977 Murray the K became the technical advisor for the unauthorized stage production, *Beatlemania,* and later played the role of himself in the Beatle-related movie *I Want To Hold Your Hand* in 1978.

Keats, Pamela
Costume designer for Wings' World Tour and 1979 British Tour.

113

Kebaka, Remi
Nigerian musician who plays percussion on the album BAND ON THE RUN. Ironically, the recordings were done in Britain after Wings returned from Nigeria, where they were threatened with a lawsuit if any local musicians were used on the album.

"Keep Looking That Way"
Unreleased Beatles song recorded in 1962.

"Keep Your Hands off My Baby"
Goffin and King composition which The Beatles performed on the "Saturday Club" radio show in January of 1963.

Keifer, Lee
Engineer for John's album ROCK 'N' ROLL.

Kelly, Freda
President of the original Liverpool Beatles Fan Club established in 1961. Freda later became the Liverpool area secretary for the Official Beatles Fan Club.

Kelly, George
Former butler to Paul in 1967. Kelly had his experiences with the "drug taking, orgy throwing" Beatle published after he quit the job due to the unsavory atmosphere. Paul claims Kelly was fired.

Kelly, John
Photographer whose glossy portraits are included in the album THE BEATLES. Kelly is also credited with taking the photographs in the MAGICAL MYSTERY TOUR album package and was the official photographer at Paul's wedding in 1969.

Keltner, Jim
Percussionist who worked with The Beatles on many of their solo productions. Keltner appeared on stage at the Concert for Bangla Desh as codrummer with Ringo and at the One to One concert. He also contributed his talents on the albums LIVING IN THE MATERIAL WORLD, DARK HORSE, EXTRA TEXTURE, IMAGINE, SOMETIME IN NEW YORK CITY, MIND GAMES, WALLS AND BRIDGES, RINGO, RINGO'S ROTOGRAVURE, and GOODNIGHT VIENNA. Keltner can be seen in the promo film clip for "This Song" playing the role of the judge.

Kemp, Astrid Kirschner
German photographer who was engaged to the late ex-Beatle Stuart Sutcliffe. Astrid photographed The Beatles during their visits to Hamburg in the early sixties. The Beatles greatly admired Astrid's work and her style was later imitated on the cover photos for their albums WITH THE BEATLES and MEET THE BEATLES. Astrid's innovative ideas were also responsible for having The Beatles brush their hair forward.

After Stu's death, Astrid remained a close friend of The Beatles. In 1968 she photographed George for his WONDERWALL album. Paul has stated that no photographer has since captured The Beatles on film in the way Astrid did.

Kennedy, Adrienne
Coauthor of the London theatrical production based on John's book, *In His Own Write,* along with John and Victor Spinetti.

Kennedy Center for the Performing Arts
Washington D.C. hall where Jimmy Carter's 1977 Presidential Inauguration Ball was held in January of that year. John and Yoko were among the guests.

Kentucky Minstrels, The
Group which John's paternal grandfather headed in the late 1800s.

Kenwood
Sixty-acre home in Surrey, England purchased by John in 1964. The tudor mansion, located in London's stockbroker belt, was bought for forty thousand pounds. The Lennons lived here for four years until John and Cynthia separated in 1968.

Kestrals, The
Group on the bill with The Beatles during their 1963 British Tour with Helen Shapiro.

Keys, Bobby
Musician on whose album BOBBY KEYS George and Ringo contribute their talents. In 1975 Keys recorded "Give Me the Key" for Ring O' Records. He also performed on the albums ALL THINGS MUST PASS, THE CONCERT FOR BANGLA DESH, SOMETIME IN NEW YORK CITY, WALLS AND BRIDGES, RINGO, and GOODNIGHT VIENNA.

Kids Are Alright, The
1979 documentary movie on the Who in which Ringo appears. Ringo did several radio and TV spots to promote the movie.

Killan, Buddy
Record producer who worked with Wings in Nashville in 1974.

Kinfawn
George's bungalow in Esher, England, purchased in 1965 for £30,000. The home included five bedrooms, three reception rooms, and a heated swimming pool. In 1977, George and Pattie had the bungalow psychedelicized with paintings and murals adorning the exterior of the house. The Harrisons lived here until 1968.

King Curtis Band
Group that appeared on the bill with The Beatles on their 1965 North American Tour. In 1971 King Curtis played saxophone on John's IMAGINE album. He died one week after those recording sessions.

King Features
Company which produced The Beatles cartoon television series and the *Yellow Submarine* movie.

King, Soloman
Musician on whose record Ringo's hand-clapping is heard. Ringo's contribution occurred when he wandered into King's recording studio while taking a break from The Beatles' recording session for "Revolution" at EMI studios.

King, Ted
Disc jockey who was the first to air "Love Me Do" on BBC radio in 1962.

King, Tony
Chief A and R man for Apple Records, replacing Peter Asher in 1969.

Kings College Hospital
Birthplace of Paul and Linda's daughter, Stella, on September 13, 1971.

Kinnear, Roy
Actor who portrays Algernon in the movie *Help!*

Kirschner, Astrid
See Astrid Kemp.

Kinney, Norman
Engineer of the EXTRA TEXTURE album.

Kite, Mr.
Circus performer character in the song "Being for the Benefit of Mr. Kite."

Kitty
Character referred to in the song "Rock Show."

Klaatu
Canadian group whose mysteriously packaged and anonymously credited album, released on Capitol Records in 1976, spurred the hoax that The Beatles had reunited under this assumed name. The group sold a million records under this pretense.

The word Klaatu was first seen on the cover of Ringo's album GOODNIGHT VIENNA.

Klein, Allen
Born December 18, 1931. Allen Klein became The Beatles' manager in February of 1969 after previously managing The Rolling Stones, among other artists.

Klein was first called upon by John, in 1968, to check on his personal financial situation. John admired Klein's New York City streetwise manner and forthright business tactics. When The Beatles discovered their Apple management company was on the verge of bankruptcy, they set about appointing a financial advisor to audit their books. Their original selection of New York law firm Eastman and Eastman was soon overruled when John, and eventually George and Ringo, were swayed toward Klein. By a vote of three to one, Allen Klein was installed as Apple's manager. Due to a three-year agreement, signed in May 1969, Klein was entitled to 20 percent of The Beatles' earnings.

Paul was the dissenting Beatle in the appointment of Klein as The Beatles' representative. He refused Klein's counsel and instead pledged his allegiance to his original choice of Eastman and Eastman, who had also become his in-laws through his marriage to Linda Eastman. Klein was left to negotiate on behalf of Apple and The Beatles minus Paul, who would have no part of Klein's dealings. This controversy within Apple's ranks hindered many of its business transactions.

Allen Klein's major contribution as The Beatles' manager was to renegotiate a breakthrough recording contract between EMI Records and The Beatles. The contract proved to be the most profitable ever devised for an artist by a record company up until that time. (See EMI.) The Beatles were delighted with the deal and even Paul was quick to sign the agreement Klein had devised.

In May of 1973 Allen Klein's company, ABKCO, offered to buy Apple but the deal fell through. By this time The Beatles did not see fit to keep Klein on as manager and another internal shake-up was imminent. Klein felt he was still entitled to his share of The Beatles' earnings for projects on which he worked during his time at Apple. He sued The Beatles over the matter of his commission, and four years later, in January 1977, the case was settled out of court with The Beatles (including Paul) paying Klein $4.2 million.

On October 11, 1977, Allen Klein was indicted for tax evasion by New York Federal Court. He allegedly did not declare $216,000 in revenue earned from the sale of Beatle records between 1970 and 1972. In April 1979, Klein was convicted on charges of tax evasion and was later sentenced to serve two months, out of a two-year sentence, in prison.

Knight, Ian
Stage designer for the 1975–76 Wings' World Tour.

Knoop, Herr
German police chief responsible for deporting The Beatles from Germany in 1960 during their first engagement in Hamburg. Paul and Pete Best were the first to be deported for criminal negligence when a fire accidentally started in their dressing room; George was also deported for being underage and having no working papers.

Kohara, Roy
Art director and designer for the albums EXTRA TEXTURE, WALLS AND BRIDGES, ROCK 'N' ROLL, and SHAVED FISH. Kohara also worked on the album THE BEATLES AT THE HOLLYWOOD BOWL.

"Komm, Gib Mir Deine Hand"
The Beatles' German rendition of "I Want to Hold Your Hand." The song appears on the albums SOMETHING NEW and THE BEATLES RARITIES (Britain).

Koobas, The
Group that appeared with The Beatles on their 1965 British Tour.

Koschmider, Bruno
German owner of the Indra and Kaiserkeller clubs where The Beatles performed in Hamburg in 1960. Koschmider was allegedly responsible for instigating The Beatles' deportation from the country because they left his club in order to perform at another German club.

Kosh, John
Designer of the booklet included in the LET IT BE album package. Kosh designed the albums BEAUCOUPS OF BLUES, RINGO'S ROTOGRAVURE, and BAD BOY.

Kraft, Dean
New York psychic healer John and Yoko visited in the mid-seventies.

"Kreen-Akore"
Written by: Paul McCartney
Recorded by: Paul
Lead singer: None (Instrumental)
Year first released: 1970
Record label: Apple
Album: McCARTNEY
· Paul was inspired to write this song after watching a television documentary about the African Kreen-Akore tribe.

Krishna Consciousness Movement
Organization to which George donated money in 1969. Members of this movement accepted four awards on behalf of The Beatles at the Disc and Music Awards ceremony in 1969.

Krishna, the Supreme Personality of Godhead
Book for which George wrote the introduction.

L

Lacey, Alfred
Actor who portrayed the lawn mower in the movie *Help!*

Ladders, The
Name which The Beatles, minus Paul, were planning to use after the group formally split in 1970. For a short time John, George, and Ringo considered reforming with Klaus Voorman replacing Paul.

"Lady Gaye"
Written by: Richard Starkey, Vini Poncia, and Clifford T. Ward
Recorded by: Ringo
Lead singer: Ringo
Year first released: 1976
Record label: Polydor (Britain); Atlantic (U.S.)
Album: RINGO'S ROTOGRAVURE
Single: B side of "Hey Baby"

"Lady Madonna"
Written by: Lennon/McCartney
Recorded by: The Beatles
Lead singer: Paul
Year first released: 1968
Record label: Parlophone (Britain); Capitol (U.S.)
Album: THE BEATLES AGAIN
       THE BEATLES 1967–1970
       WINGS OVER AMERICA
Single: Britain and U.S.
Performances: Promo film clip
       1975–76 Wings' World Tour
· Last Beatles single to be released on Parlophone and Capitol.
· Tissue and comb effect, which is heard in the chorus, was accomplished by The Beatles cupping their hands around their mouths while singing.
· Paul designed the advertisements for this record release.

Lady Mitchell Hall
Concert hall in Cambridge, England, where John and Yoko staged a concert on March 2, 1969. This was John and Yoko's first public performance together. The act consisted of Yoko on vocals and John on guitar; it was recorded and can be heard on the album UNFINISHED MUSIC NO. 2: LIFE WITH THE LIONS.

Lagos, Nigeria
African city where Paul, Linda, and Denny Laine recorded the album BAND ON THE RUN. In September of 1973 Wings arrived in Lagos after suffering the sudden loss of members Denny Seiwell and Henry McCullough, when they quit the group just before leaving to record the album. Paul was determined to go on with the recording despite his "broken wings," and the record was made with the three remaining members. From the onset, the group was plagued with problems in the city, including monsoons, illness, knifepoint muggings, and plagiarism threats by local musicians. Despite the overwhelming odds confronting Wings, the album was completed and became the group's most critically acclaimed release.

Laine, Denny
Born Brian Hines on September 29, 1944. Denny, along with Paul and Linda, formed the nucleus of Wings, after joining the band in 1971. Denny Laine first gained notoriety as a musician and composer with the Moody Blues in the 1960s. It was during that time that he first met Paul and The Beatles and became friendly with the group. Denny has composed several songs which Wings have recorded, the most successful being "Mull of Kintyre," which he cowrote with Paul in 1977. In 1979, after nine years with Wings, Denny announced his plans to pursue his own musical interests with the release of a solo album titled JAPANESE TEARS.

Lambert, Kenneth
Twenty-eight-year-old man who was killed at Miami Airport by police when he threatened officials with a toy gun and demanded the release of his idol, Paul McCartney, when Paul was being held in a Japanese jail in 1980.

LAND'S END
Jimmy Webb album on which Ringo plays drums.

Larkin, Rochelle
Author of the book *The Beatles Yesterday . . . Today . . . Tomorrow.*

Larry the Dwarf
One of the characters Ringo portrayed in the movie *200 Motels.*

Larsen, Neil
Keyboard player on the album GEORGE HARRISON.

"Las Brisas"
Written by: Richard Starkey and Nancy Andrews
Recorded by: Ringo
Lead singer: Ringo
Year first released: 1976
Record label: Polydor (Britain); Atlantic (U.S.)
Album: RINGO'S ROTOGRAVURE

LASSO FROM EL PASSO
Kinky Friedman album on which Ringo plays drums.

Last Waltz, The
Documentary movie of The Band's last performance filmed on Thanksgiving Day, 1977. Ringo was a special guest at the performance and sat in on drums.

Lategan, Barry
Photographer who took the cover photo for the album WILD LIFE.

Lawrence, Jack
Composer who wrote the 1940s hit "Linda" in honor of young Linda Eastman. It was Linda's father, Lee, who suggested Lawrence write the song in lieu of payment for his legal services. McCartney Productions now owns the publishing rights to "Linda" and all of the Jack Lawrence song catalogue.

Lawrie, Billy
Composer who cowrote two songs with Ringo: "Rock and Roller" and the unreleased "Where Are You Going?"

Lazarus
Ringo's childhood nickname given to him by his grandfather because of the many illnesses Ringo experienced as a boy.

"Lazy Dynamite"
Written by: Paul McCartney
Recorded by: Wings
Lead singer: Paul
Year first released: 1973
Record label: Apple
Album: RED ROSE SPEEDWAY
· Second part of the four-song medley.

Lear
Character on whom the writer in "Paperback Writer" bases his story.

"Learning How to Love You"
Written by: George Harrison
Recorded by: George
Lead singer: George
Year first released: 1976
Record label: Dark Horse
Album: 33⅓
Single: B side of "This Song"
           B side of "Crackerbox Palace" in the U.S.
· Tribute to Herb Alpert, whom George credits as the inspiration for this song. George admired Alpert's recording "This Guy's In Love" and wrote his song to sound similar in style. Ironically, it was Alpert's record label, A&M, which chucked George from the company, just prior to the release of the album 33⅓.

Leary, Timothy
LSD guru of the late sixties. Leary inspired John's writing of the song "Come Together" when John thought it could be used as a campaign slogan should Leary decide to run for the governorship of California. Leary also performs on John's recording "Give Peace a Chance."

"Leave It"
Mike McGear song which was written by his brother, Paul, and appears on the album McGEAR.

Lee, Alvin
Musician who plays on George's album DARK HORSE. Lee recorded a cover version of George's "So Sad," with George playing guitar on the recording.

Lee, Christopher
Actor who appears in the cover photo of the Wings album BAND ON THE RUN.

Lee, Debbie
Singer on the bill with The Beatles on the 1963 Chris Montez/Tommy Roe Tour of Britain.

Lee, Peggy
Singer/composer who recorded Paul's composition "Let's Love," which Paul also produced. Paul brought the song to Peggy Lee as a gift when she invited him and Linda to her home for dinner in 1974. Paul credits Peggy Lee's rendition of "Till There Was You" with inspiring him to include it in The Beatles' early repertoire.

Leiber, Steve
Production coordinator for the Concert for Bangla Desh.

Leicester Arts Festival
Event Paul supported in 1967 by donating his time to publicize and attend the festival held at the Royal Garden Hotel in London.

"Lend Me Your Comb"
Song written by Tworney, Wise, and Weisman, which The Beatles sang during their early performances and is included on the album THE BEATLES LIVE AT THE STAR CLUB. George sings lead on this song. The song was performed on the BBC show "Pop Go The Beatles."

LenMac Enterprises
Publishing company formed in 1963 to handle the publishing rights to the first fifty-nine songs written by John Lennon and Paul McCartney. In 1965 Northern Songs took over LenMac and changed the name to Maclen Publishing.

Lennon, Alfred

Father of John Lennon. Fred Lennon divorced John's mother, Julia, when John was three years old and proceeded to sail off as a ship steward, not to see his son again for another twenty years. When Mr. Lennon realized his son had become rich and famous, he showed up at John's house only to be shown the door by his son. John later chose to forgive his father and to assist him financially until his death in 1970.

Lennon, Cynthia

See Cynthia Twist.

Lennon, John Ono

Born October 9, 1940, at Liverpool's Oxford Maternity Hospital, John Winston Lennon was the only child of Alfred and Julia Lennon.

When John was three years old his father, who worked as a seaman, drifted off into oblivion leaving his wife and baby son to fend for themselves. John's mother soon realized that caring for John was a full-time job, leaving no room in her life for the fun and frivolity she so thrived on. Julia decided it would be best for her sister Mimi and Mimi's husband, George Smith, to raise John, while she retained visiting rights. The Smiths became John's foster parents, rearing him as their own child. Mrs. Smith (Aunt Mimi) was a loving but stern parent, who tried her best to instill in John the sense of discipline and responsibility so lacking in his natural parents.

As John grew older his mischievous irreverence toward authority became more apparent. His high intellect set him apart from the other children in his class and left John bored with his schoolwork. His teachers, no match for his wit, were exasperated by John's disrespectful behavior and daredevil antics. The only school subjects at which John excelled were art and literature. His vast imagination combined with artistic skills resulted in drawings of one beyond his years. John also enjoyed reading, spending hours in his room with the likes of Lewis Carroll and James Thurber. He joined the staff of his school newspaper and contributed to it with his own illustrated short stories.

John first began showing signs of musical interest during Liverpool's skiffle craze in the early fifties. He had already mastered the harmonica during his childhood years, and now with the emergence of rock 'n' roll John was determined to become part of this new and exciting music. He taught himself to play the guitar by applying the banjo chords his mother had previously showed him. The music became an all-consuming interest to John as, much to his aunt's dismay, he abandoned whatever slight interest he might have had at school, and devoted himself entirely to making music. John had found that his thirst for action could now be quenched only by rock 'n' roll.

In 1955 John formed his first musical group, The Quarrymen. The name was taken from his high school as were the members of the band. It was while playing with The Quarrymen that John was introduced to two younger would-be musicians, Paul McCartney and George Harrison. The two boys soon joined The Quarrymen, which would eventually evolve into The Beatles.

When John was seventeen years old, his mother was killed when she was hit by a car. She and John had, at that time, just started to reestablish their relationship and this final separation devastated him. Music became even more important to John, serving as the outlet for his deep frustrations. He married Cynthia Powell, his girlfriend of four years in 1962. Though Cynthia was pregnant at the time, John was not pressured into the marriage, but accepted his responsibility willingly and looked forward to the prospect of becoming a father. Their son, Julian, was born in April of 1963. Though content with his wife and son, The Beatles still remained John's true love. All of his energies were put into his music making and songwriting.

As The Beatles' popularity spread worldwide, John's reputation as a profound lyricist was being established. His social statements veiled in symbolic imagery displayed a poetic genius, as his tender love ballads revealed a vulnerable and sensitive side of John rarely seen in public. The image of the "mind" behind The Beatles was given more credence with the publication of John's two books, *In His Own Write* and *A Spaniard in the Works*. The books consisted of short stories, poems, and illustrations laced throughout with a sarcasm and irreverence thinly disguised in absurd language use and nonsensical situations. The critics and public alike lauded the author, and the books were best sellers.

John was soon to become famous for his outstanding candor—especially during The Beatles' press conferences, which differed from other celebrity interviews of the time due to the refreshing honesty of all four group members.

Though John could not be more pleased by the financial gains which accompanied his success, he began resenting the lack of privacy he had to endure. He hated the pressures of fame and the demands put upon him as a spokesman for a generation; with the public scrutinizing his every move to find some clue for a future fad. John started to feel as though The Beatles were going stale as the rigors of touring reduced the group to repeating the same songs time and again to a chorus of deafening screams. He began to want a fresh excitement in his life, away from the superficial world of fame. Though music was still the mainstay of his life, John felt he was at a crossroads and once again began to search for something more. No matter what he tried to do to gain fulfillment, whether by artificial or spiritual means, John kept coming up feeling alienated and dissatisfied with the course his life was taking.

Yoko Ono, an avant-garde artist living in London, entered John's life in late 1966. John offered to finance her art exhibit, as he admired her strange yet thought-provoking style. They began working on art projects together and gradually fell in love. John decided to leave his wife Cynthia to be with Yoko. This action spurred great criticism of John—both public and private. The press had a field day with his "shameful" behavior in leaving his pretty English wife and young son for the love of a Japanese "weirdo" involved in strange and incomprehensible art projects. George and Paul frowned upon Yoko's strong influence on John, both personally and professionally. This friction and jealousy within the group caused John to feel alienated from The Beatles and their music. He became enthralled with the concept of experimental sounds and progressive music. The Beatles could no longer satisfy John's personal taste in musical structure.

Following his divorce from Cynthia, John and Yoko married in March, 1969, and embarked on a public honeymoon, taking to their beds to promote world peace. John legally changed his middle name from Winston to Ono to demonstrate his oneness with Yoko. Through his love for her, John was beginning to feel secure enough to finally let down his defenses. With the help of psychologist Arthur Janov's primal therapy program, John strove to vent his inner fears and vulnerabilities. This release of repressed pain was displayed in his first solo album, JOHN LENNON/PLASTIC ONO BAND. Much of the material on the album dealt with his disillusionment and resentment of loved ones including The Beatles, especially Paul. The album became a critical success, setting a trend among songwriters to become more introspective in their compositions.

John and Yoko visited America in 1971. John felt an instant affinity with the excitement and action inherent in New York City. Yoko introduced him to many of the artists and musicians she had known from her early days in the city. They soon became involved with the antiwar movement and contributed time and effort, attending rallies and recording songs to help the cause. It wasn't long before the Lennons decided to make New York their home.

In 1972, the One to One organization for retarded children held a benefit concert which John and Yoko headlined. At this time, unbeknownst to John and Yoko, a confidential memo sent to the U.S. attorney general, John Mitchell, in Washington had branded them political activists and, therefore, undesirable aliens. This put into effect the thinly disguised United States government's persecution of John and Yoko.

Since Yoko was an American citizen, the United States Immigration and Naturalization Department decided to zero in on John and began proceedings to deport him for his prior drug conviction. The next four years of court battles and appeals caused John and Yoko much personal strife as well as hundreds of thousands of dollars. One of their appeals to remain in the country stemmed from the custody battle Yoko was involved in with her ex-husband, Anthony Cox. The Lennons found themselves fighting for their home and her child. The emotional stress was intense and in 1974 John and Yoko separated. The pressures, plus their respective artistic temperaments, had taken their toll on the couple. John left New York to lead the bachelor life in California. The Lennons stayed apart approximately twelve months and then reunited. They soon had more reason to be joyous, when, after three miscarriages during the course of their relationship, Yoko gave birth to a son, Sean Ono Lennon, in 1975. John and Yoko soon found that good things come in threes when, in July of 1976, John was finally granted his visa to reside in the United States.

Today John, Yoko, and Sean live on New York's upper West Side, leading private lives away from the public eye. In 1979, after almost five years of self-imposed exile from the media, John and Yoko took out a full page ad in newspapers in New York, London, and Tokyo. The ad was a love letter to people still interested in their lives, explaining their lifestyle and the fact that they are content to stay at home. The ad appeared just one week after Paul, George, and Ringo gained public attention when they reunited to play together at a private party outside of London. Rumors of John being sighted in various recording studios still abound, but John has consistently denied plans to record again.

Lennon, John Charles Julian

Son of John and Cynthia Lennon; born April 8, 1963. Julian was the first child to be born to any of The Beatles.

Lennon, Julia Stanley

Mother of John Lennon. Julia and John's father, Alfred, were married for a short time and separated when John was a small boy. Shortly after their separation, Julia moved in with another man and left John in the care of her sister and brother-in-law. Julia finally divorced Alfred and give birth to two daughters, Julia and Jacqueline, while still living with her male companion. Although she lived only a few blocks away, Julia had little contact with John until he reached his early teens. He continued to live with his Aunt Mimi, while he and his mother were reestablishing a relationship. John loved Julia and found they shared many interests. Like John, Julia had an adventurous spirit and they both had a deep interest in music. Julia encouraged John's musical ambitions and it was she who bought him his first guitar.

	REGISTRATION DISTRICT *Liverpool South.*								
1940.	BIRTH in the Sub-district of *Abercromby*			in the *County Borough* of *Liverpool*					
Columns:—	1	2	3	4	5	6	7	8	9	10
No.	When and where born	Name, if any	Sex	Name, and surname of father	Name, surname, and maiden surname of mother	Occupation of father	Signature, description, and residence of informant	When registered	Signature of registrar	Name entered after registration
83.	Ninth October 1940. Liverpool Maternity Hospital	John Winston	Boy	Alfred Lennon	Julia Lennon formerly Stanley	Steward (Steamship) 9 Newcastle Road Liverpool 15.	A. Lennon Father 9 Newcastle Road Liverpool 15.	Eleventh November 1940.	J R Kirkwood Registrar	

John Winston Lennon's birth certificate.

John with Cynthia, his first wife, at home, 1964.
(*Henry Grossman/Transworld*)

A happy John drives his new car off the
display floor at a 1967 London motor show.
(*Keystone Press Agency*)

John and Yoko in Beverly Hills, 1970.
(*Lucille Azzarito, courtesy of Pattie O'Neil.*)

John and son Julian at the filming of the
Rolling Stones' "Rock 'N' Roll Circus," 1968.
(*Keystone Press Agency*)

Promoting Yoko's book,
Grapefruit, 1971
(*Sylvia Purbs*)

John and Yoko arrive at Alice Tully Hall, New York, 1972. (*Robin Titone*)

John shows off t-shirt given to him by fans, New York, 1973. (*Robin Titone*)

John Lennon and Harry Nilsson at benefit for The March of Dimes, Central Park, 1974. (*Robin Titone*)

John and Yoko reunited at
1975 Grammy Awards.
(*Vinnie Zuffante*)

John and Yoko going home to the Dakota,
New York, 1976. (*Robin Titone*)

John, 1976. The day after receiving his
"green card." (*Robin Titone*)

The Lennons stroll with son,
Sean, New York, 1976.
(*Vinnie Zuffante*)

Robin Titone)

From her knowledge of the banjo, she taught John banjo chords, which he applied to his guitar.

In 1958 Julia was killed by an off-duty police car in front of John's home on Menlove Avenue. Her tragic, untimely death shattered John, who felt that he was just beginning to know his mother. Throughout his career, John has written several songs expressing his feelings toward his mother including, "Julia," "Mother," and "My Mummy's Dead."

Lennon, Sean Ono
First child born to John and Yoko on October 9, 1975, at New York Hospital. Dubbed "the all-American boy" by his father, Sean's birth helped to secure John's residency permit in the United States.

Lennon, Yoko Ono
Born in Japan on February 18, 1934, Yoko is the wife of John Lennon and mother of their son, Sean. Yoko, the daughter of a wealthy banking family, was educated and groomed in the upper-class traditions of her conservative Japanese background. At age nineteen, Yoko and her family moved to America and settled in the affluent New York suburb of Scarsdale. Yoko continued her college education, but dropped out before graduating. She married a struggling Japanese musician and the couple moved to Greenwich Village, where Yoko began cultivating her artistic ambitions. She soon became known as one of New York's most respected avant-garde artists. Her marriage of five years ended in divorce as Yoko delved deeper into her work. She soon married producer Anthony Cox, with whom she had a daughter, Kyoko, in 1963. Yoko traveled to Japan and England to promote her "concept art." In 1964 a book of her poetry, *Grapefruit,* was published. By this time Yoko and Cox had separated, and Cox was given custody of the child.

John and Yoko first met at a London art gallery in 1966. John was impressed by Yoko's intellect and will, which were traits he had previously thought almost nonexistent in the female gender. In fact, upon getting to know Yoko, John began to see in her a female version of himself. The two began collaborating on artistic endeavors, and John sponsored most of Yoko's projects.

Yoko was signed to Apple in 1968. She and John soon realized that their mutual admiration had developed into a deep love for one another. Though they were both still legally married to others, they decided to declare their love publicly and weather the imminent stormy times ahead. Yoko was attacked by press and public as the fiend who had broken up John's happy home. She dealt with the insults and consternation from John's closest friends, who resented her strong hold on John. She had become a source of friction within The Beatles, as they resented her constant presence, especially in the recording studio. Yoko was an opinionated woman with

ideas of her own who would not sublimate her ego to please anyone else—a trait which was totally contrary to the behavior The Beatles had come to expect in women. Through it all, John and Yoko stood firm in their love for one another. With John's encouragement Yoko kept on contributing ideas and inspired him to broaden his outlook in music, art, and politics. The couple was ostracized for appearing nude together on their album cover for TWO VIRGINS and also for living together and starting a family without the benefit of marriage. (Yoko suffered two miscarriages prior to their marriage.) Yoko and John dismissed all of the public outcry and lived their lives as they saw fit. After both obtained their divorces, John and Yoko were married on March 20, 1969. They decided to make use of the inevitable publicity which would follow the event, and spent their honeymoon in full view of the world as they embarked on their "Bed-in for Peace" campaign. From their bedroom suite John and Yoko gave a week of interviews denouncing war and violence.

In 1971 John and Yoko moved to New York City. Yoko introduced John to New York's hip underground and the two became involved in the political activist movement. Their left-wing views and peace efforts subsequently caused them to come to the attention of the U.S. government as subversives. In 1972 John was ordered to leave the country by the Immigration and Naturalization Department. Yoko found herself in an emotional and legal quandry. Not only was her husband facing deportation, but it was at this time that she became involved in a heated legal battle with her ex-husband to gain custody of their child, Kyoko.

After two years of great stress, in and out of courts, John and Yoko separated in 1974. The split sent John to Los Angeles, and Yoko remained in New York. They remained apart for over a year before reconciling. Their son Sean was born soon after.

Today John, Yoko, and Sean live quietly in Manhattan. The couple, who had lived a fish-bowl existence for so many years, now shun publicity, preferring to keep their family life private. Yoko is presently a director of Apple Corps Ltd, representing John.

"As usual there's a great woman behind every idiot. I feel overwhelmed." John.

Lennon Factor, The
Book written by Paul Young; published by Stein and Day in 1972.

Lennon Play: In His Own Write, The
Book version of the play based on John's two books. The theatre production was adapted by John, Adrienne Kennedy, and Victor Spinetti. The book was published by Simon and Schuster in 1968.

Lennon Remembers
Book of interviews with John compiled by *Rolling Stone* editor Jann Wenner. The series of interviews were given to the newspaper and ran in three parts entitled "Working Class Hero" in 1971. The book was published in 1971 by Straight Arrow Press. John objected to the printing of the book when he was excluded from any percentage of the profits.

LEON RUSSELL
Album on which Ringo plays drums.

Les Ambassadeurs
Restaurant in London where a private party was held in honor of The Beatles after they received their MBE medals in 1965. In 1969 Ringo and the cast of *The Magic Christian* celebrated the completion of the film here. Paul and Linda and John and Yoko also attended the party. Paul celebrated at Les Ambassadeurs once again when on October 24, 1979, a party was given to honor Paul by the *Guinness Book of Records*. (See *Guinness Book of World Records*.)

Les Stewart Quartet
Band in which George was a member in 1958. It was while playing with this group that George was scheduled to perform at Liverpool's Casbah club. When a problem arose with two other members, George suggested his two friends, John and Paul, fill in. The group used John's old band's name, The Quarrymen, for the performance and began playing together regularly from then on.

Leso
Greek Island which The Beatles planned to purchase in 1967. The island was to be a haven for The Beatles and their families to live on and establish their own community. The dealings fell through during the final negotiations. The island came up again when, in 1969, it was discovered that the name Leso is written in the floral arrangement on the album cover of SGT. PEPPER. It was to become another in the series of clues which supposedly signified Paul's so-called death.

Lester, Richard
Director of The Beatles movies *A Hard Day's Night* and *Help!*. Lester also directed John in the movie *How I Won the War*.

"Let 'Em In"
Written by: Paul McCartney
Recorded by: Wings
Lead singer: Paul
Year first released: 1976
Record label: Parlophone (Britain); Capitol (U.S.)
Album: WINGS AT THE SPEED OF SOUND
WINGS OVER AMERICA
WINGS GREATEST

Single: Britain and U.S.
Performances: 1975–76 Wings' World Tour
- Song starts off with the sound of an actual doorbell, which was given to Paul by drummer Joe English.

Let It Be
A ninety-minute film of The Beatles at work in the recording studio and in concert. Released through United Artists; produced by Neil Aspinall and Apple Films; directed by Michael Lindsay-Hogg. The Beatles chose to document their work in the recording studio in order to fulfill their three-movie contract with United Artists.

The resulting film was in sharp contrast to The Beatles' previous movies, which were filled with fun and merriment. *Let It Be* was a glimpse of a somber Beatles during their most trying time just prior to their breakup. The movie climaxes with a rooftop concert given by The Beatles on January 30, 1969, at the Apple Building on Saville Row.

Film Notes
- Filming began on January 2, 1969 and finished three weeks later on January 30, 1969.
- When filming first began, the cameras were positioned at a distance from The Beatles while they worked in the studio, and telephoto lenses were employed to capture the action on film. As time went on and the group became more comfortable and less self-conscious, the film crew was able to get in close to capture The Beatles at work.
- The scene in which George and Paul are seen arguing over a guitar riff resulted in George leaving the group for three days. Filming was halted until George returned.
- The movie was originally intended as a television special on the making of the album.
- The rooftop concert was almost edited from the movie in order to be shown separately as a promotional film.
- The movie premiered in London on May 20, 1970, with none of The Beatles in attendance. Jane Asher and Cynthia Lennon were among the celebrities who attended the opening.

LET IT BE
Artist: The Beatles
Producer: Phil Spector
Year first released: 1970
Record label: Apple
Tracks: 12
"Two of Us"
"I Dig a Pony"
"Across the Universe"
"I Me Mine"

"Dig It"
"Let It Be"
"Maggie Mae"
"I've Got a Feeling"
"One after 909"
"The Long and Winding Road"
"For You Blue"
"Get Back"

- Originally titled "Get Back," the original album lineup went as follows:
  "One after 909"
  "Save the Last Dance for Me"
  "Don't Let Me Down"
  "I Dig a Pony"
  "I've Got a Feeling"
  "Get Back"
  "For You Blue"
  "Teddy Boy"
  "Two of Us"
  "Maggie Mae"
  "Dig It"
  "Let It Be"
  "The Long and Winding Road"
- The lineup was changed when producer Phil Spector was brought in to salvage the hours of recorded tapes which The Beatles were dissatisfied with. Paul was furious with Spector's rearrangement of his recordings and disassociated himself from the production.
- A pictorial book including movie dialogue was included in all the album packages in every country but the U.S. When the album was reissued the picture book was eliminated from all editions.
- The album won a Grammy Award.

"Let It Be"
Written by: Lennon/McCartney
Recorded by: The Beatles
Lead singer: Paul
Year first released: 1970
Record label: Apple
Album: LET IT BE
         THE BEATLES 1967–1970
Single: Britain and U.S.
Performances: *Let It Be* movie
               1979 Wings' British Tour.
- The single version differs from the album track. George Martin produced the single in which George plays lead guitar and The Beatles perform without orchestration. Phil Spector's album version has John on lead guitar and an added string accompaniment with a vocal chorus.
- "Mother Mary" in the song as a reference to Paul's late mother.

"Let It Down"
Written by: George Harrison
Recorded by: George

Lead singer: George
Year first released: 1970
Record label: Apple
Album: ALL THINGS MUST PASS

"Let Me Roll It"
Written by: Paul McCartney
Recorded by: Wings
Lead singer: Paul
Year first released: 1973
Record label: Apple
Album: BAND ON THE RUN
         WINGS OVER AMERICA
Single: B side of "Jet" in Britain
          Second B side of "Jet" in the U.S.
Performances: 1975–76 Wings' World Tour
- Paul admits that this song sounds like one of John's, though he claims the similarities in style were coincidental.

"Let's Go On Flying"
Instrumental track which is heard on John and Yoko's album UNFINISHED MUSIC NO. 2: LIFE WITH THE LIONS. The song was recorded live at Cambridge, London in 1969.

"Let's Love"
Paul McCartney composition recorded by Peggy Lee. Paul wrote this song especially for Peggy Lee to record. He also produced the record.

"Let the Rest of the World Go By"
Written by: J. Keirn Brennan/Ernest R. Ball
Recorded by: Ringo
Lead singer: Ringo
Year first released: 1970
Record label: Apple
Album: SENTIMENTAL JOURNEY

"Letting Go"
Written by: Paul McCartney
Recorded by: Wings
Lead singer: Paul
Year first released: 1975
Record label: Parlophone (Britain); Capitol (U.S.)
Album: VENUS AND MARS
         WINGS OVER AMERICA
Single: Britain and U.S.
Performances: 1975–76 Wings' World Tour
               Promo film clip
- Single version is shorter than the album track.

Levis, Caroll
British television producer who, in the 1950s, hosted the program "Discoveries." In 1959 John, Paul, and George auditioned for the show at Liverpool's Empire Theatre,

where they were booked by Levis to appear live on the program aired in Manchester. They performed on the local broadcast billed as Johnny and the Moondogs. Because of a time problem, the Moondogs could not stay for the second part of the show to find out the results of the contest, since they were forced to leave to catch the train back to Liverpool.

Levy, Morris
Owner of the publishing company Big Seven Music, which owns the Chuck Berry song "You Can't Catch Me." In the Beatles song "Come Together" two lines were taken from Berry's song and John was sued by Levy. Instead of hassling through the courts, John agreed to record three of Levy's company's songs on his upcoming oldies album. When plans were changed and John decided to first release his WALLS AND BRIDGES album, Levy got edgy and released John's tapes himself on an album called ROOTS (Adam VIII). This turn of events forced Capitol Records to release John's ROCK 'N' ROLL album quickly to divert sales from ROOTS.

Levy sued John for breach of contract, fraud, and antitrust violation. Capitol, EMI, and John countersued. In January 1976 the case came to trial and Levy's oral contract was denied. Two months later John was awarded $45,000 by the court in his damage suit filed against Levy.

Lewis, Brian
Consultant to Apple Corps Ltd. in 1968.

Lewis, Vic
Managing director of Nems Enterprises. Lewis was appointed to this position after the death of Brian Epstein in 1967.

Lickie, John
Coengineer on the album JOHN LENNON/PLASTIC ONO BAND.

LIES AND ALIBIS
Guthrie Thomas album on which Ringo plays and sings background vocals.

Life of Brian
Monty Python movie in which George invested 4 million dollars and coproduced. The movie was released in 1979 to rave reviews and some controversy concerning the movie's irreverence. George appears briefly in the film.

"Light That Has Lighted the World, The"
Written by: George Harrison
Recorded by: George
Lead singer: George

Year first released: 1973
Record label: Apple
Album: LIVING IN THE MATERIAL WORLD

"Like Dreamers Do"
Lennon/McCartney song The Beatles performed at their Decca Records audition in 1962. It was later recorded by the Applejacks.

Lil
The name which Rocky Raccoon's girlfriend prefers to be called.

Linda's Pictures
Book of photographs taken by Linda McCartney during her career as a rock photographer. It includes various artists, among them The Beatles and Paul, in addition to private family shots. Published by Alfred A. Knopf in 1976 and by Ballantine in soft-cover.

Lindsay-Hogg, Michael
Director of The Beatles movie *Let It Be*. Lindsay-Hogg also directed The Beatles in their promotional films for "Paperback Writer," "Revolution," and "Hey Jude." In 1978 Michael Lindsay-Hogg directed Wings in their promo clip "London Town."

Lingasong
Production company which released THE BEATLES LIVE AT THE STAR CLUB album.

"Lipstick Traces (on a Cigarette)"
Written by: N. Neville
Recorded by: Ringo
Lead singer: Ringo
Year first released: 1978
Record label: Polydor (Britain); Portrait (U.S.)
Album: BAD BOY
Single: U.S.

Lisson Gallery
London art gallery where John sponsored Yoko's exhibition "Yoko plus Me" in 1967.

"Listen the Snow Is Falling"
B side of John's "Happy Xmas (War Is Over)" single. Written by Yoko Ono and produced by John, Yoko, and Phil Spector.

"Listen To What the Man Said"
Written by: Paul McCartney
Recorded by: Wings
Lead singer: Paul
Year first released: 1975
Record label: Parlophone (Britain); Capitol (U.S.)
Album: VENUS AND MARS
          WINGS OVER AMERICA

Single: Britain and U.S.
Performances: 1975–76 Wings' World Tour

Lisztomania
Movie directed by Ken Russell in 1975. Ringo plays a cameo role in this film starring Roger Daltrey.

Litchfield, David
Director of the unreleased Wings film *The Sound of One Hand Clapping*.

Litherland Town Hall
Concert hall in Liverpool where The Beatles performed on December 27, 1960. This was the group's first appearance in Liverpool since their return from Germany. The show was played to the largest audience The Beatles had ever performed to up until that time, and The Beatles felt this marked their success in Liverpool. In July of 1961 The Beatles performed at the Litherland Town Hall once again for one concert with Gerry and the Pacemakers. (See Beatmakers.)

"Little Child"
Written by: Lennon/McCartney
Recorded by: The Beatles
Lead singer: John
Year first released: 1963
Record label: Parlophone (Britain); Capitol (U.S.)
Album: WITH THE BEATLES
MEET THE BEATLES

Little George
Photographer portrayed by George Clayton in the movie *Magical Mystery Tour*.

"Little Lamb Dragonfly"
Written by: Paul McCartney
Recorded by: Wings
Lead singer: Paul
Year first released: 1973
Record label: Apple
Album: RED ROSE SPEEDWAY
· Paul was first inspired to compose this song after the death of one of his sheep on his farm.

Little Malcolm and His Struggle against the Eunuchs
Movie produced by George in 1974. The film premiered at the Berlin Film Festival and won the Silver Bear Award. It also won a gold medal at the Atlanta Film Festival.

"Little Queenie"
Chuck Berry song which The Beatles perform on the album THE BEATLES LIVE AT THE STAR CLUB. Paul sings lead.

Little Richard
American composer/singer, who greatly influenced The Beatles during their early days. Paul credits Little Richard with inspiring much of his own vocal style in his rock efforts, as exhibited in renditions of "Long Tall Sally" and "Kansas City." In 1962 The Beatles performed in Britain on the bill with Little Richard.

"Little Woman Love"
Written by: Paul and Linda McCartney
Recorded by: Wings
Lead singer: Paul
Year first released: 1972
Record label: Apple
Single: B side of "Mary Had a Little Lamb"
Performances: Performed in medley with "C Moon" on the TV special "James Paul McCartney"
1973 Wings' British Tour

"Live and Let Die"
Written by: Paul McCartney
Recorded by: Wings
Lead singer: Paul
Year first released: 1973
Record label: Apple
Album: WINGS OVER AMERICA
WINGS GREATEST
Single: Britain and U.S.
Performances: "James Paul McCartney" TV special
1975–76 Wings' World Tour
· Title song for the James Bond movie *Live and Let Die*.
· Originally the producers of the movie did not want Paul and Wings to record the song. They preferred female voices for the movie soundtrack. Paul made it clear that if he writes it, he sings it.
· George Martin and his orchestra perform on the recording, which Martin also produced. A soundtrack album for the film was also released.
· The song was nominated for an Academy Award and won a Grammy Award.

LIVE PEACE IN TORONTO
See PLASTIC ONO BAND/LIVE PEACE IN TORONTO

Liverpool
Port city in the north of England with a population of one million. This large industrial metropolis, two hundred miles northwest of London, is the birthplace of John Lennon, Paul McCartney, George Harrison, and Ringo Starr.

Liverpool Art College
School which was attended by John in 1958. He majored in lettering and met his first wife, Cynthia, while at the school.

Liverpool Institute

School which was attended by George and Paul. The building was also the home of the Liverpool Art College, where John was attending school. On November 23, 1979, Wings gave a special concert for the students and faculty of the Liverpool Institute. The show was held at the Royal Court Theatre in Liverpool. Two hundred of Paul's family members attended the performance.

"Liverpool Lou"

British folk song recorded by the Scaffold; produced by Paul.

LIVING IN THE MATERIAL WORLD

Artist: George Harrison
Producer: George and Phil Spector
Year first released: 1973
Record label: Apple
Tracks: 11
"Give Me Love"
"Sue Me, Sue You Blues"
"The Light That Has Lighted the World"
"Don't Let Me Wait Too Long"
"Who Can See It?"
"Living in the Material World"
"The Lord Loves the One"
"Be Here Now"
"Try Some, Buy Some"
"The Day the World Gets 'Round"
"That Is All"
• Ringo plays drums on this album.

"Living in the Material World"

Written by: George Harrison
Recorded by: George
Lead singer: George
Year first released: 1973
Record label: Apple
Album: LIVING IN THE MATERIAL WORLD
• George mentions the names of the other three Beatles in this song.

Lockheed Electra

Aircraft which The Beatles used during their 1965 North American tour. On August 22, enroute to Portland, Maine, from Minneapolis, one of the plane's engines caught fire with the full Beatle entourage on board. The plane was able to land safely, but was then put out of commission.

Lockwood, Sir Joseph

Chairman of EMI, the record company which The Beatles were contracted to from 1962 through 1976. Paul is still contracted to EMI in Britain and Europe.

Loka Productions

George's production company.

Lomax, Jackie

Liverpool musician who was one of the first artists signed to Apple Records. His record "Sour Milk Sea," released in 1968, was written and produced by George and was one of Apple's first releases included in their four-record package "Our First Four." George worked very closely with Lomax, producing his recording "How the Web Was Woven" and the album IS THIS WHAT YOU WANT?. Paul produced his song "Thumbing a Ride."

Lomax Alliance

Liverpool group managed by Brian Epstein in 1967. Jackie Lomax, who went on to sign with Apple, was the leader of this band.

Lon and Derek Van Eaton

Apple artists who recorded the album BROTHER for Apple Records in 1972. George produced and worked on the album, with Ringo helping out on drums. The Van Eaton brothers helped out on George's and Ringo's respective albums DARK HORSE and GOODNIGHT VIENNA.

London Arts Gallery

Exhibit hall where John's lithographs were on display during January of 1970. The drawings depicted scenes from John and Yoko's wedding and private life. The lithographs were confiscated by the police for possible violation of the Obscene Public Act. The case was brought to court, where it was ruled that the lithographs were not obscene and they were returned to John.

LONDON HOWLIN' WOLF SESSIONS

Album on which Ringo performs.

London Palladium

Famed concert venue where The Beatles performed on October 13, 1963. The show, headlined by The Beatles, was broadcast live to the nation. The Beatles received national press coverage and by the following day Beatlemania was in full gear throughout Great Britain. The Beatles appeared here again on January 12, 1964, and in July of 1964 performed here for the "Night of 100 Stars" show.

London Pavilion

Theatre which premiered The Beatles movies *A Hard Day's Night* (July 6, 1964), *Help!* (July 29, 1965), *How I Won the War* (October 18, 1967), *Yellow Submarine* (July 17, 1968), and *Let It Be* (May 20, 1970).

London Symphony Orchestra, The

Orchestra which performs on The Beatles' "A Day in the Life." During the recording, the musicians were asked to play off key in order for The Beatles to achieve the desired effect in the song. When the orchestra recorded the album TOMMY, Ringo did the vocals on two tracks.

LONDON TOWN
Artist: Wings
Producer: Paul
Year first released: 1978
Record label: Parlophone (Britain); Capitol (U.S.)
Tracks: 14
  "London Town"
  "Cafe on the Left Bank"
  "I'm Carrying"
  "Backwards Traveller"
  "Cuff Link"
  "Children Children"
  "Girlfriend"
  "I've Had Enough"
  "With a Little Luck"
  "Famous Groupies"
  "Deliver Your Children"
  "Name and Address"
  "Don't Let It Bring You Down"
  "Morse Moose and the Grey Goose"
- On this album Paul collaborated on more compositions with the group members than on any previous Wings recording.
- Nine songs were recorded on a yacht docked in the Caribbean Sea off the Virgin Islands. The boat was installed with recording equipment rented from a recording studio in America.
- Drummer Joe English and guitarist Jimmy McCulloch left the band just prior to the album's release.

"London Town"
Written by: McCartney/Laine
Recorded by: Wings
Lead singer: Paul
Year first released: 1978
Record label: Parlophone (Britain); Capitol (U.S.)
Album: LONDON TOWN
Single: Britain and U.S.
Performances: Promo film clip

London University
British academy which requested that Ringo become its honorary president in 1964.

"Lonely Man"
Song written by Robert J. Purvis and Mal Evans. It was composed for the movie *Little Malcolm and His Struggle Against the Eunuchs,* which was produced by George. Splinter recorded the song.

"Lonely Old People"
Written by: Paul McCartney
Recorded by: Wings

Lead singer: Paul
Year first released: 1975
Record label: Parlophone (Britain); Capitol (U.S.)
Album: VENUS AND MARS
- Second part of the medley which includes the song "Treat Her Gently."

"Long and Winding Road, The"
Written by: Lennon/McCartney
Recorded by: The Beatles
Lead singer: Paul
Year first released: 1970
Record label: Apple
Album: LET IT BE
        THE BEATLES 1967–1970
        LOVE SONGS
        WINGS OVER AMERICA
Single: U.S.
Performances: *Let It Be* movie
               1975–76 Wings' World Tour
- Single version was produced by George Martin and differs from the album track which was produced by Phil Spector.
- Paul was dissatisfied with Spector's version because he added female voices and dramatic orchestration.
- Movie version has different lyrics than record versions.

Long and Winding Road, The
Film footage of The Beatles, produced by Neil Aspinall, which was intended for commercial release, but was shelved indefinitely.

Longest Cocktail Party, The
Book written by Richard DiLello; published by Playboy Press. The book describes the author's first-hand experience with the inner workings of Apple Corps, Ltd.

"Long Haired Lady"
Written by: Paul and Linda McCartney
Recorded by: Paul and Linda
Lead singer: Paul
Year first released: 1971
Record label: Apple
Album: RAM

Long Lane Jewish Cemetery
Liverpool cemetery where Brian Epstein is buried.

"Long Long Long"
Written by: George Harrison
Recorded by: The Beatles
Lead singer: George
Year first released: 1968
Record label: Apple
Album: THE BEATLES

"Long Tall Sally"
Written by: Johnson, Penniman, and Blackwell
Recorded by: The Beatles
Lead singer: Paul
Year first released: 1964
Record label: Parlophone (Britain); Capitol (U.S.)
Album: THE BEATLES SECOND ALBUM
THE BEATLES LIVE AT THE STAR
   CLUB
THE BEATLES ROCK AND ROLL
   MUSIC
THE BEATLES AT THE HOLLYWOOD
   BOWL
THE BEATLES RARITIES (Britain)
EP: LONG TALL SALLY
Performances: 1964 February U.S. Tour
   1964 Summer North American Tour
   "Around The Beatles" TV show, 1964
   1964 Christmas Shows
   1965 European Summer Tour
   1973 Wings' British Tour
   "James Paul McCartney" TV show,
      1973 (U.S. version)
- This song was used as the finale to many of The Beatles' concerts.
- Paul sang this song in his first public appearance at the age of twelve, at a holiday camp with his family.

LONG TALL SALLY (EP)
Artist: The Beatles
Producer: George Martin
Year first released: 1964
Record label: Parlophone
Tracks: 4
   "Long Tall Sally"
   "I Call Your Name"
   "Slow Down"
   "Matchbox"

"Look At Me"
Written by: John Lennon
Recorded by: John Lennon/Plastic Ono Band
Lead singer: John
Year first released: 1970
Record label: Apple
Album: JOHN LENNON/PLASTIC ONO BAND

Lopez, Trini
Performer on the bill with The Beatles at the Olympia Theatre in Paris in 1964.

"Lord Loves the One, The"
Written by: George Harrison
Recorded by: George
Lead singer: George
Year first released: 1973
Record label: Apple
Album: LIVING IN THE MATERIAL WORLD

LOS COCHINOS
Cheech and Chong album on which George plays guitar.

"Loser's Lounge"
Written by: Bobby Pierce
Recorded by: Ringo
Lead singer: Ringo
Year first released: 1970
Record label: Apple
Album: BEAUCOUPS OF BLUES

"Los Paranois"
Intended title for The Beatles' "Sun King."

"Loup (1st Indian on the Moon)"
Written by: Paul McCartney
Recorded by: Wings
Lead singer: None (Instrumental)
Year first released: 1973
Record label: Apple
Album: RED ROSE SPEEDWAY

"Love"
Written by: John Lennon
Recorded by: John Lennon/Plastic Ono Band
Lead singer: John
Year first released: 1970
Record label: Apple
Album: JOHN LENNON/PLASTIC ONO BAND

"Love Comes to Everyone"
Written by: George Harrison
Recorded by: George
Lead singer: George
Year first released: 1979
Record label: Dark Horse
Album: GEORGE HARRISON

"Love Don't Last Long"
Written by: Chuck Howard
Recorded by: Ringo
Lead singer: Ringo
Year first released: 1970
Record label: Apple
Album: BEAUCOUPS OF BLUES

"Love in Song"
Written by: Paul McCartney
Recorded by: Wings
Lead singer: Paul
Year first released: 1975
Record label: Parlophone (Britain); Capitol (U.S.)
Album: VENUS AND MARS
Single: B side of "Listen To What the Man Said"
- In this song Paul uses the same bass which was used on the Elvis recording of "Heartbreak Hotel."

"Love in the Open Air"
Title of the music Paul scored for the 1967 movie *The Family Way*. The soundtrack appears on the album THE FAMILY WAY, with the George Martin Orchestra performing. George Martin, who produced the song, later released it as a single for EMI, as did the movie producers for Decca Records.

"Love Is a Many Splendored Thing"
Written by: Webster and Fain
Recorded by: Ringo
Lead singer: Ringo
Year first released: 1970
Record label: Apple
Album: SENTIMENTAL JOURNEY
• Arranged by Quincy Jones.

"Love Is Strange"
Written by: McDaniel/Baker
Recorded by: Wings
Lead singer: Paul
Year first released: 1971
Record label: Apple
Album: WILD LIFE

Love Letters to The Beatles
Book of fan letters written to The Beatles; edited by Bill Adler and published by Putnam in 1964.

"Lovely Linda, The"
Written by: Paul McCartney
Recorded by: Paul
Lead singer: Paul
Year first released: 1970
Record label: Apple
Album: McCARTNEY
• Paul claims to have recorded this song with the intent of testing his equipment.

"Lovely Rita"
Written by: Lennon/McCartney
Recorded by: The Beatles
Lead singer: Paul
Year first released: 1967
Record label: Parlophone (Britain); Capitol (U.S.)
Album: SGT. PEPPER'S LONELY HEARTS CLUB BAND
• Paul was amused with the American meter maids when on a visit to the States and was inspired to compose the song.

Lovely Starlet
Actress played by Maggie Wright in the film *Magical Mystery Tour*.

"Love Me Do"
Written by: Lennon/McCartney
Recorded by: The Beatles
Lead singer: Paul
Year first released: 1962
Record label: Parlophone (Britain); Vee Jay, Capitol (U.S.)
Album: PLEASE PLEASE ME
INTRODUCING THE BEATLES
THE EARLY BEATLES
THE BEATLES 1962–1966
LOVE SONGS
THE BEATLES RARITIES (U.S.)
EP: THE BEATLES' HITS
Single: Britain and U.S.
Performances: "Ed Sullivan Show" (TV), 1964
"Around The Beatles" (TV), 1964
• The Beatles' first British single.
• It is one of the songs The Beatles sang at their audition with EMI's record producer George Martin on June 6, 1962. Pete Best was the drummer at the audition, but was ousted from the group before their first actual recording session. Ringo was brought in as his replacement and, because George Martin was unsure of his ability, he asked studio musician Andy White to sit in on the first session. The song was recorded with White on drums and Ringo on tambourine and again with Ringo on drums.
• On the British single Ringo's drumming is heard, but the version with White's drumming was released on the album cuts in Britain and the U.S. Later, White's version was rereleased as the British single. Ringo's drumming appears on the version on THE BEATLES RARITIES.
• The song was recorded on September 11, 1962.

Love Me Do
Book written by Michael Braun; published by Penguin Books in 1964. John has stated that this book, more than any other, gave a true account of the Beatles years.

"Love Minus Zero/No Limit"
Bob Dylan song which he performed at the matinee performance at the Concert for Bangla Desh.

"Love of the Loved"
Cilla Black song written by Lennon/McCartney. This was one of John and Paul's earlier efforts which The Beatles performed for their Decca Records audition in 1962.

"Love Scene/Crying"
Written by: George Harrison
Recorded by: George
Lead singer: None (Instrumental)
Year first released: 1968
Record label: Apple
Album: WONDERWALL

LOVE SONGS
Artist: The Beatles
Producer: George Martin (Phil Spector for "The Long and Winding Road")
Year first released: 1977
Record label: Parlophone (Britain); Capitol (U.S.)
Tracks: 25 (Two-record set)
   "Yesterday"
   "I'll Follow the Sun"
   "I Need You"
   "Girl"
   "In My Life"
   "Words of Love"
   "Here, There, and Everywhere"
   "Something"
   "And I Love Her"
   "If I Fell"
   "I'll Be Back"
   "Tell Me What You See"
   "Yes It Is"
   "Michelle"
   "It's Only Love"
   "You're Gonna Lose That Girl"
   "Every Little Thing"
   "For No One"
   "She's Leaving Home"
   "The Long and Winding Road"
   "This Boy"
   "Norwegian Wood"
   "You've Got to Hide Your Love Away"
   "I Will"
   "P.S. I Love You"
- This album package includes a twenty-eight page lyric booklet.
- Cover photo for the album is the famed Avedon picture of The Beatles, which was first released in 1967 and published in *Look* magazine. The photo shown on the cover differs from the original photograph, with Paul the most prominent on the album.

"Love You To"
Written by: George Harrison
Recorded by: The Beatles
Lead singer: George
Year first released: 1966
Record label: Parlophone (Britain); Capitol (U.S.)
Album: REVOLVER
- No other Beatle performs on this song.

Lovine, Jimmy
Assistant engineer on the albums WALLS AND BRIDGES and ROCK 'N' ROLL.

Lowlands Club
Liverpool club where, in 1958, George practiced music with his band, the Les Stewart Quartet.

Low Park Farm
Farmland located adjacent to Paul's Scottish farm. Paul purchased this property in early 1970 in order to insure the security of his original farm (High Park) against trespassers.

L7
Term Paul uses in "C Moon" which was originally from a Sam the Sham and the Pharaohs' song "Wooly Bully." L7 is a symbol for square (joining the L and 7 forms a square shape). C moon is therefore the opposite of L7.

"Luck of the Irish"
Written by: John Lennon and Yoko Ono
Recorded by: John and Yoko
Lead singer: John
Year first released: 1972
Record label: Apple
Album: SOMETIME IN NEW YORK CITY
Performances: John Sinclair Benefit Concert, 1971
- Written in response to the British government's intervention in Ireland.

Lucky Spot
Horse that Paul and family purchased in Texas while on tour in 1976. They "spotted" the Appaloosa stallion along the roadside and stopped off to inquire whether they could purchase it.

"Lucille"
Little Richard song which Paul performed in concert on Wings' 1972 University Tour and at the December 29 benefit concert for Kampuchean refugees in 1979.

Lucy
Name of the guitar which was given as a gift to George by friend Eric Clapton in 1968.

"Lucy in the Sky with Diamonds"
Written by: Lennon/McCartney
Recorded by: The Beatles
Lead singer: John
Year first released: 1967
Record label: Parlophone (Britain); Capitol (U.S.)
Album: SGT. PEPPER'S LONELY HEARTS CLUB BAND
   THE BEATLES 1967–1970
- This song precipitated a public controversy concerning the initials in the title—LSD. Though the song's surrealistic imagery and fantasy-like quality helped to fuel the drug-related theory, The Beatles insisted the analogies were coincidental. John claimed that the title actually came from his four-year-old son, Julian, who had painted a picture and called it *Lucy in the Sky with Diamonds*. Regardless of The Beatles' denials, the song was banned by the BBC.

- Elton John released this song in 1974 with John helping out on vocals. The two also performed the song on stage at Madison Square Garden during Elton's concert.

"Lunchbox and Odd Sox"
Unreleased Wings song, recorded during the VENUS AND MARS sessions.

Lush, Richard
Engineer on the albums JOHN LENNON/PLASTIC ONO BAND and RED ROSE SPEEDWAY.

Luther, Martin
Character in Wings' song "Let 'Em In."

Lutton, Davy
Drummer who performed with Paul, Linda, Denny Laine, and Jimmy McCulloch in France in 1972 at the recording session of "Seaside Woman." After the single was released Lutton auditioned for Wings as a permanent member, but did not join.

"Lumberjack Song, The"
Monty Python song which George broadcast over the PA system prior to each of his concerts on his 1974 Dark Horse Tour. In 1976 George joined Monty Python on stage at New York's City Center to perform this song. He later produced their recording.

Lyceum Ballroom Theatre
London concert hall where John and Yoko staged a "Peace for Christmas" concert on December 15, 1969. The proceeds went to the U.N. Children's Fund (UNICEF). Performing with John at the concert were George, Eric Clapton, Delaney and Bonnie, Billy Preston, Alan White, Klaus Voorman, and Keith Moon.

A "War Is Over" billboard was erected behind the stage. The performance can be heard on the album SOMETIME IN NEW YORK CITY.

Lympne Castle
Estate in Kent, England where Wings recorded some of the tracks on their album BACK TO THE EGG.

Lynch, Kenny
Singer on the bill with The Beatles on the Helen Shapiro tour of Britain in 1963. He also appears in the cover photo of the Wings album BAND ON THE RUN.

Lyndon, John
Director in charge of Nems theatre presentations in 1967. Lyndon staged Brian Epstein's Sunday concerts at the Saville Theatre. He later went on to manage the Apple Boutique.

Lynn, Harry
Concert promoter who booked The Beatles for their first American concert at the Washington Coliseum on February 11, 1964.

Lynn, Vera
English singer on whose record "Don't You Remember When" Ringo plays tambourine.

Lynton, Rod
Rhythm guitarist who worked on George's album ALL THINGS MUST PASS and John's album IMAGINE.

M

Macbeth, David
Performer on the bill of The Beatles May–August 1963 British Tour.

Maclen Music
Music publishing company formed in 1965 to collect the songwriting royalties paid John and Paul for their compositions. The company was originally called LenMac.

Macmillan, Ian
Photographer who took the photos on the album cover for ABBEY ROAD.

Madryn Street (9)
Address of the Liverpool home where Richard Starkey was born on July 7, 1940.

Maharishi Mahesh Yogi
Indian guru who is the leader of the Transcendental Meditation movement. The Maharishi was introduced to The Beatles in 1967 when Pattie Harrison first attended his lecture and then convinced her husband George and the others to look into his teachings. The Beatles attended his London lecture on August 24, 1967, and were so impressed that they agreed to go to a college retreat in Wales to learn more about the Maharishi's method of attaining inner tranquility. The Beatles and their wives, with the exception of Maureen, who had just given birth to son Jason, journeyed to Wales with the guru and were initiated into the society, vowing to keep their bodies pure of chemicals and instead expand their minds through the spiritual nature of TM. The trip was cut short when, on August 27, the news of Brian Epstein's sudden death sent The Beatles home to London to deal with the personal and professional loss.

After the death of their manager the group turned to the Maharishi for spiritual guidance and enlightenment. In February of 1968 they left England and traveled to India to meditate at the Maharishi's retreat in Rishikesh. The Beatles and their wives spent weeks in India meditating and relaxing in the holiday camp setting in the Himalayas.

It was during their stay in India that Ringo and Maureen were the first to become disenchanted with the rigors of meditating and opted instead to go home and spend their time with their kids.

Paul and Jane were the next to go. Though John and George stayed a while longer, disillusionment with the Maharishi began to interfere with their studies. After spending time with the teacher, The Beatles began to realize the guru was merely mortal and could not live up to their supernatural expectations. It was after their return from India that The Beatles broke their ties with Maharishi Mahesh Yogi.

Mahon, George
Artist who designed the back cover of the album SGT. PEPPER'S LONELY HEARTS CLUB BAND. Mahon also designed the Apple Records' logo which appeared on the record label. The two sides of the "apple" took him six months to perfect.

"Maggie Mae"
Written by: (Public Domain)
Recorded by: The Beatles
Lead singer: John and Paul
Year first released: 1970
Record label: Apple
Album: LET IT BE
- A traditional Liverpool sing-along song which The Beatles performed as early as their Quarrymen years.

Magic Christian, The
Movie starring Peter Sellers and Ringo Starr. The movie, filmed in 1969, was produced by Dennis O'Dell; directed by Joseph McGrath; and distributed by Commonwealth United Films. It premiered on December 11, 1969, at the Odeon Kensington with Ringo and Maureen plus John and Yoko in attendance.

The movie soundtrack was recorded by Apple band Badfinger, with the theme song "Come and Get It" written by Paul.

Magical Mystery Tour
The Beatles' sixty-minute color movie which they produced, directed, and starred in. The film was released through Apple Films in 1967 at a cost of $100,000.

Magical Mystery Tour was The Beatles' first attempt at movie making on their own. Paul devised the concept for the musical fantasy while visiting America in 1967 for Jane Asher's birthday. He laid out the blueprints for the movie while on a plane en route to Los Angeles. When he returned to London he presented the plan to the other Beatles, who agreed to produce the project. The film would be an improvised musical travelogue with the emphasis on adventure and spontaneity rather than scripted and rehearsed material. Each of The Beatles contributed their own ideas for individual segments to be shot during the mystery tour.

Filming began on September 11, 1967, as The Beatles, camera crew, actors, and friends took off to make a movie with no script and little experience, but plenty of enthusiasm. The filming went on for two weeks as the Magical Mystery Tour bus traveled through the south of England, stopping periodically wherever the setting seemed most interesting.

137

After six weeks of editing hundreds of hours of movie footage, the film was set to The Beatles' music, which was written for the soundtrack, and edited down to sixty minutes. It premiered on British television on Boxing Day, December 26, 1967. The movie was broadcast in black and white, though it was shot in color. The reviews were unanimously negative, criticizing the amateur production as "blatant rubbish" with a "lack of continuity and senseless plot enhanced only by The Beatles' music." It was the Beatles' first nonsuccess and they did not take the harsh criticism too kindly. Paul especially was hurt and disappointed by the cruel reception given his brainchild. The Beatles argued that the black and white broadcast was not conducive to the picturesque scenes in the movie, and the conventionally schooled critics could not appreciate their free-style technique in directing the movie. The film was given a second chance when it was aired on television again on January 5, 1968, and this time it was shown in color. The critics were still unimpressed and worldwide distribution plans were cancelled.

Some years later the film was released for distribution in theatres, and has since developed a huge following, lending credence to The Beatles' original claim that the concept was ahead of its time.

Film Notes

- The title song, "Magical Mystery Tour," was recorded in April 1967, five months before the film went into production.
- Due to the death of Brian Epstein in August of 1967, The Beatles cancelled plans to travel to India in September and instead decided to go ahead with a group project. *Magical Mystery Tour* was The Beatles' first venture without a manager.
- Paul and Ringo were the main directors of the movie, with each of The Beatles lending supervision and instruction in all aspects of production.
- Along with the actors and technical crew accompanying The Beatles on the trip, were roadies Neil and Mal, Paul's brother, Mike McGear, and a host of Beatles Fan Club area secretaries. All appear in the movie.
- During the second week of filming George came down with the flu and the bus was delayed two days before he was well enough to continue on the journey.
- The "Blue Jay Way" sequence was filmed, in part, in Ringo's Weybridge garden. Ringo's dog, Tiger, appears in this scene.
- Paul's "Fool on the Hill" segment was shot in Nice, France, without the other Beatles present. Paul flew to Nice alone to take advantage of the sunny climate and scenic backdrop, but was soon beset by serious legal and financial problems. Paul's troubles started when he realized he had forgotten his passport and had to have it sent air freight while he was detained at French Customs. (He had already charmed his way

past English authorities.) More problems arose when the hotel in which he was staying refused to accept Paul's credit and also would not advance him the money to pay his other debts, such as car rentals, etc., when he discovered he had left his wallet home. Paul had to wire home for money before he could continue work on the film.
- The Beatles held a party at the Royal Lancaster Hotel on December 17, 1967, where the movie was previewed to all the guests. Linda Eastman attended the party and took photos of Paul the next day for the book she was working on with J. Marks, *Rock and Other Four-Letter Words*.

MAGICAL MYSTERY TOUR
Recorded by: The Beatles
Producer: George Martin
Year first released: 1967
Record label: Capitol
Tracks: 11
    "Magical Mystery Tour"
    "The Fool on the Hill"
    "Flying"
    "Blue Jay Way"
    "Your Mother Should Know"
    "I Am the Walrus"
    "Hello Goodbye"
    "Strawberry Fields Forever"
    "Penny Lane"
    "Baby You're a Rich Man"
    "All You Need Is Love"
- U.S. release.
- The album package includes a booklet of photos and descriptions from the movie.

MAGICAL MYSTERY TOUR (EP)
Recorded by: The Beatles
Producer: George Martin
Year first released: 1967
Record label: Parlophone
Tracks: 6
    "Magical Mystery Tour"
    "Your Mother Should Know"
    "I Am the Walrus"
    "The Fool on the Hill"
    "Flying"
    "Blue Jay Way"
- Released as a two-record set in Britain.
- A color photo booklet accompanied the release.
- The EP's distribution was discontinued in 1976 and was replaced by the U.S. album version.

"Magical Mystery Tour"
Written by: Lennon/McCartney
Recorded by: The Beatles
Lead singer: Paul
Year first released: 1967

Record label: Parlophone (Britain); Capitol (U.S.)
Album: MAGICAL MYSTERY TOUR
      THE BEATLES 1967–1970
EP: MAGICAL MYSTERY TOUR
Performances: *Magical Mystery Tour* movie
- This song was conceived by Paul when on holiday to visit girlfriend Jane while she was on tour in America.

MAGIC CIRCLE, THE
One of the tentative titles for the album RUBBER SOUL.

Magil, Lil
Heroine in the song "Rocky Raccoon."

"Magneto and Titanium Man"
Written by: Paul McCartney
Recorded by: Wings
Lead singer: Paul
Year first released: 1975
Record label: Parlophone (Britain); Capitol (U.S.)
Album: VENUS AND MARS
      WINGS OVER AMERICA
Single: B side of "Venus and Mars"/"Rock Show" in Britain.
Performances: 1975–76 Wings' World Tour.
- Influenced by the Marvel Comic Book characters.
- Drawings of the cartoon characters were screened on stage while Wings performed this song.

Magritte, René
Artist whose painting was reproduced as a backdrop to Wings' live performance of "Maybe I'm Amazed" during the 1975–76 World Tour. It was Magritte's painting of an apple that inspired Paul to use this symbol as Apple's logo.

Maidenhead Hospital
Hospital where George and Pattie were taken after being injured when their car hit a light pole during a blackout on the highway in February, 1972. Pattie suffered a fractured rib and a concussion; George was treated for a head wound and lacerations, but was soon released. Due to the power cut in the area, Pattie had to be transferred to another hospital, the Nuffield Nursing Home.

Mailer, Norman
American author who testified as a character witness on behalf of John during John's deportation proceedings.

"Maisy Jones"
Unreleased Beatle song which was recorded during the RUBBER SOUL sessions.

Maltz, Steve
Apple accountant who was the first to warn The Beatles that Apple was approaching serious financial trouble in 1969.

"Mamunia"
Written by: Paul McCartney
Recorded by: Wings
Lead singer: Paul
Year first released: 1973
Record label: Apple
Album: BAND ON THE RUN
Single: B side of "Jet" in U.S.
- The spelling is a bit different but the name is from a Marrakesh hotel in which Paul once stayed.
- The theme of the song was taken from a saying on a plaque Paul saw in Lagos, Nigeria.

Manhattan Transfer
Recording group on whose album COMING OUT Ringo plays drums.

"Men of the Decade"
Television documentary aired in Britain on December 31, 1968. The show profiled John F. Kennedy, Mao Tse Tung, and John Lennon.

"Man Like Me, A"
Written by: R. O'Lochlainn
Recorded by: Ringo
Lead singer: Ringo
Year first released: 1978
Record label: Polydor (Britain); Portrait (U.S.)
Album: BAD BOY
Performances: "Ringo" TV special, 1978

Manning, Richard
Artist who painted the album cover for WINGS OVER AMERICA.

"Man We Was Lonely"
Written by: Paul McCartney
Recorded by: Paul
Lead singer: Paul
Year first released: 1970
Record label: Apple
Album: McCARTNEY
- Autobiographical contents about Paul and Linda, premarriage.

"Man Who Found God on the Moon, The"
Mike McGear song which Paul cowrote with brother Mike for the album McGEAR. Paul also performs on the cut.

Man Who Gave The Beatles Away, The
Book written by Allan Williams and William Marshall; published by MacMillan and Ballantine in 1975. Williams was The Beatles' first booking agent and this book is an account of his days with the group.

Maguire, Marie
Family friend of the Starkeys who cared for and tutored Ringo during his childhood illnesses when he was away from school.

"March of the Meanies"
Instrumental by George Martin which appears on the soundtrack album YELLOW SUBMARINE.

Marcos, Mrs. Ferdinand
Wife of the president of the Philippines when, in 1966, The Beatles toured the country. A controversy concerning Mrs. Marcos and the group was spurred by an insult she suffered when The Beatles did not show up at the palace after they were invited to a reception in their honor. Though The Beatles claimed they were never made aware of the invitation, and apologized for the misunderstanding, the first family and their countrymen considered the snub highly insulting. The people of Manila were furious and retaliated by giving The Beatles an angry farewell. At the airport they were harassed and physically threatened. Paul later commented, "I wouldn't want my worst enemy to go to Manila."

Marcus, Ken
Photographer who took the inner sleeve photo on George's album LIVING IN THE MATERIAL WORLD.

Mardas, Alex
Greek inventor who was signed to Apple's electronics division in 1968. Known as "Magic Alex," The Beatles believed his genius would be responsible for electronic inventions that would revolutionize the recording industry. He became a close friend of the group, accompanying them on their travels around the world during the late sixties.

Mardas never did succeed in getting his inventions out of the workshop and onto the market. His most infamous contribution to Apple was the designing of an elaborate recording studio which turned out to be void of electrical outlets. The opening of the studio was delayed considerably until the wiring system could be redone.

Mardin, Arif
Record producer responsible for Ringo's albums RINGO'S ROTOGRAVURE and RINGO THE 4TH.

Margary, Mr.
Owner of Lympne Castle in England, where Wings recorded portions of the album BACK TO THE EGG. Margary is heard on the track "The Broadcast" reciting prose.

Maria, Vera
Eighteen-year-old Czechoslovakian pop singer who, although signed to Apple in 1968, never released any records.

Marsden, Beryl
Performer on the bill with The Beatles on their 1965 December British Tour.

Marsden, Gerry
Leader of the Liverpool group Gerry and the Pacemakers. In 1964, John and Gerry cowrote a book of jokes, but their mutual manager, Brian Epstein, nixed the project due to the off-color humor and style. Brian felt the book would not be in keeping with their teen idol image. In 1973 Gerry appeared briefly in the TV special "James Paul McCartney."

Marsh, Tony
Performer on the bill with The Beatles during the Chris Montez/Tommy Roe Tour of Britain in the spring of 1963. He again toured with The Beatles on their 1963 British Summer Tour.

Marshall, William
Coauthor, along with Alan Williams, of the book *The Man Who Gave The Beatles Away*.

"Martha My Dear"
Written by: Lennon/McCartney
Recorded by: The Beatles
Lead singer: Paul
Year first released: 1968
Record label: Apple
Album: THE BEATLES
- Title is a tribute to Paul's beloved old English sheep dog, Martha, which he bought in 1966.
- Despite the title, the song's contents deal with a broken love affair and is, as Mal Evans said, "a ballad for a lover."

Martin, George
Record producer who produced all of The Beatles' recordings (with the exception of LET IT BE) and is credited with discovering The Beatles for Parlophone Records in 1962.

George Martin was born in England in 1926. An accomplished musician, he specialized in the oboe, which he studied under the tutelage of Margaret Asher, the mother of Jane and Peter. In 1950 Martin began working as Artists and Repertoire Man for Parlophone Records, a division of EMI.

On June 6, 1962 The Beatles tested for George Martin at EMI studio 3 on London's Abbey Road. Coming at a time when the company was looking for new talent to boost sales, Martin recognized The Beatles' innovative sound and promising talent. He signed The Beatles to Parlophone Records, and on September 11, 1962 "Love Me Do" was recorded, with Martin as producer.

By 1965 George Martin decided to leave EMI in order to work as a free agent. He gambled that The Beatles would still want him to work with them, which they did, and he was paid well for his services, rather than salaried by the record company. He also formed his own production company with three associate record engineers called Associated Independent Recordings (AIR).

George Martin was an integral part of The Beatles' recordings. In the beginning all facets of the production were left to Martin, as he orchestrated and transposed the music which The Beatles could only express verbally. As the group became more adept at recording skills, Martin took a back seat in the studio, but he remained a well-respected advisor and aide in all their productions. Aside from producing The Beatles' records, Martin produced Paul's solo work for the movie *The Family Way*. He also arranged and orchestrated the instrumental versions of The Beatles' songs which appeared in the soundtrack of the movie *A Hard Day's Night*. The instrumental music for the movie *Yellow Submarine* was also composed and arranged by George Martin.

After The Beatles broke up, Martin again teamed up with Paul when, in 1973, the two collaborated on the soundtrack music to the James Bond movie *Live and Let Die*. In 1976 he became a partner in Chrysalis Records. Martin's most recent Beatle-related activities were his work on the album THE BEATLES AT THE HOLLYWOOD BOWL and the arrangement and production for the soundtrack to the 1978 movie *Sgt. Pepper's Lonely Hearts Club Band*. In 1979 George Martin's autobiography, *All You Need Is Ears,* was published.

Martin, Loretta
Character in the song "Get Back."

Martin, Rose
Paul's housekeeper who has worked for him since 1967. The title of the album RED ROSE SPEEDWAY was inspired by Rose.

Marvin, Hank
Actor who was Ringo's double in the TV show "Ringo."

"Mary Had a Little Lamb"
Written by: Paul McCartney
Recorded by: Wings
Lead singer: Paul
Year first released: 1972
Record label: Apple
Single: Britain and U.S.

Performances: Promo film clip
"James Paul McCartney" TV show
1972 Wings Over Europe Tour
- Paul put to music the nursery rhyme about loyalty, which he felt described the special relationship between himself and his ever-faithful fans.
- He was originally inspired to do the song when his baby daughter Mary enjoyed hearing her name being sung.
- Paul's kids sing along on the chorus.

Marylebone Register Office
London office where Paul and Linda were married on March 12, 1969. Paul's brother, Mike, although an hour late, stood as best man with Mal Evans as a witness and daughter Heather as flower girl. No other family members attended the ceremony.

Mary Frampton and Friends: Rock 'n' Roll Recipes
Book by Mary Frampton (Pete's ex) which includes the culinary recipes of Linda McCartney, Ringo, George, and Pattie Clapton.

Masked Melody Makers, The
Original name for Paul's father's jazz band in the twenties. It was later changed to Jim Mac's Jazz Band.

Mason, Dave
British musician heard on George's album ALL THINGS MUST PASS and Wings' VENUS AND MARS. George also performs on Mason's album IT'S LIKE YOU NEVER LEFT.

Massey and Coggins
Liverpool firm where Paul worked winding electrical coils in the late fifties.

"Matchbox"
Written by: Carl Perkins
Recorded by: The Beatles
Lead singer: Ringo
Year first released: 1964
Record label: Parlophone (Britain); Capitol (U.S.)
Album: SOMETHING NEW
ROCK AND ROLL MUSIC
THE BEATLES LIVE AT THE STAR CLUB
THE BEATLES RARITIES (Britain)
EP: LONG TALL SALLY
Single: U.S.

Material World Foundation
Charity founded by George to which he contributed the proceeds from several cuts on the album LIVING IN THE MATERIAL WORLD.

Matsuo, Tasuko
Japanese lawyer who in 1980 represented Paul during his incarceration in a Tokyo jail after being busted for drugs. (See Tokyo Metropolitan Police Office.)

Matthew, Brian
British disc jockey and television personality who first brought The Beatles to the attention of the nation via his television program "Thank Your Lucky Stars." The Beatles also appeared frequently on his radio shows, "Saturday Club" and "Easy Beat."

In 1972 Matthew put together an in-depth thirteen-hour radio series "The Beatles Story." The program was aired on the BBC and consisted of music and interviews chronicling The Beatles' career. The program was later syndicated in the U.S.

Matthew Street (10)
Liverpool location of the famed Cavern club. The Beatles played here hundreds of times as regulars at The Cavern during the early sixties.

Maxon, Jack
Engineer on the album WINGS OVER AMERICA.

"Maxwell's Silver Hammer"
Written by: Lennon/McCartney
Recorded by: The Beatles
Lead singer: Paul
Year first released: 1969
Record label: Apple
Album: ABBEY ROAD
· A rehearsal of this song is performed in the movie *Let It Be.*
· Both George and John dislike the song.

"Maya Love"
Written by: George Harrison
Recorded by: George
Lead singer: George
Year first released: 1974
Record label: Apple
Album: DARK HORSE
Single: B side of "This Guitar (Can't Keep From Crying)"
Performances: 1974 North American Dark Horse Tour

"Maybe I'm Amazed"
Written by: Paul McCartney
Recorded by: Paul
Lead singer: Paul
Year first released: 1970
Record label: Apple
Album: McCARTNEY
            WINGS OVER AMERICA

Single: Live version released in Britain and U.S. (1977)
Performances: Promo film clip
            "James Paul McCartney" TV special
            1972 Wings over Europe Tour
            1973 Wings' British Tour
            1975–76 Wings' World Tour
            1979 Wings' British Tour
· Capitol Records released a special 12" record with four different versions of the song for radio air play.

MBE
Most Excellent Order of the British Empire award which was bestowed upon The Beatles on October 26, 1965.

The announcement that The Beatles would be given MBEs for their aid in boosting the British economy was made on June 12, 1965. Though many distinguished British subjects protested the award being squandered on mere rock musicians, the Queen persisted and presented the medals personally to the Beatles at Buckingham Palace. The Beatles and their families accepted the honor proudly, though John did have his doubts about the "prestige" involved and his father advised him not to accept it at all.

On November 23, 1969, John sent back his MBE after first sending his chauffeur to Bournemouth to take the medal off his Aunt Mimi's mantel. John stated that he was returning the award in protest against the British involvement in Biafra, Nigeria, and Vietnam. He also added that it didn't help matters that his latest record "Cold Turkey" was slipping down the charts in Britain.

McBean, Angus
Photographer who took the cover photo for the albums PLEASE PLEASE ME, INTRODUCING THE BEATLES, and the EP THE BEATLES HITS. Years later, in 1969, The Beatles posed again as they did for PLEASE PLEASE ME. McBean took the photo which was intended for the cover of the album GET BACK (LET IT BE), but it was decided against and instead used for the album THE BEATLES 1962–1966 and THE BEATLES 1967–1970.

McCARTNEY
Artist: Paul McCartney
Producer: Paul
Year first released: 1970
Record label: Apple
Tracks: 14
    "The Lovely Linda"
    "That Would Be Something"
    "Valentine Day"
    "Every Night"
    "Hot As Sun"
    "Glasses"
    "Junk"
    "Man We Was Lonely"

- "Oo You"
  "Momma Miss America"
  "Teddy Boy"
  "Singalong Junk"
  "Maybe I'm Amazed"
  "Kreen-Akore"
- Paul's first solo album.
- Even though Paul was the last Beatle to release a solo album, he received the most criticism for doing so, due to his poor timing and proclamation of independence from The Beatles.
- Paul battled with the other Beatles over the release date of this album. Since The Beatles' LET IT BE was due out only two days later than McCARTNEY, The Beatles were afraid the dual releases would detract from their sales. But Paul was adamant and felt that since The Beatles' album had been held back for so long after being recorded, it wasn't fair to him to have to keep his project off the market. When Ringo went to see Paul as The Beatles' representative, an ambassador of goodwill, not only did Paul refuse to work out a timetable with him, but he threw him out of his house. Subsequently, the McCARTNEY album was released on schedule.
- Included in the British album release was a copy of a self-interview in which Paul discussed his feelings about his life apart from The Beatles and stated the group had officially split up.
- Paul plays all of the instruments on the album and Linda is the only other voice on the harmonies. It was a homemade recording on a 4-track recording machine. Though Paul stressed the album symbolized "home, family, and love," the critics were not very impressed and felt he pushed the point a bit too far.

McCartney, Angela Williams
Second wife of Paul's late father, James. Angela and James were married on November 24, 1964, after a courtship of only one week. Mrs. McCartney (twenty years her husband's junior) brought with her her five-year-old daughter, Ruth, whom Paul's dad adopted. They remained happily married until Mr. McCartney's death in 1976. After her husband's death Mrs. McCartney became a partner in a public relations firm. Paul has since broken ties with his stepmother, feeling that she was capitalizing on the McCartney name.

McCartney, Heather
Born December 31, 1963; Paul and Linda's eldest daughter. Heather, Linda's daughter from a previous marriage, was adopted by Paul in 1969.

McCartney, James
Father of Paul McCartney.

Jim McCartney was a young musician in his own time, heading a jazz band, Jim Mac's Band. It was from Jim that Paul believes he inherited his musical ability and he credits his dad with instilling in him an appreciation of music from his early years. Mr. McCartney was left alone to raise his two sons after the death of his wife in 1956. A cotton salesman drawing a meager salary, Jim was more than happy when Paul became successful enough to inform him that he could retire. Mr. McCartney died on March 10, 1976.

McCartney, James Louis
First son born to Paul and Linda, on September 12, 1977.

McCartney, James Paul
Paul, born in Liverpool on June 18, 1942, was the first son of James and Mary McCartney. His birth was a dramatic event at Walton Hospital, where Paul's mother had previously worked as a midwife. Aside from the special attention given the child, due to his mother's VIP status on the ward, Paul was born in a state of white asphyxia (lack of oxygen) and had to be resuscitated to life. After Paul's startling debut, life took an ordinary turn for the McCartneys and, eighteen months later, another son, Michael, completed the family.

Music was an integral part of the household, as Paul's father, a one-time jazz musician, encouraged his sons to appreciate the art. He gave his children piano lessons, but neither boy displayed much interest, and all formal instruction was soon discontinued. As Paul was entering his teens, though, two major events occurred which were to affect and subsequently change the course of his life. Rock 'n' roll music was sweeping Britain by the mid-fifties and, with it came the emergence of young, amateur musicians who formed their own groups in the hopes of one day making it to the top. Paul too became infected with the music fever and set about teaching himself to play the guitar. He would practice endlessly to reproduce the sounds of his favorite recording artists, such as Elvis Presley and Little Richard, and discovered that mastering the instrument came easier to himself than to his friends, who were also aspiring to their rock 'n' roll dreams. In 1956, tragedy struck the McCartneys when Paul's mother died suddenly of cancer. The emotional grief the family suffered was compounded by the economic strain from the loss of the income Mrs. McCartney had brought in as a nurse. Although Paul's father did his best to keep his sons in tow during these trying times, the boys were left much on their own, while their dad worked long hours to support the family. By this time, Paul had already become a member of a band called The Quarrymen, headed by another would-be-musician, two years his senior—John Lennon. Paul was asked to join the band in 1955, when he had sufficiently impressed John with his musical expertise after they met at a village fete where The Quarrymen were performing. Paul later brought along his schoolmate George Harrison, with whom he often practiced guitar, and he too was inducted into the group. Music became the nucleus of Paul's existence, as he let his school studies take a back seat to this all-consuming passion. His father's hopes for Paul to pursue a career in teaching were soon put to rest when he realized his son's infatuation with music was more than just a passing fancy. Paul and his fellow band members used his home as their headquarters (a practice which was later to become standard Beatles protocol), discussing plans and rehearsing new material. By this time, Paul was obsessed with the development of the group and was the first to introduce an original composition into their repertoire.

When bass player Stu Sutcliffe left the group in 1961, Paul switched from guitar and piano to bass guitar. He tackled the instrument with the driving enthusiasm characteristic of him, and created a unique sound which added yet another dimension to enhance the group's sound. When The Beatles' line-up became complete, Paul stayed on as bassman, although through the years he learned to master many instruments and utilized his talents to the fullest in the recording studio.

As the group's popularity flourished, Paul became The Beatles' unofficial public relations representative. He was the most concerned for the group to maintain a healthy image and went out of his way to insure this result. By nature Paul was a private person who disguised his innermost feelings with a glimmering facade of congeniality. His willingness to please, coupled with his natural charm, was a valuable asset in The Beatles' dealings with their fans and the ever-present press corps.

By 1963, The Beatles had moved to London to be closer to their work. Paul began a steady relationship with actress Jane Asher, who was from an upper-class London family. After a short time, he was invited to live with her family in their five-story home, where he resided for three years before he and Jane moved into his own home in St. John's Wood. Paul made the transition from provincial rocker to man about town with relative ease. He immediately began a campaign in self-improvement, with Jane as his tutor and guide in a crash course in culture. Determined to absorb all of the social graces inherent in his new upper-class environment, Paul grasped every opportunity to broaden his horizons. He sought to be respected as a serious musician and accepted into the established musical community. His tender and poetic ballads were helping The Beatles gain the appreciation of the general public, who, up until that time, had only regarded the group as mop-topped rock 'n' rollers. But Paul never forgot his roots. His songwriting skills encompassed all styles—from the raunchiest rockers to the sweetest love songs. With fact and fiction interwoven in his lyrics, the "man of a thousand voices" could appeal to most everybody at some time.

Although Paul's hip image gave him trend-setter status in music and fashion, he never totally abandoned the working-class values on which he was raised. It was this conservatism which at first kept Paul the sole holdout when most of his colleagues were experimenting with the use of drugs. Not wishing to remain the social outcast among his cohorts, Paul finally relented and joined in on the psychedelic festivities. He became enamored with the mind-expanding potential he discovered in LSD, and went as far as to advocate its use to promote world peace. It wasn't until he faced public condemnation for his admitted involvement with drugs, plus the physical effects of one too many trips, that Paul decided to refrain from the use of heavy drugs.

After the death of manager Brian Epstein in 1967, it was Paul's main concern that The Beatles should continue to develop musically and branch out into other areas. Even before Brian's death, it was Paul who had conceived of The Beatles' own management company, Apple, and who began planning its development. He took it upon himself to keep the group alive by constantly thinking of new frontiers for The Beatles to conquer. It was this incessant driving and coaxing which the other Beatles began to resent. Though Paul's intentions were admirable, it was his overbearing way which annoyed the others. They complained that their own egos had to be put under in order to comply with Paul's musical tastes. By 1968 Paul's personal as well as professional world was beginning to crumble. His engagement to Jane ended and The Beatles were gradually drifting apart. John had by this time fallen in love with Yoko Ono and his allegiance to the group was on the wane. Paul was becoming bored with studio work and was eager for The Beatles to perform live again. It was Paul who thrived most on the contact with an audience, and the unwillingness of the others, especially George, served to frustrate him even more. Paul felt he was fighting a losing battle and there was nothing he could do about it; he had lost control.

Linda Eastman and her five-year-old daughter, Heather, entered Paul's life during this time of confusion. Paul looked to Linda for the acceptance and security that he felt was lacking in his life. Linda and Heather provided a ready-made family in which he could relax and do some soul searching. They were married in 1969 and settled down quietly, retreating to Paul's Scottish farm, where they led a reclusive existence away from the emotional and legal hassles involving the dissolution of the Beatles, which he had initiated. It was during this time out from the public life that a rumor started that Paul might indeed be dead and the known public figure only a double replacing him. The death hoax was given credence by the changed Paul, who not only looked different in appearance but sounded different musically, as exhibited on his toned-down, laid-back McCARTNEY album.

The birth certificate of
James Paul McCartney.

CERTIFIED COPY OF AN ENTRY OF BIRTH

GIVEN AT THE GENERAL REGISTER OFFICE,
SOMERSET HOUSE, LONDON

Application Number 652302

REGISTRATION DISTRICT   Liverpool North

1942 BIRTH in the Sub-district of Walton Park in the County Borough of Liverpool

No.	When and where born	Name, if any	Sex	Name, and surname of father	Name, surname, and maiden surname of mother	Occupation of father	Signature, description, and residence of informant	When registered	Signature of registrar	Name entered after registration

CERTIFIED to be a true copy of an entry in the certified copy of a Register of Births in the District above mentioned.
Given at the GENERAL REGISTER OFFICE, SOMERSET HOUSE, LONDON, under the Seal of the said Office, the 17th day of July 1968

BX 524344

*See note overleaf

Paul, his father, Jim, and brother, Mike.
Liverpool, 1963. (*Keystone Press Agency*)

Paul shortly after receiving the news of
Brian Epstein's death, August, 1967.
(*London Daily Express*)

Jane Asher displays the engagement ring
given to her by Paul, 1968.
(*Keystone Photo Agency*)

Photographer Linda Eastman interviews Paul at Sgt. Pepper press party, 1967. She later would become his wife. (*Keystone Photo Agency*)

Paul and family: wife, Linda, daughters Stella, Mary, and Heather at Heathrow Airport, 1974. (*Pictorial Parade*)

A delighted father, Paul leaves the hospital after the birth of his son, James, in 1977. (*Robin Titone*)

Paul at London party celebrating the completion of Wings' British Tour, 1973. (*Robin Titone*)

Paul and daughter, Stella, 1974. (*Goldie Friede*)

Paul switches to drums at Wings party, 1973. (*Robin Titone*)

Paul at Wings final U.S. concert,
Los Angeles, June, 1976.
(*Robin Titone*)

Wings, 1978. Laurence Juber, Denny Laine, Linda, Paul, Steve Holly.

Paul and Linda in front of their
London home, 1977. (*Goldie Friede*)

Paul and son, James Louis, New York, 1978.
(*Goldie Friede*)

Paul McCartney, 1977. (*Goldie Friede*)

Paul is included in *Guinness Book of World Records,* 1979. (*Transworld Features Syndicate*)

Paul and Linda pose with Linda's single, New York, 1977. (*Robin Titone*)

Paul on Christmas holiday in New York, 1974. (*Robin Titone*)

In 1971 Paul formed a new group, Wings. In this endeavor, Paul sought to reestablish himself as a musician and again summoned all of his energies into developing the group. After many professional and emotional setbacks in the four-year struggle to regain his musical esteem, Paul and Wings finally achieved critical acclaim in 1973 with the release of the album BAND ON THE RUN. Paul has since become the highest paid recording artist in the industry and was honored by the *Guinness Book of World Reecords* for proving the most successful composer of all time. Along with Paul's career ambitions, he prides himself on being a devoted father, who includes his children (Heather, Mary, Stella, and James Louis) whenever his work takes him on the road.

In 1979 Paul was granted a visa to perform in Japan, after several denials due to previous drug convictions. It was at the Tokyo airport, where he landed in January 1980 with Wings and his family, that Paul was arrested for allegedly smuggling 7.7 ounces of marijuana into the country. He was remanded into custody and remained in jail for nine days, while his family nervously waited at a nearby hotel. Paul was released without conviction on the grounds of his being an illegal alien (his visa was confiscated at the airport) and therefore deported from the country. He left Japan, losing millions of dollars owed in ticket refunds and promoters' costs for the ill-fated tour. Since Paul's return home from Japan, Wings has temporarily suspended all future endeavors, while Paul concentrates on a solo album.

McCartney, Linda Eastman
Born September 24, 1941, Linda is the wife of Paul McCartney and mother of their four children, Heather, Mary, Stella, and James Louis.

Linda was born to a well-to-do family in Scarsdale, New York. Her father, Lee Eastman, a prominent lawyer, sent Linda to the best of schools and encouraged her to work hard at getting the most out of life. Linda's mother, Louise, died in an air crash when Linda was eighteen. She soon married a fellow student, Melville See, with whom she moved to Arizona. The marriage lasted a year, and Linda returned to New York with her baby daughter Heather.

Linda soon developed an interest in photography, a vocation she realized could open many doors. She enjoyed being in the company of celebrities, especially rock stars, and established herself as the house photographer for the Fillmore East, New York's hippest rock house in the sixties.

Linda first photographed The Beatles in 1965 when she flew to Austria to shoot the group on the set of their movie *Help!*. Apparently no fast friendship developed, as Linda cites her first recollection of meeting Paul in 1966 at The Beatles' Shea Stadium concert. One year

after the concert Linda accompanied writer J. Marks on an excursion to London to gather material for an upcoming book. She spent the month of December 1967 photographing The Beatles and reacquainting herself with Paul. It is said that it was John whom Linda had at first set her sights on, but when she realized his disinterest, she transferred her feelings to Paul. Paul, though well acquainted with Linda at this time, had gone ahead and become engaged to Jane Asher. Linda left London disappointed but still determined to "make the most out of her life." Paul and Linda's next meeting occurred in May of 1968, when Paul and John came to New York to discuss business plans for Apple. It was during this time that Linda slipped Paul her phone number at a press conference. She later introduced Paul to her four-year-old daughter, whom Paul fell head over heels in love with. The threesome spent a few days together, but at the end of the stay Paul again returned to London alone. The separation was short-lived, as one month later Linda was invited to visit Paul while he was on business in Los Angeles. It was at this time that Paul was on the rebound after his engagement to Jane had been broken. Linda spent a week of sun and fun with Paul in Los Angeles and then returned to New York, puzzled and worried by Paul's lack of commitment to her. The waiting went on until November of that year, when Paul came to New York, and Linda and Heather went back to London with him.

Though four months had gone by, with much time to prepare, the wedding, which took place on March 12, 1969, occurred in a state of disorganization. The groom found himself scrambling around town to buy a wedding band on the night before the ceremony. No family members, except Paul's brother, who arrived an hour late to stand as best man, attended the wedding; nor did any of the other Beatles.

The marriage got off to a shaky start, as it was during this time that Paul had become involved in the emotion-packed legal struggles with The Beatles. Linda was left with a very depressed and despondent husband, whose world seemed to be coming down around him. During the first year the family (baby Mary was born in August) moved to Scotland to keep out of the limelight. It was here that Linda encouraged Paul to make it on his own and believe in himself. Her confidence and support helped him to get back on his feet, and within a year of the dissolution of The Beatles (a move Linda strongly advised) Paul was making plans for a new group. This time Paul decided his wife would double as music partner. Though Linda had no skills as a musician, she was invited into the new band, Wings. She began taking piano lessons when Paul found tutoring her himself too trying an ordeal.

The band and their music were subject to great criticism from public and press, mostly due to the inclusion of Linda. Her lack of musical experience, evident on record and in concert, made her the focal point for attack. Through it all Linda persevered. With Paul's support, she refused to be put under by mere public opinion. Together they "believe[d] that we can't be wrong" and stood fast on their decision.

Today Linda and Paul live in England and Scotland when not touring or traveling the world. She continues her photography, taking pictures for the Wings Fan Club calendar booklets and chronicling the family's travels through her camera's lens. In 1977 a collection of her rock photos was published in the book *Linda's Pictures.*

McCartney, Mary
First child born to Paul and Linda, on August 28, 1969.

McCartney, Mary Patricia Mohin
Mother of Paul. Mrs. McCartney worked as a midwife throughout Paul's childhood. She died suddenly of cancer in October of 1956.

McCartney, Michael
See Michael McGear.

McCartney, Paul
See James Paul McCartney.

McCartney, Ruth
Daughter of Paul's stepmother, Angela, and adopted by Paul's father in 1965. In the late seventies Ruth was a member of the group Talent.

McCartney, Stella
Second child born to Paul and Linda, on September 13, 1971.

McCulloch, Jimmy
Late member of Wings who played lead guitar for the group. Jimmy is featured in the albums VENUS AND MARS, WINGS AT THE SPEED OF SOUND, WINGS OVER AMERICA, and LONDON TOWN. He is also featured on the single "Junior's Farm."

Jimmy McCulloch first played with Paul and Linda in Paris in 1972. Along with Denny Laine and drummer Davy Lutton, the group recorded Linda's composition "Seaside Woman." He didn't see Paul again until 1974, when Paul called on him to help out on the album McGEAR, which he was producing for his brother. When Jimmy's band Stone the Crows split up, Paul took the opportunity to ask him to join Wings.

While with Wings Jimmy recorded two of his compositions, "Medicine Jar" and "Wino Junko." He also appeared with Wings on their successful world tour from 1975 through 1976. It was Jimmy's alleged broken finger which delayed the start of Wings' American tour in

1976. In 1977 Jimmy left Wings after a dispute with Paul and went on to form his own band. In September of 1979 Jimmy McCulloch was found dead of unknown causes.

McCullough, Henry
Lead guitarist for Wings from 1972 through 1974. Henry joined Wings after he stopped performing with Joe Cocker's Grease Band. Paul had just recorded his album WILD LIFE and was looking for a guitarist who could contribute a heavier lead guitar sound to perform in the band. Denny Laine recommended McCullough to Paul and he was soon a member of Wings. Henry's first record with Wings was "Give Ireland Back To the Irish." He toured with Wings on their 1972 Wings Over Europe Tour and played lead on the album RED ROSE SPEEDWAY, which Wings also promoted with a British tour in 1973. Later that year, just before Wings was scheduled to record BAND ON THE RUN, Henry left the group without any prior notice. He later stated he quit because of musical differences he had with Paul and his dissatisfaction in playing in a band with an amateur such as Linda. Ironically, after leaving Wings, Henry signed with George's record company Dark Horse.

McDonald, Phil
Engineer who worked with The Beatles on their album ABBEY ROAD. He also worked with three Beatles on their solo works, including, ALL THINGS MUST PASS, LIVING IN THE MATERIAL WORLD, EXTRA TEXTURE, DARK HORSE, 33⅓, GEORGE HARRISON, JOHN LENNON/PLASTIC ONO BAND, IMAGINE, WINGS OVER AMERICA, and BACK TO THE EGG.

McDougal, Dwarf
Pseudonym John uses on his song "Nobody Loves You When You're Down and Out."

McDougall, John
Former owner of Paul's Scottish farm Low Gate Farm. McDougall was later hired by Paul as caretaker.

McFall, Ray
Owner and promoter of The Cavern when The Beatles played as the house band in the early sixties.

McGear, Michael
Born Michael McCartney on January 7, 1944, the younger brother of Paul McCartney. Mike changed his surname to McGear for professional purposes when he entered the entertainment world in 1964. Mike, an artist in his own right, is a member of the comedy/musical group The Scaffold, and for a time was in the group Grimms. Paul and Mike were close brothers as they were growing up, even sharing an interest in music. Mike was Paul's

first musical partner when as children they performed at amateur shows as the Nurk Twins.

Aside from his recording success with The Scaffold, Mike has worked on solo projects apart from the group. In 1968 he teamed up with Scaffold member Roger McGough for an album coproduced by Paul called McGOUGH AND McGEAR. In 1974 Paul produced and cowrote many of the songs on Mike's solo album McGEAR.

Michael still resides in Liverpool and is the father of three girls.

McGivern, Maggie
Waitress at London's discotheque Revolution, where she met Paul in 1968. The two dated and traveled to Greece together.

McGOUGH AND McGEAR
Mike McGear and Roger McGough album which was produced by Paul.

McGough, Roger
Member of the group The Scaffold, of which Paul's brother, Michael, is a member. Paul produced his album McGOUGH AND McGEAR and in 1974 Paul and McGough cowrote the song "The Casket" for Paul's brother's album McGEAR.

McGovern, Geraldine
Ex-fiancée of Ringo. They split up before his marriage to Maureen.

McKenzie, Father
Clergyman in the song "Eleanor Rigby." Paul picked the name at random from a phone directory after deciding to forego his original choice of Father McCartney. He felt using his own name might suggest his life was synonymous with that of a lonely priest.

McLagan, Ian
Musician on whose album TROUBLEMAKER Ringo appears.

McMouse, Bruce
Cartoon character whom Paul created for an unreleased film of Wings' 1972 Concert Tour. The setting of the film takes place under the concert stage, where Bruce and his family (wife Yvonne, kids Soily, Swooney, and Swat) live. Bits of animation are spliced together with concert footage of Wings performing on stage. The movie, entitled *The Bruce McMouse Show,* was intended for a television special.

McPeake Family, The
Folk group that performed at the party given by The Beatles for the preview showing of *Magical Mystery Tour.* The McPeakes were invited after John and Paul had seen them perform on television and were impressed with their talent.

"Mean Mr. Mustard"
Written by: Lennon/McCartney
Recorded by: The Beatles
Lead singer: John
Year first released: 1969
Record label: Apple
Album: ABBEY ROAD

"Meat City"
Written by: John Lennon
Recorded by: John
Lead singer: John
Year first released: 1973
Record label: Apple
Album: MIND GAMES
Single: B side of "Mind Games"

Mecca Ballroom
Location in London's Leicester Square, where Paul and Wings threw a gala celebration on November 8, 1971. The party was to preview and promote Wings' first album WILD LIFE.

"Medicine Jar"
Written by: Jimmy McCulloch and Colin Allen
Recorded by: Wings
Lead singer: Jimmy
Year first released: 1975
Record label: Parlophone (Britain); Capitol (U.S.)
Album: VENUS AND MARS
WINGS OVER AMERICA
Performances: 1975–76 Wings' World Tour

MEET THE BEATLES
Artist: The Beatles
Producer: George Martin
Year first released: 1964
Record label: Capitol
Tracks: 12
"I Want to Hold Your Hand"
"I Saw Her Standing There"
"This Boy"
"It Won't Be Long"
"All I've Got to Do"
"All My Loving"
"Don't Bother Me"
"Little Child"
"Till There Was You"
"Hold Me Tight"
"I Wanna Be Your Man"
"Not a Second Time"
· U.S. release
· It was the first million-selling Beatle album in the U.S.

Mellers, Wilfred
Author of the book *Twilight Of the Gods,* a study of The Beatles' music.

"Mellow Yellow"
Donovan song on which Paul can be heard singing background vocals.

"Memphis"
Chuck Berry song which The Beatles performed for their Decca audition in 1962. On February 23, 1972, John performed the song with Chuck Berry when they both guested on "The Mike Douglas Show" on television in the U.S.

Mendelsohn, Jack
Screenwriter for the movie *Yellow Submarine.*

Mendelsohn, John
Author of the book *Paul McCartney: A Biography in Words and Pictures.*

Mendes, Carlos
Singer who recorded Paul's composition "Penina" in 1969. Mendes was given the song when he overheard Paul singing it and remarked that he liked the tune.

Menlove Avenue (251)
Address of the home in Liverpool where John lived with his Aunt Mimi.

"Men, Men, Men"
Yoko Ono song appearing on her FEELING THE SPACE album; John does vocals.

Mercury Theatre
Theatre in Bayswater, London, where The Beatles held a special photo session intended for use by the Official Beatles Fan Club and *Beatles Book Monthly.* The photos featured The Beatles around a piano with a friendly parrot.

Merlin the Magician
Character portrayed by Ringo in the 1974 movie *Son of Dracula,* starring Harry Nilsson.

Mersey Beat
Liverpool music paper which, in 1961, was the first to acknowledge and support the struggling young Beatles. The *Mersey Beat* kept a close eye on the local talent and loyally reported on all their doings. John contributed his views to the paper in zany articles under the name Beatcomber. It was in the newspaper's first issue that John wrote an article called "How The Beatles Were Formed."

Mersey Beat: The Beginning of The Beatles
Book edited by *Mersey Beat* editor Bill Harry; published by Omnibus Press in 1978. The book is a compilation of a variety of the articles and information reported on The Beatles from their earliest days in Liverpool.

Merseybeats, The
Liverpool group which was on the bill with The Beatles for their last performance at The Cavern on August 3, 1963.

"Mess, The"
Written by: Paul McCartney
Recorded by: Wings
Lead singer: Paul
Year first released: 1973
Record label: Apple
Single: B side of "My Love"
Performances: 1972 Wings' University Tour
1972 Wings' European Tour
"James Paul McCartney" TV Show
1973 Wings' British Tour
• Recorded live.

Messenger Out of the East
Documentary film on Indian culture coproduced by George and Ravi Shankar. The film includes a sequence where Ravi instructs George on the sitar.

Meters, The
Band hired by Paul to perform at his party aboard the *Queen Mary* in March 1975. The Meters also performed at a Wings press party in New Orleans during the recording sessions of VENUS AND MARS.

Michaels, Ross
Author of the book *George Harrison Yesterday and Today.*

Michael Sammes Singers
Choir which sings on "I Am the Walrus."

"Michelle"
Written by: Lennon/McCartney
Recorded by: The Beatles
Lead singer: Paul
Year first released: 1965
Record label: Parlophone (Britain); Capitol (U.S.)
Album: RUBBER SOUL
A COLLECTION OF BEATLES OLDIES
THE BEATLES 1962–1966
LOVE SONGS
EP: NOWHERE MAN
• French translation courtesy of Mrs. Ivan Vaughn. Mrs. Vaughn was a French teacher and supplied Paul with the French lyrics.
• The song won a Grammy Award.

"Microbes"
Written by: George Harrison
Recorded by: George
Lead singer: None (Instrumental)
Year first released: 1968
Record label: Apple
Album: WONDERWALL

Middlesex Hospital
Hospital in which Ringo was admitted for "intestinal problems" on September 8, 1969. He was released on September 11.

Midlands Hotel Restaurant
Hotel where The Beatles were ejected in February 1963 while on tour with Helen Shapiro. When the group sat down at a table in their leather attire, the management asked them to leave for being improperly dressed.

Midsummer Night's Dream, A
Shakespeare play which The Beatles perform in part on their 1964 television special "Around The Beatles." In this humorous rendition Ringo portrayed the lion, George–Moonshine; Paul–Pyramus, and John–Thisbe (the maiden Pyramus loves).

Mike Cotton Sound, The
Performers on the bill of The Beatles' Christmas shows in 1964.

Miles
Coowner of the Indica Art Gallery. In 1978 he compiled the book *Beatles in Their Own Words*.

Milligan, Spike
Author and comedian who wrote scripts for the British radio program, "The Goon Show." When the scripts were later published in a book, John favorably reviewed it in *The New York Times Book Review* section. "The Goon Show" was a favorite of all The Beatles. Milligan was responsible for the World Wildlife Charity album, on which the Beatles contributed the song "Across the Universe."

Millings, Dougie
The Beatles' tailor during the early sixties. Millings appeared in the movie *A Hard Day's Night* and worked as head of the tailoring department in its production. He also designed The Beatles outfits for the wax replicas which were put on display at London's Madame Tussaud's.

Mills, Mrs.
Paul's housekeeper in 1967.

MIND GAMES
Artist: John Lennon
Producer: John
Year first released: 1973
Record label: Apple
Tracks: 12
    "Mind Games"
    "Tight A$"
    "Aisumasen (I'm Sorry)"
    "One Day (At a Time)"
    "Bring On the Lucie (Freda People)"
    "Nutopian International Anthem"
    "Intuition"
    "Out of the Blue"
    "Only People"
    "I Know"
    "You Are Here"
    "Meat City"
• For this album John used the same band as on Yoko's album, FEELING THE SPACE.
• John went into the studio without having lyrics for most of the songs. Many were written as he was singing them.

"Mind Games"
Written by: John Lennon
Recorded by: John
Lead singer: John
Year first released: 1973
Record label: Apple
Album: MIND GAMES
            SHAVED FISH
Single: Britain and U.S.
Performances: Promo film clip

"Mine for Me"
Song written by Paul and recorded by Rod Stewart.

Minoff, Lee
One of the screenwriters of the *Yellow Submarine* movie.

"Misery"
Written by: Lennon/McCartney
Recorded by: The Beatles
Lead singer: John
Year first released: 1963
Record label: Parlophone (Britain); Vee Jay and Capitol (U.S.)
Album: PLEASE PLEASE ME
            INTRODUCING THE BEATLES
            THE BEATLES RARITIES (U.S.)
EP: THE BEATLES (NO. 1)
        THE BEATLES
Single: B side of "Roll Over Beethoven" in U.S.
• This song was written for Helen Shapiro while The Beatles toured Britain with her in 1963.

"Miss O'Dell"
Written by: George Harrison
Recorded by: George
Lead singer: George
Year first released: 1973
Record label: Apple
Single: B side of "Give Me Love"
· This song refers to Apple employee Chris O'Dell.
· The phone number which George recites at the end of the record was Paul's old Liverpool number.
· George recorded this song several times and decided in the end to release the most humorous version.

Modern Jazz Quartet
Jazz band signed to Apple Records in 1969. They released two albums, UNDER THE JASMINE TREE and SPACE, before moving to another label. The Modern Jazz Quartet was the only established band to be signed by Apple.

Mods and Rockers
British ballet which was performed to the music of Lennon and McCartney in 1963.

Mollie
Character in the song "The Ballad of Sir Frankie Crisp."

"Momma Miss America"
Written by: Paul McCartney
Recorded by: Paul
Lead singer: None (Instrumental)
Year first released: 1970
Record label: Apple
Album: McCARTNEY

"Momma's Little Girl"
Unreleased Wings' song which was performed on the Wings over Europe Tour in 1972. The song was recorded by Paul with the help of one of his daughters, but was never included on an album.

"Money"
Written by: Berry Gordy and Janie Bradford
Recorded by: The Beatles
Lead singer: John
Year first released: 1963
Record label: Parlophone (Britain); Capitol (U.S.)
Album: WITH THE BEATLES
      THE BEATLES SECOND ALBUM
      LIVE PEACE IN TORONTO
      ROCK AND ROLL MUSIC
EP: ALL MY LOVING
Performances: "Sunday Night at the London Palladium," October 1963
      Toronto Rock 'n' Roll Revival Concert, 1969 (John Lennon Plastic Ono Band)
· This was one of the songs The Beatles performed for their Decca audition in 1962.
· The EP includes a different version of the song than the album cuts.
· John added the line "I want to be free" to the original version.

"Monkberry Moon Delight"
Written by: Paul and Linda McCartney
Recorded by: Paul and Linda McCartney
Lead singer: Paul
Year first released: 1971
Record label: Apple
Album: RAM
· Daughter Heather can be heard singing in the background.

Monkees, The
American television program which was based on the style of The Beatles' movies *A Hard Day's Night* and *Help!*. The group which was selected for the show soon became a success apart from the series as their records topped the charts all over the world. Though a rivalry was publicized between The Beatles and the Monkees in the press, The Beatles didn't regard the actors turned musicians with much concern. In 1967 Brian Epstein sponsored a trip to England by the Monkees to prove there were no hard feelings between the groups. All of The Beatles socialized with the group during their stay and a party hosted by Paul was given in honor of the Monkees at London's Speakeasy nightclub.

"Monkey See-Monkey Do"
Written by: M. Franks
Recorded by: Ringo
Lead singer: Ringo
Year first released: 1978
Record label: Polydor (Britain); Portrait (U.S.)
Album: BAD BOY

Monterey Pop Festival
Rock and Roll festival which was the first of its kind and held in Monterey, California in 1967. The Beatles were on the board of directors for the planning of the concert and Paul attended a few of the meetings. Though rumors were circulating that they would attend, none of the group showed up at the festival.

Montez, Chris
Performer who along with Tommy Roe headlined The Beatles' tour of Britain in 1963. It was during this tour that The Beatles were awarded top billing, after proving that they were the crowd's favorite.

Monty Python's Flying Circus
British comedy group that has been one of The Beatles' favorites since their beginnings. George, their staunchest

supporter, used the Monty Python song "Lumberjack Song," which was broadcast over the P.A. system, to begin each of his concerts during his 1974 Dark Horse Tour. In 1975 George joined the group on stage at New York's City Center for a chorus of "Lumberjack" dressed as the others in a Canadian Mountie uniform. Their 1979 movie *Life of Brian* was financed and coproduced by George. In one of the scenes George makes a cameo appearance.

Moody Blues, The
Group on tour with The Beatles during their British tour in 1965. Wings' member Denny Laine was a member of the Moody Blues at that time.

Moon, Keith
Late drummer of the rock band the Who. Moon was a good friend of all of The Beatles and appeared at several functions with them. He appeared on stage with John at John's Lyceum Ballroom concert in 1969. In 1975 Keith accepted the Hall of Fame Grammy on behalf of The Beatles. He was a close friend of Ringo and appeared with him in the movies *That'll Be the Day* and *The Kids Are Alright*. Ringo worked on Keith's album TWO SIDES OF THE MOON. Together Ringo and Keith had their Playboy membership cards revoked because of the damages they caused during a wild party for Ringo's thirty-fifth birthday.

In 1978 Keith was found dead of an overdose. Ironically, on the eve of his death Keith Moon attended a celebration given by Paul in memory of the late Buddy Holly.

"Moondreams"
Denny Laine song for which Paul directed the promo film clip in 1977.

Moore, Scottie
Engineer on Ringo's album BEAUCOUPS OF BLUES.

Moore, Tommy
Drummer with The Beatles on their first tour of Scotland in 1960. They performed as the back-up band (the Silver Beatles) to singer Johnny Gentle.

Moptops, The
Affectionate nickname for The Beatles penned by the press in 1964.

Morgan, Dennis
President of Dark Horse Records in 1977 and associate of George.

Morgan Studios
London recording studio where Paul recorded the song "C Moon" and the album RED ROSE SPEEDWAY.

Morley, Robert
British actor who played Father Christmas at The Beatles' 1967 party for the preview of *Magical Mystery Tour*.

Morley, Rockey
Roadie in charge of the keyboard instruments on the Wings' 1975–76 World Tour.

Morris, John
Organizer of the 1972 Wings over Europe Tour.

"Morse Moose and the Grey Goose"
Written by: Paul McCartney and Denny Laine
Recorded by: Wings
Lead singer: Paul
Year first released: 1978
Record label: Parlophone (Britain); Capitol (U.S.)
Album: LONDON TOWN
· Song of the sea recorded on a yacht in the Virgin Islands.

Mortimer
New York City trio that briefly worked for Apple Records in 1969. They recorded the song "On Our Way Home," composed by Paul. The Beatles later released the song under the title "The Two of Us."

"Mother"
Written by: John Lennon
Recorded by: John Lennon/Plastic Ono Band
Lead singer: John
Year first released: 1970
Record label: Apple
Album: JOHN LENNON/PLASTIC ONO BAND
            SHAVED FISH
Single: U.S.
Performances: One to One Concert, 1972
· John vents his feelings about his late mother in this composition.
· The single and album versions differ.

"Mother Nature's Son"
Written by: Lennon/McCartney
Recorded by: The Beatles
Lead singer: Paul
Year first released: 1968
Record label: Apple
Album: THE BEATLES
· Paul recorded this autobiographical material alone in the studio with only a guitar accompaniment; the brass was added later.

Mount Pleasant Register Office
Registry located in Liverpool where John married Cynthia on August 23, 1962. George and Paul attended the ceremony.

"Move Over Ms. L"
Written by: John Lennon
Recorded by: John
Lead singer: John
Year first released: 1975
Record label: Apple
Single: B side of "Stand By Me"

MPL Communications
McCartney Productions Ltd., owned by Paul and Linda McCartney. The London office is located at 1 Soho Square and is the headquarters for the company, which is in charge of all business affairs regarding Paul and/or Wings.

MPL was first conceived by Paul in 1970 and a mention of the organization was made by him in an interview included in the press package of his album McCART-NEY. The company began in the early seventies and was run from a two-room office that progressed into a multi-million dollar operation which now occupies the entire building. Aside from Paul's musical contributions, a large part of MPL's gross profits lies in their music publishing division. Included among the thousands of songs which are owned by the company are the scores to musicals such as *Annie, Grease,* and *A Chorus Line,* plus the musical catalogues of Paul McCartney, Buddy Holly, Whale Music, Ira Gershwin, Scott Joplin, and the Edwin H. Morris Music Company.

In 1979 Paul had an exact replica of his favorite recording studio, EMI #2, at Abbey Road, built in the basement of MPL headquarters.

"Mr. Moonlight"
Written by: Roy Lee Johnson
Recorded by: The Beatles
Lead singer: John
Year first released: 1964
Record label: Parlophone (Britain); Capitol (U.S.)
Album: BEATLES FOR SALE
          BEATLES '65
          THE BEATLES LIVE AT THE STAR
              CLUB
EP: 4 BY THE BEATLES

Mr. Mustard
Pam's brother in the song "Mean Mr. Mustard."

"Mr. Policeman"
Name given by George to the water dispenser which was located in The Beatles' office suite in Apple.

"Mrs. Vandebilt"
Written by: Paul McCartney
Recorded by: Wings
Lead singer: Paul
Year first released: 1973

Record label: Apple
Album: BAND ON THE RUN

"Mr. Tambourine Man"
Bob Dylan song which he performed at the second show of the Concert for Bangla Desh and appears on the concert album.

"Mull of Kintyre"
Written by: Paul McCartney and Denny Laine
Recorded by: Wings
Lead singer: Paul
Year first released: 1977
Record label: Parlophone (Britain); Capitol (U.S.)
Album: WINGS GREATEST
Single: A side of "Girls' School" in Britain;
          B side of "Girls' School" in U.S. (later the A
              sides were switched)
Performances: Promo film clip
                1979 Wings' British Tour
• This single sold over 2.5 million copies in England, making it the biggest selling record of all time in that country. (The previous best-seller was "She Loves You," which sold 1.6 million copies). The record was a huge success all over the world except in America.
• The Mull is a cape off Scotland near Paul's farm.
• Paul used local bagpipe players on the song, which gives it an authentic Scottish anthem sound.

"Mumbo"
Written by: Paul and Linda McCartney
Recorded by: Wings
Lead singer: Paul
Year first released: 1971
Record label: Apple
Album: WILD LIFE
Performances: 1972 Wings Over Europe Tour

Murray the K Tells It Like It Is, Baby
Book written by Murray (the K) Kaufman; published by Holt, Rinehart, and Winston in 1966. Murray discusses his adventures with the group. George wrote the book's introduction.

Music and Peace Conference of the World
Festival intended to be held in Toronto in 1969 which John and Yoko were involved with. Conceived as being the greatest peace conference ever held, the idea never materialized.

"Must Do Something about It"
Written by: Paul McCartney
Recorded by: Wings
Lead singer: Joe English
Year first released: 1976
Record label: Parlophone (Britain); Capitol (U.S.)

Album: WINGS AT THE SPEED OF SOUND
- Paul gave this song to Joe to sing, as he felt his voice suited the bluesy effect desired.

Mustique
Carribean island where George planned to buy land for a vacation retreat.

"My Bonnie"
Written by: Charles Pratt
Recorded by: Tony Sheridan and The Beat Brothers
Lead singer: Tony Sheridan
Year first released: 1961
Record label: Polydor (Britain); Decca (U.S.)
Album: THE BEATLES FIRST
       IN THE BEGINNING
       THE EARLY YEARS
Single: Britain and U.S.
- Song which is indirectly responsible for the association between The Beatles and Brian Epstein. After a few requests for the record were made to him from customers in his record shop, Brian was inspired to find out who The Beatles were.
- The Beatles didn't feel it fair to later release the recording credited as The Beatles, since the company was just capitalizing on their name though they were only a back-up band working in Germany at the time of the recording.

"My Carnival"
Song written by Paul during his time in New Orleans at the Mardi Gras in 1975. The song was recorded, but not released, by Wings.

"My Love"
Written by: Paul McCartney
Recorded by: Wings
Lead singer: Paul
Year first released: 1973
Record label: Apple
Album: RED ROSE SPEEDWAY
       WINGS GREATEST
Single: Britain and U.S.
Performances: Promo film clip
             1972 Wings Over Europe Tour
             1973 Wings' British Tour
             1975–76 Wings' World Tour
             "James Paul McCartney" TV special
- One of the first songs that Paul owned the publishing rights to after The Beatles lost the publishing rights to their own songs as a result of the sale of Northern Songs Ltd. to ATV.

"My Mummy's Dead"
Written by: John Lennon
Recorded by: John Lennon/Plastic Ono Band
Lead singer: John
Year first released: 1970
Record label: Apple
Album: JOHN LENNON/PLASTIC ONO BAND
- John recorded this song alone with his tape recorder. The childlike manner reflects his feelings as he brings the album full circle from the anguished opening track "Mother" to the realized acceptance of "My Mummy's Dead."

Myrtle Street Children's Hospital
Liverpool hospital where Ringo spent time when he was six years old for a burst appendix and peritonitis. He was in a coma for weeks and on the brink of death. Ringo spent eleven months here convalescing from his illness.

Mysterioso, L'Angelo
Pseudonym George used on the Cream song "Badge," cowritten by George, and the Jack Bruce album SONGS FOR A TAILOR.

"My Sweet Lord"
Written by: George Harrison
Recorded by: George
Lead singer: George
Year first released: 1970
Record label: Apple
Album: ALL THINGS MUST PASS
       THE CONCERT FOR BANGLA DESH
       THE BEST OF GEORGE HARRISON
Single: Britain and U.S.
Performances: Concert for Bangla Desh, 1971
             Promo film clip
             1974 Dark Horse Tour
- George was sued by Bright Tunes Music for the release of this song, which they claimed plagiarized their song melody from the 1963 recording "He's So Fine." Though George lost the case, it was ruled that any melody borrowing was done unintentionally. George parodied the situation in court in his later release "This Song."
- George produced Billy Preston's version of the song.
- John speculated that it must have been with God's help that the record did so well.
- George wrote this song while on tour with Delaney and Bonnie.

N

Nakamaura, Mike
The Beatles' road manager for their 1966 concert tour of Japan.

"Name and Address"
Written by: Paul McCartney
Recorded by: Wings
Lead singer: Paul
Year first released: 1978
Record label: Parlophone (Britain); Capitol (U.S.)
Album: LONDON TOWN
• This tribute to Elvis was composed prior to his death in 1977.

Nancy
Lil Magill's nickname in the song "Rocky Raccoon."

Narita International Airport
Airport located outside Tokyo, where Paul was taken into custody on January 16, 1980, for allegedly bringing 7.7 ounces of marijuana into the country. (See Tokyo Metropolitan Police Office.)

National Milk Bar
Liverpool pub where The Beatles and Brian Epstein celebrated the news of their impending audition for EMI Records in 1962.

Native American Church of the Peyote Indians
American Indian tribe that presented George with the gift of a peace pipe in 1970. The inscription read: "Pray you smoke this pipe in peace and may great spirit bless your world. May the light of light shine in your home and your heart."

Nemperor Artists
Division of Nems Enterprises, Brian Epstein's management company, formed in 1966. American attorney Nathan Weiss went into partnership with Brian in this agency, which promoted such artists as Cream, the Bee Gees, Jimi Hendrix, and the Cyrkle.

Nems Enterprises
Management company formed by Brian Epstein in 1962.

Northern End Music Stores was a chain of shops owned by the Epstein family in Liverpool. When Brian began managing The Beatles he established Nems Enterprises to handle their finances. Of the ten thousand shares held in Nems, Brian owned seven thousand, his brother Clive owned two thousand, and The Beatles divided the remaining thousand shares. Nems acted as The Beatles agent in collecting royalties paid to the group from all records and sales of merchandise relating to The Beatles. Twenty-five percent of the group's earnings went to Brian as his agent's fee.

After the death of Brian Epstein in 1967, Clive Epstein became director of Nems, owning 90 percent of the company. It soon became apparent that Clive was not as talented a manager as his late brother, and he began to find his chores too much to handle. At this time, Triumph Investment Trust Bank of England offered to buy Nems from Epstein. Clive refused the offer, preferring instead to sell his shares to The Beatles through their newly formed management company, Apple. Meanwhile, Apple was in the midst of its own turmoil with a split in its ranks between managers Allen Klein and Eastman and Eastman. Though The Beatles were eager to purchase Epstein's shares in Nems, the conflicting stipulations for the deal set forth by their dual management finally made Epstein back away and accept Triumph's offer after all. Nems was sold to Triumph Investment Trust in 1969 despite The Beatles' last minute attempts to gain control of their parent company.

The Beatles were furious over the Nems sellout and refused to shell out their 25 percent agent's fee to a company now owned by a banking firm. They instructed EMI Records to, from now on, send The Beatles' record royalties directly to Apple and bypass Nems completely. The matter was brought to court when Triumph sued The Beatles in order to see to it that their contractual commitment to Nems be honored. Triumph was also pushing to gain total control of Nems by buying out The Beatles' remaining 10 percent of the shares. While the battle raged on, a compromise was sought by the record company caught in the middle of the proceedings, as all The Beatles' royalties were temporarily deposited in a bank pending the outcome of the court ruling. An agreement was reached when Allen Klein, representing The Beatles, worked out a deal with Triumph. Triumph Investment Trust was to collect £700,000 plus 25 percent of The Beatles' royalties already deposited in the bank. The Beatles also paid Triumph for Nems shares in The Beatles' film company, Suba Films. This, plus an agreement by The Beatles to pay Triumph 5 percent of their royalties earned from 1972 to 1976, persuaded Triumph to drop their claim for Nems's 25 percent share of the royalties for the next nine years. They also gave up all other rights regarding The Beatles. The Beatles sold their remaining 10 percent of Nems to Triumph in exchange for Triumph shares worth over £400,000.

New Cabaret Artists Club
Liverpool strip club where in 1960 The Beatles provided a week of back-up music for Shirley the Stripper.

Newfield, Joanne
Personal secretary to Brian Epstein. She was the first to discover Brian dead in his home in 1967.

Newman, Del
Musician who provided the orchestral arrangements for the album GEORGE HARRISON.

Newmark, Andy
Drummer who appeared on George's 1974 North American Dark Horse Tour. Newmark also worked on the albums: DARK HORSE, EXTRA TEXTURE, and GEORGE HARRISON.

Newsweek
U.S. weekly publication which was the first American magazine to carry a cover story on The Beatles, on February 4, 1964. The proposed group photo session intended for use on the cover went awry when George couldn't attend due to illness. The picture that was subsequently used was a composite shot of the group from photos of the individual members.

"New York City"
Written by: John Lennon
Recorded by: John
Lead singer: John
Year first released: 1972
Record label: Apple
Album: SOMETIME IN NEW YORK CITY
Performances: One to One Concert, 1972
• John penned this ode to his adopted hometown.

NEW YORK CONNECTION
Tom Scott album on which George plays guitar.

New York Hospital
Birthplace of John and Yoko's son Sean, born October 9, 1975.

New York Philharmonic Orchestra, The
Paul conducted members of this orchestra on his album RAM. They appear on the songs, "Uncle Albert/Admiral Halsey," "Long Haired Lady," and "Back Seat of My Car."

New York Times **Neediest Fund**
Organization set up to aid the poor at Christmastime, to which Paul and Linda donated $10,000 in 1979.

Next, The
Rock group headed by drummer Zak Starkey, son of Ringo Starr.

"Next Time You Feel Important, The"
B side of the single "That's My Life" recorded by John's dad, Freddie Lennon, in 1965.

Nichol, Jimmy
Drummer who substituted for Ringo during The Beatles' 1964 tour of the Netherlands, Australia, and Hong Kong. Nichol, an ex-member of Georgie Fame and the Blue Flames, sat in for Ringo when he fell ill with tonsilitis. On July 19, 1964, Nichols appeared on the bill with all four Beatles.

Nicholas/Helmer
Translators of "I Want to Hold Your Hand" for The Beatles' German recording "Komm, Gib Mir Deine Hand."

Nicholas/Montague
Handled the translation of the song "She Loves You" for The Beatles' German version "Sie Liebt Dich."

Nicola
Five-year-old girl who is one of The Beatles' traveling companions on their *Magical Mystery Tour*. She appears in the scene on the bus with John, George, and the balloon.

"Night and Day"
Written by: Cole Porter
Recorded by: Ringo
Lead singer: Ringo
Year first released: 1970
Record label: Apple
Album: SENTIMENTAL JOURNEY

"Night Before, The"
Written by: Lennon/McCartney
Recorded by: The Beatles
Lead singer: Paul
Year first released: 1965
Record label: Parlophone (Britain); Capitol (U.S.)
Album: HELP!
           ROCK AND ROLL MUSIC
Performances: The Beatles performed this song on the Salisbury Plains in *Help!*

"Night Time"
Escorts song which Paul produced.

Nilsson, Harry
American singer/composer who first became associated with The Beatles in 1968 when John and Paul proclaimed Nilsson their favorite artist/group after hearing his rendition of their song "You Can't Do That."

Nilsson has since become a personal friend of The Beatles, spending leisure time in their company and working with them. Ringo produced Nilsson's *Son of Dracula* movie and subsequent album. John coproduced Nilsson's album PUSSYCATS, for which he wrote the song "Mucho Mungo." Ringo plays drums and sings on Nilsson's album DUIT ON MON DEI and his song "Kojack Columbo." Both Ringo and George play on SON OF SCHMILSSON. Harry Nilsson has also contributed his talents to The Beatles' solo albums: RINGO, GOODNIGHT VIENNA (on which he wrote "Easy for Me"), RINGO'S ROTOGRAVURE, and WALLS AND BRIDGES.

In 1974 one of the better-known incidents involving Nilsson and John occurred when the two were roommates in Los Angeles during John's separation from Yoko. The much publicized event took place at the L.A. night spot the Troubador, from which John and Harry were ejected after becoming drunk and disorderly during a Smothers Brothers show.

In 1979 the house Ringo was living in in Los Angeles, which was rented from Harry Nilsson, was destroyed in a fire. Ringo got out safely, but his possessions and Beatle memorabilia were destroyed.

"Nineteen Hundred and Eighty-Five"
Written by: Paul McCartney
Recorded by: Wings
Lead singer: Paul
Year first released: 1973
Record label: Apple
Album: BAND ON THE RUN
Single: B side of "Band on the Run" in the U.S.

"No Bed for Beatle John"
Song which appears on John and Yoko's album UNFINISHED MUSIC NO. 2: LIFE WITH THE LIONS. It was recorded in 1968 at London's Queen Charlotte Hospital, where Yoko was being treated for her ill-fated pregnancy. The song was improvised with no musical accompaniment as John and Yoko read aloud the numerous newspaper clippings reporting their current situation.

"Nobody I Know"
Lennon/McCartney song recorded by Peter and Gordon.

"Nobody Loves You When You're Down and Out"
Written by: John Lennon
Recorded by: John
Lead singer: John
Year first released: 1974
Record label: Apple
Album: WALLS AND BRIDGES
• This is the only song on the album recorded in Los Angeles.

"Nobody's Child"
Song on which The Beatles backed Tony Sheridan during their recording sessions in Hamburg, Germany in 1961. The song was later released as the B side of "Ain't She Sweet." It also appears on the albums: THE BEATLES FIRST, THE EARLY YEARS, and THE BEATLES FEATURING TONY SHERIDAN: IN THE BEGINNING.

Noebel, David A.
Author of the anti-Beatle books, *Communism, Hypnotism and The Beatles* (1965) and *The Beatles: A Study in Sex, Drugs and Revolution* (1968).

"No No Song"
Written by: Hoyt Axton
Recorded by: Ringo
Lead singer: Ringo
Year first released: 1974
Record label: Apple
Album: GOODNIGHT VIENNA
         BLAST FROM YOUR PAST
Single: Britain and U.S.
Performances: "Smothers Brothers Show" (TV), 1975

NO ONE'S GONNA CHANGE OUR WORLD
Album released by The World Wildlife Foundation in 1969. On this recording, various artists contributed their talents to raise money for the preservation of wildlife. The Beatles donated their first recording of "Across the Universe," which was different than the second recording that appears on the LET IT BE album.

"No Reply"
Written by: Lennon/McCartney
Recorded by: The Beatles
Lead singer: John
Year first released: 1964
Record label: Parlophone (Britain); Capitol (U.S.)
Album: BEATLES FOR SALE
         BEATLES '65
EP: BEATLES FOR SALE

Norm
Road manager portrayed by Norman Rossington in the movie *A Hard Day's Night*.

Northern Songs Ltd.
Music publishing company formed by Brian Epstein and Dick James in 1963 to handle the publishing rights to The Beatles' songs.

In 1965 Northern Songs went on the open market with five million shares of stock issued. John and Paul owned 30 percent of the shares, George and Ringo owned 1.5 percent, and Nems (Epstein's management company) owned 7.5 percent. The other major stockholder in the company was The Beatles' original music publisher, Dick James, who owned 37 percent of the holdings.

By 1969 Northern Songs Ltd. was worth over $20 million. At this time, without informing The Beatles, Dick James sold his shares in the company to Associated Television. With ATV now a major stockholder, equaling The Beatles in the number of shares held, a power struggle to gain control of Northern Songs emerged. The Beatles were determined to keep their music publishing firm under their own control. They resented the idea of ATV profiting from their music. Both ATV and The Beatles began a drive to buy out the remaining independent shareholders in the company in order to acquire the majority of stock and ultimately gain control. The Beatles' negotiations were greatly hampered by their own conflict in management, which was going on simultaneously. Due to the dissension and confusion among their own advisors, The Beatles' dealings fell through, and ATV was able to gain the necessary shares in the company which gave them control of Northern Songs.

The Beatles, disgusted in defeat, refused to carry on as minor shareholders in their own publishing company while producing music to furnish the profits for ATV. In October of 1969 The Beatles sold their remaining stock in Northern Songs to ATV for over $5 million and relinquished all the publishing rights to their music.

"Norton"
Mike McGear song cowritten with brother Paul, who also helps out on vocals.

"Norwegian Wood"
Written by: Lennon/McCartney
Recorded by: The Beatles
Lead singer: John
Year first released: 1965
Record label: Parlophone (Britain); Capitol (U.S.)
Album: RUBBER SOUL
            THE BEATLES 1962–1966
            LOVE SONGS
· John credits a clandestine affair he was having at the time with the inspiration for this composition.
· The Beatles used a sitar for the first time on this song.

NO SECRETS
Carly Simon album on which Paul and Linda help out with some back-up vocals.

"Not a Second Time"
Written by: Lennon/McCartney
Recorded by: The Beatles
Lead singer: John
Year first released: 1963
Record label: Parlophone (Britain); Capitol (U.S.)
Album: WITH THE BEATLES
            MEET THE BEATLES

"Note You Never Wrote, The"
Written by: Paul McCartney
Recorded by: Wings
Lead singer: Denny Laine
Year first released: 1976
Record label: Parlophone (Britain); Capitol (U.S.)
Album: WINGS AT THE SPEED OF SOUND
· Only song written by Paul on which Denny sings lead.

"Not Guilty"
Written by: George Harrison
Recorded by: George
Lead singer: George
Year first released: 1979
Record label: Dark Horse
Album: GEORGE HARRISON
· This song was originally slated for THE BEATLES album, but it was dropped from the line-up at the last minute.

"Nothin' Shakin' "
Song performed by The Beatles on which George sang lead in Hamburg, Germany in 1962. It appears on the album THE BEATLES LIVE AT THE STAR CLUB.

"No Time or Space"
Side two of ELECTRONIC SOUND.

"Not Only—But Also"
British television program on which John guested on December 26, 1966. He cameoed as a lavatory attendant in a comedy skit.

Nottingham University
Wings' first public appearance was given here on February 9, 1972. It was the first stop on the Wings' tour of Britain, which consisted mostly of unannounced performances at college campuses. Students were charged fifty pence admission to the Nottingham concert.

"Not Unknown"
Unreleased song composed by George and recorded by The Beatles during the SGT. PEPPER sessions.

"Now Hear This Song of Mine"
Song written and recorded by Paul and Linda in 1971. The song was never released commercially, but one thousand copies were distributed for promotional purposes for RAM.

NOWHERE MAN (EP)
Artist: The Beatles
Producer: George Martin
Year first released: 1966
Record label: Parlophone

Tracks: 4
      "Nowhere Man"
      "Drive My Car"
      "Michelle"
      "You Won't See Me"

"Nowhere Man"
Written by: Lennon/McCartney
Recorded by: The Beatles
Lead singer: John
Year first released: 1965
Record label: Parlophone (Britain); Capitol (U.S.)
Album: RUBBER SOUL (Britain)
      "YESTERDAY" ... AND TODAY
      THE BEATLES 1962–1966
EP: NOWHERE MAN
Single: U.S.
Performances: 1965 British Tour
      1966 Summer World Tour
- This is one of the few Beatle songs to be recorded in only one take.
- John later confessed he felt disappointed in the lyrics, which he thought seemed trite.

"No Words"
Written by: McCartney/Laine
Recorded by: Wings
Lead singer: Paul and Denny
Year first released: 1973
Record label: Apple
Album: BAND ON THE RUN
Performances: 1979 Wings' British Tour
- The song started off as a Denny Laine composition, but Paul pitched in to help finish it off.

"#9 Dream"
Written by: John Lennon
Recorded by: John
Lead singer: John
Year first released: 1974
Record label: Apple
Album: WALLS AND BRIDGES
      SHAVED FISH

Single: Britain and U.S.
- The number 9 is considered by John to symbolize his personal existence. The number keeps turning up throughout John's life, starting with the month and day of his birth. It was during his separation from Yoko (also born on a 9 day) that John wrote this song, hoping that the numerical force of the title would aid in their reunion.

Nurk Twins
Name used by John and Paul for a performance they gave in 1960 during a brief separation from The Beatles. They played one engagement at Bending in Berkshire and, after a cool reception, the Beatles were hastily reformed.

The name Nurk Twins was also used by Paul and his brother, Michael, when, as children, they performed together at amateur functions.

Nutopia
Conceptual country created by John and Yoko in 1973 during their immigration problems with the U.S. government. John announced the formation of Nutopia at a press conference at the New York American Bar Association. The country "has no boundaries, no land, no passports, only people." The Nutopian flag would be a tissue.

Nutopian Embassy
Plaque which hangs on the door of John's New York apartment.

"Nutopian International Anthem"
Three seconds of silence on John's MIND GAMES album.

Nuttall, David
Apple employee who stood as a witness for John and Yoko's wedding in Gibraltar in 1969. Nuttall took the official wedding photos.

Nutter, Tommy
British designer who tailored and designed The Beatles' clothing.

O

Obber, Horst
Waiter at Hamburg's Star Club during The Beatles' visit in 1962. Obber sings lead on two numbers with The Beatles on the album THE BEATLES LIVE AT THE STAR CLUB. His vocals can be heard on the songs "Be-Bop-a-Lula" and "Halleluja."

Obertourn
Austrian ski resort where The Beatles resided with their wives during the filming of the movie *Help!*.

"Ob-la-di, Ob-la-da"
Written by: Lennon/McCartney
Recorded by: The Beatles
Lead singer: Paul
Year first released: 1968
Record label: Apple
Album: THE BEATLES
        THE BEATLES 1967–1970
Single: Released in America in 1976
- The title for the song was borrowed from a reggae band of the same name.
- This song was originally intended to be a single, but it was voted down by John and George, who felt it too trite.

O'Boogie, Dr. Winston
Pseudonym John uses on his MIND GAMES album. O'Boogie's philosophies later appear on John's WALLS AND BRIDGES album and in *Interview* magazine, when John conducted a mock interview with himself using this name.

O'Brien, Denis
Business manager for George's Dark Horse Records and presently one of the directors of Apple.

"Occapella"
Written by: Allen Toussaint
Recorded by: Ringo
Lead singer: Ringo
Year first released: 1974
Record label: Apple
Album: GOODNIGHT VIENNA

Ocean, Humphrey
Cartoonist hired by Paul, in 1975, to sketch the Wings' 1975–76 World Tour. His drawings appear on the record sleeve for WINGS AT THE SPEED OF SOUND.

O'Cean, John
Pseudonym which John uses on Yoko's album FEELING THE SPACE.

"Octopus's Garden"
Written by: Richard Starkey
Recorded by: The Beatles
Lead singer: Ringo
Year first released: 1969
Record label: Apple
Album: ABBEY ROAD
        THE BEATLES 1967–1970
Performances: *Let It Be* movie
               "Ringo" TV special, 1978

O'Dell, Chris
Former Apple secretary whom George immortalizes in his composition "Miss O'Dell."

O'Dell, Dennis
Associate producer for the movie *A Hard Day's Night*. O'Dell also worked on the Beatle-related movies, *The Family Way* and *The Magic Christian*. In 1969 The Beatles appointed O'Dell manager of Apple Films. The Beatles refer to O'Dell in their song "You Know My Name (Look Up The Number)."

O'Duffy, Alan
Engineer who worked on Paul's album VENUS AND MARS.

O'Ghurkin, Dr. Winston
John goes under this name on his song "Going Down On Love."

O'Hara, George
Pseudonym used by George on Gary Wright's albums FOOTPRINT and THAT WAS ONLY YESTERDAY. He uses this alias again on Nicky Hopkins's album THE TIN MAN WAS A DREAMER.

O'Hara-Smith, George
Pseudonym used by George on the Ashton, Gardner, and Dyke album I'M YOUR SPIRITUAL BREADMAN.

Oh Calcutta!
Theatre production for which John wrote one act.

"Oh Darling"
Written by: Lennon/McCartney
Recorded by: The Beatles
Lead singer: Paul
Year first released: 1969
Record label: Apple
Album: ABBEY ROAD
- The raspy quality in Paul's voice was acquired by singing at the top of his lungs for a week prior to the recording.

165

"Oh Happy Day"
Song recorded by the Edwin Hawkins Singers, which George credits as his inspiration for "My Sweet Lord."

"Oh My Love"
Written by: John Lennon and Yoko Ono
Recorded by: John
Lead singer: John
Year first released: 1971
Record label: Apple
Album: IMAGINE
Performances: *Imagine* film
· George plays guitar on this song.

"Oh My My"
Written by: Richard Starkey and Vini Poncia
Recorded by: Ringo
Lead singer: Ringo
Year first released: 1973
Record label: Apple
Album: RINGO
            BLAST FROM YOUR PAST
Single: U.S.

Ohnothimagen
Phrase which appears on the album sleeve and label for George's album EXTRA TEXTURE. George coined the phrase in reference to the unfavorable notices he received on his previous album (DARK HORSE) and tour.

O'Horgan, Tom
Director of the *Sgt. Pepper's Lonely Hearts Club Band* theatre production in 1975.

"Oh Woman Oh Why"
Written by: Paul McCartney
Recorded by: Paul
Lead singer: Paul
Year first released: 1971
Record label: Apple
Single: B side of "Another Day"
· In this song Paul's "choir boy" image goes awry.

"Oh Yoko"
Written by: John Lennon
Recorded by: John
Lead singer: John
Year first released: 1971
Record label: Apple
Album: IMAGINE
Performances: *Imagine* film

166

Okin, Earl
Singer who opened the show for Wings on the first night of their 1979 British Tour.

Okura Hotel
Tokyo hotel where Linda McCartney and her four children resided during Paul's jail stay in January 1980.

"Old Brown Shoe"
Written by: George Harrison
Recorded by: The Beatles
Lead singer: George
Year first released: 1969
Record label: Apple
Album: THE BEATLES AGAIN
            THE BEATLES 1967–1970
Single: B side of "The Ballad of John and Yoko"

"Old Dirt Road"
Written by: John Lennon
Recorded by: John
Lead singer: John
Year first released: 1974
Record label: Apple
Album: WALLS AND BRIDGES

"Old Siam, Sir"
Written by: Paul McCartney
Recorded by: Wings
Lead singer: Paul
Year first released: 1979
Record label: Parlophone (Britain); Columbia (U.S.)
Album: BACK TO THE EGG
Single: Britain
Performances: 1979 British Tour
                Promo film clip/"Back to the Egg"
                TV special

"Old Time Relovin' "
Written by: Richard Starkey and Vini Poncia
Recorded by: Ringo
Lead singer: Ringo
Year first released: 1978
Record label: Polydor (Britain); Portrait (U.S.)
Album: BAD BOY
Single: B side of "Lipstick Traces (On a Cigarette)"

Oliver, Jack
Ex-manager of Apple Records.

Olympia Theatre
Concert hall in Paris where The Beatles performed for three weeks in January of 1964.

Olympic Studios
Studio in Barnes, England where The Beatles worked on the song "Baby You're a Rich Man" and laid down the first track for "All You Need Is Love."

"One After 909"
Written by: Lennon/McCartney

Recorded by: The Beatles
Lead singer: John
Year first released: 1970
Record label: Apple
Album: LET IT BE
Performances: *Let It Be* movie
· Album version differs from the performance seen in the movie.
· This song was originally written during John and Paul's schooldays in Liverpool.

"One and One Is Two"
Song written by John and Paul and recorded by The Strangers with Mike Shannon in 1964. Unlike the previous hits composed by The Beatles for others, this song never made its way onto the charts.

"One and Only, The"
Unreleased song which was written by Paul in 1964 during a holiday in the Virgin Islands with girlfriend Jane, plus Ringo and Maureen.

"One Day (at a Time)"
Written by: John Lennon
Recorded by: John
Lead singer: John
Year first released: 1973
Record label: Apple
Album: MIND GAMES
· This song was also recorded by Elton John in 1975 with John assisting on guitar and background vocals.

One Day at a Time
Book written by Anthony Fawcett and published by Grove Press in 1976. Fawcett chronicles his two years spent as personal assistant to John and Yoko from 1969 through 1971.

One Hand Clapping
See *Sound of One Hand Clapping, The.*

"One More Kiss"
Written by: Paul McCartney
Recorded by: Wings
Lead singer: Paul
Year first released: 1973
Record label: Apple
Album: RED ROSE SPEEDWAY

"One of the Beautiful People"
Original title for "Baby You're a Rich Man."

ONE OF THOSE DAYS IN ENGLAND
Roy Harper album on which Paul and Linda sing background vocals.

One to One Benefit Concert
Charity concert organized by journalist Geraldo Rivera held on August 30, 1972, to aid mentally handicapped children. John and Yoko headlined this event for the matinee and evening performances at New York's Madison Square Garden. Other artists appearing on the bill included Stevie Wonder, Roberta Flack, and Sha Na Na.

Besides appearing on the bill, John and Yoko also contributed $60,000 worth of tickets, which were distributed free to the volunteers who had helped solicit funds. The concert raised over $500,000 in proceeds to be turned over to the One to One organization.

A telecast of the event was aired on December 15, 1972.

John and Yoko's set included sixteen numbers:
  "New York City"
  "It's So Hard"
  "Sisters O Sisters"
  "Woman Is the Nigger Of the World"
  "Now or Never"
  "Well Well Well"
  "Instant Karma"
  "Mother"
  "We're All Water"
  "Born in a Prison"
  "Come Together"
  "Imagine"
  "Open Your Box"
  "Cold Turkey"
  "Hound Dog"
  "Give Peace a Chance"

"Only a Northern Song"
Written by: George Harrison
Recorded by: The Beatles
Lead singer: George
Year first released: 1969
Record label: Apple
Album: YELLOW SUBMARINE
· The title of this song is a pun on The Beatles' music publishing company, Northern Songs.
· This song was written by George in one hour when The Beatles found themselves one song short.

"Only You (and You Alone)"
Written by: Buck Ram and Ande Rand
Recorded by: Ringo
Lead singer: Ringo
Year first released: 1974
Record label: Apple
Album: GOODNIGHT VIENNA
        BLAST FROM YOUR PAST
Single: Britain and U.S.
· John plays guitar on this song, which he suggested that Ringo record.

"Only You Know and I Know"
Delaney and Bonnie song on which George plays guitar.

Ono, Yoko
See Yoko Ono Lennon.

"On Our Way Home"
Original title given The Beatles' song "Two of Us." It was recorded under this title by Apple artist, Mortimer.

"On Safari with Whide Hunter"
Short story written by John and Paul, which appears in John's book *In His Own Write.*

"On the Bed"
Written by: George Harrison
Recorded by: George
Lead singer: Instrumental
Year first released: 1968
Record label: Apple
Album: WONDERWALL

"Ooh Baby (You Know That I Love You)"
Written by: George Harrison
Recorded by: George
Lead singer: George
Year first released: 1975
Record label: Apple
Album: EXTRA TEXTURE

"Oo-Wee"
Written by: Richard Starkey and Vini Poncia
Recorded by: Ringo
Lead singer: Ringo
Year first released: 1974
Record label: Apple
Album: GOODNIGHT VIENNA
Single: B side of "Snookeroo" in Britain
           B side of "Goodnight Vienna" in U.S.

"Oo-Wee Baby I Love You"
Bobby Hatfield song on which Ringo plays drums.

"Oo You"
Written by: Paul McCartney
Recorded by: Paul
Lead singer: Paul
Year first released: 1970
Record label: Apple
Album: McCARTNEY

"Open Your Box"
Yoko Ono composition which is the B side of "Power to the People" in Britain. The song was banned from the British airwaves due to its sexual allusions, though Yoko claimed her statements were political, not sexual, in na-

ture. The title was later changed to "Hirake." This song was performed by John and Yoko at the One to One Concert in 1972.

O'Reggae, Dr. Winston
John's pseudonym on his song "Steel and Glass."

O'Rahilly, Ronan
Business advisor for Apple in 1968. O'Rahilly had previously worked as the program director for the pirate radio station Radio Caroline. When the rock music station was forced off the air by the British government, The Beatles voiced their regrets and hired O'Rahilly in sympathy.

Orbison, Roy
American singer/composer who toured Britain with The Beatles in May of 1963. It was during this tour that, despite the worldwide popularity of the recording star (Orbison), The Beatles were given top billing for the first time in their career. Orbison is credited by The Beatles as being influential to their early musical style.

"Oriental Nightfish"
Song composed by Linda McCartney which is performed by Wings in the animated movie of the same name. The film ran at the Cannes Film Festival in May of 1978. The song was never released commercially.

Ormsby-Gore, Lord
British ambassador who in 1964 hosted an Embassy reception for The Beatles when they visited Washington, D.C., for their first American concert.

"Ornaments in the 20th Century"
Exhibition held in 1978 at New York's Smithsonian Cooper-Hewitt Museum. The show featured the psychedelic Rolls Royce John purchased in 1966.

"Our First Four"
Title The Beatles gave to the first four Apple records produced by the company in 1968. The four singles, consisting of: "Hey Jude"/"Revolution"—The Beatles, "Those Were the Days"/"Turn, Turn, Turn"—Mary Hopkin, "Sour Milk Sea"/"The Eagle Laughs At You"—Jackie Lomax, and "Thingumybob"/"Yellow Submarine"—The Black Dyke Mills Brass Band, were packaged and presented to members of the Royal Family and Parliament.

"Our World"
A six-hour television spectacular featuring live performances from around the world via satellite on June 25, 1967. The Beatles represented Britain on the broadcast and they chose to televise the recording session for their new song "All You Need Is Love." The song was written

especially for this worldwide performance as The Beatles' message to the masses. In order to enhance the "flower power" atmosphere, The Beatles were joined in EMI studio #1 by a host of celebrated friends, including Mick Jagger and Donovan.

"Out of the Blue"
Instrumental included on the "Apple Jam" portion of George's album ALL THINGS MUST PASS.

"Out of the Blue"
Written by: John Lennon
Recorded by: John
Lead singer: John
Year first released: 1973
Record label: Apple
Album: MIND GAMES
• Inspired by Yoko, this is one of John's most beautiful love songs.

"Out on the Streets"
Written by: Richard Starkey and Vini Poncia
Recorded by: Ringo
Lead singer: Ringo

Year first released: 1977
Record label: Polydor (Britain); Atlantic (U.S.)
Album: RINGO THE 4TH

Owen, Alun
Liverpool writer of the screenplay for The Beatles' first movie, *A Hard Day's Night*. Owen spent several days observing the group on tour in order to get a reasonably accurate portrayal of The Beatles and their life on the road.

Oxfam
Children's fund to which The Beatles donated time and money throughout the 1960s. The Beatles encouraged public donations, as family members and friends campaigned for the charity with luncheons and salvage drives. John designed Christmas cards for Oxfam sales and in 1976 he donated the proceeds from an exhibition of his psychedelic Rolls Royce to the organization.

Oxford Maternity Hospital
Hospital in Liverpool where John was born during an air raid at seven o'clock in the morning on October 9, 1940.

P

Paar, Jack
Televison personality who was the first to broadcast a film of The Beatles on his show in America, on January 3, 1964. The taped segment filmed in concert in England was aired one month prior to The Beatles live performance on "The Ed Sullivan Show" and went virtually unnoticed.

Paddington Green Police Station
John and Yoko were brought here on October 18, 1968, after a drug raid uncovered cannabis in their home. In addition to possession of drugs, John was charged with obstructing the arrest. Although John claimed the drugs had been planted because he was informed of the bust three weeks before it happened, he pleaded guilty in order to obtain a quick settlement and protect Yoko from any involvement. On November 28, 1968, John was fined £150.

Page, Jimmy
Led Zeppelin member mentioned in Paul's song "Rock Show."

Pang, May
Personal assistant to John and Yoko in 1973 and 1974. During John's separation from Yoko, May Pang worked exclusively for John and became his constant companion. She also worked as the production coordinator on John's albums WALLS AND BRIDGES and ROCK 'N' ROLL.

Paolozzi, Eduardo
Artist who tutored the late Beatle Stu Sutcliffe, and whose works were reproduced in the album package for RED ROSE SPEEDWAY. Paolozzi's art work is also included in *The Beatles Illustrated Lyrics*. Paul owns a Paolozzi sculpture.

"Paperback Writer"
Written by: Lennon/McCartney
Recorded by: The Beatles
Lead singer: Paul
Year first released: 1966
Record label: Parlophone (Britain); Capitol (U.S.)
Album: A COLLECTION OF BEATLES OLDIES
         THE BEATLES AGAIN
         THE BEATLES 1962–1966
Single: Britain and U.S.
Performances: Promo film clip
                1966 Summer World Tour
• Background vocals include the falsetto harmonies of "Frere Jacques."

Paperback Writer
Fictional account of The Beatles past and future written by Mark Shipper and published by Sunridge Press, a division of Grosset and Dunlap, in 1978.

Paramounts, The
Group on the bill with The Beatles on their 1965 tour of Britain. They later changed their name to Procol Harum.

Paramount Theatre
New York City concert hall where The Beatles held a benefit performance to aid United Cerebral Palsy on September 20, 1964.

Pariser, Alan
Photographer whose works are included in THE CONCERT FOR BANGLA DESH album package.

Parker, Bertrum
Headmaster at the Liverpool Institute (the school Paul and George attended) who, after hosting Paul and Wings' benefit concert for the school in 1979, severely criticized Paul when he was busted for possession of marijuana in Japan two months later.

Parkins, Brenda
Photographer who, on March 12, 1974, was allegedly struck by John while photographing him in Los Angeles. She filed a complaint against John, but the charges were later dropped so as not to affect John's pending immigration action. A settlement was reached out of court.

Parkinson, Michael
British talk show host who appears on the BAND ON THE RUN album cover photo.

Parlophone Records
British record label which distributed The Beatles' records from 1962 to 1976 and all of Paul's solo recordings. (See EMI.)

Parnes, Larry
British rock 'n' roll concert promoter in the 1950s whose clientele included Cliff Richard and Tommy Steele. In 1959 John, Paul, George, and Stu plus stand-in drummer Johnny Hutchinson auditioned for Parnes under the name The Silver Beatles. Though Parnes was not overly impressed with their performance, he saw enough talent in the group to offer the boys a two-week engagement touring Scotland as back-up band for singer Johnny Gentle. This was The Beatles' first performance outside of England.

Parsons, Allan
Engineer who worked on the SGT. PEPPER album and later helped Paul with his albums WILD LIFE and RED ROSE SPEEDWAY.

"Party"
Unreleased song written by Ringo and Harry Nilsson.

"Party Seacombe"
Written by: George Harrison
Recorded by: George
Lead singer: None (Instrumental)
Year first released: 1968
Record label: Apple
Album: WONDERWALL

Pascall, Jeremy
Coauthor of the book *The Beatles: The Fabulous Story of John, Paul, George, and Ringo* and author of the book *Paul McCartney and Wings.*

Partridge, Kenneth
Interior decorator who worked on John and Cynthia's Weybridge home in 1965.

Patrolman's Benevolent Association
New York City organization to which John and Yoko contributed money during a 1979 drive to equip the city's police with bulletproof vests.

Paul McCartney: A Biography in Words and Music
Book written by rock critic John Mendelsohn; published by Sire-Chappal in 1977.

Paul McCartney and Wings
Two books were published under this title and both share the same parent publishing company, Music Sales. *Paul McCartney and Wings* written by Tony Jasper was distributed by Chartwell Books and the other *Paul McCartney and Wings,* written by Jeremy Pascall, was distributed by Octopus Press. The books share a similar format, but include different text and pictures.

Paul McCartney: Beatle with Wings
Book written by Martin A. Grove; published by Manor Books in 1978.

Paul McCartney in His Own Words
Book consisting of an interview between Paul and author journalist Paul Gambaccini. The book published by Flash Books is an expanded version of an interview which was done for *Rolling Stone* magazine.

Paul McCartney Story, The
Book written by George Tremlett; published by Futura Publications Limited (Britain) and Popular Library (U.S.).

Paul Raymond Revue Bar
Club in Soho, London where the stripper scene for the movie *Magical Mystery Tour* was filmed.

Pease, Gayleen
Teenager who, in 1969, was invited by The Beatles to sing background vocals on their recording "Across the Universe." Gayleen was one of the fans waiting outside the studio to get a glimpse of The Beatles when they sent a scout out to enlist the fans' help in getting female voices for the record. This version of "Across the Universe" appears on the benefit album NO ONE'S GONNA CHANGE OUR WORLD and THE BEATLES RARITIES.

Peel, David
New York City hippie/minstrel who, in 1971, became friends with John and Yoko and was subsequently signed to Apple Records. Peel is mentioned in John's song "New York City" and John and Yoko produced his album THE POPE SMOKES DOPE.

"Peggy Sue"
Written by: Buddy Holly, Jerry Allison, and Norman Petty
Recorded by: John
Lead singer: John
Year first released: 1975
Record label: Apple
Album: ROCK 'N' ROLL

Penguin John Lennon, The
Paperback version of John's two books, *In His Own Write* and *A Spaniard in The Works,* combined into one edition. The book was published by Penguin Books in 1966.

"Penina"
Song written by Paul and recorded by Carlos Mendez and the Dutch group Jotta Herre.

"Penny Lane"
Written by: Lennon/McCartney
Recorded by: The Beatles
Lead singer: Paul
Year first released: 1967
Record label: Parlophone (Britain); Capitol (U.S.)
Album: MAGICAL MYSTERY TOUR
         THE BEATLES 1967–1970
         THE BEATLES RARITIES (U.S.)
Single: Britain and U.S.
Performances: Promo film clip
• The Beatles' sentimental journey home. Penny Lane is a street in Liverpool.
• The song was originally recorded with a trumpet solo at the end and distributed for promotional purposes. The trumpet ending was deleted from the commercial release and did not appear again until its release on THE BEATLES RARITIES.

Pentagon Paper Defense Fund
Organization formed to help raise money for the defense of Daniel Ellsburg and Anthony Russo, who were being

prosecuted by the U.S. government for leaking classified information to the press. John, Yoko, George, and Ringo attended a party given to raise money for this fund.

"People and Places"
Northern England television program on which The Beatles made their televison debut in 1962, via a film of them performing from The Cavern.

Pepperland
Fictional village which is the setting for the movie *Yellow Submarine*. George Martin composed the "Pepperland" theme song, which appears on the YELLOW SUBMARINE album.

"Pepperland Laid Waste"
Instrumental composition by George Martin, which appears on the YELLOW SUBMARINE album.

Perkins, Carl
Musician/composer who had three of his compositions recorded by The Beatles: "Matchbox," "Honey Don't," and "Everybody's Trying to Be My Baby." The Beatles' admiration for Perkins was evident as far back as 1959 when George used the name "Carl" Harrison as his stage name. For Carl Perkins's forty-sixth birthday Paul presented him with a large guitar-shaped cake. In 1969 John performed Perkins's "Blue Suede Shoes" at the Toronto Rock 'n' Roll Revival Concert, which appears on his LIVE PEACE IN TORONTO album.

Perry, Richard
American record producer who worked with Ringo on his RINGO and GOODNIGHT VIENNA albums. Perry helped to arrange for the other three Beatles to appear on the album RINGO. Perry also arranged Ringo's recording "Sentimental Journey."

Peter and Gordon
British duo that recorded the Lennon/McCartney compositions. "World without Love," "Nobody I Know," and "I Don't Want to See You Again." They also recorded the McCartney composition "Woman" in 1966. Peter and Gordon performed on the bill with The Beatles on their 1966 tour of Germany and Japan.

Peter Jay and the Jaywalkers
Group on the bill with The Beatles for their 1963 British Winter Tour.

Phil and Don
Everly Brothers who are mentioned in the song "Let 'Em In."

Phoenix House
American drug rehabilitation center which helped Paul secure his U.S. work visa in 1974 after his drug convictions in England. In turn Paul donated the proceeds from one of his 1976 New York concerts to Phoenix House.

"Photograph"
Written by: Richard Starkey and George Harrison
Recorded by: Ringo
Lead singer: Ringo
Year first released: 1973
Record label: Apple
Album: RINGO
          BLAST FROM YOUR PAST
Single: Britain and U.S.

"Picasso's Last Words"
Written by: Paul McCartney
Recorded by: Wings
Lead singer: Paul and Denny
Year first released: 1973
Record label: Apple
Album: BAND ON THE RUN
          WINGS OVER AMERICA
Performances: 1975–76 Wings' World Tour
• Paul wrote this at the request of actor Dustin Hoffman, who was curious about Paul's songwriting technique. Hoffman suggested Picasso's last words "drink to me, drink to my health, you know I can't drink anymore" as a topic for Paul to compose a song about.

"Picture of You, A"
Joe Brown song which The Beatles performed on the "Here We Go" radio series in Britain in 1962.

"Piggies"
Written by: George Harrison
Recorded by: The Beatles
Lead singer: George
Year first released: 1968
Record label: Apple
Album: THE BEATLES
• George started this song in 1966, but left it unfinished, until he rediscovered the composition in his parents' home two years later. With his mother's help he completed the song.

Pilcher, Norman
Scotland Yard detective who led the drug raid on the homes of John in 1968 and George in 1969. Pilcher was later removed from his position on the police force for improper behavior as a police officer.

"Pink Litmas Paper"
Unreleased Beatles song written by George during the SGT. PEPPER recording sessions.

172

Pinsker, Harold
Chief financial advisor for The Beatles' company Apple in 1968. Pinsker is sung about by Paul in a mock rendition of "Hare Krishna," which was recorded during the LET IT BE sessions.

Pirmington, Patricia
Author of the children's book *The Beatles.*

Pisshole Artistes, The
Name George, Mick Ralphs, Boz Burrell, Simon Kirke, Ian Paice, and Jan Lords gave themselves when they played a benefit performance at Christmastime 1978 in the town of Pisshole, England.

PLACE I LOVE, THE
Splinter album produced by George and released on his Dark Horse Record label.

Plant, Robert
Member of Led Zeppelin, who joined Wings on stage at London's Hammersmith Odeon, on December 29, 1979, for a benefit concert for Kampuchea.

Plastic Ono Band
Group formed by John and Yoko when John began recording and performing apart from The Beatles. The group was first credited by John on his "Give Peace a Chance" single and was introduced to the public in the form of robots at London's Chelsea Town Hall in July 1969. On September 13, 1969, the group, consisting of John, Yoko, Eric Clapton, Klaus Voorman, and Allan White appeared for the first time in concert at the Toronto Rock 'n' Roll Revival Concert. The Plastic Ono Band was the name given to John's various back-up musicians throughout the years, even though the band members changed from album to album.

PLASTIC ONO BAND/LIVE PEACE IN TORONTO 1969, THE
Artist: The Plastic Ono Band
Producer: John and Yoko
Year first released: 1969
Record label: Apple
Tracks: 8
    "Blue Suede Shoes"
    "Money"
    "Dizzy Miss Lizzie"
    "Yer Blues"
    "Cold Turkey"
    "Give Peace a Chance"
    "Don't Worry Kyoko (Mummy's Only Looking for her Hand in the Snow)"
    "John, John (Let's Hope For Peace)"
• Live recording of The Plastic Ono Band's performance at the Toronto Rock 'n' Roll Concert in September 1969.

Plastic Ono Elephant's Memory Band
New York group, Elephant's Memory, was dubbed this title while working as the back-up band for John and Yoko in 1972.

Plastic Ono Nuclear Band
Name John coined for musicians who worked on the WALLS AND BRIDGES album.

Plastic Ono Supergroup
Name John used for his performance at the Lyceum Ballroom in 1969. Among the members of the Supergroup were George Harrison, Keith Moon, and Eric Clapton. Their concert was recorded and appears on the SOMETIME IN NEW YORK CITY album. The album also features a group photograph on the centerfold cover.

Plastic UFOno Band
Group John credits on his MIND GAMES album.

PLAYING POSSUM
Carly Simon album on which Ringo plays drums.

Plaza Hotel
New York hotel in which The Beatles stayed during their first visit to America in 1964. The exclusive establishment booked their reservation under the assumption that The Beatles were British businessmen, but were soon loudly awakened to the truth when they found thousands of teenagers camped outside the hotel during the group's entire stay. The Beatles and their entourage occupied suites 1209 through 1216.

"Please Mr. Postman"
Written by: Berry Gordy, Brian Holland, and Robin Bateman
Recorded by: The Beatles
Lead singer: John
Year first released: 1963
Record label: Parlophone (Britain); Capitol (U.S.)
Album: WITH THE BEATLES
            THE BEATLES SECOND ALBUM
EP: 4 BY THE BEATLES
Performances: "Big Night Out" TV show
                    1965 British Tour

PLEASE PLEASE ME
Artist: The Beatles
Producer: George Martin
Year first released: 1963
Record label: Parlophone
Tracks: 14
    "I Saw Her Standing There"
    "Misery"
    "Anna"

"Chains"
"Boys"
"Ask Me Why"
"Please Please Me"
"Love Me Do"
"P.S. I Love You"
"Baby It's You"
"Do You Want to Know a Secret"
"A Taste of Honey"
"There's a Place"
"Twist and Shout"

- PLEASE PLEASE ME was the first British album released by The Beatles. It was recorded at EMI Studios in London in fourteen consecutive hours.
- In retrospect, Paul feels this album best represents The Beatles' style.

"Please Please Me"
Written by: Lennon/McCartney
Recorded by: The Beatles
Lead singer: John
Year first released: 1963
Record label: Parlophone (Britain); Vee Jay and Capitol (U.S.)
Album: PLEASE PLEASE ME
INTRODUCING THE BEATLES
JOLLY WHAT! THE BEATLES AND FRANK IFIELD
THE EARLY BEATLES
THE BEATLES 1962–1966
EP: THE BEATLES HITS
Single: Britain and U.S.
Performances: 1964 Winter American Tour
"Around The Beatles" TV show
"Ed Sullivan Show" (TV), 1964

- The Beatles' first number one song in Britain; it reached that position after approximately seven weeks on the charts.
- The "Please Please Me" single in America was released in 1964 on the Vee Jay label. It wasn't until late 1965 that Capitol Records released the song.
- In the stereo version a mistake can be heard as John and Paul sing different words.

"Plug Me In"
Instrumental jam which appears on George's ALL THINGS MUST PASS album as part of the "Apple Jam" record.

Pobjoy, Mr.
Liverpool high school teacher who worked closely with John as his art tutor and helped him get admitted into art college.

Pocket Beatles Complete
Book of Beatles' music published by Wise Publications in 1979.

Podrazik, Wally
Coauthor of The Beatles discographies *All Together Now* and *The Beatles Again*.

Polak, Richard
Photographer of the photos on Ringo's album SENTIMENTAL JOURNEY.

Polaris
Western-style hotel and restaurant in India where John, George, and their wives and friends stopped to eat on their way to the Maharishi's retreat in Rishikesh in 1968.

Polydor
Record company which released the German and British pressings of The Beatles' work with Tony Sheridan in 1962 and in America in 1970. After Ringo left Apple, Polydor became the distributor of Ringo's British releases. The album THE BEATLES TAPES FROM THE DAVID WIGG INTERVIEWS was also released on the Polydor label.

"Polythene Pam"
Written by: Lennon/McCartney
Recorded by: The Beatles
Lead singer: John
Year first released: 1969
Record label: Apple
Album: ABBEY ROAD
- The sister of "Mean Mr. Mustard."

Poncia, Vini
Musician/composer who cowrote several songs with Ringo, including: "Devil Woman," "Oh My My," "Oo-Wee," "All by Myself," "Cryin'," "Lady Gaye," "Wings," "Gave It All Up," "Out in the Streets," "It's No Secret," "Gypsies in Flight," "Simple Love Song," and "Who Needs a Heart." Poncia appears on Ringo's albums RINGO, GOODNIGHT VIENNA, RINGO'S ROTOGRAVURE, RINGO THE 4TH, and BAD BOY.

POPE SMOKES DOPE, THE
David Peel album which was released on Apple Records and was produced by John and Yoko.

"Pop Go The Beatles"
1963 BBC radio series starring the Beatles. The program featured interviews and live performances lasting over fifteen weeks on the air.

"Pops Alive"
Series of concerts promoted by Brian Epstein in 1964. As a part of the program The Beatles performed for two shows on May 31, 1964, at London's Prince of Wales Theatre.

Portrait Records
Division of Columbia Records (U.S.) to which Ringo is contracted. Ringo signed with the company in 1978 and his first release on Portrait was the BAD BOY album.

POSTCARD
Mary Hopkin album produced by Paul and released on Apple Records. Paul performs on the record and contributed to the album cover design by writing the postcard, which lists the songs. Linda McCartney is the cover photographer.

Powell, Cynthia
Maiden name of John's ex-wife, Cynthia. (See Cynthia Twist.)

"Power Cut"
Written by: Paul McCartney
Recorded by: Wings
Lead singer: Paul
Year first released: 1973
Record label: Apple
Album: RED ROSE SPEEDWAY
• Inspired by the extensive power cuts Britain was experiencing at the time.

"Power to the People"
Written by: John Lennon
Recorded by: John and the Plastic Ono Band
Lead singer: John
Year first released: 1971
Record label: Apple
Album: SHAVED FISH
Single: Britain and U.S.
Performances: Benefit Concert for John Sinclair, 1971

Presley, Elvis
Late legendary singer and performer whose unique rock and roll style and sound heavily influenced The Beatles in their formative years. The Beatles first met their idol, "the Coca Cola of singers" as John said, while on tour in America in 1965. They were invited by Elvis to visit his Los Angeles home, and most of the evening was spent playing Monopoly, although they did manage to get some jamming in before the night's end.

Preston, Billy
Musician who was the first non-Beatle to be credited on a Beatles' record ("Get Back") for his musical contributions. Preston first met The Beatles while he was performing in Germany in 1962 as a member of Little Richard's band. He sat in on The Beatles' recording session on January 22, 1969, during the filming of the movie *Let It Be,* in which he appears. Billy Preston was signed to Apple Records and his albums THAT'S THE WAY GOD PLANNED IT and ENCOURAGING WORDS were produced by George. George also performs on Preston's albums I WROTE A SIMPLE SONG and IT'S MY PLEASURE. Billy Preston was among the many guest performers at George's production for The Concert for Bangle Desh in 1971 and again worked with George on his 1974 Dark Horse tour. He appears on several Beatle solo albums, including: ALL THINGS MUST PASS, THE CONCERT FOR BANGLA DESH, EXTRA TEXTURE, DARK HORSE, 33⅓, SOMETIME IN NEW YORK CITY, RINGO, and GOODNIGHT VIENNA.

Price, Vincent
Actor who portrayed the hypnotist in the 1978 television special "Ringo."

Priestly, Jack
Filmmaker who shot the footage for the "Wings over the World" television special which was aired in 1979.

Primal Institute, The
Los Angeles institute where John and Yoko spent four months in therapy in 1970. (See Arthur Janov.)

Prince of Wales Theatre
Theatre in London where The Beatles performed as a part of the Royal Variety Performance on November 4, 1963. They later performed here again in concert on May 31, 1964.

Princess Grace Hospital
Hospital in Monaco where Ringo was treated for an intestinal blockage in April of 1979. His operation required laser beam surgery to correct the problem.

Proby, P.J.
Recording artist who recorded the Lennon/McCartney composition "That Means a Lot." Proby appears in the TV film *Around The Beatles.*

Professor Longhair (Henry Bird)
Late musician referred to by Paul in the song "Rock Show." Paul visited the Professor while in New Orleans in 1975 and later invited him to perform at his VENUS AND MARS party held on the *Queen Mary* in Long Beach, California. The performance was recorded and released on the album LIVE ON THE QUEEN MARY, which Paul coproduced.

In 1977 Paul attended a Professor Longhair concert in London and can be seen wearing a commemorative T-shirt on the poster included in the LONDON TOWN album.

"P.S. I Love You"
Written by: Lennon/McCartney
Recorded by: The Beatles

Lead singer: Paul
Year first released: 1962
Record label: Parlophone (Britain); Vee Jay and Capitol (U.S.)
Album: PLEASE PLEASE ME
        INTRODUCING THE BEATLES
        THE EARLY BEATLES
        LOVE SONGS
EP: ALL MY LOVING
Single: B side of "Love Me Do"
• Performed at the audition for Parlophone Records in 1962
• Paul wrote this song in letter format first and then added the music.
• On the original single, session drummer Andy White sat in on drums and Ringo played tambourine. Producer George Martin decided to use White as drummer for fear the "new Beatle" might not be professional enough to handle a recording session.

"Pure Gold"
Written by: Paul McCartney
Recorded by: Ringo
Lead singer: Ringo
Year first released: 1976
Record label: Polydor (Britain); Atlantic (U.S.)
Album: RINGO'S ROTOGRAVURE
• Paul and Linda contribute background vocals.

"Pure Smokey"
Written by: George Harrison
Recorded by: George
Lead singer: George
Year first released: 1976
Record label: Dark Horse
Album: 33⅓
Single: B side of "True Love" in Britain
• Tribute to one of George's idols, Smokey Robinson.

PUSSYCATS
Harry Nilsson album coproduced by John in 1974. John also performs on the record.

Putland, Michael
Photographer of the inner sleeve of the British version of the BEST OF GEORGE HARRISON album. Putland's photos also appear in THE BEATLES TAPES album package.

Putnam, Curly
Owner of the Nashville ranch Paul and family rented while the McCartneys were in town to record in 1974.

"Python on Song"
Monty Python record which was produced by George.

Q

Quarry Bank High
School in Liverpool which John attended as a teenager.

Quarrymen, The
John's first formal group, which he formed in 1955. The original line-up included Pete Shotton, Nigel Whalley, Eric Griffiths, Len Gary, Colin Hanson, Rodney Davis, and leader John Lennon. The name Quarrymen was taken from the school which they attended, Quarry Bank High. In the summer of 1955, Paul was introduced to John through a mutual friend and was soon asked by John to join his band. Approximately one year later, Paul brought along his schoolmate George to meet John and to hear The Quarrymen perform. Though George was only thirteen and a baby by John's standards, his musical ability could not be denied and he too was invited to join The Quarrymen. The group played dance halls and social meetings on and off for two years, but due to the constant replacement of members they eventually disbanded. The break-up was short-lived, however, when John and Paul reunited with George to work as substitute players in George's band, The Les Stewart Quartet. For the performance, they used the original Quarrymen name. Shortly after this regrouping, The Quarrymen title was dropped and the name was changed to The Beatles.

Quayle, Anna
Actress who played the role of Millie ("she looks more like him than I do") in *A Hard Day's Night*.

Queen Charlotte's Hospital
Hospital in Hammersmith, London where Ringo and Maureen became parents three times. Their son Zak was born on September 13, 1965, their son Jason was born on August 19, 1967, and their daughter Lee was born on November 17, 1970.

Yoko had her first miscarriage at Queen Charlotte's, on November 21, 1968. John stayed in her room throughout her stay, and the cover photo for their album UNFINISHED MUSIC NO. 2: LIFE WITH THE LIONS was taken here.

Queen Elizabeth Hotel
Hotel in Montreal, Canada where, in 1969, John and Yoko held their "bed-in." The record "Give Peace a Chance" was recorded in their room, suite 1742.

Queen Elizabeth II
Ocean liner on which Ringo, Maureen, and children Zak and Jason traveled to America with the cast of *The Magic Christian*. They left England on May 16, 1969 and arrived in New York on May 22. John and Yoko were scheduled on the voyage, but due to visa problems they had to cancel their trip.

Queen Mary
Ocean liner, converted into a hotel, which is permanently docked in Long Beach, California. In March of 1975, Paul and Linda threw a party on the *Queen Mary* to celebrate the completion of their album VENUS AND MARS. The guest list included Bob Dylan, Micky Dolenz, Ryan O'Neal, Carole King, Cher, Paul Williams, Blair Sabol, Shecky Green, Dean Martin, and George Harrison. This was the first public meeting between the two Beatles since The Beatles' break-up.

Quickly, Tommy
Performer on the bill with The Beatles on their May–August 1963 British Tour, 1964 British Fall Tour, and their first Christmas show, in December of 1963. Quickly recorded the Lennon/McCartney composition "Tip of My Tongue."

Quoram Restaurant
Restaurant in Denver, Colorado, where, on April 5, 1967, Jane Asher celebrated her twenty-first birthday. Jane was in America touring with the Old Vic company. The party's guest list included the cast of her acting company and special guest Paul McCartney, who flew in from London for the occasion.

R

Radha Krishna Temple
London-based religious organization which George became involved with in the late sixties. In addition to contributing time and money to the Krishna devotees, George also signed them to Apple Records in 1969. Their album RADHA KRISHNA TEMPLE was produced by George and released in 1971.

"Radio"
Working title of the Wings song "Reception."

"Radio Play"
Album cut on John and Yoko's UNFINISHED MUSIC NO. 2: LIFE WITH THE LIONS.

Radle, Carl
Bass guitarist who worked with George on his albums ALL THINGS MUST PASS and EXTRA TEXTURE. In 1971, Radle was invited by George to appear at The Concert for Bangla Desh, and his performance can be heard on the concert album.

Raga
1971 documentary film on the music of Ravi Shankar. The movie was released by Apple Films and included an appearance by George; he is shown being instructed on sitar by Shankar.

RAGA
Soundtrack album for the movie *Raga*. The album was produced by George for Apple Records.

"Rain"
Written by: Lennon/McCartney
Recorded by: The Beatles
Lead singer: John
Year first released: 1966
Record label: Parlophone (Britain); Capitol (U.S.)
Album: THE BEATLES AGAIN
      THE BEATLES RARITIES (Britain)
Single: B side of "Paperback Writer"
Performances: Promo film clip
- With this song The Beatles started a trend of using backward tape loops. The last verse of the song was mistakenly inserted backwards into John's home tape recorder, and when he liked the eerie effect, the loop was intentionally included in the final recording.

Rainbow, The
Name for the group John, Paul, and George formed in 1958. They used this name for a short time when they had discarded The Quarrymen title after John no longer attended Quarry Bank High.

"Rainbow Lady"
Song cowritten by Paul McCartney and Michael McGear. It appears on Paul's brother's album McGEAR, with Paul helping on vocals.

RAM
Artist: Paul and Linda McCartney
Producer: Paul and Linda
Year first released: 1971
Record label: Apple
Tracks: 12
    "Too Many People"
    "3 Legs"
    "Ram On"
    "Dear Boy"
    "Uncle Albert/Admiral Halsey"
    "Smile Away"
    "Heart of the Country"
    "Monkberry Moon Delight"
    "Eat At Home"
    "Long Haired Lady"
    "Ram On"
    "Back Seat of My Car"
- This was the first album to be recorded by Paul outside of London. All of the tracks were recorded in New York City.
- Paul and Linda share equal billing in the production of RAM, going halvsies on composing and producing credits. The couple also designed the album cover.

"Ram On"
Written by: Paul McCartney
Recorded by: Paul and Linda
Lead singer: Paul
Year first released: 1971
Record label: Apple
Album: RAM
- This song is heard twice on the album; in its entirety and again as a reprise.

Ramone, Paul
Stage name used by Paul on The Beatles' first tour of Scotland in 1960. The name was brought up again by Paul years later as a pseudonym on the Steve Miller song "My Dark Hour" and again in a slightly altered form as Paul's song "Ram On." The group The Ramones took their name from Paul's nickname.

Ransome-Kuti, Fela
Nigerian musician who accused Paul of exploiting the African music sound while Paul was in Lagos to record the album BAND ON THE RUN.

Rapple
Division of Apple Records which released the soundtrack album SON OF DRACULA.

Rrats, Ognir
Ringo Starr spelled backwards. Ognir was the fictional character portrayed by Ringo in his 1978 TV special "Ringo."

"Raunchy"
Instrumental composition by Justice Manker, which George played to John and Paul in 1956 to prove his expertise on guitar. By impressing them with his skill, George was soon asked to join the Quarrymen, despite John's initial reservations about his young age.

Rawle, Side
Head of the hippie commune to which John provided, lease-free, his Irish island for the group to live on in 1969.

Ray McVay and His Band
Orchestra that performed at the costume ball for Wings' launching of their first album, WILD LIFE, at the Empire Ballroom in 1971.

"Ready Teddy/Rip It Up"
Written by: Robert Blackwell and John Marascalco
Recorded by: John
Lead singer: John
Year first released: 1975
Record label: Apple
Album: ROCK 'N' ROLL

Rebels, The
Musical group George organized and performed with prior to joining John and Paul in The Quarrymen. The other members included George's brother Peter and three schoolmates.

"Reception"
Written by: Paul McCartney
Recorded by: Wings
Lead singer: Instrumental
Year first released: 1979
Record label: Parlophone (Britain); Columbia (U.S.)
Album: BACK TO THE EGG
· Paul's aim was to produce sounds similar to a radio's reception as you turn the dial trying to find something to listen to.

Record Plant—East and West
Recording studios located in New York and Los Angeles. It was here that John worked on the albums: IMAGINE, SOMETIME IN NEW YORK CITY, MIND GAMES, WALLS AND BRIDGES, and ROCK 'N' ROLL. Record Plant also supplied Paul with the equipment for the recording of the album LONDON TOWN, while Wings visited the Virgin Islands.

Recruiting Sergeant
Character played by Victor Spinetti in the Beatles' movie *Magical Mystery Tour*.

"Red Lady Too"
Written by: George Harrison
Recorded by: George
Lead singer: George
Year first released: 1968
Record label: Apple
Album: WONDERWALL

Red Price Band
Group on the bill with The Beatles on tour with Helen Shapiro in Britain in 1963.

RED ROSE SPEEDWAY
Artist: Paul McCartney and Wings
Producer: Paul McCartney
Year first released: 1973
Record label: Apple
Tracks: 12
    "Big Barn Bed"
    "My Love"
    "Get On the Right Thing"
    "One More Kiss"
    "Little Lamb Dragonfly"
    "Single Pigeon"
    "When the Night"
    "Loop (1st Indian on the Moon)"
    "Hold Me Tight"
    "Lazy Dynamite"
    "Hands of Love"
    "Power Cut"
· The title for this album was inspired by the McCartneys' housekeeper, Rose.
· It was originally intended as a double album, but Paul's business consultant persuaded him to release one record instead.
· The Harley-Davidson motorcycle pictured on the album cover was ordered especially for the photo session.
· Though the album received mixed reviews, it was with this release that Wings began commanding the public's respect.

"Red Sails in the Sunset"
The Beatles performed this ballad in their repertoire during their early years. It appears on the album THE BEATLES LIVE AT THE STAR CLUB.

Reece's Cafe
John and bride Cynthia held their wedding reception here on August 23, 1962. Paul and George along with Brian Epstein attended the celebration.

Reeperbahn
Main thoroughfare in Hamburg, Germany, where among the beer halls and strip joints stood The Top Ten, The Kaiserkeller, The Star Club, and The Indra. These nightclubs all served as training grounds for The Beatles during the early sixties.

Release
Organization set up in England to prevent drug abuse. Paul and Wings did a benefit concert for Release in March of 1973, after Paul was convicted for growing cannabis on his Scottish farm.

Remains, The
Group that toured on the bill with The Beatles on their 1966 North American Summer Tour.

Rembrandt
Name of the home in Cheshire, Liverpool, which Paul bought for his father in 1964.

"Remember"
Written by: John Lennon
Recorded by: John and the Plastic Ono Band
Lead singer: John
Year first released: 1970
Record label: Apple
Album: JOHN LENNON/PLASTIC ONO BAND

"Remember Love"
Yoko Ono composition which was released as the B side of John's single "Give Peace a Chance."

"Reminiscing"
The Beatles performed this King Curtis song while working in Germany during the early sixties. The song appears on the album THE BEATLES LIVE AT THE STAR CLUB.

Remo Four
British group that appeared on the bill with The Beatles on their 1964 British Fall Tour. In 1968 these musicians were among the orchestra which recorded the music for George's WONDERWALL album. George later reciprocated by producing an album for the Remo Four.

Replica Studio
Recording studio built for Paul in the basement of his MPL London headquarters. The portable studio was finished in 1978 after being constructed as an exact duplicate of EMI studio #2, where The Beatles and Wings recorded regularly. It was due to EMI being unavailable to Paul on one occasion that Replica was built as a reliable standby. Wings recorded parts of their album BACK TO THE EGG here.

"Revolution"
Written by: Lennon/McCartney
Recorded by: The Beatles
Lead singer: John
Year first released: 1968
Record label: Apple
Album: THE BEATLES
           THE BEATLES AGAIN
           THE BEATLES 1967–1970
           ROCK AND ROLL MUSIC
Single: B side of "Hey Jude"
Performances: "Frost on Sunday" TV show, September 1968
                "The Smothers Brothers Comedy Hour" TV show, October 1968
- This song was recorded and released in two different versions. The single, which was released first, is the faster version with a hard rock sound. The album version, which was actually recorded first and appears on THE BEATLES, is titled "Revolution 1" and differs in tempo and background vocals from the single.
- The fast version was recorded with John lying on his back while singing on the studio floor.
- In this song John expresses his strong yet ambivalent feelings on how to achieve political change.

"Revolution 9"
Written by: Lennon/McCartney
Recorded by: The Beatles
Lead singer: None (Musical montage)
Year first released: 1968
Record label: Apple
Album: THE BEATLES
- With this cut John experiments in avant-garde sound as he interweaves disjointed tape loops in order to achieve the nightmarish effect of his personal revolution. Number 9 symbolizes John's self-concept.
- This track was created and mastered solely by John and Yoko with no involvement by the other Beatles, who at first rejected the piece but eventually saw things John's way.

REVOLVER
Artist: The Beatles
Producer: George Martin
Year first released: 1966
Record label: Parlophone (Britain); Capitol (U.S.)
Tracks: 14—Britain
          11—U.S.

Britain

"Taxman"
"Eleanor Rigby"
"I'm Only Sleeping"
"Love You To"
"Here, There and Everywhere"

"Yellow Submarine"
"She Said, She Said"
"Good Day Sunshine"
"And Your Bird Can Sing"
"For No One"
"Dr. Robert"
"I Want to Tell You"
"Got to Get You Into My Life"
"Tomorrow Never Knows"

U.S.

"Taxman"
"Eleanor Rigby"
"Love You To"
"Here, There and Everywhere"
"Yellow Submarine"
"She Said, She Said"
"Good Day Sunshine"
"For No One"
"I Want to Tell You"
"Got to Get You Into My Life"
"Tomorrow Never Knows"
- This album took one month to record and was the last Beatles album to contain different songs on the European and American versions.
- With this release The Beatles' individual musical preferences become more apparent in their contrasting styles. George is given more room for his compositions on this album (three songs) than on previous recordings.
- Contrary to popular belief, the album title does not refer to a weapon but rather to the motion of the record spinning on the turntable.
- Album won a Grammy Award.

Richard, Thaddeus
Musician who performed in the horn section for Wings' 1975–76 World Tour and 1979 British Tour. Richard also appears on the albums, WINGS OVER AMERICA and BACK TO THE EGG.

"Richard Cory"
Written by: Paul Simon
Recorded by: Wings
Lead singer: Denny Laine
Year first released: 1976
Record label: Parlophone (Britain); Capitol (U.S.)
Album: WINGS OVER AMERICA
Performances: 1975–76 Wings' World Tour
- This was the only song included in the Wings' World Tour line-up which was not one of their original compositions.

Richards, Emil
Percussionist who was a member of George's back-up band during his 1974 Dark Horse Tour. Richards also appears on the albums DARK HORSE, 33⅓, and GEORGE HARRISON.

Richenberg, Leonard
Managing director of Triumph Investment Trust when the company took control of The Beatles' Nems Organization in 1969. (See Nems.)

Richie
Name used by Ringo for his appearance on the LONDON HOWLIN' WOLF SESSION album.

Richmond Jazz Festival
Musical event which John and George attended on August 8, 1965. The Beatles' film company, Suba Films, recorded the concert, which was aired on British television.

Richoroony Ltd.
One of Ringo's music publishing companies.

Richter, Dan
Personal assistant to John and Yoko from 1969 to 1970. Richter accompanied John to Toronto where he filmed the Plastic Ono Band's performance at the Rock 'n' Roll Revival Concert in 1969. He is also credited with the cover photo of John's album JOHN LENNON/PLASTIC ONO BAND.

Ricky and the Red Streaks
Name Paul devised for The Beatles to use in 1969. The plan was to use this name for billing purposes when the group showed up at concert halls unannounced. They would then be able to perform and at the same time avoid the Beatlemania syndrome. Ironically, the name is very similar to Linda's subsequent group, Suzy and the Red Stripes.

Righteous Brothers, The
Duo that appeared with The Beatles on their 1964 American Tour.

RING AROUND THE POPS
Album released through the Braille Foundation in 1966, consisting of interviews with The Beatles during their 1966 North American Tour.

RINGO
Artist: Ringo Starr
Producer: Richard Perry
Year first released: 1973
Record label: Apple
Tracks: 10
    "I'm the Greatest"
    "Hold On (Have You Seen My Baby)"
    "Photograph"

"Sunshine Life for Me (Sail Away Raymond)"
"You're Sixteen"
"Oh My My"
"Step Lightly"
"Six O'Clock"
"Devil Woman"
"You and Me (Babe)"
- Ringo's best-selling solo album.
- For the first time since the split all four Beatles contribute compositions and musical accompaniment on one album. George, John, and Ringo worked together in the recording studio in Los Angeles, while Paul recorded his parts separately in London.
- An instrumental version of the album performed on synthesizer was recorded by David Hentschel and released in 1975 on Ring O' Records.

"Ringo"
A sixty-minute comedy/musical television program aired only in the U.S., starring Ringo Starr, along with a cast of luminaries including George, Art Carney, Vincent Price, Angie Dickenson, John Ritter, and Carrie Fisher. The show, loosely based on the classic *The Prince and the Pauper* was broadcast on April 26, 1978.

Ring O' Records
Record company started by Ringo in 1974. Ringo never recorded for the label, but he lined up several of his favorites including Bobby Keys, David Hentschel, Carl Grossman, Graham Bonnet, and Col. Doug Boogie to record for Ring O' Records. The label never successfully got off the ground and in 1978 the company halted record distribution and was converted into a production company. (See Able Label.)

Ringo or Robin Ltd. (ROR)
Furniture design company formed by Ringo and partner Robin Cruikshank in 1970. Some of the contemporary designs manufactured by the company include dining tables with adjustable seats for children, Rolls Royce ashtrays, and futuristic fireplaces.

Ringo's Roadside Attraction
Back-up band that performed with Ringo in the concert segment of his 1978 television special "Ringo."

RINGO'S ROTOGRAVURE
Artist: Ringo Starr
Producer: Arif Mardin
Year first released: 1976
Record label: Polydor (Britain); Atlantic (U.S.)
Tracks: 11
    "A Dose Of Rock and Roll"
    "Hey Baby"
    "Pure Gold"
    "Cryin' "
    "You Don't Know Me At All"

    "Cookin' "
    "I'll Still Love You"
    "This Be Called A Song"
    "Las Brisas"
    "Lady Gaye"
    "Spooky Weirdness"
- Ringo's first release for Polydor and Atlantic.
- Though Ringo got help from the likes of Peter Frampton, Harry Nilsson, and Dr. John, not to mention contributions from the other Beatles, the album was not as successful as its predecessors.
- A collection of photos on the inner sleeve includes shots of Ringo's children and John and Paul.

Ringo Starrtime
Title of Ringo's solo set during his performance with Rory Storme and the Hurricanes in 1961.

RINGO THE 4TH
Artist: Ringo Starr
Producer: Arif Mardin
Year first released: 1977
Record label: Polydor (Britain); Atlantic (U.S.)
Tracks: 10
    "Drowning in The Sea of Love"
    "Tango All Night"
    "Wings"
    "Gave It All Up"
    "Out on the Streets"
    "Can She Do It Like She Dances"
    "Sneaking Sally through the Alley"
    "It's No Secret"
    "Gypsies in Flight"
    "Simple Love Song"
- Ringo's last album for Atlantic Records.

"Ringo's Theme"
Instrumental version of the Lennon/McCartney composition "This Boy." The music was recorded by the George Martin Orchestra and heard on the soundtrack for the movie *A Hard Day's Night* and appears on the U.S. album A HARD DAY'S NIGHT. The music was dubbed "Ringo's Theme" because it accompanied Ringo's "parading" scene in the movie.

Rita
Lovely meter maid whom Paul sings about in the song "Lovely Rita."

Ritchie
Alias for Ringo on the STILLS album.

Ritter, John
Actor who portrayed Ringo's agent in the TV special "Ringo."

Ritz Hotel
London hotel where Paul and Linda held their wedding luncheon on March 12, 1969.

Rivera, Geraldo
American television journalist who was responsible for organizing the One to One benefit concerts to aid the mentally handicapped. On August 30, 1972 John and Yoko headlined the concert, which was hosted by Rivera. He later testified as a character witness for John at his Immigration proceedings in 1976.

In June of 1976 Geraldo Rivera interviewed Paul and Linda on his TV show "Good Night America." Paul and Linda were interviewed again by Rivera in 1979 (after Paul received his award from the Guinness Book) on the "20/20" TV show.

Riviera Idlewild Hotel
Hotel located in Queens, New York. In 1964 The Beatles stayed here before returning to London after completing their summer tour in the U.S. It was during their stay at the Riviera Idlewild that The Beatles were first introduced to Bob Dylan when he visited them in their room. On that same night, a row between Brian Epstein and publicist Derek Taylor terminated Taylor's job.

Robbins, Jessie
British actress who played Ringo's Aunt Jessie in the movie *Magical Mystery Tour*.

Robbins, Kate
Cousin of Paul's, she recorded the song "Tomorrow" from the theatrical production of *Annie*.

Robert Frazer Gallery
Mayfair London art gallery where John held his "You Are Here" exhibition dedicated to Yoko Ono on July 19, 1968. It was here that John and Yoko first publicly proclaimed their love for one another. Owner Robert Frazer was an artist friend of The Beatles', and they backed him financially on several art ventures.

Robinson, Smokey
American soul singer whom George greatly admires and professes to "be madly in love with." George's song "Pure Smokey" is dedicated to Robinson, as George delivers a performance reminiscent of Smokey on the record.

"Rock and Roll Circus"
Unreleased British TV program starring The Rolling Stones. John and Yoko attended the filming, which took place on December 11, 1968, and they both appear in the film. John made a guest appearance on the show as part of the supergroup band that performed.

"Rock and Roller"
Billy Lawrie song cowritten by Ringo Starr. It appears on Lawrie's album SHIP IMAGINATION.

"Rock and Roll Music"
Written by: Chuck Berry
Recorded by: The Beatles
Lead singer: John
Year first released: 1964
Record label: Parlophone (Britain); Capitol (U.S.)
Album: BEATLES FOR SALE
         BEATLES '65
         ROCK AND ROLL MUSIC
EP: BEATLES FOR SALE
Performances: 1964 Christmas Shows
               1965 European Summer Tour
               1966 Summer Tour

ROCK AND ROLL MUSIC
Artist: The Beatles
Producer: George Martin (and Phil Spector)
Year first released: 1976
Record label: Parlophone (Britain); Capitol (U.S.)
Tracks: 28
    "Twist and Shout"
    "I Saw Her Standing There"
    "You Can't Do That"
    "I Wanna Be Your Man"
    "I Call Your Name"
    "Boys"
    "Long Tall Sally"
    "Rock and Roll Music"
    "Slow Down"
    "Kansas City"
    "Money (That's What I Want)"
    "Bad Boy"
    "Matchbox"
    "Roll Over Beethoven"
    "Drive My Car"
    "Dizzy Miss Lizzie"
    "Anytime At All"
    "Everybody's Trying to Be My Baby"
    "The Night Before"
    "I'm Down"
    "Revolution"
    "Back in the USSR"
    "Helter Skelter"
    "Taxman"
    "Got to Get You into My Life"
    "Hey Bulldog"
    "Birthday"
    "Get Back"
- This double album is a collection of songs that were handpicked by the record company without The Beatles' consent or permission.
- John had offered to help make the package more pre-

sentable by doing the cover illustration himself, but amazingly he was turned down by the company.
• All selections (except "Get Back," which was produced by Phil Spector) were produced by George Martin and remixed to give the album a stereo sound.
• Capitol Records spent more money promoting this album than on any of their previous releases.

"Rock and Roll People"
Johnny Winter song written by John Lennon which appears on Winter's album JOHN DAWSON WINTER III.

"Rockestra Theme"
Written by: Paul McCartney
Recorded by: Wings
Lead singer: None (Instrumental)
Year first released: 1979
Record label: Parlophone (Britain); Columbia (U.S.)
Album: BACK TO THE EGG
Performances: 1979 Wings' Concert for Kampuchea
• This song was recorded by Wings with the help of such notable musicians as:
    Guitars: Pete Townshend, David Gilmore, Hank Marvin, plus Denny Laine and Lawrence Juber
    Drums: John Bonham, Kenney Jones, and Steve Holly
    Percussion: Ray Cooper, Tony Carr, Speedy Acquaye, and Maurice Pert
    Bass: Paul McCartney, Bruce Thomas, and Ronnie Lane
    Keyboards: John Paul Jones, Gary Brooker, Tony Ashton, and Linda McCartney
    Horns: Howie Casey, Thaddeus Richard, Tony Dorsey, and Steve Howard
• The song won a Grammy for the best instrumental in 1979.
• The recording session was filmed for posterity.

"Rock Island Line"
Song performed by George and Paul Simon during the rehearsals for the television program "Saturday Night Live" in November of 1976. The song was not included in the broadcast.

ROCK 'N' ROLL
Artist: John Lennon
Producer: Phil Spector and John Lennon
Year first released: 1975
Record label: Apple
Tracks: 13
    "Be-Bop-a-Lula"
    "Stand By Me"
    "Ready Teddy"/"Rip It Up"
    "You Can't Catch Me"

    "Ain't That a Shame"
    "Do You Want to Dance"
    "Sweet Little Sixteen"
    "Slippin' and Slidin' "
    "Peggy Sue"
    "Bring It On Home to Me"/"Send Me Some Lovin' "
    "Bony Maronie"
    "Ya Ya"
    "Just Because"
• John recorded this album because he had always had a desire to record the songs that inspired him in his youth.
• Work first began on the album in 1973, but due to conflicts between John and producer Phil Spector, the project was dropped after half of the tracks had been recorded. John began work again on the album, on his own, in 1974, but the release date was postponed indefinitely due to the release of WALLS AND BRIDGES. The album was finally released when a bootleg comprised of John's acetates was put out first (see Morris Levy), forcing John and his record company to push up the release date in order to kill the bootleg sales.

Rockpile
Group that performed on the bill with Wings at the London Hammersmith Odeon benefit concert for Kampuchea on December 29, 1979.

"Rock Show"
Written by: Paul McCartney
Recorded by: Wings
Lead singer: Paul
Year first released: 1975
Record label: Parlophone (Britain); Capitol (U.S.)
Album: VENUS AND MARS
          WINGS OVER AMERICA
Single: In medley with "Venus and Mars"
Performances: 1975–76 Wings' World Tour
• Paul wrote this song specifically to be used as the opening number for Wings' concert tour.

"Rocky Raccoon"
Written by: Lennon/McCartney
Recorded by: The Beatles
Lead singer: Paul
Year first released: 1968
Record label: Apple
Album: THE BEATLES
• Ironically, this "western" music style narrative was written while The Beatles were visiting India and soaking up the Far Eastern culture.
• John is featured on harmonica.

Roducer, P.
Pseudonym used by George for the album SPLINTER.

Roe, Tommy
American singer who toured with The Beatles on their 1963 tour of Britain. In 1964 Roe again worked with the group on the bill during their winter U.S. tour, and their spring tour of Britain. It was during this tour that Roe was involved in a "row" with John on the bus trip between gigs. John began the fight over a remark Roe made. It took the entire entourage to pry the two apart but all was forgotten by the journey's end.

Rolling Stones, The
British group whose first hit record, "I Wanna Be Your Man," was written for them by Lennon/McCartney.

The Rolling Stones' bad boy image sharply contrasted with The Beatles' clean-cut persona and the press consistently tried to create a rivalry between the two groups. Nevertheless, the two most successful names in rock music remained personal friends, occasionally appearing on each other's records. "Welcome Rolling Stones" is written on the front cover of The Beatles SGT. PEPPER album, as the Stones reciprocate with their album cover montage including The Beatles' pictures on THEIR SATANIC MAJESTIES REQUEST.

In 1966 the Stones were on the bill with The Beatles at the New Musical Express Poll Winners Concert.

"Roll Over Beethoven"
Written by: Chuck Berry
Recorded by: The Beatles
Lead singer: George
Year first released: 1963
Record label: Parlophone (Britain); Capitol (U.S.)
Album: WITH THE BEATLES
          THE BEATLES SECOND ALBUM
          ROCK AND ROLL MUSIC
          THE BEATLES AT THE HOLLYWOOD
             BOWL
          THE BEATLES LIVE AT THE STAR
             CLUB
EP: 4 BY THE BEATLES
Single: U.S.
Performances: 1964 Winter American Tour
                1964 Summer North American Tour

Romeo, Vincent
Wings's first manager.

Romero, Rudy
Recording artist whose album TO THE WORLD features George on guitar and background vocals.

Ronettes, The
American group that appeared on the bill of The Beatles' 1966 North American tour.

ROOTS
Bootleg version of John's album ROCK 'N' ROLL. The unauthorized release includes two songs which do not appear on John's album: "Angel Baby" and "Be My Baby." (See Morris Levy.)

Rory
Roadie who practices voodoo in the Wings song "Famous Groupies."

Rose
A friend of the defendant in the song "Maxwell's Silver Hammer."

Rose, Bettina
National secretary for England's Official Beatles Fan Club.

Rosenbaum, Helen
Author of the book *The Beatles Trivia Quiz Book.*

"Rosetta"
Foremost song which Paul produced in 1969.

Rossington, Norman
Actor who played Norm, The Beatles' road manager, in the movie *A Hard Day's Night.*

Rowe, Dick
Decca Records executive who was responsible for rejecting The Beatles' bid to record for the company in 1962.

Royal, The
Hotel located in London's Russell Square. The Beatles stayed here for one night, January 1, 1962, on the eve of their Decca recording audition.

Royal Caribbean Steel Band, The
Liverpool band which was one of the first to travel to Hamburg in 1960 to perform at the German clubs. It was during their visit to Hamburg that they informed Beatles' friend/agent Allan Williams of the work available in Germany for struggling Liverpool bands. It was because of this that Williams was inspired to book The Beatles into Hamburg.

Royal Lancaster Hotel
London hotel in which, on December 21, 1967, a "fancy dress" party was held to celebrate the premiere of The Beatles' film production *Magical Mystery Tour.* All of the guests arrived in costume including Paul and girlfriend Jane dressed as the Pearly King and Queen; John as a fifties style Teddy boy rocker, with wife Cynthia dressed as an Edwardian lady; Ringo arrived as a Regency buck, along with wife Maureen, who came as an Indian squaw; and George dressed as a cavalry officer,

accompanied by wife Pattie, the Eastern dancer. Linda Eastman also attended the party.

The *Magical Mystery Tour* film was screened here for the first time, prior to the public showing on national television.

On July 17, 1968 this hotel again hosted a Beatles' celebration, this time for the opening of the movie *Yellow Submarine*.

Royle, Derek
Actor who played the part of the coach courier in the movie *Magical Mystery Tour*.

R.S.
Pseudonym used by Ringo on the David Hentschel album STARTLING MUSIC.

RUBBER SOUL
Artist: The Beatles
Producer: George Martin
Year first released: 1965
Record label: Parlophone (Britain); Capitol (U.S.)
Tracks: 14—Britain; 12—U.S.

Britain

"Drive My Car"
"Norwegian Wood"
"You Won't See Me"
"Nowhere Man"
"Think for Yourself"
"The Word"
"Michelle"
"What Goes On"
"Girl"
"I'm Looking Through You"
"In My Life"
"Wait"
"If I Needed Someone"
"Run For Your Life"

U.S.

"I've Just Seen a Face"
"Norwegian Wood"
"You Won't See Me"
"Think For Yourself"
"The Word"
"Michelle"
"It's Only Love"
"Girl"
"I'm Looking Through You"
"In My Life"
"Wait"
"Run for Your Life"
• The title of the album was conceived by Paul as a pun on white artists trying their hand at soul music.
• The album marked a milestone in The Beatles'

recording career, as it was the first in the transition from electrified rock 'n' roll to a more sophisticated musical and lyrical content with an accoustical emphasis.

Rude Studios
Recording studio built on Paul's Scottish farm in 1975. Denny Laine's solo album HOLLY DAYS, produced by Paul, was recorded here. The name was later changed to Spirit of Ranachan Studios.

"Rudolf the Red-Nosed Reggae"
Written by: J. Marks
Recorded by: Paul McCartney
Lead singer: None (Instrumental)
Year first released: 1979
Record label: Parlophone (Britain); Columbia (U.S.)
Single: B side of "Wonderful Christmastime"
• Although Paul was a member of Wings, he recorded and released this song and the A side of the single, "Wonderful Christmastime," under his own name.
• Reggae version of the classic Christmas song.

"Run for Your Life"
Written by: Lennon/McCartney
Recorded by: The Beatles
Lead singer: John
Year first released: 1965
Record label: Parlophone (Britain); Capitol (U.S.)
Album: RUBBER SOUL
• John has stated that in retrospect this is not one of his favorite songs.

"Run of the Mill"
Written by: George Harrison
Recorded by: George
Lead singer: George
Year first released: 1970
Record label: Apple
Album: ALL THINGS MUST PASS

Rupert the Bear
British cartoon character which McCartney Productions bought the rights to in 1970. Paul intends to produce a film based on the character.

Russell, Ethan
Photographer whose pictures appear in the LET IT BE album jacket and the accompanying booklet (not released in the U.S.) of photos and dialogue. His work is also included in the book *The Beatles Illustrated Lyrics*.

Russell, Leon
American recording artist who performed on stage with George and friends at the 1971 Concert for Bangla Desh. Russell had previously recorded his rendition of George's song "Beware of Darkness," and it was on this

number that George and Leon alternated lead vocals during the concert. Russell later worked on George's album, EXTRA TEXTURE, while George and Ringo helped out on Leon Russell's album LEON RUSSELL.

Russell, William
Liverpool playwright who authored the play *John, Paul, George, Ringo and Bert*. The Beatles unanimously deplored the production, especially Paul, who felt his character was not depicted correctly. In 1978 Paul hired Russell to write the screenplay for the Wings movie *Band On the Run*.

Rustics, The
Group on the bill with The Beatles on their 1964 British Fall Tour.

Rutles, The
Satirical group that starred in the 90-minute film spoof on The Beatles, "All You Need Is Cash." The group, comprised of Neil Innes (Ron Nasty), Eric Idle (Dirk McQuickly), Rikki Fataar (Stig O'Hara), and John Halsey (Barry Wom), portrayed characters based on The Beatles and performed original material, written by Neil Innes, based on The Beatles' music. The show aired in the U.S. on March 22, 1978, and included a cameo appearance by George.

The idea for The Rutles was conceived by Eric Idle, who first presented a film of the group performing which was shown on the TV show "Saturday Night Live."

S

Sacher Hotel
Hotel in Vienna, Austria, where John and Yoko held a press conference to promote Yoko's film, *Rape*. The conference took place on March 31, 1969, with John and Yoko fielding questions from inside a bag.

"Sad Michael"
Short story, written by John, which is included in his book *In His Own Write*. The phrase "A Hard Day's Night" appears for the first time in this work.

Sailor Sam
Character mentioned in the Wings' songs "Band on the Run" and "Helen Wheels."

"Saints, The
Recording on which The Beatles backed singer Tony Sheridan in Germany in 1961. The song was produced by Bert Kaempfert and was released as the B side of "My Bonnie." The song also appears on the albums: THE BEATLES FIRST, THE BEATLES: THE EARLY YEARS, and THE BEATLES FEATURING TONY SHERIDAN, IN THE BEGINNING.

Salisbury, Mike
Photographer/designer of the cover for the album GEORGE HARRISON.

Salisbury Plain
English site of the ancient structure Stonehenge. In May of 1965 The Beatles filmed a recording sequence here, which is included in the movie *Help!*.

"Sally G"
Written by: Paul McCartney
Recorded by: Wings
Lead singer: Paul
Year first released: 1974
Record label: Apple
Single: B side of "Junior's Farm"
· This song was written and recorded in Nashville, where Wings was spending a "working holiday" recording new material.
· It is said to have been inspired by a country singer whom Paul met during his visit to Tennessee.

Samala
Boat docked in the Virgin Islands which Paul rented to accomodate members of Wings during the recording of the album LONDON TOWN.

Sanders, E. R.
Registrar who married Paul and Linda on March 12, 1969.

Sandy Lane Beach
Area in Barbados where George and Pattie honeymooned in February 1966.

"San Ferry Anne"
Written by: Paul McCartney
Recorded by: Wings
Lead singer: Paul
Year first released: 1976
Record label: Parlophone (Britain); Capitol (U.S.)
Album: WINGS AT THE SPEED OF SOUND

"Saturday Club"
BBC radio series on which The Beatles appeared a total of ten times from 1963 to 1965.

"Save the Last Dance for Me"
Nilsson recording which was produced by John. The original Drifters' ballad is cited by Paul as the musical influence behind his composition "Hey Jude." In 1969 this song was slated by The Beatles to be included on their GET BACK album.

Saville, Jimmy
British disc jockey who appeared on the bill with The Beatles at their 1964 Christmas shows in England.

Saville Row (3)
London address where The Beatles opened their Apple Headquarters in 1968. The three-story Georgian townhouse served as home to the Apple offices until 1972, when it closed for renovation. (It was never to reopen at this location.) In January of 1969 The Beatles held their rooftop concert here; their performance appears in the movie *Let It Be*.

Saville Theatre
Theatre in London purchased by Brian Epstein in April, 1965 for the purpose of showcasing pop and rock performances. The Beatles held their press reception here after receiving their MBE medals in 1965. In 1967, the Saville was the setting for The Beatles promo film "Hello, Goodbye."

"Savoy Truffle"
Written by: George Harrison
Recorded by: The Beatles
Lead singer: George
Year first released: 1968
Record label: Apple
Album: THE BEATLES
· This song is dedicated to Eric Clapton's sweet tooth as George lectures on the evils of junk food.

"Say You Don't Mind"
Denny Laine composition which Wings performed on their 1972 and 1973 tours.

Scaduto, Anthony
Author of the book *The Beatles.*

Scaffold, The
Liverpool comedy/musical group comprised of Paul's brother, Michael McGear, Roger McGough, and John Gorman. Paul produced their hit single "Liverpool Lou" in 1974.

Scala, The
Concert hall located in Soho, London. It was here that The Beatles filmed the concert sequence for their movie *A Hard Day's Night.*

Scandinavia Hall
Concert hall in Gothenburg, Sweden, where Wings were playing on August 12, 1972, when the Swedish police busted Paul before the group could return to the stage for an encore. Paul, Linda, Denny Seiwell, and a secretary were arrested and held overnight for questioning after marijuana was discovered in a package addressed to the group which was mailed into the country. Paul called the British Consulate for help. They were all released after being fined a total of £720.

"Scared"
Written by: John Lennon
Recorded by: John
Lead singer: John
Year first released: 1974
Record label: Apple
Album: WALLS AND BRIDGES
• John bares his nervous soul in this therapeutic outburst of paranoia.

Scarfe, Gerald
British cartoonist whose papier-mâché Beatle replicas were pictured on the cover of *Time* magazine in September, 1967. Scarfe later married Paul's ex, Jane Asher.

Scene II Act II
Title of the London theatre production of John's short stories taken from his book *In His Own Write.* The play was performed for one night in December 1967.

Schaffner, Nicholas
Author of the books *The Beatles Forever* and *The Boys from Liverpool: John, Paul, George, Ringo.*

Schaper, Bob
Engineer on Ringo's BAD BOY album.

Schaumburg, Ron
Author of the book *Growing Up with The Beatles.*

Schnee, Bill
Engineer who worked on the albums RINGO and GOODNIGHT VIENNA.

Schultheiss, Tom
Author of the book *A Day in the Life.*

Schwartz, Francie
Author of the book *Body Count,* in which one chapter deals with her romance with Paul during the summer of 1968.

Scotch and Coke
"Fave" Beatle beverage during the swinging sixties.

Scott, Ken
Engineer who worked on George's album ALL THINGS MUST PASS.

Scott, Tom
Saxophone player who worked with The Beatles on many of their solo efforts. He appears on George's albums EXTRA TEXTURE, DARK HORSE, and 33⅓ (which he also helped produce). In 1974 Scott accompanied George on his North American Dark Horse Tour, in which he was a featured performer. Tom Scott has also worked with Ringo on his albums RINGO and BAD BOY, and he is featured on sax in Paul's song "Listen To What the Man Said." George plays guitar on Scott's recording "Appolonia."

SCOUSE THE MOUSE
Children's story album featuring Ringo in the title role. The album was released in December 1977, and the story was written by actor Donald Pleasance.

"Scrambled Eggs"
Working title for "Yesterday."

"Scumbag"
Instrumental track which appears on John's album SOMETIME IN NEW YORK CITY. The music was recorded live at the Fillmore East in 1971, when John and Yoko joined Frank Zappa on stage in a surprise appearance.

"Sea Dance"
Unreleased Wings song recorded during the VENUS AND MARS album sessions.

"Sea of Monsters"
George Martin composition which is heard in the movie *Yellow Submarine* and on the soundtrack album.

"Sea of Time, and Sea of Holes (Medley)"
George Martin composition which is heard in the movie *Yellow Submarine* and on the soundtrack album.

"Sea of Time, Music, Science, Monsters, Consumer Products, Nowhere, Green, Phrenology, and Holes"
The seas in which the Yellow Submarine travels on its journey from Liverpool to Pepperland in *Yellow Submarine.*

"Searchin"
Leiber and Stoller song which The Beatles performed at their audition for Decca Records in January, 1962. Paul sang lead.

Sea Saint Studios
Recording studios located in New Orleans where Paul and Wings recorded the album VENUS AND MARS in 1975. The studio was recommended to Paul by singer Paul Simon.

"Seaside Woman"
Song written by Linda McCartney in 1971. The song was performed by Wings several times in concert, but was not released by the group until 1977 under the alias Suzy and the Red Stripes. It was released in the U.S. by Epic Records (a division of Columbia Records) while Wings was still signed to Capitol Records, and distributed in a special limited edition in Britian in 1979. An animated film based on this song was released in 1979.

See, Melville
Ex-husband of Linda McCartney, and the father of her daughter, Heather.

"See Yourself"
Written by: George Harrison
Recorded by: George
Lead singer: George
Year first released: 1976
Record label: Dark Horse
Album: 33⅓

Sefton General
Hospital in Liverpool where John's son Julian was born in 1963.

Segal, Erich
Contributing screenwriter for the movie *Yellow Submarine.*

Seiwell, Denny
Original drummer for Wings from 1971 to 1974. Seiwell was an American session musician who auditioned for Paul in New York during the recording of Paul's album RAM. After working on the album, Seiwell was invited to join Paul's newly formed band, Wings. During his membership in the group, Denny Seiwell appeared on two Wings albums, WILD LIFE and RED ROSE SPEEDWAY. He is also the drummer on the recordings "Mary Had a Little Lamb"/"Little Woman Love," "Hi, Hi Hi"/"C Moon," and "Give Ireland Back to the Irish." Seiwell toured with Wings on their 1972 and 1973 British and European Tours. He left the group in 1974, after experiencing personal disagreements with the McCartneys.

Sellen, Ted
Roadie who worked on the 1975–76 Wings' World Tour.

Sellers, Peter
British comedy actor who costarred with Ringo in the movie *The Magic Christian.* In 1965 Sellers presented The Beatles with their Grammy awards on the set of their movie *Help!.* He also appeared with the group on the 1965 television special "The Music Of Lennon and McCartney." Sellers can be seen walking with George on the inner cover photo of the album DARK HORSE.

Seltaeb
U.S. agency licensed by Brian Epstein's company Nems in 1964 to oversee and collect royalties from the sale of all Beatle-related merchandise in America. The name Seltaeb is "Beatles" spelled backwards.

Semolina Pilchard
He climbed the Eiffel Tower in the song "I Am the Walrus."

SENTIMENTAL JOURNEY
Artist: Ringo
Producer: George Martin
Year first released: 1970
Record label: Apple
Tracks: 12
    "Sentimental Journey"
    "Night and Day"
    "Whispering Grass"
    "Bye Bye Blackbird"
    "I'm a Fool to Care"
    "Stardust"
    "Blue Turning Grey over You"
    "Love Is a Many Splendored Thing"
    "Dreams"
    "You Always Hurt the One You Love"
    "Have I Told You Lately That I Love You"
    "Let the Rest of the World Go By"
- On this first solo album by any of The Beatles, Ringo chose songs that "his mother should know" with hopes that the rest of the world might also appreciate this sentimental journey through the past.
- The album contains tunes arranged by many of Ringo's celebrated friends including Paul McCartney, Maurice Gibb, Quincy Jones, and Richard Perry.

"Sentimental Journey"
Written by: Brown, Homer, and Green
Recorded by: Ringo

Lead singer: Ringo
Year first released: 1970
Record label: Apple
Album: SENTIMENTAL JOURNEY
Performances: Promo film clip

Seven Queens of England
Book written by Geoffrey Trease. In 1953 Paul won this book as a Coronation Day prize from his school for the best written essay in his class.

Sextette
1978 movie starring Mae West and featuring Ringo. The film did not receive widespread distribution until 1979.

"Sexy Sadie"
Written by: Lennon/McCartney
Recorded by: The Beatles
Lead singer: John
Year first released: 1968
Record label: Apple
Album: THE BEATLES
- The Beatles parody their involvement with the guru Maharishi Mahesh Yogi in this song.

"Sgt. Pepper's Inner Groove"
Two seconds left off the U.S. SGT. PEPPER album and later released on THE BEATLES RARITIES album (U.S.) in 1980.

SGT. PEPPER'S LONELY HEARTS CLUB BAND
Artist: The Beatles
Producer: George Martin
Year first released: 1967
Record label: Parlophone (Britain); Capitol (U.S.)
Tracks: 13
      "Sgt. Pepper's Lonely Hearts Club Band"
      "With a Little Help from My Friends"
      "Lucy in the Sky with Diamonds"
      "Getting Better"
      "Fixing a Hole"
      "She's Leaving Home"
      "Being for the Benefit of Mr. Kite"
      "Within You Without You"
      "When I'm Sixty-four"
      "Lovely Rita"
      "Good Morning, Good Morning"
      "Sgt. Pepper's Lonely Hearts Club Band Reprise"
      "A Day in the Life"
- SGT. PEPPER was the first Beatles' release to be distributed worldwide in its uniform and unabridged context.
- The record took over seven hundred hours to record with a production cost of $75,000, an amount unheard of in record production costs up until that time.
- In this first "rock concept" album, The Beatles invite

their audience to tune in on the soundtrack to their imaginary show. The lavish orchestration and descriptive imagery mark a departure from The Beatles' original rock roots, as the album becomes a vehicle for the bridging of the gap between popular and classical music.
- The album became the theme of a generation as The Beatles revolutionized the rock music industry with its production.
- The record comes gift-wrapped in an elaborately designed collage of luminaries assembled on the album cover to witness The Beatles' finest achievement. The back cover proudly displays the lyrics to all of the songs. Brian Epstein protested the album's packaging, but The Beatles' concept won out.
- Originally titled DR. PEPPER'S . . . until The Beatles realized an American soft drink claimed that name.
- The album won four Grammy Awards.

Sgt. Pepper's Lonely Hearts Club Band"
Written by: Lennon/McCartney
Recorded by: The Beatles
Lead singers: John and Paul
Year first released: 1967
Record label: Parlophone (Britain); Capitol (U.S.)
Album: SGT. PEPPER'S LONELY HEARTS CLUB BAND
            THE BEATLES 1967–1970
Single: Rereleased in 1978 as a medley with "With a Little Help from My Friends"
Performances: George, Paul, and Ringo performed this song together on May 19, 1979, at the wedding reception for Eric and Pattie Clapton.
- Part of the songwriting royalties went to The Beatles' assistant, Mal Evans.

Shake
Assistant manager of The Beatles, played by John Junkin in the movie *A Hard Day's Night.*

Shambudas, Mr.
Student of Ravi Shankar who instructed George on the sitar in 1966.

Sha Na Na
Group which appeared on the bill with John and Yoko at the One to One Concert in 1972.

Shankar, Kumar
Nephew of Indian musician Ravi Shankar. Kumar worked as assistant engineer on George's albums DARK HORSE, 33⅓, and GEORGE HARRISON. He also appeared on stage on George's 1974 Dark Horse Tour.

Shankar, Ravi

Indian musician responsible for tutoring George in the foundations of Eastern music and culture.

Shankar, a master of the sitar, invited George to visit India in 1966 to begin private lessons on the sitar. The two soon became close friends, with George's reverence for his teacher inspiring him to introduce Ravi and his artistry to the Western world. Shankar was signed to Apple Records in 1971. Ravi requested that George help his homeland during its civil war and therefore George organized the charity concert for Bangla Desh. Ravi Shankar and his orchestra were among the musicians who appeared on the concert bill in 1971.

All of Shankar's recordings released on Apple and subsequently on Dark Horse were produced by George. Ravi Shankar's releases include: "Joi Bangla"/"Oh Bhavgowan," RAGA (soundtrack to the film), IN CONCERT 1972, SHANKAR FAMILY AND FRIENDS, and RAVI SHANKAR'S MUSIC FESTIVAL FROM INDIA. In 1974 Ravi Shankar and his Indian musicians were the opening act on George's North American Dark Horse Tour.

SHANKAR FAMILY AND FRIENDS

Ravi Shankar album produced by George and released on his Dark Horse label.

Shannon, Del

American singer who performed on the bill with The Beatles in 1963. He was also the first to record a Beatles composition. His cover version of "From Me to You" was released in the U.S. in 1963, prior to The Beatles' first visit to America. The song was a mild success on the charts.

Shapiro, Helen

Singer who headlined The Beatles' first tour of Britain in 1963.

SHAVED FISH

Artist: John Lennon
Producer: John, Yoko, and Phil Spector
Year first released: 1975
Record label: Apple
Tracks: 12

"Give Peace a Chance"
"Cold Turkey"
"Instant Karma"
"Power to the People"
"Mother"
"Woman Is the Nigger of the World"
"Imagine"
"Whatever Gets You through the Night"
"Mind Games"
"#9 Dream"

"Happy Xmas (War Is Over)"
"Give Peace a Chance"
· A collection of John's greatest hits.

Shaw, John

Photographer of the front cover of Paul's BACK TO THE EGG album.

Shears, Billy

Fictional character who heads Sgt. Pepper's Lonely Hearts Club Band and is portrayed by Ringo on the SGT. PEPPER album. The name comes up again when Ringo refers to himself as Billy Shears in the song "I'm the Greatest."

Shea Stadium

New York City ballpark where The Beatles performed on August 15, 1965, and on August 23, 1966. Their first appearance here drew the largest crowd that ever attended a music concert. They played to an audience of sixty thousand people, with two thousand more being turned away for lack of seating capacity. The highest priced ticket went for $5.65. The Beatles grossed $300,000 in 1965, which for that time was an unprecedented amount in concert proceeds. The concert was filmed for posterity and was considered by The Beatles to be the pinnacle of their touring career.

The *Beatles at Shea Stadium* film was aired on British television in March 1966 and in January 1967 in America. The film of The Beatles' 1966 Shea Stadium concert was never aired on American television.

Sheba

Name of the Bengal tiger who frightens Ringo in the movie *Help!*.

"She Came In through the Bathroom Window"

Written by: Lennon/McCartney
Recorded by: The Beatles
Lead singer: Paul
Year first released: 1969
Record label: Apple
Album: ABBEY ROAD
· Paul claims to have been inspired to write this song by a true experience which occurred when a fan entered his home uninvited.
· Paul's original idea was to have singer Joe Cocker record the composition, which he did following the release of The Beatles' recording.

"Sheik of Araby"

Song written by T. Snyder, F. Wheeler, and H. Smith. The Beatles performed this number at their Decca audition in 1962, with George singing lead.

"Sheila"

Tommy Roe song which The Beatles included in their repertoire at the Star Club in Germany. It appears on the U.S. version of the album THE BEATLES LIVE AT THE STAR CLUB.

"She Loves You"
Written by: Lennon/McCartney
Recorded by: The Beatles
Lead singer: John
Year first released: 1963
Record label: Parlophone (Britain); Swan and Capitol (U.S.)
Album: THE BEATLES SECOND ALBUM
     A COLLECTION OF BEATLES OLDIES
     THE BEATLES 1962–1966
     THE BEATLES AT THE HOLLYWOOD
       BOWL
     THE BEATLES RARITIES (Britain)
EP: THE BEATLES MILLION SELLERS
Single: Britain and U.S.
Performances: Royal Variety Performance, November 1963
     "Ed Sullivan Show," (TV), February 1964
     1964 February North American Tour
     1964 Summer World Tour
     "Around The Beatles" TV show, 1964
     A Hard Day's Night movie
- The Beatles' first U.S. hit.
- The catch phrase "yeah, yeah, yeah," included in the lyrics, soon became one of The Beatles' trademarks. Paul's father had suggested changing it to "yes, yes, yes," so it could maintain British dignity.

Shenson, Walter
Producer of The Beatles' movies *A Hard Day's Night* and *Help!*.

Shepherd, Billy
Author of the book *The True Story of The Beatles.* Shepherd was also a contributing writer for *The Beatles Book Monthly* magazine.

Sheridan, Tony
British singer for whom The Beatles performed as back-up band at the Top Ten club in Hamburg in 1961. The Beatles' first professional recording session occurred when they recorded with Sheridan while in Germany. "My Bonnie"/"The Saints" was released as a single and many of their other recorded songs appear on the albums THE EARLY YEARS, IN THE BEGINNING, and THE BEATLES FIRST.

In 1978, Sheridan returned to the stage at The Star Club in Hamburg, and George and Ringo both attended his opening night performance.

"She Said She Said"
Written by: Lennon/McCartney
Recorded by: The Beatles

Lead singer: John
Year first released: 1966
Record label: Parlophone (Britain); Capitol (U.S.)
Album: REVOLVER
- This song was inspired by the line "I know what it's like to be dead" which American actor Peter Fonda continuously repeated at a party John and George attended in Los Angeles.

"She's a Woman"
Written by: Lennon/McCartney
Recorded by: The Beatles
Lead singer: Paul
Year first released: 1964
Record label: Parlophone (Britain); Capitol (U.S.)
Album: BEATLES '65
     THE BEATLES AT THE HOLLYWOOD
      BOWL
     THE BEATLES RARITIES (Britain)
Single: Britain and U.S.
Performances: 1964 Christmas shows
     1965 European and North American Tours
     1965 British Winter Tour
     1966 Summer World Tour

"She's Leaving Home"
Written by: Lennon/McCartney
Recorded by: The Beatles
Lead singer: Paul
Year first released: 1967
Record label: Parlophone (Britain); Capitol (U.S.)
Album: SGT. PEPPER'S LONELY HEARTS CLUB BAND
- Paul claims to have been inspired to write this song after reading a newspaper article on teenage runaways.
- The Beatles do not play any of the instruments on this track.

"She's My Baby"
Written by: Paul McCartney
Recorded by: Wings
Lead singer: Paul
Year first released: 1976
Record label: Parlophone (Britain); Capitol (U.S.)
Album: WINGS AT THE SPEED OF SOUND

"Shimmy Shake"
Song written by Joe South and Billy Land which The Beatles sang at the Star Club in 1962 and appears on the album THE BEATLES LIVE AT THE STAR CLUB. Paul sings lead on this number.

Shipper, Mark
Author of the fictional book about The Beatles, *Paperback Writer*.

"Shirley's Wild Accordion"
Instrumental song written by The Beatles and performed by accordionist Shirley Evans in the film *Magical Mystery Tour*.

"Shot of Rhythm and Blues"
Song The Beatles performed on "Pop Go The Beatles" in June 1963.

Shotten, Pete
Original member of The Quarrymen in 1955. Shotten, The Beatles' friend since childhood, remained close with the group after they became successful. In 1965 John and George purchased a supermarket for their old classmate Pete to manage. When The Beatles opened their Apple Boutique in 1967, they appointed Shotten manager.

"Shout"
Isley Brothers song which was performed by The Beatles on their 1964 television special "Around The Beatles." Their rendition featured each Beatle alternating on lead vocals.

Showco
Dallas company which provided the sound system and lighting facilities for the 1975–76 Wings' World Tour and part of their 1979 British Tour.

Shrimpton, Stephen
Managing director of McCartney Productions Ltd.

Sia, Joseph
Photographer whose pictures appear in the SOMETIME IN NEW YORK CITY album package.

"Side by Side"
British radio series on which The Beatles performed several times.

"Sie Liebt Dich"
The Beatles' German rendition of "She Loves You," which Swan released as a single in America in 1964. Years later it appeared on THE BEATLES RARITIES album. The song was recorded in Paris in 1964.

"Silent Homecoming"
Written by: Sorrells Pickard
Recorded by: Ringo
Lead singer: Ringo
Year first released: 1970
Record label: Apple
Album: BEAUCOUPS OF BLUES

Silkie, The
Group that recorded the Lennon/McCartney composition "You've Got to Hide Your Love Away." The Beatles were present at the studio and contributed to the recording by supplying musical accompaniment and production assistance.

"Silly Love Songs"
Written by: Paul McCartney
Recorded by: Wings
Lead singer: Paul
Year first released: 1976
Record label: Parlophone (Britain); Capitol (U.S.)
Album: WINGS AT THE SPEED OF SOUND
          WINGS OVER AMERICA
          WINGS GREATEST
Single: Britain and U.S.
Performances: 1975–76 Wings' World Tour
                Promo film clip
• Paul defends his romantic writing style against the advocators of "heavy" lyrics.
• Wings' first stab at the disco sound.

Silly Willy
Character in the Wings song "Rock Show."

Silver, Charles
Business partner of The Beatles' former music publisher, Dick James. Silver and James coowned 37 percent of The Beatles' music publishing company, Northern Songs Ltd.

Silver Beatles, The
Name used by The Beatles on their first tour (of Scotland) as back-up band to singer Johnny Gentle in 1960. For the occasion, they also changed their individual names to suit their new celebrity status. The line-up went as follows: Carl (George) Harrison, Paul (McCartney) Ramon, and Stu (Sutcliffe) deStyl. John was the only one to keep his given name.

Simmons, Kathy
Model who was romantically involved with George after his separation from wife Pattie in 1974.

Simon, Carly
American singer on whose song "Night Owl" Paul and Linda sing background vocals. Ringo is the drummer on Carly's song "More and More."

Simon, Paul
American singer/composer who, in 1975, hosted the American television show, "Saturday Night Live," on which George guest starred. Together they performed two numbers, "Homeward Bound" and "Here Comes the Sun." In 1973, Paul McCartney wrote a full-page favorable review of the *Paul Simon Songbook,* and two years later Denny Laine and Wings chose to perform a Simon composition, "Richard Cory," on their world tour.

Simple Life Leisure Suits
Company that hired Ringo to sing a promotional tune for their TV commerical. The commercial was aired on Japanese television in 1977.

"Simple Love Song"
Written by: Richard Starkey and Vini Poncia
Recorded by: Ringo
Lead singer: Ringo
Year first released: 1977
Record label: Polydor (Britain); Atlantic (U.S.)
Album: RINGO THE 4TH

"Simply Love You"
Song on the McGEAR album which Paul cowrote with his brother, Mike McGear.

"Simply Shady"
Written by: George Harrison
Recorded by: George
Lead singer: George
Year first released: 1974
Record label: Apple
Album: DARK HORSE
· Autobiographical song which George wrote after he and his wife Pattie split up.

"Singalong Junk"
Written by: Paul McCartney
Recorded by: Paul
Lead singer: None (Instrumental)
Year first released: 1970
Record label: Apple
Album: McCARTNEY
· Instrumental version of "Junk."

"Singing Om"
Written by: George Harrison
Recorded by: George
Lead singer: None (Chorus)
Year first released: 1968
Record label: Apple
Album: WONDERWALL

"Single Pigeon"
Written by: Paul McCartney
Recorded by: Wings
Lead singer: Paul
Year first released: 1973
Record label: Apple
Album: RED ROSE SPEEDWAY

"Sing One for the Lord"
Song written by George Harrison and recorded by Billy Preston.

"Sisters, O Sisters"
Written by: Yoko Ono
Recorded by: John and Yoko/Plastic Ono Band with Elephant's Memory
Lead singer: Yoko
Year first released: 1972
Record label: Apple
Album: SOMETIME IN NEW YORK CITY
Single: B side of "Woman Is the Nigger of the World"
Performances: John Sinclair Benefit Concert, Ann Arbor, Mich., 1971
One to One Concert, N.Y., 1972

Sister Suzy
Character in the Wings song "Let 'Em In."

"Six O'Clock"
Written by: Paul and Linda McCartney
Recorded by: Ringo
Lead singer: Ringo
Year first released: 1973
Record label: Apple
Album: RINGO
· Paul and Linda first recorded this song and then sent the recording to Ringo. Ringo then recorded his version, incorporating Paul and Linda's voices into the final mix as background vocals.
· On the test pressing and tape versions of the RINGO album an additional verse, with Paul and Linda, is included but was edited out of the album.

Skellern, Peter
British singer on whose album HARD TIMES George performs.

"Slippin' and Slidin' "
Written by: Penniman, Bocage, Collins, and Smith
Recorded by: John
Lead singer: John
Year first released: 1975
Record label: Apple
Album: ROCK 'N' ROLL
Performances: Promo film clip
"Salute to Lew Grade" TV special, 1975
· John performed the song wearing a two-faced mask in order to symbolize his feelings about the "true" personality of the guest of honor, Sir Lew. (See Lew Grade.)
· Song was originally slated for release as a single and promo copies were sent to disc jockeys before John decided not to release it.

"Slow Down"
Written by: Larry Williams
Recorded by: The Beatles
Lead singer: John
Year first released: 1964

Record label: Parlophone (Britain); Capitol (U.S.)
Album: SOMETHING NEW
      ROCK AND ROLL MUSIC
      THE BEATLES RARITIES (Britain)
EP: LONG TALL SALLY
Single: B side of "Matchbox" in U.S.

"Smile Away"
Written by: Paul McCartney
Recorded by: Paul
Lead singer: Paul
Year first released: 1971
Record label: Apple
Album: RAM

SMILEY SMILE
Beach Boys album on which Paul coproduced one cut.

Smith, A
One of the pseudonyms Paul used as the composing credit for the song "Woman."

Smith, George
Late husband of John's Aunt Mimi, who, along with his wife, helped raise John.

Smith, Legs Larry
Member of the Bonzo Dog Doo Dah Band to whom George dedicates his song "His Name is Legs."

Smith, Mike
Producer for Decca Records who, in 1961, arranged for The Beatles to audition for the company. Despite Smith's enthusiasm, Decca rejected The Beatles.

Smith, Mimi
John's aunt who raised him after his parents left when he was three years old. Mimi acted as a loving parent whose straitlaced views often clashed with those of her rebellious nephew. Mimi's favorite saying about John's preoccupation with music throughout the years was "The guitar's alright as a hobby, John, but you'll never make a living of it." In 1965 John presented his aunt with a plaque inscribed with these words and a beautiful home in Bournemouth, England, in which to hang it.

Smith, Norman
The Beatles' recording engineer who worked at EMI recording studios from 1963 to 1968. Smith later launched his own performing career as Hurricane Smith.

Snare, Richie
Alias used by Ringo on Nilsson's album SON OF SCHMILSSON.

"Sneaking Sally through the Alley"
Written by: Allen Toussaint
Recorded by: Ringo
Lead singer: Ringo
Year first released: 1977
Record label: Polydor (Britain); Atlantic (U.S.)
Album: RINGO THE 4TH

"Snookeroo"
Written by: Elton John and Bernie Taupin
Recorded by: Ringo
Lead singer: Ringo
Year first released: 1974
Record label: Apple
Album: GOODNIGHT VIENNA
Single: B side of "No No Song"
• This song was written specifically for Ringo to record for his album.

"Snow Is Falling All the Time"
Yoko's song which she and John performed at their 1969 concert in Cambridge, England. The performance was recorded and appears on the album UNFINISHED MUSIC NO. 2: LIFE WITH THE LIONS.

Snyder, Tom
American talk show host who interviewed John, and Paul and Linda on his "Tomorrow" TV show. John guested on his show live in 1974; Paul and Linda's segment was taped via satellite from London, where they were doing their concert tour in 1979.

"Soft-Hearted Hana"
Written by: George Harrison
Recorded by: George
Lead singer: George
Year first released: 1979
Record label: Dark Horse
Album: GEORGE HARRISON
Single: B side of "Blow Away" in U.S.
• George wrote the lyrics to this song while in Hawaii.
• The name Hana was taken from a section of the Hawaiian island, Maui, where George holidayed.
• Portions of the song were recorded at a small pub in Henley, England.

"Soft Touch"
Written by: George Harrison
Recorded by: George
Lead singer: George
Year first released: 1979
Record label: Dark Horse
Album: GEORGE HARRISON
Single: B side of "Blow Away" in Britain

"So Glad to See You Here"
Written by: Paul McCartney
Recorded by: Wings

Lead singer: Paul
Year first released: 1979
Record label: Parlophone (Britain); Columbia (U.S.)
Album: BACK TO THE EGG
Performances: Promo film clip
• Guest artists on this cut include the "rockestra" crew.

"Soily"
Written by: Paul McCartney
Recorded by: Wings
Lead singer: Paul
Year first released: 1976
Record label: Parlophone (Britain); Capitol (U.S.)
Album: WINGS OVER AMERICA
Single: B side of live version of "Maybe I'm Amazed"
released in 1977
Performances: 1972 Wings Over Europe Tour
1973 Wings' British Tour
1975–76 Wings' World Tour

"Soldier of Love"
Song The Beatles performed on "Pop Go The Beatles" in July of 1963.

Solters and Roskin
United States public relations firm which represented Wings in 1976. Paul fired the agents after learning that the firm was also handling the publicity for The International Committee to Reunite The Beatles.

"Some Kind of Friendly"
Original title for the song "Don't Pass Me By."

"Some Other Guy"
Song included in The Beatles' repertoire during their early years at Liverpool's Cavern club. The Beatles were filmed performing this song for their television debut on the program "People and Places" in England in 1962.

"Some People Never Know"
Written by: Paul and Linda McCartney
Recorded by: Wings
Lead singer: Paul
Year first released: 1971
Record label: Apple
Album: WILD LIFE
Performances: 1972 Wings Over Europe Tour
• One of Paul's answers to John's "How Do You Sleep?"

"Something"
Written by: George Harrison
Recorded by: The Beatles
Lead singer: George
Year first released: 1969
Record label: Apple

Album: ABBEY ROAD
THE CONCERT FOR BANGLA DESH
LOVE SONGS
THE BEATLES 1967–1970
THE BEST OF GEORGE HARRISON
Single: Britain and U.S.
Performances: The Concert for Bangla Desh, 1971
George's 1974 North American Dark
Horse Tour
Promo film clip
• This song was the first Harrison composition to be released as the A side of a Beatles single.
• George was inspired by his wife Pattie, who appears, along with George and the other Beatle couples, in the 1969 film clip promoting the song.
• The first line of the song was taken from the James Taylor composition "Something in the Way She Moves."

SOMETHING NEW
Artist: The Beatles
Producer: George Martin
Year first released: 1964
Record label: Capitol
Tracks: 11
"I'll Cry Instead"
"Things We Said Today"
"Any Time at All"
"When I Get Home"
"Slowdown"
"Matchbox"
"Tell Me Why"
"And I Love Her"
"I'm Happy Just to Dance with You"
"If I Fell"
"Komm, Gib Mir Deine Hand"
• American album compiled from various British releases.

SOMETIME IN NEW YORK CITY
Artist: John and Yoko/Plastic Ono Band/Elephant's
Memory
Producer: John, Yoko, and Phil Spector
Year first released: 1972
Record label: Apple
Tracks: 16
"Woman Is the Nigger of the World"
"Sisters, O Sisters"
"Attica State"
"Born in a Prison"
"New York City"
"Sunday Bloody Sunday"
"Luck of the Irish"
"John Sinclair"
"Angela"
"We're All Water"

"Cold Turkey"
"Don't Worry Kyoko"
"Well . . . (Baby Please Don't Go)"
"Jam Rag"
"Scumbag"
"Au"
- John's most politically oriented musical package.
- The album's radical leanings helped to pigeonhole John as a "subversive" by the U.S. government.

Sommerville, Brian
Beatles' publicist in 1964. A disagreement with George, which resulted in a drink being thrown in Sommerville's face, precipitated his parting with the group.

"Song for John"
Yoko Ono composition which she and John performed live at Cambridge, England, in 1969. It appears on their album, UNFINISHED MUSIC NO. 2: LIFE WITH THE LIONS.

SONGS FOR A TAILOR
Jack Bruce album on which George appears.

SON OF ALWAYS
Intended title for the Wings album BAND ON THE RUN.

Son of Dracula
1974 movie produced by Ringo, starring Harry Nilsson. Ringo invested $800,000 in this rock/horror film in which he also played the role of Merlin the Magician. The movie premiered in Atlanta, Georgia and soon after was not heard of again.

The soundtrack to the film was released in 1974 and was coproduced by Ringo, Nilsson, and Richard Perry. George helped out on one cut ("Daybreak").

Son of Harry
Alias under which George plays guitar on the Dave Mason album, IT'S LIKE YOU NEVER LEFT.

SON OF SCHMILSSON
Harry Nilsson album on which George and Ringo both contribute their talents.

"So Sad"
Written by: George Harrison
Recorded by: George
Lead singer: George
Year first released: 1974
Record label: Apple
Album: DARK HORSE

Sound of One Hand Clapping, The
Documentary movie of Wings recording their album VENUS AND MARS, while visiting Nashville in 1974.

The film, directed by David Litchfield, is an MPL production and was never released commercially.

Sound Shop Studios
Recording studios located in Nashville, Tennessee. Paul and Wings worked on their album VENUS AND MARS here.

Sounds Incorporated
British band that appeared on the bill with The Beatles during their 1964 British Fall Tour, 1964 Christmas Shows, and 1965 North American Summer Tour. Their horn accompaniment is featured on The Beatles song, "Good Morning, Good Morning."

"Sound Stage of Mind"
Instrumental George performed on his Dark Horse Tour.

"Sour Milk Sea"
Song written by George and recorded by Apple artist Jackie Lomax. The record, which was produced by George, was part of the "Our First Four" package distributed by Apple.

Southern Trail
Yacht which The Beatles used while on holiday in Miami in 1964.

South Ocean Boulevard
Site of John and Yoko's million dollar Palm Beach mansion, purchased in 1979.

Spaniard in the Works, A
John's second book, published by Jonathan Cape (Britain) and Simon and Schuster (America) in 1965. The book's content is very similar in style to the works contained in John's first book, *In His Own Write*, published one year earlier.

SPARK IN THE DARK
Alpha Band album on which Ringo plays drums.

Spector, Phil
Record producer and arranger who first worked with The Beatles as a group on their album LET IT BE in 1970. Spector was called in by John to mix and arrange the finished tapes, which had been recorded and discarded by The Beatles the previous year. This decision to call in Spector caused a controversy within The Beatles ranks since it was a departure from their usual producer, George Martin. Spector's lavish orchestrations were especially not appreciated by Paul, who preferred the original and less ostentatious recordings.

Phil Spector had first worked with John when he produced "Instant Karma." It was this experience which inspired John to call Spector in to salvage the LET IT

BE tapes. Spector also produced John's songs "Happy Xmas (War Is Over)" and "Power to the People" and John's albums JOHN LENNON/PLASTIC ONO BAND, IMAGINE, and SOMETIME IN NEW YORK CITY. In 1974, John and Phil Spector cowrote a song called "Here We Go Again" while producing John's album ROCK 'N' ROLL. The song was never released. Spector worked with George on the production of the albums ALL THINGS MUST PASS and THE CONCERT FOR BANGLA DESH.

Spector, Ronnie
Former member of the 1960s group The Ronettes and ex-wife of record producer Phil Spector. Ronnie Spector was signed to Apple Records in 1971. She recorded the George Harrison composition "Try Some, Buy Some," which George also coproduced.

Speedy Prompt Delivery
Liverpool parcel delivery service which employed Paul in 1960. Loading packages on and off trucks was how Paul supplemented his income after he first returned from Hamburg with The Beatles. The job lasted approximately two weeks.

Spinetti, Victor
British actor/comedian who appeared in The Beatles movies *A Hard Day's Night* (the television director), *Help!* (the mad scientist), and *Magical Mystery Tour* (the sergeant). Spinetti also appears on The Beatles' 1967 Christmas record and also makes a brief appearance in the Wings promo film clip for "London Town." In 1968 Spinetti coauthored the theatre production based on John's book, *In His Own Write.*

"Spin It On"
Written by: Paul McCartney
Recorded by: Wings
Lead singer: Paul
Year first released: 1979
Record label: Parlophone (Britain); Columbia (U.S.)
Album: BACK TO THE EGG
Single: B side of "Getting Closer" (U.S.)
B side of "Old Siam, Sir" (Britain)
Performances: "Back to the Egg" TV special, 1979
1979 Wings' British Tour

Spinoza, Dave
Session musician who worked on Paul's RAM and John's MIND GAMES.

Spirit of Ranachan Studio
Recording studio built on Paul's farm in Scotland; formally known as Rude Studios. Wings recorded parts of BACK TO THE EGG here.

"Spirits of Ancient Egypt"
Written by: Paul McCartney
Recorded by: Wings
Lead singer: Paul and Denny Laine
Year first released: 1975
Record label: Parlophone (Britain); Capitol (U.S.)
Album: VENUS AND MARS
WINGS OVER AMERICA
Performances: 1975–76 Wings' World Tour

Splinter
First group to have a record released on George's Dark Horse record label. The two-man band, comprised of Bill Elliot and Bob Purvis, was discovered by The Beatles' assistant Mal Evans in 1973. He felt their style was appropriate for recording a song for the film George was producing at the time, *Little Malcolm and his Struggle against the Eunuchs.* When George heard Splinter, he was impressed with their sound and began working in the studio with the group. After producing the song "Lonely Man" for the film, George went on to produce their entire album, THE PLACE I LOVE. Splinter's album was released on Dark Horse in 1974 and George continued to work with the group on all their subsequent recordings released on his record label.

Splinter's Bill Elliot was a part of John's Elastic Oz Band, singing on the recording "God Save Us" in 1971.

"Spooky Weirdness"
One minute and twenty-five seconds of said title appearing on RINGO'S ROTOGRAVURE album.

Spooner, James Douglas
Receiver who was appointed by London's High Court, in 1971, to handle Apple's monies pending the outcome of the lawsuit between Paul and the other Beatles. (See Apple.)

Sport, Speed and Illustrated
Book written by John in 1947. Its contents included John's writings, drawings, and cartoons.

Stallworth, Paul
Bass guitarist who worked on George's album EXTRA TEXTURE. Stallworth was partially responsible for the album's title. The name came about during a word game in which George and Stallworth were participating.

Stamp, Justice
Judge who presided throughout the court battle between Paul, The Beatles, and Apple Corps Ltd. (See Apple.)

"Stand By Me"
Written by: Ben E. King, Jerry Leiber, and Mike Stoller
Recorded by: John

Lead singer: John
Year first released: 1975
Record label: Apple
Album: ROCK 'N' ROLL
Single: Britain and U.S.
Performances: Promo film clip

Star Band
House band of Hamburg's Star Club. In 1962, following his split from Rory Storme and The Hurricanes, Ringo became the drummer of the Star Band.

Star Club
Nightclub in Hamburg, Germany where The Beatles headlined from April through June 1962. It was during this engagement that they were notified that their recording contract with Parlophone Records had been secured.

The Beatles returned to The Star Club again in November 1962 and for the last time in December of the same year. Their final engagement was amateurishly recorded and released fifteen years later on the album THE BEATLES LIVE AT THE STAR CLUB.

"Stardust"
Written by: Hoagy Carmichael and Mitchell Parish
Recorded by: Ringo
Lead singer: Ringo
Year first released: 1970
Record label: Apple
Album: SENTIMENTAL JOURNEY
• Arrangement of this song was done by Paul.

Starkey, Jason
Second son born to Ringo and Maureen on August 19, 1967.

Starkey, Lee
Third child and only daughter of Ringo and Maureen. Lee was born on November 17, 1970.

Starkey, Maureen
Born Mary Cox on August 4, 1946; ex-wife of Ringo Starr and mother of their three children, Zak, Jason, and Lee.

Maureen grew up in Liverpool and as a teenager frequented The Cavern club to watch The Beatles perform. The first Beatle she made contact with was Paul, when she kissed him on a dare while the group was setting up for a performance. She began dating Ringo in 1962. While The Beatles were touring the world and recording in London, Maureen remained home in Liverpool, working as a hairdresser. The two kept up their long-distance romance and in 1965, Ringo and Maureen married on February 11. Maureen and Ringo, of all the Beatle couples, were the most conventional and family-oriented. They moved next door to the Lennons in Weybridge and set about raising their family. Maureen spent her leisure time sketching and embroidering. Her art works were admired and proudly displayed among friends. Maureen would faithfully answer Ringo's fan mail and attended Beatle concerts whenever possible. Her main concern was her husband and children, and she was the only Beatle wife to wait up for her husband, with dinner prepared, after he returned home from recording sessions lasting into the early morning. It was agreed by all that Ringo and "Mo" were the perfect couple, leading a contented family life. But by 1973 life had changed drastically for Ringo and Maureen. The Beatles had split up and Ringo was left to his own devices as a solo artist. Maureen stayed home with the children as Ringo set out to the U.S. to further his recording career. It was at this time that the once happy marriage began to go sour. Ringo spent most of his time pursuing his own interests in Los Angeles while six thousand miles separated him from Maureen and the kids. Maureen filed for divorce, and in July 1975 the marriage ended. Today Maureen still lives in England and is raising their three children. Ringo and Maureen have remained close friends, with Ringo just recently purchasing a new home in London for Maureen and the children.

Starkey, Richard
Born on July 7, 1940 in Dingle, Liverpool, to Richard and Elsie Starkey.

Ringo was the last member to join The Beatles. He was admitted to the group in 1962, just prior to the signing of The Beatles' first recording contract with Parlophone Records. He had previously worked as the drummer in a Liverpool group called Rory Storme and The Hurricanes, which at the time were The Beatles' key rivals. Ringo became friendly with The Beatles during their simultaneous excursions to Hamburg, Germany, where many Liverpool groups were booked in the German clubs. He sat in on drums for The Beatles on several occasions and when The Beatles decided to fire their regular drummer, Pete Best, Ringo was offered the job. Though he did enjoy playing with his friends, it was the twenty-five pound a week salary offer which was the deciding factor in accepting the position with The Beatles. Ringo debuted with The Beatles in Liverpool to a riotous reception from angry fans upset by Best's ouster from the group. It wasn't long before Ringo's charm and talent won over many more fans and proved to be a major force behind The Beatles' popularity. Though he still felt the outsider, being the last to join the group, ironically it was Ringo's name which was soon to become the household word associated with The Beatles.

Ringo (Richie), an only child, was three years old when his parents divorced. He grew up in Liverpool's toughest section, spending most of his childhood in and out of

The birth certificate of Richard Starkey.

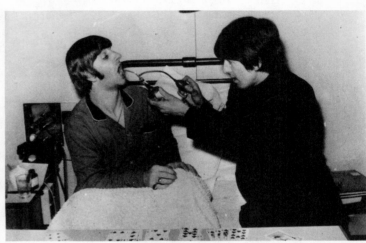

Dr. George attending to Ringo during his hospital stay for a tonsilectomy, December, 1964. (*Keystone Press Agency*)

BX 524341

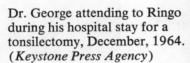

Ringo at home with son, Jason, 1967. (*Henry Grossman/Transworld*)

Maureen, Zak, and Ringo, 1967.
(*Henry Grossman/Transworld*)

Ringo, 1976. (*Atlantic Records*)

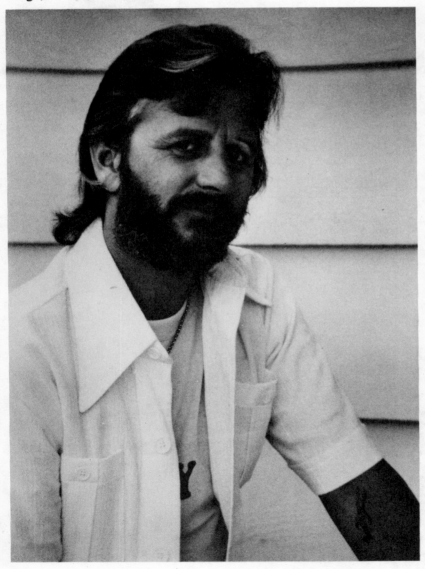

Ringo and date, daughter, Lee,
at Los Angeles party, 1977.
(*Transworld Features Syndicate*)

(*Goldie Friede*)

Ringo strolls with Nancy Andrews,
New York, 1977. (*Vinnie Zuffante*)

Ringo at promotional party for
BAD BOY, New York, April 1978.
(*Robin Titone*)

Arriving at Kennedy Airport,
July 1979. (*Robin Titone*)

hospitals with various illnesses. During one of his hospital stays Ringo became interested in drumming and formed his first band, with some children in the ward. This started Ringo's preoccupation with the drums and, until his parents bought him a drum set at fourteen, he'd improvise on tin cans and pieces of wood.

Ringo's mother married Harry Graves in 1953. Mr. Graves helped Ringo with his musical ambitions by giving him moral support and booking his bands into local clubs and lodge meetings. By age fifteen, Ringo left school and supported himself by taking drumming jobs with various groups. He soon became a full-time drummer with the Liverpool rock band Rory Storme and The Hurricanes. He grew a mustache and beard and soon was reputed for his off-beat style, in manner as well as drumming technique. It wasn't long before The Beatles, too, became aware of Ringo Starr and offered him membership in the group.

In 1965, Ringo married his eighteen-year-old Liverpool sweetheart, Maureen Cox, and they later became parents of three children: Zak, Jason, and Lee. Ringo thrived on married life and made no secret of the fact that his life centered around his family.

As Ringo's basic drumbeat formed the solid backbone of The Beatles music, his easygoing disposition provided the necessary balance in blending The Beatles' personalities into a cohesive unit. His warmth and good nature was the essence of The Beatles' public image, and was emphasized in The Beatles' two motion pictures in which Ringo "starred."

Stemming from his new-found acting talent, Ringo went on to appear in various movies after the group stopped performing together. During this post-Beatle period, Ringo recorded several solo albums, experimenting in country-western and big band sounds. Though the breakup of The Beatles and their close friendship hurt Ringo personally, he refused to let it hurt his professional life. His greatest musical acclaim came in 1973 when he recorded the album RINGO. The record consisted of songs which perfectly suited Ringo's singing style, with contributions by some of the music industry's greatest artists, including Paul, John, and George. In 1975, Ringo and Maureen divorced. He left his residence in England and today Ringo commutes between homes in the U.S. and Monte Carlo. Ringo continues to record and in 1978 his musical-comedy talents were displayed on the NBC television special "Ringo." In 1979, much of Ringo's Beatle collection and personal possessions were destroyed in a fire at his rented home in Los Angeles.

Starkey, Richard
Father of Ringo Starr. Mr. and Mrs. Starkey divorced in 1943 when Ringo was three years old.

Starkey, Zak
First child born to Ringo and Maureen on September 13, 1965.

Starlett, Wendy
Character in the movie *Magical Mystery Tour.*

Starr, Ringo
Stage name adopted by Richard Starkey due to his great affection for American Western culture and his passion for wearing many rings. (See Richard Starkey.)

Steckler, Al
Production coordinator of the albums IMAGINE, SOMETIME IN NEW YORK CITY, and THE CONCERT FOR BANGLA DESH.

"Steel and Glass"
Written by: John Lennon
Recorded by: John
Lead singer: John
Year first released: 1974
Record label: Apple
Album: WALLS AND BRIDGES
• For this song John uses a variation of the same music he used in his song about Paul ("How Do You Sleep?"). The new lyrics were directed at Allen Klein.

Steele, Tommy
British performer who appeared on the bill with The Beatles for the Royal Variety Show on November 4, 1963.

"Step Inside Love"
Theme song for the "Cilla" (Black) British television program. The song was written by John and Paul in 1968, specifically for the program, and recorded by Cilla Black. Paul plays guitar on the recording and can be seen in the song's promotional film clip.

"Step Lightly"
Written by: Richard Starkey
Recorded by: Ringo
Lead singer: Ringo
Year first released: 1973
Record label: Apple
Album: RINGO
Single: B side of "Oh My My"

Steve Miller Band
Group whose song "My Dark Hour" features Paul on drums, bass guitar, and background vocals under the alias Paul Ramon.

Stevens, Andy
Engineer who worked on the album JOHN LENNON/PLASTIC ONO BAND.

205

Stevens, Joe
Photographer employed by Paul to photograph the 1972 Wings' European tour.

Stewart, Jackie
Race car driver and sports commentator whose book *Faster* inspired the title of George's song of the same name. Besides being George's close friend, Stewart began instructing George in the art of racing in 1979.

Stewart, Rod
Rock artist for whom Paul composed the song "Mine for Me" to record. In November 1974, Paul and Linda joined Stewart and the Faces on stage at the Lewisham Odeon in England to sing the song.

Stewart also recorded the McCartney composition "Maybe I'm Amazed."

Stigwood, Robert
Entrepreneur and president of the Robert Stigwood Organization (RSO). In 1966, Stigwood was hired by Brian Epstein to scout out new talent for his company, Nems Enterprises. After Epstein's death in 1967, Stigwood left Nems' management agency, with his discoveries the Bee Gees and Eric Clapton, to form his own organization. Stigwood was also responsible for bringing the play *John, Paul, George, Ringo and Bert* to the London stage in 1975 and the movie *Sgt. Pepper's Lonely Hearts Club Band* to the screen in 1978.

Stills, Stephen
Musician/composer who in 1969 cowrote two songs with George, Ringo, and Doris Troy: "Gonna Get My Baby Back" and "You Give Me Joy Joy." The songs appear on the album DORIS TROY, released on Apple Records. In 1971 Ringo played drums on the Stephen Stills album STILLS.

St. John's Wood Church
Church in London where Paul and Linda had their marriage blessed following their wedding on March 12, 1969.

Stockton Wood Road Primary
School located in the Speke section of Liverpool which was the first school Paul attended.

Storme, Rory (and The Hurricanes)
Early 1960s Liverpool group in which Ringo played drums. Rory Storme and his group were at the time more popular than The Beatles. The Hurricanes were playing on the same bill as The Beatles when Ringo and The Beatles started jamming together at the Kaiserkeller club in Hamburg, Germany. In 1972, Rory Storme, along with his mother, died in a bizarre double suicide.

St. Pauli
District of Hamburg, Germany, where The Beatles lived during their stay in 1961.

St. Peter's Choir
Liverpool church choir in which John sang as a child.

STRAIGHT UP
Badfinger album which George helped produce.

Stramsact
British agency licensed and approved by Nems, in 1964, to regulate the sales of Beatle merchandise and issue licenses to various British manufacturers. Stramsact paid royalties to Nems on all transactions.

"Strawberry Fields Forever"
Written by: Lennon/McCartney
Recorded by: The Beatles
Lead singer: John
Year first released: 1967
Record label: Parlophone (Britain); Capitol (U.S.)
Album: MAGICAL MYSTERY TOUR
            THE BEATLES 1967–1970
Single: B side of "Penny Lane"
· John took the title for this song from a girls' school in Liverpool.
· Two versions of this song were recorded, and the final product was a combination of the two.
· The strange hypnotic, hallucinogenic theme makes use of backward tape loops and numerous overdubs to gain the dreamlike effect.
· John claims "Strawberry Fields Forever" is one of his most personal statements.

Strawberry Studios
Studio in Stockport, England, where Paul produced his brother's album, McGEAR.

St. Silas Primary
Liverpool school which was the first school Ringo attended.

Suba Films
Company formed through Nems in 1964 to handle The Beatles' percentage profits on all their movie productions.

"Sue Me, Sue You Blues"
Written by: George Harrison
Recorded by: George
Lead singer: George
Year first released: 1973
Record label: Apple
Album: LIVING IN THE MATERIAL WORLD
Performances: 1974 Dark Horse Tour

- This song was written during and about the legal hassles between The Beatles.
- Jesse Ed Davis recorded and released this composition one year prior to George's release.

"Suicide"
Unfinished composition which Paul claims to have started writing at the age of fifteen. It appears as part of an instrumental on the McCARTNEY album.

Sullivan, Ed
Late American newspaper columnist and television host. Sullivan was the first to present The Beatles "live" to the U.S. via his nationally broadcast television program in 1964.

It was in London, in 1963, that Sullivan first became aware of The Beatles' popularity in Europe. In November he signed a contract for The Beatles to appear on his show for three performances at a price of approximately ten thousand dollars.

On February 9, 1964, live from New York, The Beatles first appeared on the "Ed Sullivan Show." Seventy-three million people across the country tuned in that night to witness the new phenomenon called The Beatles. It was reported that during the hour in which the show was aired the country experienced the lowest crime rate, among teenagers, of the decade. The second segment was performed from Miami, Florida, on February 16 and the third taped performance was aired on February 23, 1964. Through the years, promo film clips of Beatle songs have appeared on his show.

In 1965, Ed Sullivan hosted The Beatles once again. This time he introduced the group to over fifty-five thousand people gathered for The Beatles' concert at Shea Stadium in New York City.

"Summertime"
One of the first songs recorded by The Beatles while working as a back-up band in Germany.

"Sunday Blood Sunday"
Written by: John Lennon and Yoko Ono
Recorded by: John and Yoko
Lead singer: John
Year first released: 1972
Record label: Apple
Album: SOMETIME IN NEW YORK CITY
- This song was written in protest of the "Bloody Sunday" massacre which occurred in Ireland on January 3, 1972.

Sundown Playboys
Short-lived group signed to Apple Records in 1972. While with the label, the Sundown Playboys released the record "Saturday Night Special."

Sunny Heights
Name of the Weybridge home where Ringo and his family lived from 1965 to 1968. He purchased the house for £35,000.

"Sun King"
Written by: Lennon/McCartney
Recorded by: The Beatles
Lead singer: John, Paul, and George
Year first released: 1969
Record label: Apple
Album: ABBEY ROAD
- The Beatles combine languages and dialects in this romantic-sounding nonsense song.

Sunset Sound
Los Angeles recording studio in which Ringo recorded portions of his RINGO album.

"Sunshine Life for Me (Sail away Raymond)"
Written by: George Harrison
Recorded by: Ringo
Lead singer: Ringo
Year first released: 1973
Record label: Apple
Album: RINGO

"Sure to Fall"
Song performed by The Beatles during their early acts circa 1962.

"Surprise, Surprise (Sweet Bird of Paradox)"
Written by: John Lennon
Recorded by: John
Lead singer: John
Year first released: 1974
Record label: Apple
Album: WALLS AND BRIDGES
- In the title, Paradox refers to a restaurant (of the same name) which Yoko worked in while living in Greenwich Village during the sixties.

Surrey
London suburb where John, George, and Ringo plus respective families set up housekeeping during the middle to late sixties.

Sutcliffe, Stuart
Original member of The Beatles, who died on April 10, 1962, just prior to the group's success.

Stu first met John while they were both attending the Liverpool College of Art. The young artist, with the complex intellect, soon gained John's respect and they became fast friends. Though Stu's artistic talents at the school were unparalleled, John persuaded him to pursue a musical career by joining his rock 'n' roll band. It was

Stu who suggested the name "The Beetles" as a takeoff on Buddy Holly's Crickets, and—when John changed the spelling—the group became The Beatles.

In 1960, The Beatles, with Stu on bass guitar, visited Germany to perform in Hamburg. The following year, Stu fell in love with a German girl, Astrid Kirschner, and decided to remain in Germany to continue his art studies when The Beatles returned to England. Stu's friendship with The Beatles remained strong, as they corresponded and always visited whenever in Germany.

At the age of twenty-one Stu developed a brain tumor and died. His death was a great shock to The Beatles, especially to John, who had looked up to Stu and loved him like a brother. Up until Stu's death, John was still planning for Stu to rejoin The Beatles. Today Stuart Sutcliffe's paintings are displayed in art galleries throughout England.

Sutton, Margret
Author of the children's book, *We Love You, Beatles.*

Suzy and the Red Stripes
Alias for Linda McCartney and Wings on the record "Seaside Woman." The pseudonym was thought up while on a Jamaican holiday, where Linda was nick-named Suzy by the local natives. "Red Stripe" was taken from her favorite brand of beer.

"Suzy Parker"
Improvised song which The Beatles performed in the movie *Let It Be.*

Swan Records
American record company which released "She Loves You" in the U.S. in 1963. Swan was given the contract after Vee Jay Records (The Beatles' first U.S. distributor) decided to stop distribution.

Swanson, Gloria
American actress who testified, in 1976, on John's behalf during his U.S. immigration hearings.

SWAT
Anti-Beatles organization formed in 1964. "Students to Wipe Away Trash" picketed New York's Carnegie Hall when The Beatles performed there.

"Sweet Georgia Brown"
Song recorded by Tony Sheridan and The Beatles in Germany in 1961. It appears on the recordings YA YA, THE BEATLES FIRST, THE EARLY YEARS, IN THE BEGINNING, and was also released as a single.

"Sweet Little Sixteen"
Written by: Chuck Berry
Recorded by: John
Lead singer: John
Year first released: 1975
Record label: Apple
Album: ROCK 'N' ROLL
       THE BEATLES LIVE AT THE STAR
       CLUB
• This song was a favorite in the Beatles' early performing repertoire.

Swenson, John
Author of the book *The Beatles Yesterday and Today.*

Swiss Cottage
Steak house located in London where, in 1962, The Beatles and producer George Martin celebrated the completion of their first recording "Love Me Do."

Sybilla's
London discotheque co-owned by George in 1966. The club was named in honor of Sybil Burton, who had, two years earlier, dubbed her New York disco Arthur, the name George called his hair in *A Hard Day's Night.* All of The Beatles attended the club's opening on June 27, 1966.

Sydell, Ira
Head of security for The Beatles' American tours.

T

"Tabla and Pakavaj/In the Park"
Written by: George Harrison
Recorded by: George
Lead singer: None (Instrumental)
Year first released: 1968
Record label: Apple
Album: WONDERWALL

Taj Mahal Hotel
Hotel where George and Pattie stayed during their visit to India in the fall of 1966. They were forced to leave the hotel after a short stay due to the crowds of fans who discovered their location and began camping outside.

"Take Good Care of My Baby"
Song The Beatles performed at their Decca Records audition in 1962.

Talent for Loving, A
Movie script which was tentatively planned for The Beatles' third feature film in 1965. After serious consideration, this comedy-western script was rejected.

"Talent Spot, The"
BBC radio program which was the first to present The Beatles' performances from London in 1962.

Talk of the Town
London nightclub where Ringo filmed his "Sentimental Journey" promo film clip in March of 1970.

"Tandoori Chicken"
Song cowritten by George and Phil Spector which was recorded by Ronnie Spector.

"Tango All Night"
Written by: Steve Hague and Tom Seufert
Recorded by: Ringo
Lead singer: Ringo
Year first released: 1977
Record label: Polydor (Britain); Atlantic (U.S.)
Album: RINGO THE 4TH

Tarrant County Convention Center
Location of the first Wings concert in America, in Fort Worth, Texas. This May 3, 1976, engagement began Wings' two month tour of the United States.

"Taste of Honey, A"
Written by: Rich Marlow and Bobby Scott
Recorded by: The Beatles
Lead singer: Paul
Year first released: 1963

Record label: Parlophone (Britain); Vee Jay and Capitol (U.S.)
Album: PLEASE PLEASE ME
INTRODUCING THE BEATLES
THE EARLY BEATLES
THE BEATLES LIVE AT THE STAR
CLUB
EP: TWIST AND SHOUT
THE BEATLES
• One of the songs The Beatles performed in their early days, which they also recorded for an album.
• Their live version, which appears on THE BEATLES LIVE AT THE STAR CLUB, makes it possible for the public to witness how similar the studio version is to their early rendition.

Taverner, John
Classical music composer and conductor who was signed to Apple Records in 1970. His Apple releases included THE WHALE and CELTIC REQUIEM.

Tavern on the Green
Restaurant located in New York's Central Park. It was here that John and Yoko held a celebration in honor of Yoko's performance at Lincoln Center in 1972. In August, John and Yoko celebrated their One to One performance at the Tavern.

In 1978 and 1979 the Lennons gave their son Sean a birthday party here.

"Taxman"
Written by: George Harrison
Recorded by: The Beatles
Lead singer: George
Year first released: 1966
Record label: Parlophone (Britain); Capitol (U.S.)
Album: REVOLVER
ROCK AND ROLL MUSIC
THE BEST OF GEORGE HARRISON
• Paul plays lead guitar on this song.

Taylor, Alistair
Onetime assistant to Brian Epstein and employee of Nems Enterprises. Taylor was a witness at the signing of the contract between The Beatles and Brian in 1961. He was later employed by The Beatles as office manager of Apple Corps Ltd. but left the company in 1969.

Taylor, Alvin
Drummer who worked on George's 33⅓ album.

Taylor, Derek
Former personal assistant to Brian Epstein and press agent for The Beatles.

In 1964, while employed by the British newspaper, *The Daily Express,* Taylor was assigned to cover The Beatles on their concert engagement in Paris. There he transcribed George's personal experiences for the newspaper. Derek was soon hired by Brian to help write his speeches and work as The Beatles' press officer. He also helped Brian write his autobiography *A Cellarful of Noise.*

It was while The Beatles were touring America for the second time, in 1964, that Derek and Brian had a disagreement which led to Derek's resignation.

Taylor again became involved with The Beatles in 1967 when he was appointed head press officer for Apple Corps Ltd. Ironically, he was fired by Allen Klein in 1970 only a year after he recommended Klein for the position of manager of The Beatles.

In 1973, Taylor authored the book, *As Time Goes By,* an account of his work prior, during, and after his association with The Beatles.

At present, Derek Taylor is employed by Warner Bros. Records and assisted George in the writing of his autobiography, *I Me Mine.*

Taylor, James
One of the first discoveries signed to Apple Records in 1968. Taylor recorded one album for the label (JAMES TAYLOR) before leaving the company along with his mentor Peter Asher because he felt Apple had neglected his career in favor of The Beatles' dealings. He was eventually sued by Apple for $5 million for breach of contract, an action which Paul later stated he regretted taking.

Paul contributes background vocals to Taylor's albums JAMES TAYLOR and WALKING MAN.

Taylor, Ted (Kingsize)
Liverpool singer who taped a Beatles' performance at the Star Club in Germany in 1962. Taylor offered Brian Epstein the tapes for sale but Brian rejected them due to the poor quality. In 1977 these tapes reappeared on the album THE BEATLES LIVE AT THE STAR CLUB.

Teachers' Training College
Transcendental Meditation Institute located in Bangor, Wales, where, on August 26, 1967, The Beatles were initiated into the meditation program. It was while visiting here that they were informed of the death of Brian Epstein.

"Teddy Boy"
Written by: Paul McCartney
Recorded by: Paul
Lead singer: Paul
Year first released: 1970
Record label: Apple
Album: McCARTNEY
• The Beatles recorded this song intended for LET IT BE.

Tee, Richard
Musician who plays keyboards on George's album 33⅓.

"Tell Me If You Can"
Unreleased song written by Tony Sheridan and Paul.

"Tell Me What You See"
Written by: Lennon/McCartney
Recorded by: The Beatles
Lead singer: John and Paul
Year first released: 1965
Record label: Parlophone (Britain); Capitol (U.S.)
Album: HELP! (Britain)
       BEATLES VI
       LOVE SONGS

"Tell Me Why"
Written by: Lennon/McCartney
Recorded by: The Beatles
Lead singer: John
Year first released: 1964
Record label: Parlophone (Britain); United Artists and Capitol (U.S.)
Album: A HARD DAY'S NIGHT
       SOMETHING NEW
EP: EXTRACTS FROM THE FILM A HARD DAY'S NIGHT
Performances: In the film *A Hard Day's Night*

"Tell the Truth"
A Derek and the Dominoes song on which George plays guitar.

"Ten Years after on Strawberry Jam"
Song written by Paul and Linda and recorded by The Scaffold. Paul produced this song.

Terry-Gore, Reverend Noel
Reverend who blessed Paul and Linda's marriage on March 12, 1969.

Terry Young Six
Group that appeared on the bill with The Beatles for their 1963 British tour.

Tetragrammation
American company which distributed John and Yoko's album UNFINISHED MUSIC NO. 1: TWO VIRGINS after Capitol turned it down.

"Thanks for the Pepperoni"
Instrumental jam which appears on George's ALL THINGS MUST PASS album.

"Thank You Girl"
Written by: Lennon/McCartney
Recorded by: The Beatles

Lead singer: John
Year first released: 1963
Record label: Parlophone (Britain); Vee Jay and Capitol (U.S.)
Album: JOLLY WHAT!
          THE BEATLES AND FRANK IFIELD
             ON STAGE
          THE BEATLES SECOND ALBUM
          THE BEATLES RARITIES (Britain)
EP: THE BEATLES HITS
Single: B side of "From Me to You"
B side of "Do You Want to Know a Secret"(U.S.)

"Thank Your Lucky Stars"
British television show which in January 1963 was responsible for giving The Beatles national exposure for the first time. Their appearance was arranged by The Beatles' music publisher Dick James.

"That Is All"
Written by: George Harrison
Recorded by: George
Lead singer: George
Year first released: 1973
Record label: Apple
Album: LIVING IN THE MATERIAL WORLD

"That'll Be the Day"
Buddy Holly song, which was the first tune John learned to play on his guitar.

That'll Be the Day
Movie featuring Ringo Starr, David Essex, and Keith Moon. This 1973 film was written by Ray Connally; directed by Claude Whatham; and produced by David Puttnam and Sanford Lieberson.

"That Means a Lot"
P.J. Proby song written by Lennon/McCartney.

"That's Alright Mama"
Song The Beatles performed on the "Pop Go The Beatles" radio series in 1963.

"That's a Nice Hat-Cap"
Original title for the song "It's Only Love." When George Martin and his orchestra recorded the song they used this title.

"That's My Life (My Love and My Home)"
Song written and recorded by John's father, Freddie Lennon. The record was released in 1965.

THAT'S THE WAY GOD PLANNED IT
Billy Preston album and song which was produced by George. The song of the same name was performed by Preston at The Concert for Bangla Desh and appears on the concert album.

THAT WAS ONLY YESTERDAY
Gary Wright album on which George plays guitar.

"That Would Be Something"
Written by: Paul McCartney
Recorded by: Paul
Lead singer: Paul
Year first released: 1970
Record label: Apple
Album: McCARTNEY

Theatre Three Productions
Agency which handled the promotion for The Beatles' Carnegie Hall concerts in February 1964.

"There's a Place"
Written by: Lennon/McCartney
Recorded by: The Beatles
Lead singer: John
Year first released: 1963
Record label: Parlophone (Britain); Vee Jay and Capitol (U.S.)
Album: PLEASE PLEASE ME
          INTRODUCING THE BEATLES
          THE BEATLES RARITIES (U.S.)
EP: TWIST AND SHOUT
Single: B side of "Twist and Shout" in the U.S.

"Things We Said Today"
Written by: Lennon/McCartney
Recorded by: The Beatles
Lead singer: Paul
Year first released: 1964
Record label: Parlophone (Britain); Capitol (U.S.)
Album: A HARD DAY'S NIGHT (Britain)
          SOMETHING NEW
          THE BEATLES AT THE HOLLYWOOD
             BOWL
EP: EXTRACTS FROM THE ALBUM A HARD
          DAY'S NIGHT
Single: B side of "A Hard Day's Night" in Britain
Performances: 1964 North American Tour
• This song was written by Paul while he was vacationing with Jane Asher, Ringo, and Maureen in the Bahamas in 1964.

"Thingumybob"
Lennon/McCartney instrumental recorded by the Black Dyke Mills Band in 1968 and produced by Paul.

"Think for Yourself"
Written by: George Harrison
Recorded by: The Beatles
Lead singer: George
Year first released: 1965
Record label: Parlophone (Britain); Capitol (U.S.)

211

Album: RUBBER SOUL
      THE BEST OF GEORGE HARRISON
- Paul uses a fuzz bass on this number.

"Thinking of Linking"
Unreleased Beatles song recorded in 1962.

"Think It Over"
Buddy Holly song which Johnny and the Moondogs performed on the Caroll Levis television show "Discoveries" in 1959.

THIRTY THREE AND ⅓
Artist: George Harrison
Producer: George Harrison (assisted by Tom Scott)
Year first released: 1976
Record label: Dark Horse
Tracks: 10
    "Woman Don't You Cry For Me"
    "Dear One"
    "Beautiful Girl"
    "This Song"
    "See Yourself"
    "It's What You Value"
    "True Love"
    "Pure Smokey"
    "Crackerbox Palace"
    "Learning How to Love You"
- George's first album to be released on his own record label.
- The album's title is a pun on the record' playing speed and George's age while recording the album.

"This Be Called a Song"
Written by: Eric Clapton
Recorded by: Ringo
Lead singer: Ringo
Year first released: 1976
Record label: Polydor (Britain); Atlantic (U.S.)
Album: RINGO'S ROTOGRAVURE

"This Boy"
Written by: Lennon/McCartney
Recorded by: The Beatles
Lead singer: John
Year first released: 1964
Record label: Parlophone (Britain); Capitol (U.S.)
Album: MEET THE BEATLES
    A HARD DAY'S NIGHT (instrumental version) (U.S.)
    LOVE SONGS
    THE BEATLES RARITIES (Britain)
EP: FOUR BY THE BEATLES
Single: B side of "I Want to Hold Your Hand" (Britain)
Performances: "Sunday Night at the London Palladium," October 1963

"Ed Sullivan Show" (TV), February 1964
1964 Winter American Tour

"This Guitar (Can't Keep From Crying)"
Written by: George Harrison
Recorded by: George
Lead singer: George
Year first released: 1975
Record label: Apple
Album: EXTRA TEXTURE
Single: Britain and U.S.
- George's sequel to his "While My Guitar Gently Weeps."
- The song was written while George was on holiday in Hawaii.

"This Song"
Written by: George Harrison
Recorded by: George
Lead singer: George
Year first released: 1976
Record label: Dark Horse
Album: 33⅓
Single: Britain and U.S.
Performances: Promo film clip
- This song parodies the plagiarism suit by Bright Tunes Music brought against George for "stealing" the tune for "My Sweet Lord" from an early sixties song "He's So Fine."
- The promo film clip for "This Song" depicts a mock trial, with George handling his own defense.

Thomas, Chris
Onetime assistant engineer to George Martin. Thomas worked with The Beatles on their album THE BEATLES. In 1979 he coproduced the Wings album BACK TO THE EGG and the single "Daytime Nighttime Suffering."

Thomas, Guthrie
Recording artist whose album LIES AND ALIBIS features Ringo on a few cuts.

Thompson, Jay
Author whose book *I Am Also a You* includes an introduction written by John.

Thorne, Ken
Composer of the musical score for the Beatles movie *Help!*. His compositions are included on the American HELP! soundtrack album.

Thorton, Fradkin, and Unger
Group whose song "God Bless California" features Paul on bass guitar and background vocals. In 1977, Leslie Fradkin became part of the original cast of the Broadway production, *Beatlemania,* portraying George.

THOSE WERE THE DAYS
Mary Hopkin's album which Paul helped produce, and the title of her first single released on the Apple label. The single was a huge success for the newly established record company and for The Beatles' protégée, Mary Hopkin.

"Three Cool Cats"
One of the songs The Beatles sang at their 1962 Decca audition. George sings lead.

365 Days of Sean
Title of a book which John and Yoko planned to publish in 1976. It was to consist of photos of their son Sean taken every day of the first year of his life.

"3 Legs"
Written by: Paul McCartney
Recorded by: Paul
Lead singer: Paul
Year first released: 1971
Record label: Apple
Album: RAM
· The other Beatles felt this song was a snide commentary about them.

Thrillington, Percy
Recording artist whose album was released by MPL Productions. The record, an instrumental version of the RAM album, contains a brief bio of Mr. Thrillington claiming that he was an Irish bandleader. Many people have speculated that Thrillington might be a pseudonym for McCartney, since Thrillington was and is unknown in the industry.

"Thumbin' a Ride"
Song recorded by Apple artist Jackie Lomax and produced by Paul.

Thurmond, Strom
South Carolina Republican Senator who, in 1972, sent a message to United States Attorney General John Mitchell accusing John Lennon of subversive politics Concerning the United States government. Thurmond had been misinformed about John's plans to attend a massive peace demonstration at the 1972 Republican convention and was prompted to take action against him. It was this government intervention that put pressure on the United States Immigration and Naturalization Service to deport John.

"Ticket to Ride"
Written by: Lennon/McCartney
Recorded by: The Beatles
Lead singer: John
Year first released: 1965

Record label: Parlophone (Britain); Capitol (U.S.)
Album: HELP!
A COLLECTION OF BEATLES OLDIES
THE BEATLES 1962–1966
THE BEATLES AT THE HOLLYWOOD BOWL
Single: Britain and U.S.
Performances: 1965 European Summer Tour
1965 North American Summer Tour
"Ed Sullivan Show" (TV), September 1965
1965 British Winter Tour
Soundtrack of *Help!* film
· One of John's personal favorites.
· Paul plays lead guitar on this song.

"Tight A$"
Written by: John Lennon
Recorded by: John
Lead singer: John
Year first released: 1973
Record label: Apple
Album: MIND GAMES

"Till There Was You"
Written by: Meredith Wilson
Recorded by: The Beatles
Lead singer: Paul
Year first released: 1963
Record label: Parlophone (Britain); Capitol (U.S.)
Album: WITH THE BEATLES
MEET THE BEATLES
THE BEATLES LIVE AT THE STAR CLUB (U.S.)
Performances: 1962 Decca Records audition
Royal Variety Performance, November 1963
"Ed Sullivan Show" (TV), February 1964
1964 American Winter Tour
"Big Night Out" TV show, 1964
· This song was included in The Beatles' early repertoire in England and Germany. Paul's admiration of Peggy Lee's recording inspired him to include it in The Beatles' act.

"Time to Hide"
Written by: Denny Laine
Recorded by: Wings
Lead singer: Denny
Year first released: 1976
Record label: Parlophone (Britain); Capitol (U.S.)
Album: WINGS AT THE SPEED OF SOUND
WINGS OVER AMERICA
Performances: 1975–76 Wings' World Tour

TIN MAN WAS A DREAMER, THE
Nicky Hopkins album which features George on guitar.

Tiny Tim
American singer who made a guest apperance on The Beatles 1968 Christmas record singing his own rendition of "Nowhere Man." In the summer of 1968 Apple sponsored its first concert, The Beatles Present Tiny Tim, which took place at London's Albert Hall.

"Tip of My Tongue"
Song written by John and Paul and recorded by Tommy Quickly in 1963.

"Tired of Midnight Blue"
Written by: George Harrison
Recorded by: George
Lead singer: George
Year first released: 1975
Record label: Apple
Album: EXTRA TEXTURE
- This song was originally titled "Midnight Blue" until George learned about Melissa Manchester's hit song of the same name.

Titanium Man
Comic book character who became the subject of Paul's song, "Magneto and Titanium Man."

Titelman, Russ
Coproducer (along with George) of the GEORGE HARRISON album.

Titone, Robin
Coauthor of the book *The Beatles A to Z*.

Tittenhurst Park
Eighteenth century Georgian mansion, located in Ascot, England, which John purchased in May 1969 for £150,-000. In August of 1969, John and Yoko moved into the estate, which included in its seventy acres, four cottages and a heated swimming pool. The mansion, which was John and Yoko's home prior to their residency in New York, also served as Ringo's home for a short period in 1973.

"Together"
Track on John and Yoko's UNFINISHED MUSIC NO. 1: TWO VIRGINS album.

"To Know Her Is to Love Her"
Song written by Phil Spector which The Beatles included in their stage acts in England and Germany in the early sixties. It was one of the numbers they chose to record at their audition for Decca Records in 1962. The song also appears on the album THE BEATLES LIVE AT THE STAR CLUB.

Tokyo Metropolitan Police Office
Jailhouse in Japan which Paul was taken to and held in custody for nine days after his arrest at Narita Airport, Japan, on January 16, 1980. The arrest took place after authorities found 7.7 ounces of marijuana in Paul's possession upon arrival in the country for an 11-day concert tour with Wings. Paul was taken to the Police Office in handcuffs and placed in a small cell with only the barest necessities at his disposal. Even a request for a guitar was denied as he spent his days reading and waiting. He was held without bail while Japanese officials pondered whether to press charges, with the knowledge that a possible conviction would carry with it a prison sentence of up to eight years.

On January 25, Paul was released and ordered to leave Japan. The release was obtained on the grounds that Paul was an illegal alien since his visa had been taken from him at the airport. He could therefore be deported and a solution to the sticky situation could be appreciated on all sides.

Paul was still accountable for the losses suffered by the concert promoters and ticket holders, which amounted to millions of dollars, since Paul's tour insurance had expired just prior to the Japan trip.

TOMMY
Rock opera written by Peter Townshend and recorded by the Who. In 1972 the TOMMY score was recorded by the London Symphony Orchestra and Chamber Choir with guest vocalists. Ringo appears on two cuts on this album.

"Tomorrow"
Written by: Paul and Linda McCartney
Recorded by: Wings
Lead singer: Paul
Year first released: 1971
Record label: Apple
Album: WILD LIFE

"Tomorrow Never Knows"
Written by: Lennon/McCartney
Recorded by: The Beatles
Lead singer: John
Year first released: 1966
Record label: Parlophone (Britain); Capitol (U.S.)
Album: REVOLVER
- Originally titled "The Void," Ringo suggested the eventual title and they all agreed.
- The song's concepts were based on the teachings of the *Tibetan Book of the Dead*.
- Sixteen tape machines simultaneously running at different speeds aided in the strange sound effects. The birdlike noises on the record are actually a tape loop of Paul laughing.

"Tonight"
Written by: I. McLagan and J. Piggeon
Recorded by: Ringo
Lead singer: Ringo
Year first released: 1978
Record label: Polydor (Britain); Portrait (U.S.)
Album: BAD BOY

Tonight
Film produced by Ringo and Nancy Andrews in which Ringo performs. The movie shot in 1978 has not yet been released.

"Tonight Show, The"
American television program on which John and Paul were guests on May 14, 1968. It was on this show that they took the opportunity to announce the formation of their new management company, Apple Corps Ltd., located in England. They pledged Apple's assistance to all struggling artists, and the following day it was reported that all U.S. flights to London were booked to capacity.

"Too Bad about Sorrows"
One of John and Paul's earliest songs. It was never recorded.

"Too Many People"
Written by: Paul McCartney
Recorded by: Paul and Linda
Lead singer: Paul
Year first released: 1971
Record label: Apple
Album: RAM
Single: B side of "Uncle Albert/Admiral Halsey"
• John was offended by this song, feeling that Paul was referring to him and Yoko.

"Too Much Monkey Business"
Chuck Berry song which The Beatles performed on the radio shows "Saturday Club," "Pop Go The Beatles," and "Side by Side," in Britain in 1963.

"Top of the Pops"
British radio and television music series on which The Beatles were guests many times.

Top Ten Club
Hamburg club, managed by Peter Eckhorn, in which The Beatles performed during 1960 and 1961. The Beatles' first engagement at the Top Ten was in August 1960. While still performing at another German club, the Kaiserkeller, The Beatles were offered a better deal to work at the Top Ten. The change in clubs was short-lived, when, due to immigration problems, allegedly precipitated by angry owners of The Kaiserkeller, half the group was deported back to England. In March of 1961, The Beatles were invited back to Germany to play a three-month engagement at the Top Ten. It was during these seven-night-a-week performances that The Beatles feel their skill and style was perfected.

Torment, Mel
Pseudonym used by John on his song "Scared."

Toronto Rock 'n' Roll Revival Concert
Concert headlined by John and the Plastic Ono Band on September 13, 1969. The band was hastily assembled by John and Yoko in order to back them at the concert. The band consisted of Eric Clapton, Klaus Voorman, and Alan White. (See Varsity Stadium.)

TO THE WORLD
Rudy Romero album on which George assists on guitar and background vocals.

"Touch Me"
Song written by Yoko Ono which appears as the B side of the single "Power to the People" in the U.S.

Toussaint, Allen
Musician and record producer who worked with Wings on their album VENUS AND MARS in 1975. The group recorded the album at Toussaint's Sea Saint Studios in New Orleans.

Allen Toussaint composed "Occapella," which was recorded by Ringo and appears on the GOODNIGHT VIENNA album.

Townshend, Pete
Member of the Who who appears on the Wings album BACK TO THE EGG as a part of the rockestra. He also performed with Wings at London's Hammersmith Odeon on December 29, 1979 at the concert for Kampuchea.

"Toy Boy"
Short story written by John which appeared in the December 1965 issue of *McCall's* magazine.

"To You"
Written by: Paul McCartney
Recorded by: Wings
Lead singer: Paul
Year first released: 1979
Record label: Parlophone (Britain); Columbia (U.S.)
Album: BACK TO THE EGG

Track Records
British company which pressed and distributed John and Yoko's UNFINISHED MUSIC NO. 1: TWO VIRGINS in 1968. The record company was contacted when EMI wasn't willing to handle the controversial album.

215

"Tragedy"
Thomas Wayne song which was recorded by Wings, but was never released.

Transcendental Meditation
See Maharishi Mahesh Yogi.

Trash
Originally called White Trash; this group was signed to Apple Records in 1969. (See White Trash.)

"Treat Her Gently"
Written by: Paul McCartney
Recorded by: Wings
Lead singer: Paul
Year first released: 1975
Record label: Parlophone (Britain); Capitol (U.S.)
Album: VENUS AND MARS

Tree Top Hotel
Hotel in Nairobi, Africa, where Paul stayed while on holiday in 1966.

Tremlett, George
Author of the books *The Paul McCartney Story* and *The John Lennon Story*.

Trinidad, Olivia
Pet name used by George, referring to his wife Olivia.

Trinidad is Olivia's middle name.

Trident Studio
London recording studio where The Beatles worked on THE BEATLES and "Hey Jude." It was at this studio, too, that some work was done on ALL THINGS MUST PASS and BAND ON THE RUN.

Triumph Investment Trust
Banking firm which purchased Brian Epstein's management company, Nems, in 1969. (See Nems.)

Troubador
Los Angeles night club. In March 1974, John and Harry Nilsson were ejected from the club for drunken and disorderly conduct during a Smothers Brothers performance.

TROUBLEMAKER
Ian McLagan album on which Ringo appears.

Troy, Doris
Artist signed to Apple Records in 1969. Her recordings for Apple included "Get Back," "Jacob's Ladder" (arranged by George), "Ain't That Cute" (cowritten and produced by George), "Vaya Con Dios" (with George on guitar), "Gonna Get My Baby Back" and "You Give Me Joy Joy" (both cowritten with George and Ringo and Steven Stills). One album, DORIS TROY, was released during Doris Troy's affiliation with Apple Records.

"True Love"
Written by: Cole Porter
Recorded by: George Harrison
Lead singer: George
Year first released: 1976
Record label: Dark Horse
Album: 33⅓
Single: Britain
Performances: Promo film clip

True Story of The Beatles, The
Book written by Billy Shepherd and published by Bantam Books in 1964.

"Try Some, Buy Some"
Written by: George Harrison
Recorded by: George
Lead singer: George
Year first released: 1973
Record label: Apple
Album: LIVING IN THE MATERIAL WORLD
· This song was first recorded by Ronnie Spector, produced by Phil Spector, and released by Apple Records in 1971. George was so impressed with Spector's production that for his own version he just sang over the original.
· George and Phil Spector produced both versions.

Tucker, Keith
Artist, specializing in surrealistic seascapes, who met Paul and Linda in Hawaii. Tucker sold the McCartneys several paintings, and he was later contracted to design the 1976 Wings' tour T-shirts.

Turberville, Danny
Assistant engineer for John's SOMETIME IN NEW YORK CITY album.

Turner, Shelly
Linda McCartney's friend, who became Paul's secretary in 1972.

Turpentine
Name Paul seriously considered calling his new band in 1971. After a seventy-nine-year-old fan dissuaded Paul from the idea, the group was named Wings instead.

Tuxedo Brass Band
Group that worked with Paul in New Orleans in 1975. They recorded "Baby Face" together, which was also filmed for the movie *The Sound of One Hand Clapping*. Neither the song nor the film were ever released.

"Twenty-Flight Rock"
Eddie Cochran song which Paul performed for John in 1955 at their first meeting. Paul included this song in the Wings' repertoire on their 1979 British Winter Tour.

Twickenham Studios
British movie studio where The Beatles filmed segments for their movies *A Hard Day's Night, Help!* and *Let It Be.* Twickenham was also used for the filming of The Beatles' "Hey Jude" performance and film clip. Portions of the movie *The Magic Christian,* which Ringo starred in, were filmed here.

Twilight of the Gods
Book about The Beatles' music written by Wilfred Mellers; published by Viking Press, Schirner in 1973.

"Twist and Shout"
Written by: Bert Russell and Phil Medley
Recorded by: The Beatles
Lead singer: John
Year first released: 1963
Record label: Parlophone (Britain); Vee Jay and Capitol (U.S.)
Album: PLEASE PLEASE ME
    INTRODUCING THE BEATLES
    THE EARLY BEATLES
    ROCK AND ROLL MUSIC
    THE BEATLES LIVE AT THE STAR CLUB (Britain)
    THE BEATLES AT THE HOLLYWOOD BOWL
EP: TWIST AND SHOUT
Single: U.S.; Live version from the Star Club performance released in Britain in 1977
    B side of "Back in the USSR" in 1976 (Britain)
Performances: "Sunday Night at the London Palladium" October 1963
    Royal Variety Performance, November 1963
    "Ed Sullivan Show" (TV), February 1964
    1964 North American Winter Tour
    1964 North American Summer Tour
    1964 British Christmas Shows
    1965 European Summer Tour
    1965 North American Tour

TWIST AND SHOUT (EP)
Artist: The Beatles
Producer: George Martin
Year first released: 1963
Record label: Parlophone
Tracks: 4
    "Twist and Shout"

"A Taste of Honey"
"Do You Want to Know a Secret"
"There's a Place"

Twist, Cynthia Lennon
Born Cynthia Powell on September 10, 1939: John's first wife and the mother of their son, Julian.

Cynthia was born in Blackpool, an affluent suburb of Liverpool. She first met John at age eighteen, when they were both attending the Liverpool College of Art. Cynthia was a diligent student, who did not mix with John's crowd, which she looked upon with disdain. John's only contact with Cynthia was to tease her for her snobbish, high-class airs. Eventually the two realized an attraction for one another and began dating. Though they were seemingly mismatched, according to their friends, they each found a stability within the relationship—which soon grew into love. John relied on "Cyn" for her strength and honesty, which helped to see him through his struggling times, both emotional and professional.

In 1962 Cynthia became pregnant. She refused to use the child to pressure John into marriage and gave him the option as to which course to take. They were married on August 23, 1962, at a simple civil ceremony with Paul and George as the only friends in attendance. Their son, John Charles Julian, was born the following April. At first they tried to keep their marriage a secret, but the press soon found out.

Cynthia was the first "Beatle-wife" and quickly learned that the best way to cope was to keep out of the spotlight. She did her best to make her family's homelife as normal as possible, while warding off jealous fans and overzealous reporters. Cynthia, of all the Beatle women, was the most conventional by nature. She was still the butt of the crowd's jokes as they kidded her good-naturedly about being a "square" for not partaking in the drug scene. It was partly this conflict in interests, combined with John's restless nature, which started to put a strain on their marriage.

Though John was content with his family, his fascination and subsequent love for artist Yoko Ono soon took precedence over his marriage to Cynthia. Cynthia moved out of the family's Weybridge home in 1968 and filed for a divorce, which came through on November 8, 1968.

Cynthia married Italian businessman Roberto Bassinini in 1970. She had been friendly with Bassinini and his family since 1968 (a relationship John cited as helping to strain their marriage). The marriage was not a happy one and they were soon divorced. Cynthia is now married to John Twist and lives in Wales along with son Julian. In 1978 she published her memoirs on John and the Beatles in the book, *A Twist of Lennon,* under the name Cynthia Lennon.

Twist, John
Husband of Cynthia Lennon. John and Cynthia were married in 1977 and live in Wales with Cynthia's son, Julian (from her marriage to John Lennon).

Twist of Lennon, A
Book written by John's ex-wife Cynthia Lennon; published by Star Books in 1978 (Britain) and Avon in 1980 (U.S.)

200 Motels
1971 Frank Zappa movie in which Ringo played the dual roles of Larry the Dwarf and Frank Zappa. This surrealistic interpretation of the life of a rock star was written by Frank Zappa and directed by Tony Palmer. The film was produced by Jerry Good and Herb Cohen.

TWO MAN BAND
Album recorded by Dark Horse group Splinter. The album was coproduced by George and Dennis Morgan, with George also lending his talents on guitar.

"Two Minutes of Silence"
Cut on John and Yoko's album UNFINISHED MUSIC NO. 2: LIFE WITH THE LIONS.

"Two of Us"
Written by: Lennon/McCartney

Recorded by: The Beatles
Lead singer: Paul
Year first released: 1970
Record label: Apple
Album: LET IT BE
Performances: In the *Let It Be* movie, which also served as a promo film clip
- Song was performed twice in the movie. Once during rehearsal, with John and Paul improvising and giving the song a lift by changing the tempo. The second movie version is also the album's version.
- Before The Beatles released this song, they had given it to the group Mortimer to record.

TWO SIDES OF THE MOON
Keith Moon album, which was coproduced by Mal Evans and features Ringo on drums and occasional vocal accompaniment.

TWO VIRGINS
(See UNFINISHED MUSIC NO. 1: TWO VIRGINS.)

Tyler, Tony
Coauthor of the book, *The Beatles: An Illustrated Record*.

Tyringham
Town in Massachusetts where John and Yoko have a vacation home.

U

"Uncle Albert/Admiral Halsey"
Written by: Paul and Linda McCartney
Recorded by: Paul and Linda
Lead singer: Paul
Year first released: 1971
Record label: Apple
Album: RAM
          WINGS GREATEST
Single: U.S.
Performances: Soundtrack to the TV special "James Paul McCartney"
- Written about Paul's late uncle, who was noted in the family for his familiarity with the bible and the bottle.
- The song was awarded a Grammy.

Uncle Ernie
Character Ringo portrayed in the London Symphony Orchestra's version of the Who's TOMMY. Also one of the names mentioned in Paul's song "Let 'Em In."

Uncle Ian
Another uncle mentioned in "Let 'Em In."

Undertakers, The
Group on the bill of The Beatles' 1963 British Tour.

"Under the Mersey Wall"
Side one of George's album ELECTRONIC SOUND.

UNFINISHED MUSIC NO. 1: TWO VIRGINS
Artist: John Lennon and Yoko Ono
Producer: John and Yoko
Year first released: 1968
Record label: Apple
Tracks: 12
    "Two Virgins 1–10"
    "Together"
    "Hush a Bye Hush a Bye"
- John and Yoko's first recording collaboration.
- The album consists of John and Yoko's avant-garde sounds in experimental music.
- The album jacket displays John and Yoko posing together in the nude (front and rear). It took John five months to gain the other Beatles' approval for the album cover. The photographs caused such a controversey that The Beatles' record company, EMI, refused to handle the album. Small independent labels distributed the album, which was packaged in brown paper wrappings.

- Paul wrote the caption on the album cover which reads: "When two great Saints meet it is a humbling experience. The long battles to prove he was a Saint."

UNFINISHED MUSIC NO. 2: LIFE WITH THE LIONS
Artist: John Lennon and Yoko Ono
Producer: John and Yoko
Year first released: 1969
Record label: Zapple
Tracks: 9
    "Song for John"
    "Cambridge 1969"
    "Let's Go On Flying"
    "Snow Is Falling All the Time"
    "Don't Worry Kyoko"
    "No Bed for Beatle John"
    "Baby's Heartbeat"
    "Two Minutes of Silence"
    "Radio Play"
- First album recorded on Apple's experimental sound division, Zapple.
- Side one was recorded live at Cambridge, England.
- Side two was recorded in Queen Charlotte Hospital prior to Yoko's miscarriage.

United Artists
American movie company with which The Beatles signed a contract in 1964, agreeing to star in three feature films. The Beatles movies released through United Artists included *A Hard Day's Night, Help!,* and *Let It Be. Yellow Submarine,* The Beatles' animated film, was also released by the company. A HARD DAY'S NIGHT soundtrack album was released on the United Artists record label.

University College Hospital
London hospital where, on December 2, 1964, Ringo had his tonsils removed. It was during this stay that Ringo proposed marriage to his Liverpool sweetheart, Maureen Cox.

On February 7, 1969, George had his tonsillectomy at this hospital.

University Tour
Unofficial title of Wings' 1972 British tour. The group played unannounced gigs at random universities throughout England.

URBAN SPACEMAN
Bonzo Dog Band album which includes the song "I'm the Urban Spaceman," which was produced by Paul, under the alias Apollo C. Vermouth.

V

"Valentine Day"
Written by: Paul McCartney
Recorded by: Paul
Lead singer: Instrumental
Year first released: 1970
Record label: Apple
Album: McCARTNEY

Valerie
Character who fights for Maxwell's freedom in the song "Maxwell's Silver Hammer."

Valley View Farm
Three-hundred-and-sixteen acre dairy farm, located in New York, purchased by John and Yoko in 1978.

Van Winkle, Dixon
Engineer credited on Paul's RAM and RED ROSE SPEEDWAY albums.

Varsity Stadium
Arena in Toronto, Canada and the site of the Toronto Rock 'n' Roll Revival Concert, featuring John Lennon and the Plastic Ono Band. The event, which took place on September 13 and 14, 1969, was responsible for assembling such notable musicians as Eric Clapton, Klaus Voorman, and Alan White—the Plastic Ono Band. For the concert, the group hurriedly put together an act consisting of a few fifties rockers and some of John's compositions. Since it was all arranged within a day's notice, the band had to rehearse on the plane en route from London to Toronto. Their concert performance was filmed and recorded, and later released as an album titled LIVE PEACE IN TORONTO.

Vartan, Sylvie
Performer on the bill with The Beatles during their engagement in 1964 at the Olympia Theatre in Paris.

Vaughn, Ivan
Friend of The Beatles since their school days. Vaughn attended the Liverpool Institute with Paul and was responsible for John and Paul's first meeting, when Vaughn brought Paul to see John's group, The Quarrymen.

Even after The Beatles attained worldwide fame, they retained their friendship with Vaughn. When The Beatles were considering forming an Apple school, Vaughn, who was a teacher, was to be employed at their educational facility. In 1968, Ivan Vaughn accompanied Paul on an Apple promotional trip to America.

Vaughn, Janet
Wife of Ivan Vaughn, an old friend of The Beatles since their teenage years. Ms. Vaughn, who spoke French fluently, helped Paul write the French verses of the song "Michelle."

"Vaya Con Dios"
Doris Troy song, released on Apple Records, on which George plays guitar.

Vee Jay Records
First American record company authorized to issue Beatle records in the U.S., in 1963. Through their two-year association with The Beatles, Vee Jay released a total of five Beatle albums: INTRODUCING THE BEATLES; JOLLY WHAT! THE BEATLES AND FRANK IFIELD; THE BEATLES VS. THE FOUR SEASONS; SONGS, PICTURES, AND STORIES OF THE FABULOUS BEATLES; and HEAR THE BEATLES TELL ALL; six singles: "Please Please Me"/"Ask Me Why," "From Me to You"/"Thank You Girl," "Please Please Me"/"From Me to You," "Do You Want to Know a Secret"/"Thank You Girl," "Twist and Shout"/"There's a Place," and "Love Me Do"/"P.S. I Love You"; and one EP: THE BEATLES.

VENUS AND MARS
Artists: Wings
Producer: Paul McCartney
Year first released: 1975
Record label: Parlophone (Britain); Capitol (U.S.)
Tracks: 13
 "Venus and Mars"
 "Rock Show"
 "Love in Song"
 "You Gave Me the Answer"
 "Magneto and Titanium Man"
 "Letting Go"
 "Venus and Mars Reprise"
 "Spirits of Ancient Egypt"
 "Medicine Jar"
 "Call Me Back Again"
 "Listen To What the Man Said"
 "Treat Her Gently"/"Lonely Old People"
 "Crossroads Theme"
· First album by any of the Beatles which was not released on the Apple label; making it Paul's first solo album released on Capitol in the U.S.
· For the first time other Wings members were permitted the spotlight as lead vocalists.
· Many of album's songs were recorded in New Orleans and Los Angeles.

"Venus and Mars"
Written by: Paul McCartney
Recorded by: Wings

Lead singer: Paul
Year first released: 1975
Record label: Parlophone (Britain); Capitol (U.S.)
Album: VENUS AND MARS
Single: Britain and U.S.
Performances: 1975–76 Wings' World Tour
                Promo film clip
· Speculation has been made as to whether the song's title refers to Paul and Linda, but Paul denies this theory.

Vera
One of the fictional grandchildren Paul sings about in the song "When I'm Sixty-four."

Vermouth, Apollo C.
Pseuydonym Paul used when he produced the Bonzo Dog Band song "I'm the Urban Spacemen."

Vernon Girls
Group on the bill with The Beatles on their 1963 November/December Tour.

Vigars, Mark
Engineer who worked on WINGS AT THE SPEED OF SOUND, WINGS OVER AMERICA, LONDON TOWN, and BACK TO THE EGG albums.

Vincent, Gene
Singer who appeared on the bill with The Beatles at The Cavern in July of 1962.

Visconti, Tony
Musician/record producer who plays strings on the BAND ON THE RUN album. Visconti is also the husband of former Apple artist Mary Hopkin.

Viscounts, The
Group who toured with The Beatles on their 1963 British Tour.

"Void, The"
Original title of the song "Tomorrow Never Knows."

Vole
Magazine pertaining to environmental issues, which George helps support financially.

Vollmer, Jurgen
German photographer who met The Beatles in Hamburg in 1961. Vollmer is responsible for many of The Beatles' early stage and portrait photos, which appear in various books and magazines, and on the cover of John's ROCK 'N' ROLL album. Jurgen Vollmer can also be credited with convincing John to style his hair in the famous "Beatle cut."

Vollmer is presently living in New York and is often a guest speaker at Beatle-related gatherings.

Voorman, Klaus
German-born musician who worked for and with The Beatles from 1961 to the present day.

Klaus first came into contact with The Beatles when he was a regular customer at the Hamburg clubs where The Beatles performed. A welcome change from the drunken sailors and seedy patrons who frequented the clubs, Klaus and his friends were soon sought out by The Beatles for their companionship. The elite group of young artists and students included Beatle Stuart Sutcliffe's future fiancée, Astrid Kirschner, who had been introduced to The Beatles by Klaus. It was Klaus Voorman who was the first to wear his hair in what was to become the "Beatle haircut."

The Beatles remained close friends with Klaus, even after their return to England and eventual success. It was Klaus whom John, George, and Ringo seriously considered as a replacement for Paul on bass after he left the group early in 1970. Though he never did become a Beatle per se, Klaus (a former member of Manfred Mann) accompanied and worked with the other Beatles on most of their solo ventures. He accompanied John and Yoko as a part of their Plastic Ono Band to perform in concert at the Toronto Rock 'n' Roll Revival in 1969. He also appears on John's albums JOHN LENNON/PLASTIC ONO BAND, WALLS AND BRIDGES, and SOMETIME IN NEW YORK CITY. Klaus played bass on stage with George at the 1971 Concert for Bangla Desh, and appears on the live album. He also worked on George's ALL THINGS MUST PASS, EXTRA TEXTURE, DARK HORSE, and LIVING IN THE MATERIAL WORLD albums. Klaus helped arrange some cuts on Ringo's SENTIMENTAL JOURNEY album and later worked on RINGO, GOODNIGHT VIENNA, and RINGO'S ROTOGRAVURE. Klaus's artistic skills are displayed on the cover of REVOLVER (for which he won a Grammy) and in the lithographs printed in the RINGO album package. He also is responsible for the psychedelic mural which adorned George's Esher bungalow.

Voyager
Boat rented by Paul in New Orleans in 1975 to hold a Wings press conference while sailing on the Mississippi River.

W

"Wah-Wah"
Written by: George Harrison
Recorded by: George
Lead singer: George
Year first released: 1970
Record label: Apple
Album: ALL THINGS MUST PASS
          THE CONCERT FOR BANGLA DESH
Performance: The Concert for Bangla Desh, 1971
• George wrote this song after a particularly grueling session during the recording of the LET IT BE album. In this song, George vents his frustrations about the other Beatles.

"Wait"
Written by: Lennon/McCartney
Recorded by: The Beatles
Lead singer: John and Paul
Record label: Parlophone (Britain); Capitol (U.S.)
Year first released: 1965
Album: RUBBER SOUL

"Waiting"
Written by: Chuck Howard
Recorded by: Ringo
Lead singer: Ringo
Year first released: 1970
Record label: Apple
Album: BEAUCOUPS OF BLUES

Walker, Tony
Costume designer for the 1975–76 Wings' World Tour.

"Walking in the Park with Eloise"
Written by: James McCartney
Recorded by: The Country Hams
Lead singer: None (Instrumental)
Year first released: 1974
Record label: EMI (Britain); Capitol (US)
Single: Britain and U.S.
• This song was composed by Paul's dad in the early fifties. Paul recorded the song in deference to his dad at the suggestion of Chet Atkins, while Wings was recording in Nashville. (See Country Hams.)

WALKING MAN
James Taylor album on which Paul sings background vocals.

WALLS AND BRIDGES
Artist: John Lennon
Producer: John Lennon

Year first released: 1974
Record label: Apple
Tracks: 12
          "Going Down on Love"
          "Whatever Gets You Thru the Night"
          "Old Dirt Road"
          "What You Got"
          "Bless You"
          "Scared"
          "#9 Dream"
          "Surprise, Surprise"/"Sweet Bird of Paradox"
          "Steel and Glass"
          "Beef Jerky"
          "Nobody Loves You When You're Down and Out"
          "Ya Ya"
• The album title stemmed from a public service commercial John viewed on television. The songs were recorded in New York and Los Angeles, during John's separation from Yoko.
• The album's jacket displays John's drawings from his childhood.

Wally Heider Studios
Los Angeles recording studio where Paul recorded part of his VENUS AND MARS album.

Walsh, Tom
Engineer on the WINGS OVER AMERICA album.

Walston Hall
Concert hall in Galston, Liverpool, where George was first introduced to The Quarrymen in 1956. John and Paul were members of the band at the time.

Walton and Esher Magistrates Court
Courthouse where George and Pattie were arraigned on March 18, 1969, after they were busted for illegal possession of marijuana on March 12, 1969. Pattie was at home alone when Sgt. Pilchard, accompanied by Yogi, a drug-sniffing Labrador retriever, broke into George and Pattie's home in Esher and found 750 grains of marijuana. Pattie called George, and when he arrived home, they were both formally arrested. The bust occurred on the afternoon of Paul and Linda's wedding. On March 18, 1969, they were charged and released on $240's bail each. On March 31, 1969, they returned to the courthouse and were found guilty, and each had to pay $600.

Walton Hospital
Hospital in Liverpool where Paul was born on June 18, 1942. Paul's mother was a midwife here, so she received special attention.

"War Is Over (If You Want It)"
Slogan coined by John and Yoko in 1969 as a Christmas message to the world. This chant appears on their recording "Happy Xmas (War Is Over)" and ap-

peared in newspaper ads and billboards all over the world.

On December 15, 1969, a concert given by John and Yoko at the Lyceum Ballroom was entitled "War Is Over (If You Want It)."

"Warm and Beautiful"
Written by: Paul McCartney
Recorded by: Wings
Lead singer: Paul
Year first released: 1976
Record label: Parlophone (Britain); Capitol (U.S.)
Album: WINGS AT THE SPEED OF SOUND

Warner Bros.
American record company which distributes George's Dark Horse label. George signed with the company in 1976.

Washington Coliseum
Location for The Beatles' first American concert, in Washington, D.C., on February 11, 1964. The Beatles played to an arena filled with eighty-six hundred people, the largest audience they had performed for up until that time. The only difficulty stemmed from the stage being set in the middle of the arena, causing The Beatles to alternate sides after each number. The concert was filmed.

WATER WINGS
Working title for Paul's LONDON TOWN album.

Watkins, Peter
Film producer who first suggested to John and Yoko, in 1968, that their celebrity status be employed to promote world peace.

Webb, Bernard
Alias used by Paul for the composing credit on Peter and Gordon's song "Woman." Paul was interested in finding out how a song of his would fare without the winning songwriting credit of Lennon/McCartney; hence, Bernard Webb, who was publicized as a Parisian student and a novice songwriter. Paul was pleased to see his song soon become a hit.

Webb, Jimmy
Composer/musician on whose album LAND'S END, Ringo plays drums.

"We Can Work It Out"
Written by: Lennon/McCartney
Recorded by: The Beatles
Lead singer: Paul
Year first released: 1965
Record label: Parlophone (Britain); Capitol (U.S.)

Album: "YESTERDAY" ... AND TODAY
A COLLECTION OF BEATLES OLDIES
THE BEATLES 1962–1966
Single: Britain and U.S.
Performances: Promo film clip
1965 British Tour
• Another song Paul wrote which was inspired by Jane Asher.

WEDDING ALBUM, THE
Artist: John Lennon and Yoko Ono
Producer: John and Yoko
Year first released: 1969
Record label: Apple
• First side of the album consists of John and Yoko's experimental sounds. The second side contains interviews by John and Yoko given during their bed-ins for peace.
• The package includes many souvenir reproductions from their wedding—including photos, their wedding certificate, and a photo of a piece of cake in a bag.

Weeks, Willie
Bass guitarist who performed with George on the 1974 Dark Horse Tour of North America. Weeks also appears on George's DARK HORSE, EXTRA TEXTURE, 33⅓, and GEORGE HARRISON albums. George stated he believed that Willie Weeks is the best bass player of all time.

Weet, Mandy
Actress who portrayed Wendy Winters in the film *Magical Mystery Tour.*

Weiner, Sue
Coauthor of the book *The Beatles A to Z.*

Weislieder, Manfred
Owner of The Star Club in Hamburg, where The Beatles performed in 1961 and 1962.

Weiss, Nathan
American attorney who, in 1966, became The Beatles' U.S. representative when Brian Epstein appointed him manager of Nemperor Artists in America. Shortly before Brian's death, he had requested that Weiss become his personal manager. In 1968, John and Paul stayed at Weiss's New York apartment while they were in the city to promote their newly formed company, Apple. Later that year George recorded his Christmas message to The Beatles Fan Club from Weiss's apartment.

"Well ... Baby Please Don't Go"
Song performed by John, Yoko, and Frank Zappa and the Mothers of Invention at New York's Fillmore East in 1971. The song appears on the SOMETIME IN NEW YORK CITY album.

Wells, Mary
Singer who appeared on the bill with The Beatles on their 1964 British tour and on the TV show "Around The Beatles." She recorded an album titled LOVE SONGS TO THE BEATLES.

"Well Well Well"
Written by: John Lennon
Recorded by: John
Lead singer: John
Year first released: 1970
Record label: Apple
Album: JOHN LENNON/PLASTIC ONO BAND
Performances: One to One Concert, 1972

"We Love You"
Rolling Stones song in which John and Paul sing background vocals.

We Love You Beatles
Children's book written by Margaret Sutton; published by Doubleday in 1971.

Wembley Stadium
Arena where The Beatles performed in England for the last time together, on May 1, 1966. Paul and Wings played Wembley in 1976.

Wenner, Jann
Editor and publisher of *Rolling Stone* magazine. In 1971, Wenner interviewed John and published his in-depth piece in two parts. He later compiled the interview into the book *Lennon Remembers*.

"We're All Water"
Written by: Yoko Ono
Recorded by: John and Yoko
Lead singer: Yoko
Year first released: 1972
Record label: Apple
Album: SOMETIME IN NEW YORK CITY
Performances: One to One Concert, 1972

"We're Open Tonight"
Written by: Paul McCartney
Recorded by: Wings
Lead singer: Paul
Year first released: 1979
Record label: Parlophone (Britain); Columbia (U.S.)
Album: BACK TO THE EGG

Western Recording Studios
Los Angeles studio where, in 1968, Frank Sinatra invited George and Pattie to observe his recording session. Sinatra later hosted the couple for a night on the town.

West Mallings R.A.F. Base
British Air Force base where many of the scenes from *Magical Mystery Tour* were filmed. "Aunt Jessie's Nightmare," "Sergeant Scene," "Marathon Race," "Blue Jay Way," "I Am the Walrus," "Your Mother Should Know," and the finale were all shot here.

Weybridge
Section of the London suburb of Surrey where the Lennons and the Starkeys had homes from 1964 through 1968. This section was soon to be known as the "Beatle belt."

Whadden House (#7)
Apartment building located in London at William Mews, where Ringo and Maureen lived in 1964.

Whalley, Nigel
One of the original members of The Quarrymen, the group John was in when Paul joined him in 1955. Whalley was the group's first manager.

"What Do We Really Know?"
Song Paul wrote for his brother Michael's album McGEAR. Paul can be heard on the song.

"Whatever Gets You thru the Night"
Written by: John Lennon
Recorded by: John
Lead singer: John
Year first released: 1974
Record label: Apple
Album: WALLS AND BRIDGES
        SHAVED FISH
Single: Britain and U.S.
Performances: Elton John's Madison Square Garden
               Concert, November 28, 1974.
               Promo film clip
· Elton John plays piano and shares vocals with John on this song.

"What Goes On"
Written by: Lennon/McCartney/Starkey
Recorded by: The Beatles
Lead singer: Ringo
Year first released: 1966
Record label: Parlophone (Britain); Capitol (U.S.)
Album: RUBBER SOUL (Britain)
        "YESTERDAY" . . . AND TODAY
Single: B side of "Nowhere Man" in U.S.
· The first song Ringo was given writing credit for.
· In the song John can be heard answering Ringo's "Tell me why" with "We already told you why"—a reference to their song "Tell Me Why."
· Paul instructed Ringo on how to sing the song by furnishing him with a finished recording of the song which he had done alone.

"What I Say"
Ray Charles song which The Beatles often closed their set with in their Cavern days.

"What Is Life"
Written by: George Harrison
Recorded by: George
Lead singer: George
Year first released: 1970
Record label: Apple
Album: ALL THINGS MUST PASS
        THE BEST OF GEORGE HARRISON
Single: U.S.; B side of "My Sweet Lord" in Britain
Performances: 1974 Dark Horse Tour.

"What's the New Mary Jane?"
Song intended for release on THE BEATLES album. John, George, and Ringo recorded this song without Paul.

"What You Got"
Written by: John Lennon
Recorded by: John
Lead singer: John
Year first released: 1974
Record label: Apple
Album: WALLS AND BRIDGES
Single: B side of "#9 Dream"

"What You're Doing"
Written by: Lennon/McCartney
Recorded by: The Beatles
Lead singer: Paul
Year first released: 1964
Record label: Parlophone (Britain); Capitol (U.S.)
Album: BEATLES FOR SALE
        BEATLES VI

Wheeler, Cecile
Registrar who married John and Yoko in Gibraltar on March 20, 1969.

"When Every Song Is Sung"
Original title of "I'll Still Love You," a song on RINGO'S ROTOGRAVURE album.

"When I Come to Town"
Unreleased Beatles song, recorded in 1969.

"When I Get Home"
Written by: Lennon/McCartney
Recorded by: The Beatles
Lead singer: John
Year first released: 1964
Record label: Parlophone (Britain); Capitol (U.S.)

Album: A HARD DAY'S NIGHT (Britain)
        SOMETHING NEW
EP: EXTRACTS FROM THE ALBUM A HARD DAY'S NIGHT

"When I'm Sixty-Four"
Written by: Lennon/McCartney
Recorded by: The Beatles
Lead singer: Paul
Year first released: 1967
Record label: Parlophone (Britain); Capitol (U.S.)
Album: SGT. PEPPER'S LONELY HEARTS CLUB BAND
· Paul began writing this song when he was sixteen, and finished it eight years later, for his father's sixty-fourth birthday.

"When the Night"
Written by: Paul McCartney
Recorded by: Wings
Lead singer: Paul
Year first released: 1973
Record label: Apple
Album: RED ROSE SPEEDWAY
Performances: 1973 British Tour

"Where Are You Going?"
Unreleased song written by Ringo and Billy Lawrie.

"Where Did Our Love Go?"
Written by: Holland/Dozier/Holland
Recorded by: Ringo
Lead singer: Ringo
Year first released: 1978
Record label: Polydor (Britain); Portrait (U.S.)
Album: BAD BOY

"Where Have You Been All My Life?"
Song written by Barry Mann and Cynthia Weil, which was performed by The Beatles in Germany and appears on the album THE BEATLES LIVE AT THE STAR CLUB (American version).

"While My Guitar Gently Weeps"
Written by: George Harrison
Recorded by: The Beatles
Lead singer: George
Year first released: 1968
Record label: Apple
Album: THE BEATLES
        THE CONCERT FOR BANGLA DESH
        THE BEST OF GEORGE HARRISON
Performances: Concert for Bangla Desh, 1971
               1974 Dark Horse Tour
· Eric Clapton is featured on lead guitar.

225

"Whispering Grass"
Written by: Fred & Doris Fisher
Recorded by: Ringo
Lead singer: Ringo
Year first released: 1969
Record label: Apple
Album: SENTIMENTAL JOURNEY

White, Alan
Drummer who was a member of John Lennon's Plastic Ono Band during the 1969 Toronto Rock 'n' Roll Revival Concert. He also plays on the recordings "Instant Karma," ALL THINGS MUST PASS, and IMAGINE.

White, Andy
Session drummer who was called in by producer George Martin to substitute for Ringo during The Beatles' first recording session for Parlophone Records in 1962. Martin, being unsure of the new drummer (Ringo), employed White to play on several of The Beatles' takes. Ringo ultimately got to play on the recording of "Love Me Do," but White's version appears on the British and American albums and on the single "P.S. I Love You."

WHITE ALBUM, THE
See THE BEATLES album.

White Stone Register Office
Gibraltar Register Office where John and Yoko were married on March 20, 1969.

White Trash
Recording artists signed to Apple Records in 1969. The group's name was changed to Trash to be less offensive to industry executives. Their first recording "Road to Nowhere" went nowhere, and a controversy soon brewed over their upcoming album. Paul felt it wasn't good enough to release, but his objections were overruled by John, and WHITE TRASH was released. The last song they recorded was a cover version of The Beatles' "Golden Slumbers/Carry That Weight."

Whittaker, Robert
Photographer who photographed the butcher cover and its replacement on "YESTERDAY" . . . AND TODAY. He also took the pictures for the back covers of REVOLVER and A COLLECTION OF BEATLES OLDIES.

"Who Can See It"
Written by: George Harrison
Recorded by: George
Lead singer: George
Year first released: 1973
Record label: Apple
Album: LIVING IN THE MATERIAL WORLD

"Who Has Seen the Wind"
Yoko Ono composition which appears on the B side of John's "Instant Karma" single.

"Why"
Song written by Tony Sheridan and Bill Crompton. This song was recorded by Tony Sheridan and The Beatles in 1961. It appears on the albums, THE BEATLES FIRST, IN THE BEGINNING, and THE EARLY YEARS.

"Why"
Yoko Ono song which is the B side of the single "Mother" in the U.S.

"Why Don't We Do It In the Road?"
Written by: Lennon/McCartney
Recorded by: The Beatles
Lead singer: Paul
Year first released: 1968
Record label: Apple
Album: THE BEATLES
· Improvised in the studio, this recording features Paul playing alone.

Wigg, David
British journalist who conducted a series of interviews with the Beatles from 1969 through 1973. The tapes were released on an album for Polydor Records in 1976 called THE BEATLES TAPES.

Wigmore Street (95)
Address of the first Apple offices in London, which opened in April of 1968.

Wildes, Leon
U.S. attorney who represented John during his immigration trials with the U.S. Immigration Bureau.

"Wild Honey Pie"
Written by: Lennon/McCartney
Recorded by: The Beatles
Lead singer: Paul
Year first released: 1968
Record label: Apple
Album: THE BEATLES
· This song was originally a spontaneous sing-along from The Beatles' holiday in India, which was never intended for release, but they decided to record it at the persuasion of Pattie Harrison. Paul plays the instruments on the recording.

WILD LIFE
Artist: Wings
Producer: Paul and Linda McCartney
Year first released: 1971
Record label: Apple
Tracks: 8

"Mumbo"
"Bip Bop"
"Love Is Strange"
"Wild Life"
"Some People Never Know"
"I Am Your Singer"
"Tomorrow"
"Dear Friend"
- First album recorded by Wings.
- Paul was influenced by Dylan's technique at the time, which was to record each song in one take. The whole album took only three weeks to finish, and when it received the harshest criticism of all Paul's solo endeavors, he later admitted he regretted recording it in such a slipshod manner.

"Wild Life"
Written by: Paul and Linda McCartney
Recorded by: Wings
Lead singer: Paul
Year first released: 1971
Record label: Apple
Album: WILD LIFE
Performances: 1972 Wings' European Tour
1973 Wings' British Tour
- Paul's political statement regarding conservation and ecology.

"Wild Prairie Maid"
Song recorded by Suzie & the Red Stripes (Wings), while they were visiting Paris. It was never released.

Wilk, Max
Author of the book *Yellow Submarine.*

Wilkes, Tom
Artist who designed the covers of the albums ALL THINGS MUST PASS, CONCERT FOR BANGLA DESH, LIVING IN THE MATERIAL WORLD, and DARK HORSE.

Williams, Alan
Coauthor of the book *The Man Who Gave The Beatles Away.* Williams was a Liverpool club owner and concert promoter when he became friendly with The Beatles in the late fifties. He went on to promote and book The Beatles at various engagements, including their Hamburg stints in the early sixties. He worked as their unofficial manager, representing them in business dealings up until 1961, when they broke ties over a dispute about his commission rights. In 1977 Williams helped to release THE BEATLES LIVE AT THE STAR CLUB tapes on record. He now spends much time promoting his Beatles ventures at various Beatles conventions in America and Europe.

Williams, Danny
Performer on the bill with The Beatles during the 1963 British tour featuring Helen Shapiro.

Williams, Dr. Eric
Prime minister of Trinidad-Tobago who in 1965 hosted John, Cynthia, Ringo, and Maureen when they holidayed in his country. Dr. Williams arranged a luncheon in their honor.

Williams, Larry
Late composer of The Beatles' songs "Slow Down," "Dizzy Miss Lizzie," and "Bad Boy." His "Bony Maronie" was later recorded by John on the ROCK 'N' ROLL album.

Wimpole Street (57)
London address of the Asher family home, where Paul lived from 1963 to 1966.

Winchell, Walter
American newspaper reporter who broke the story that Paul had secretly married Jane Asher in 1964. The story, which proved to be false, caused such a furor that Winchell was forced to retract the statement.

WIND OF CHANGE
Peter Frampton album on which Ringo plays drums.

"Wine, Women and Loud Happy Songs"
Written by: Larry Kingston
Recorded by: Ringo
Lead singer: Ringo
Year first released: 1970
Record label: Apple
Album: BEAUCOUPS OF BLUES

Wings
Band Paul McCartney formed after the breakup of The Beatles. The original group, consisting of Paul, his wife, Linda, Denny Laine, and Denny Seiwell, was formed on August 3, 1971, to satisfy Paul's need for a close-knit musical unit.

The group was nameless until Paul, awaiting the birth of his daughter Stella, in September of 1971, prayed for her health and came up with the group's name on the "wings of an angel."

Wings experienced a roller coaster ride to success. Their first album, WILD LIFE, was dismally received, and the band embarked on a "rehearsal" tour of British universities early in 1972 to gain confidence and polish their performance. Their itinerary was spontaneous, as the group performed in colleges with no prior announcements. Paul felt this experience was similar to his early days with The Beatles when they performed in Liverpool and Hamburg. The public, though, refused to accept less than musical perfection from Paul. So, despite the excitement of seeing a Beatle on stage, the critics and audiences were disappointed with Wings' amateur quality. Henry McCullough, a lead guitarist, was soon added to the line-up to provide the heavier sound Paul felt the group lacked. During the next two years, Wings logged in touring and recording experience, and gradually began enjoying moderate success as their music gained respect.

In 1973 Wings was scheduled to record an album in Lagos, Nigeria. Just before the band boarded the plane, two members, Henry McCullough and Denny Seiwell, decided to fly the coop, leaving the others to fend for themselves.

Paul, who had spent the last three years desperately trying to regain the success he had experienced with The Beatles, was devastated. Although he felt this would be the last straw, the resulting recording, BAND ON THE RUN, turned out to be Wings' greatest triumph. This album, on which Paul and Denny Laine played most of the instruments, gained Wings the critical acclaim which they'd been searching for for so long. This success, which came at a crucial period in Wings' career, inspired Paul to carry on with the group. Later that year, two members were added: Jimmy McCulloch (guitarist) and Geoff Britton (drummer), but Britton was soon replaced by American drummer Joe English.

Although Wings had embarked on several tours, they had yet to conquer America. In 1975 Paul finally felt his group and himself were ready to take the plunge. They began a world tour in Britain, Europe and Australia, and after a long and tedious journey, Wings was prepared for their shining moment—an American debut.

Paul dreaded the press's inevitable comparison between The Beatles and Wings, but this time everyone was in for a surprise. For the first time, Paul had risen above his past. On May 3, 1976, Wings opened their North American tour in Fort Worth, Texas, and were a smashing success. That night set the tone for the rest of the tour, and proved that Paul, with the help of The Beatles and Wings, had achieved success twice in his lifetime.

After their performances, which included a benefit in Venice, Italy, and a concert in Yugoslavia, Wings continued to soar. In 1977 they recorded "Mull of Kintyre," which became the biggest-selling single of all time in Britain.

But despite their success, Joe English and Jimmy McCulloch left Wings. Paul's determination and need for perfection led Wings to the top, but it also was re-ponsible for the constant conflicts in personalities.

Wings was, in essence, Paul's back-up band. This reality put a strain on the members, who had to repress their own egos, and left all the pressure on Paul.

In 1978 Wings acquired two new members, Laurence Juber (guitarist) and Steve Holly (drummer). They had joined up with the highest-paid recording artist in the world, when Paul signed a contract with Columbia Records in 1979. After one album, BACK TO THE EGG, the group played a tour of Britain. The reviews were mixed, and the band didn't feel that the show was strong enough to bring to America.

In January of 1980, Wings departed to Japan for a three-week concert tour, which was cancelled at the last minute, due to Paul's drug bust in Tokyo. (See Tokyo Metropolitan Police Office.)

By late February of 1980, Denny Laine, the longest surviving member of the group—aside from Paul and Linda—temporarily quit the band, claiming that Paul wasn't interested in performing any longer. Paul scratched plans for a U.S. tour with Wings and is planning to release an album of material recorded on his own.

"Wings"
Written by: Richard Starkey and Vini Poncia
Recorded by: Ringo
Lead singer: Ringo
Year first released: 1977
Record label: Polydor (Britain); Atlantic (U.S.)
Album: RINGO THE 4TH
Single: Britain and U.S.

WINGS AT THE SPEED OF SOUND
Artist: Wings
Producer: Paul McCartney
Year first released: 1976
Record label: Parlophone (Britain); Capitol (U.S.)
Tracks: 11
    "Let 'Em In"
    "The Note You Never Wrote"
    "She's My Baby"
    "Beware My Love"
    "Wino Junko"
    "Silly Love Songs"
    "Cook of the House"
    "Time to Hide"
    "Must Do Something About It"
    "San Ferry Anne"
    "Warm and Beautiful"
· First Wings album to feature each member singing lead vocals on at least one track.

Wings Fun Club
Fan club run under the supervision of McCartney Productions Ltd. It has approximately seven thousand members.

WINGS GREATEST
Artist: Wings
Producer: Paul McCartney
Year first released: 1978
Record label: Parlophone (Britain); Capitol (U.S.)
Tracks: 12
    "Another Day"
    "Junior's Farm"
    "Mull of Kintyre"
    "Silly Love Songs"
    "Live and Let Die"
    "Band on the Run"
    "Uncle Albert/Admiral Halsey"
    "My Love"
    "With a Little Luck"
    "Let 'Em In"
    "Jet"
    "Hi Hi Hi"
- The cover design cost $8,000.

WINGS OVER AMERICA
Artist: Wings
Producer: Paul McCartney
Year first released: 1976
Record label: Parlophone (Britain); Capitol (U.S.)
Tracks: 30 (3-record set)
    "Venus and Mars"
    "Rock Show"
    "Jet"
    "Let Me Roll It"
    "Spirits of Ancient Egypt"
    "Medicine Jar"
    "Maybe I'm Amazed"
    "Call Me Back"
    "Lady Madonna"
    "The Long and Winding Road"
    "Live and Let Die"
    "Picasso's Last Words"
    "Richard Cory"
    "Bluebird"
    "I've Just Seen a Face"
    "Blackbird"
    "Yesterday"
    "You Gave Me the Answer"
    "Magneto and Titanium Man"
    "Go Now"
    "My Love"
    "Listen To What the Man Said"
    "Let 'Em In"
    "Time to Hide"
    "Silly Love Songs"
    "Beware My Love"
    "Letting Go"
    "Band On the Run"
    "Hi Hi Hi"
    "Soily"

- Studio revised "live" recording of selected performances throughout Wings' 1976 U.S. Tour.

"Wings over the World"
Ninety-minute TV movie chronicling Wings' 1975–76 World Tour.

WINGS WILD LIFE
See WILD LIFE.

"Wino Junko"
Written by: Jimmy McCulloch and Allen Colin
Recorded by: Wings
Lead singer: Jimmy McCulloch
Year first released: 1976
Record label: Parlophone (Britain); Capitol (U.S.)
Album: WINGS AT THE SPEED OF SOUND

"Winston's Walk"
Unreleased song recorded by The Beatles in 1962. John sings lead.

"Winter Rose"/"Love Awake"
Written by: Paul McCartney
Recorded by: Wings
Lead singer: Paul
Year first released: 1979
Record label: Parlophone (Britain); Columbia (U.S.)
Album: BACK TO THE EGG
Performances: Promo film clip
    "Back to the Egg" TV special, 1979

Winters, Wendy
Tour bus hostess, portrayed by Mandy Weet, in the movie *Magical Mystery Tour*.

Winwood, Stevie
Musician who appears on the album GEORGE HARRISON.

"With a Little Help from My Friends"
Written by: Lennon/McCartney
Recorded by: The Beatles
Lead singer: Ringo
Year first released: 1967
Record label: Parlophone (Britain); Capitol (U.S.)
Album: SGT. PEPPER'S LONELY HEARTS CLUB
    BAND
    THE BEATLES 1967–1970
Single: Reissued in 1978 in medley with "Sgt. Pepper's Lonely Hearts Club Band"
Performances: Ringo performs a part of this song on his 1978 TV special, "Ringo."
- Original title was "Badfinger Boogie."
- Although this song was written by Paul during a separation from his girlfriend, Jane, he felt it better suited Ringo's style.

"With a Little Luck"
Written by: Paul McCartney
Recorded by: Wings
Lead singer: Paul
Year first released: 1978
Record label: Parlophone (Britain); Capitol (U.S.)
Album: LONDON TOWN
       WINGS GREATEST
Single: Britain and U.S.
Performances: Promo film clip
- Single is edited version of album track.
- Wings drummer Steve Holly debuts with the group in the promo film clip.

"Within You, Without You"
Written by: George Harrison
Recorded by: The Beatles
Lead singer: George
Year first released: 1967
Record label: Parlophone (Britain); Capitol (U.S.)
Album: SGT. PEPPER'S LONELY HEARTS CLUB
       BAND
- George espouses his Indian philosophies accompanying himself on sitar. No other Beatle appears on this recording, which George composed at the home of friend, Klaus Voorman. Contrary to popular belief, the laughter heard at the conclusion of the cut was George's idea (not the other Beatles) in order to break the serious mood created by the song.

"Without Her"
Written by: Sorrells Pickard
Recorded by: Ringo
Lead singer: Ringo
Year first released: 1970
Record label: Apple
Album: BEAUCOUPS OF BLUES

WITH THE BEATLES
Artist: The Beatles
Producer: George Martin
Year first released: 1963
Record label: Parlophone
Tracks: 14
    "It Won't Be Long"
    "All I've Got to Do"
    "All My Loving"
    "Don't Bother Me"
    "Little Child"
    "Till There Was You"
    "Please Mr. Postman"
    "Roll Over Beethoven"
    "Hold Me Tight"
    "You Really Got a Hold on Me"
    "I Wanna Be Your Man"
    "Devil in Her Heart"
    "Not a Second Time"
    "Money"
- British release.

"Woman"
McCartney song recorded by Peter and Gordon.

WOMAN
Mike McGear album which displays a portrait of Paul and Mike's mother on the cover.

"Woman Don't You Cry"
Written by: George Harrison
Recorded by: George
Lead singer: George
Year first released: 1976
Record label: Dark Horse
Album: 33⅓
Single: B side of "It's What You Value" in Britain

"Woman Is the Nigger of the World"
Written by: John Lennon and Yoko Ono
Recorded by: John and Yoko plus Elephant's Memory
       Band
Lead singer: John
Year first released: 1972
Record label: Apple
Album: SOMETIME IN NEW YORK CITY
Single: Britain and U.S.
Performances: One to One Concert, 1972
       "Dick Cavett Show" (TV), May, 1972
- This song was banned from the airwaves due to the derogatory slang in the title. John composed the song after his consciousness had been raised concerning women's rights.

"Woman of the Night"
Written by: Sorrells Pickard
Recorded by: Ringo
Lead singer: Ringo
Year first released: 1970
Record label: Apple
Album: BEAUCOUPS OF BLUES
- First pressing was misprinted on the label titled "Women of the Night." The mistake was corrected in the 1978 pressing.

Wonder, Stevie
Musician/composer who costarred with John and Yoko at the 1972 One to One concert. In 1973 Paul dedicated RED ROSE SPEEDWAY to Stevie Wonder, with the message "We love you, Stevie," printed in braille on the album's back cover.

"Wonderful Christmastime"
Written by: Paul McCartney
Recorded by: Paul
Lead singer: Paul
Year first released: 1979
Record label: Parlophone (Britain); Columbia (U.S.)
Single: Britain and U.S.

Performances: 1979 Wings British Tour
Promo film clip
• When this song was performed in concert, artificial snow fell over the stage.

WONDERWALL MUSIC
Artist: George Harrison
Producer: George
Year first released: 1968
Record label: Apple
Tracks: 12
 "Microbes"
 "Red Lady Too"
 "Tabla and Pakavaj/In the Park"
 "Drilling a Home/Guru Vandana"
 "Greasy Legs/Ski-ing and Gat Kirwani/Dream Scene"
 "Party Seacombe"
 "Love Scene/Crying"
 "Cowboy Museum"
 "Fantasy Sequins/Glass Box"
 "On the Bed"
 "Wonderwall to Be Here"
 "Singing Om"
• First album to be released on Apple Records.
• George composed this soundtrack for the movie *Wonderwall*.

"Wonderwall to Be Here"
Written by: George Harrison
Recorded by: George
Lead singer: None (Instrumental)
Year first released: 1968
Record label: Apple
Album: WONDERWALL

Wood, Charles
Coauthor of the screenplay for *Help!* and *How I Won the War*.

Wood, Ron
Musician who cowrote the song "Far East Man" with George Harrison. Wood also appears on George's DARK HORSE album. George and Paul also helped on Wood's album I'VE GOT MY OWN ALBUM TO DO.

Wood, Susan
Photographer of the front cover of the album UNFINISHED MUSIC NO. 2: LIFE WITH THE LIONS.

Wooler, Bob
Disc jockey at Liverpool's Cavern Club in the sixties. Wooler became a close friend of The Beatles during their early years and helped line up many bookings for them. In 1961 Wooler was brought along by John for moral support when The Beatles signed their contract with Brian Epstein. Ironically, Wooler was later involved in a lawsuit with John when he sued John for the injuries he sustained from a beating John gave him during a fight in 1963. The matter was settled with a £200 fee and an apology by John.

Woolton Parish Church
Liverpool church where John and Paul first met at a village fete on June 15, 1955. John and his school band, The Quarrymen, were performing at the function when a mutual friend, Ivan Vaughn, brought Paul along to see the group. Paul was impressed by the slick style of the sideburned, slightly drunk John. John remembers being impressed with Paul's guitar playing backstage and the fact that he resembled Elvis Presley.

"Word, The"
Written by: Lennon/McCartney
Recorded by: The Beatles
Lead singer: John
Year first released: 1965
Record label: Parlophone (Britain); Capitol (U.S.)
Album: RUBBER SOUL
• Predecessor to the genre of "love and peace" songs which flourished in the late sixties.

"Words of Love"
Written by: Buddy Holly
Recorded by: The Beatles
Lead singer: John and Paul
Year first released: 1964
Record label: Parlophone (Britain); Capitol (U.S.)
Album: BEATLES FOR SALE
   BEATLES VI
   LOVE SONGS
EP: BEATLES FOR SALE (NO. 2)
• Imitation is the greatest form of flattery.

"Working Class Hero"
Written by: John Lennon
Recorded by: John
Lead singer: John
Year first released: 1970
Record label: Apple
Album: JOHN LENNON/PLASTIC ONO BAND
Single: B side of "Imagine" (Britain)
• Another song to be banned or censored due to the profanities included in the lyrics of the song. The song is a scathing comment on the complacency of the masses.
• In 1971, *Rolling Stone* titled their in-depth interview with John "The Working Class Hero."

"World of Stone"
Written by: George Harrison
Recorded by: George

Lead singer: George
Year first released: 1975
Record label: Apple
Album: EXTRA TEXTURE
Single: B side of "You"

World Wild Life Fund
Charity organization to which The Beatles donated their recording "Across the Universe." The song appears on the album NO ONE'S GONNA CHANGE OUR WORLD.

"World without Love"
Lennon/McCartney composition which was the first hit record for Peter and Gordon.

Wright, Gary
Musician who appears on the albums ALL THINGS MUST PASS, LIVING IN THE MATERIAL WORLD, EXTRA TEXTURE, DARK HORSE, and 33⅓. Wright cowrote the song "If You Believe" with George and appears on the album GEORGE HARRISON.

On November 23, 1971, Gary Wright appeared on the Dick Cavett television show and performed his song "Two-faced Man" with George's accompaniment on guitar. George also appears on Wright's albums FOOTPRINT and THAT WAS ONLY YESTERDAY.

Wright, Maggie
Actress who portrayed the "Lovely Starlet" in the *Magical Mystery Tour* film.

Y

Yakus, Shelly
Coengineer of John's IMAGINE, WALLS AND BRIDGES, and ROCK 'N' ROLL albums.

Yardbirds, The
Group that appeared on The Beatles' 1964 Christmas Shows. They also performed on the bill with The Beatles for their final British concert (New Musical Express Poll Winner's Concert) in May 1966.

YA, YA
EP released by Polydor in 1962 consisting of the German recordings of The Beatles backing singer Tony Sheridan. The record includes four tracks, on which The Beatles (billed as The Beat Brothers) appear on only one: "Sweet Georgia Brown."

"Ya, Ya"
Written by: Morris Robinson, Clarence Lewis, and Lee Dorsey
Recorded by: John
Lead singer: John
Year first released: 1974
Record label: Apple
Album: WALLS AND BRIDGES
ROCK 'N' ROLL
- John first recorded this song as an impromptu jam, with his eleven-year-old son Julian sitting in on drums, for his WALLS AND BRIDGES album.
- John rerecorded this song with studio musicians for its inclusion on his oldies album, ROCK 'N' ROLL.

Year One
Name bestowed on the year 1970 by John and Yoko in their quest for world peace. On January 25, 1970 the couple sheared their heads to coincide with the announcement. The profits raised from the sale of their locks were donated to the Panther Movement.

"Years Roll Along, The"
Unreleased Beatles recording, circa 1962.

"Yellow Submarine"
Written by: Lennon/McCartney
Recorded by: The Beatles
Lead singer: Ringo
Year first released: 1966
Record label: Parlophone (Britain); Capitol (U.S.)
Album: REVOLVER
A COLLECTION OF BEATLES OLDIES
YELLOW SUBMARINE
THE BEATLES 1962–1966
Single: Britain and U.S.

- Voices of friends and family can be heard in the back-up chorus.
- The aquatic effects were created by George as he swished around a tub of water.
- In 1968 the song was released on Apple as an instrumental, recorded by the Black Dyke Mills Brass Band.

Yellow Submarine
Ninety-minute animated film based on the Lennon/McCartney song of the same name. Released in 1968 by United Artists; written by Lee Minoff, Al Brodax, Jack Mendelsohn, and Erich Segal; produced by Al Brodax; directed by George Dunning. The musical score consists of Beatle recordings and orchestrated compositions by George Martin.

Film notes:

- Though The Beatles were not actively involved with the production, they did make an appearance in the final sequence.
- The Beatles originally authorized the film under the misconception that the movie would fulfill their obligation to United Artists as the third film in their three-film contract. It was later realized that the company still required a feature film *starring* The Beatles.
- The movie premiere took place at the London Pavilion on July 17, 1968, with The Beatles in attendance.

YELLOW SUBMARINE
Artist: The Beatles
Producer: George Martin
Year first released: 1969
Record label: Apple
Tracks: 12
"Yellow Submarine"
"Only a Northern Song"
"All Together Now"
"Hey Bulldog"
"It's All Too Much"
"All You Need Is Love"
"Pepperland"
"Medley: Sea of Time and Sea of Holes"
"Sea of Monsters"
"March of the Meanies"
"Pepperland Laid Waste"
"Yellow Submarine in Pepperland"
- Soundtrack album for the movie *Yellow Submarine.*
- "Hey Bulldog" is the only song which does not appear in the U.S. version of the movie.

Yellow Submarine
Paperback book, based on the screenplay, written by Max Wilk; published by Signet in 1968.

Yellow Submarine Gift Book
Hardcover book of photos and dialogue from the movie; published by World Publishing in 1968.

"Yellow Submarine in Pepperland"
George Martin's instrumental arrangement of The Beatles' "Yellow Submarine." It appears in the *Yellow Submarine* film and on the soundtrack album.

"Yer Blues"
Written by: Lennon/McCartney
Recorded by: The Beatles
Lead singer: John
Year first released: 1968
Record label: Apple
Album: THE BEATLES
   LIVE PEACE IN TORONTO
Performances: John and the Plastic Ono Band at the
     Toronto Rock 'N' Roll Revival
     Concert, 1969
• This was the only Beatles song John included in his repertoire at the Toronto music festival.

"Yes It Is"
Written by: Lennon/McCartney
Recorded by: The Beatles
Lead singer: John
Year first released: 1965
Record label: Parlophone (Britain); Capitol (U.S.)
Album: BEATLES VI
   LOVE SONGS
   THE BEATLES RARITIES (Britain)
Single: B side of "Ticket to Ride"

"Yesterday"
Written by: Lennon/McCartney
Recorded by: The Beatles
Lead singer: Paul
Year first released: 1965
Record label: Parlophone (Britain); Capitol (U.S.)
Album: HELP! (Britain)
   "YESTERDAY" ... AND TODAY
   A COLLECTION OF BEATLES OLDIES
   THE BEATLES 1962–1966
   LOVE SONGS
   WINGS OVER AMERICA
EP: YESTERDAY
Single: U.S.; Britain (1976)
Performances: "Ed Sullivan Show" (TV), September
     1965
     1966 Summer World Tour
     "James Paul McCartney" TV show,
     1973
     1975–76 Wings' World Tour
     1979 Wings' British Tour
• Paul first composed the melody for the song, ad-libbing the lyrics "scrambled eggs" to his piano accompaniment.

• This song is cited by Paul as his personal favorite, and it has become the Beatle composition most recorded by other artists.

YESTERDAY (EP)
Artist: The Beatles
Producer: George Martin
Year first released: 1966
Record label: Parlophone
Tracks: 4
   "Yesterday"
   "Act Naturally"
   "You Like Me Too Much"
   "It's Only Love"

"YESTERDAY" ... AND TODAY
Artist: The Beatles
Producer: George Martin
Year first released: 1966
Record label: Capitol
Tracks: 11
   "Drive My Car"
   "I'm Only Sleeping"
   "Nowhere Man"
   "Dr. Robert"
   "Yesterday"
   "Act Naturally"
   "And Your Bird Can Sing"
   "If I Needed Someone"
   "We Can Work It Out"
   "What Goes On"
   "Day Tripper"
• Album created by Capitol for U.S. distribution compiled from various British releases.
• The original cover photograph ("butcher cover"), depicting The Beatles as butchers, strewn with mutilated dolls' bodies, was The Beatles' symbolism for their feelings about the chopped and mutilated album released by Capitol. They did not feel the production, slopped together from numerous sources, adequately represented their musical position at the time of release.
• The album cover was soon pulled off the shelves due to a public controversy over the "distasteful" picture and the photo was replaced by a more subdued pose. The original cover has since become a collector's item. The "butcher" photo later appeared on the Capitol album THE BEATLES RARITIES.

Yesterday Seems So Far Away
Book written by John Swenson; published by Zebra in 1977.

YOKO ONO/PLASTIC ONO BAND
Yoko album produced by John and Yoko and released on Apple in 1970. The front and back covers of the

album are identical in design to John's JOHN LENNON/PLASTIC ONO BAND.

"Yoko Plus Me"
Yoko's first art exhibit, which was financed by John in September 1967. Held at the Lisson Gallery in London, the show consisted of designs of half-finished furniture. In order to conceal their friendship from the public, John chose not to attend the exhibit.

Yolland, Peter
Producer of The Beatles' 1963 and 1964 Christmas Shows.

"You"
Written by: George Harrison
Recorded by: George
Lead singer: George
Year first released: 1975
Record label: Apple
Album: EXTRA TEXTURE
         THE BEST OF GEORGE HARRISON
Single: Britain and U.S.
· George wrote this song in 1970 with the intention of having Ronnie Spector record it. Since that recording never materialized, George decided to record it himself.

"You Always Hurt the One You Love"
Written by: Allan Roberts and Doris Fisher
Recorded by: Ringo
Lead singer: Ringo
Year first released: 1970
Record label: Apple
Album: SENTIMENTAL JOURNEY

"You and Me (Babe)"
Written by: George Harrison and Mal Evans
Recorded by: Ringo
Lead singer: Ringo
Year first released: 1973
Record label: Apple
Album: RINGO
· On this song, which closes the album, Ringo recites the names of all the people involved in the production of the album.

"You Are Here"
Written by: John Lennon
Recorded by: John
Lead singer: John
Year first released: 1973
Record label: Apple
Album: MIND GAMES

· Also the title of John's art exhibit at the Robert Frazier Gallery in 1968.

"You Can't Catch Me"
Written by: Chuck Berry
Recorded by: John
Lead singer: John
Year first released: 1975
Record label: Apple
Album: ROCK 'N' ROLL
· One of the two Berry songs which John recorded in payment of a plagiarism suit filed against him. (See "Come Together.")

"You Can't Do That"
Written by: Lennon/McCartney
Recorded by: The Beatles
Lead singer: John
Year first released: 1964
Record label: Parlophone (Britain); Capitol (U.S.)
Album: A HARD DAY'S NIGHT (Britain)
         THE BEATLES SECOND ALBUM
         ROCK AND ROLL MUSIC
Single: B side of "Can't Buy Me Love"
Performances: "Ed Sullivan Show" (TV), May 1964
                1964 North American Summer Tour
· John is featured as lead guitarist on this track.
· A twelve-string guitar is used for the first time on a Beatles song on this number.

"You Don't Know Me at All"
Written by: Dave Jordan
Recorded by: Ringo
Lead singer: Ringo
Year first released: 1976
Record label: Polydor (Britain); Atlantic (U.S.)
Album: RINGO'S ROTOGRAVURE
Performances: Promo film clip

"You Gave Me the Answer"
Written by: Paul McCartney
Recorded by: Wings
Lead singer: Paul
Year first released: 1975
Record label: Parlophone (Britain); Capitol (U.S.)
Album: VENUS AND MARS
         WINGS OVER AMERICA
Single: B side of "Letting Go"
Performances: 1975–76 Wings' World Tour
· Paul usually dedicated this number to Fred Astaire when Wings performed the song on tour.

"You Give Me Joy Joy"
Doris Troy song written by George, Ringo, Doris Troy, and Stephen Stills. It appears on the album DORIS TROY.

"You Know I Love You, Baby"
Song John performed along with Frank Zappa and the Mothers of Invention at Zappa's concert at the Fillmore East in June 1971.

"You Know My Name (Look Up the Number)"
Written by: Lennon/McCartney
Recorded by: The Beatles
Lead singer: John and Paul
Year first released: 1970
Record label: Apple
Album: THE BEATLES RARITIES
Single: B side of "Let It Be"
• This cabaret-style song was recorded in 1967 and features Brian Jones on alto sax.

"You Like Me Too Much"
Written by: George Harrison
Recorded by: The Beatles
Lead singer: George
Year first released: 1965
Record label: Parlophone (Britain); Capitol (U.S.)
Album: HELP! (Britain)
      BEATLES VI
EP: YESTERDAY

"You Never Give Me Your Money"
Written by: Lennon/McCartney
Recorded by: The Beatles
Lead singer: Paul
Year first released: 1969
Record label: Apple
Album: ABBEY ROAD
• Reference to the money hassles Paul and The Beatles were experiencing at the time.

Young, Paul
Author of the book *The Lennon Factor*.

"Youngblood"
Leiber, Stoller, and Pomus song, which The Beatles performed on "Pop Go The Beatles" radio show in June 1963. At the Concert for Bangla Desh, in 1971, Leon Russell performed this song in medley with "Jumpin' Jack Flash."

Young Island
Vacation point in the West Indies for John, Cynthia, Ringo, and Maureen in 1965.

"You Really Got a Hold on Me"
Written by: William Robinson
Recorded by: The Beatles
Lead singer: John
Year first released: 1963

Record label: Parlophone (Britain); Capitol (U.S.)
Album: WITH THE BEATLES
      THE BEATLES SECOND ALBUM
Performances: *Let It Be* movie

"You're Gonna Lose that Girl"
Written by: Lennon/McCartney
Recorded by: The Beatles
Lead singer: John
Year first released: 1965
Record label: Parlophone (Britain); Capitol (U.S.)
Album: HELP!
      LOVE SONGS
Performances: *Help!* movie

"You're Sixteen"
Written by: Richard Sherman and Robert Sherman
Recorded by: Ringo
Lead singer: Ringo
Year first released: 1973
Record label: Apple
Album: RINGO
      BLAST FROM YOUR PAST
Single: Britain and U.S.
Performances: "Ringo" TV special, 1978
• Kazoo accompaniment courtesy of Paul. When producer Richard Perry played the tapes of the RINGO album to Paul, Paul recorded the kazoo bit, adding what he thought was the needed dimension to the song.

"Your Feet's Too Big"
Song which was included in The Beatles early repertoire and which was sung at their 1962 audition for Parlophone Records. It also appears on the album THE BEATLES LIVE AT THE STAR CLUB, with Paul as lead vocalist.

"Your Love Is Forever"
Written by: George Harrison
Recorded by: George
Lead singer: George
Year first released: 1979
Record label: Dark Horse
Album: GEORGE HARRISON

"Your Mother Should Know"
Written by: Lennon/McCartney
Recorded by: The Beatles
Lead singer: Paul
Year first released: 1967
Record label: Parlophone (Britain); Capitol (U.S.)
Album: MAGICAL MYSTERY TOUR
EP: MAGICAL MYSTERY TOUR
Performances: *Magical Mystery Tour* film

"You've Got to Hide Your Love Away"
Written by: Lennon/McCartney
Recorded by: The Beatles
Lead singer: John
Year first released: 1965
Record label: Parlophone (Britain); Capitol (U.S.)
Album: HELP!
        THE BEATLES 1962–1966
        LOVE SONGS
Performances: *Help!* movie
• One of John's songs which was influenced by Bob
  Dylan.

"You've Got to Stay with Me"
Unreleased song written by George in 1972 for Cilla
Black.

"You Won't See Me"
Written by: Lennon/McCartney
Recorded by: The Beatles
Lead singer: Paul
Year first released: 1965
Record label: Parlophone (Britain); Capitol (U.S.)
Album: RUBBER SOUL
EP: NOWHERE MAN

Z

Zappa, Frank

Musician who heads the group the Mothers of Invention. On June 6, 1971, John and Yoko joined Zappa on stage at the Fillmore East, where they performed a few numbers together. Their performance was recorded and appears on the album SOMETIME IN NEW YORK CITY. The four numbers appearing on the album are "Well . . . Baby Please Don't Go," "Jamrag," "Scumbag" (written by John, Yoko, and Zappa), and "Au."

Zappa is also responsible for the movie *200 Motels,* in which Ringo played the parts of Zappa and Larry the Dwarf.

Zapple

Division of Apple Records set up to distribute experimental music records. John's UNFINISHED MUSIC No. 2: LIFE WITH THE LIONS and George's ELECTRONIC SOUNDS were released on Zapple. Another Zapple artist was poet Richard Brautigan. Zapple Records was dissolved after one year.

"Zoo Gang"

Written by: Paul McCartney
Recorded by: Wings
Lead singer: Paul
Year first released: 1974
Record label: Apple
Single: B side of "Band on the Run" in Britain

- Song was written as the theme song to a television show of the same name.

PLEASE PLEASE ME,
Parlophone, 1963.

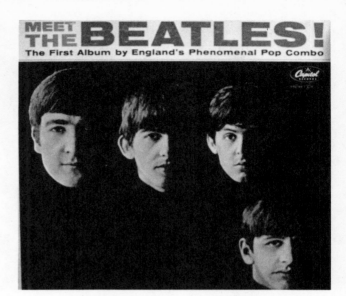

MEET THE BEATLES,
Capitol, 1964.

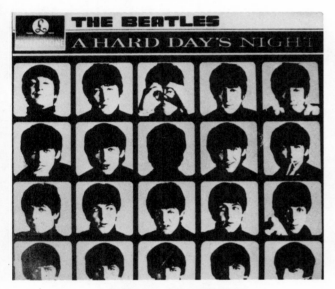

A HARD DAY'S NIGHT,
Parlophone, 1964.

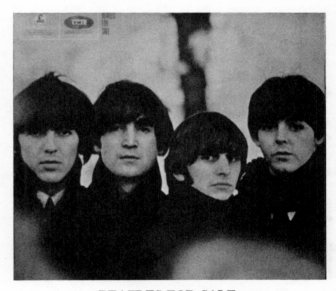

BEATLES FOR SALE,
Parlophone, 1964.

HELP!,
Capitol, 1965.

RUBBER SOUL,
Capitol, 1965.

YESTERDAY AND TODAY,
Capitol, 1966.

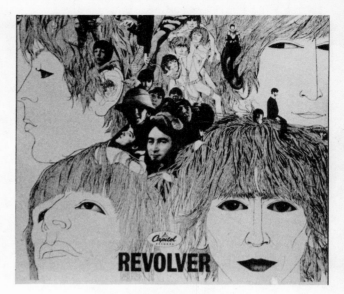

REVOLVER,
Capitol, 1966.

SGT. PEPPER'S LONELY HEARTS CLUB BAND,
Capitol, 1967.

MAGICAL MYSTERY TOUR,
Capitol, 1967.

UNFINISHED MUSIC NO. 1 TWO VIRGINS,
Tetragrammation, 1968.

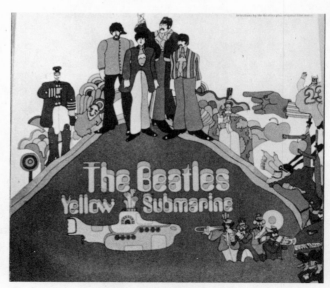

YELLOW SUBMARINE,
Apple, 1969.

ABBEY ROAD,
Apple, 1969.

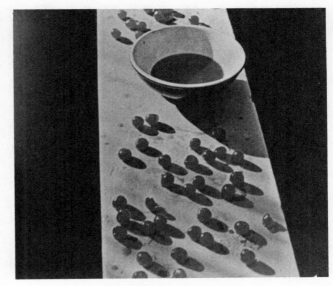

McCARTNEY,
Apple, 1970.

IN THE BEGINNING,
Polydor, 1970.

LET IT BE,
Apple, 1970.

ALL THINGS MUST PASS,
Apple, 1970.

JOHN LENNON/PLASTIC ONO BAND,
Apple, 1970.

THE BEATLES CHRISTMAS ALBUM,
Apple, 1970.

RINGO,
Apple, 1973.

BAND ON THE RUN,
Apple, 1973.

WALLS AND BRIDGES,
Apple, 1974.

ROCK 'N' ROLL,
Apple, 1975.

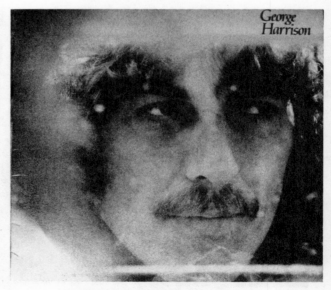

GEORGE HARRISON,
Dark Horse, 1979.

Tours

1960
The Silver Beatles tour Scotland for two weeks backing singer Johnny Gentle.
August–December: Hamburg, Germany; The Indra, the Kaiserkeller, and the Top Ten.

1961
March–July: Hamburg, Germany; Top Ten Club
Summer–Winter: Liverpool; The Cavern

1962
April–June: Hamburg, Germany; The Star Club
Summer–Fall: Northern England
December 10: On the bill with Frank Ifield (Peterborough, Embassy Theatre)
Mid-December: Hamburg, Germany; Star Club

1963
February 2–March 3: On the bill with Helen Shapiro tour of Britain
March 9–May 15: On the bill of the Chris Montez and Tommy Roe tour of Britain
May 18–October 18: Britain
October 24–October 29: Sweden
November 1–December 14: Britain

1964
January 16–February 4: Paris
February 11–February 12: Mini-tour of America
March 30–May 31: England and Scotland
June 4–August 16: Hong Kong, Denmark, Australia, New Zealand, Sweden, and Britain
August 19–September 20: America
October 9–November 10: Britain

1965
June 20–July 13: France, Italy, and Spain
August 15–August 31: America
December 3–December 12: Britain

1966
June 24–July 4: Germany, Japan, and the Philippines
August 12–August 29: America

1969
March 2: John and Yoko—Cambridge, England at Lady Mitchell Hall
September 13: John Lennon/Plastic Ono Band—Toronto Rock 'n' Roll Revival Concert, Varsity Stadium
December 5–December 15: Delaney and Bonnie tour—joined by George, Britain

1971
June 6: John and Yoko—join Frank Zappa on stage at New York's Fillmore East
August 1: The Concert for Bangla Desh (2 shows), featuring George Harrison and Ringo Starr at New York's Madison Square Garden
December 11: John and Yoko—Benefit for John Sinclair, Ann Arbor, Michigan

1972
February 9–February 23: Wings' University Tour of Britain
July 9–August 24: Wings Over Europe Tour
August 30: John and Yoko—headline One to One Concert (2 shows) at New York's Madison Square Garden

1973
March 18: Wings' benefit concert for Release at London's Hard Rock Cafe.
May 11–July 10: Wings' British Tour

1974
November 2–December 20: George's North American Dark Horse Tour

1975
September 9–November 14: Wings' tour of Britain and Australia

1976
March 20–March 26: Wings' European Tour
May 3–June 23: Wings Over America Tour
September 19–September 27: Four more European dates for Wings: Vienna, Yugoslavia, Italy, and Germany
October 19–October 21: Wings' concerts at Wembley, Empire Pool, England

1979
November 23–December 29: Wings' British Tour

Beatles Special Performances

Welcome Home Concert, December 27, 1960, Litherland Town Hall
  One-night performance upon the Beatles' return from their first trip to Hamburg, Germany.

Welcome Home Concert, June 9, 1962, Cavern Club
  Celebration upon return from The Beatles' third trip to Germany.

New Musical Express Poll Winners Concert, April 21, 1963, Wembley Empire Pool

Charity Concert for the National Society for the Prevention of Cruelty to Children, June 12, 1963, Grafton Ballroom

Final Concert at The Cavern Club, August 3, 1963

Sunday Night at the London Palladium, October 13, 1963
  First signs of Beatlemania were surfacing when hysterical fans lined up outside the theatre to catch a glimpse of The Beatles. The Beatles made the front page of the newspapers the following day. This performance was broadcast live on British TV.

Royal Variety Performance, November 4, 1963, Prince of Wales Theatre
  The Queen and other members of the Royal Family viewed the show.

Southern Fan Club Convention, December 14, 1963, Wimbledon Palais
  The Beatles performed for one half hour for three thousand fans and then mingled with the crowd.

The Beatles' Christmas Shows:
  December 21, 1963, Bradford Gaumont
  December 22, 1963, Liverpool Empire

December 24–January 11, 1964, Finsbury Park Astoria Theatre
  Shows consisted of comedy sketches and musical performances. Others on the bill were the Baron Knights with Duke D'mond, Tommy Quickly, The Fourmost, Billy J. Kramer and the Dakotas, Cilla Black and Rolf Harris. The Beatles performed nine numbers.

New Musical Express Poll Winners Concert, April 26, 1964, Wembley Stadium

Pops Alive, May 31, 1964, Prince of Wales Theatre

Night of 100 Stars (charity show), July 23, 1964, London Palladium

Charity Concert for Cerebral Palsy, September 20, 1964, Paramount Theatre (N.Y.)
  The Beatles participated in this charity concert during their second tour of America.

The Beatles' Christmas Shows, December 24, 1964–January 16, 1965, Hammersmith Odeon, London
  The Beatles again perform a few comedy skits (as they did for their previous Christmas Shows) and several musical numbers (8). The shows were performed twice nightly. Appearing on the bill with The Beatles were Freddie and the Dreamers, the Yardbirds, Elkie Brooks, Jimmy Saville, Mike Haslam, The Mike Cotton Sound, and Sounds Incorporated.

New Musical Express Poll Winners Concert, April 11, 1965, Wembley Stadium

New Musical Express Poll Winners Concert, May 1, 1966, Wembley Stadium
  This was to become The Beatles' last scheduled performance in Britain.

Rooftop Concert, January 30, 1969, Apple Building, 3 Saville Row
  Last public Beatles performance.

Various Television Appearances

1959—"Discoveries"—John, Paul, and George appear as Johnny and the Moondogs. Aired locally. (U.K.)

October 17, 1962—"People and Places"—First TV appearance by The Beatles. Aired in Manchester. (U.K.)

January 11, 1963—"Thank Your Lucky Stars"—Beatles' first national TV appearance. (U.K.)

April 16, 1963—"6.25 Show" (U.K.)

May 17, 1963—"Pops and Lennie" (U.K.)

June 29, 1963—"Thank Your Lucky Stars" (U.K.)

June 29, 1963—"Juke Box Jury"—John appears on the panel. (U.K.)

August 19, 1963—"Scene at 6:30" (U.K.)

September 7, 1963—"Big Night Out" (U.K.)

October 9, 1963—"The Mersey Beat"—Aired in London and Northern England (U.K.). Aired in rest of country November 13, 1963.

October 13, 1963—"Sunday Night at the London Palladium" (U.K.)

October 26, 1963—"Thank Your Lucky Stars" (U.K.)

November 10, 1963—"Royal Variety Performance" (U.K.)

December 7, 1963—"Juke Box Jury"—Beatles appear on panel. (U.K.)

December 22, 1963—"Thank Your Lucky Stars" (U.K.)

January 3, 1964—"Jack Paar Show"—Beatles' first TV appearance in America. Clips from a Beatles performance were shown. (U.S.)

January 12, 1964—"Sunday Night at the London Palladium" (U.K.)

February 9, 1964—"Ed Sullivan Show"—Beatles' first live appearance in the U.S. (U.S.)

February 16, 1964—"Ed Sullivan Show"—Beatles performed live from Miami. (U.S.)

February 23, 1964—"Ed Sullivan Show" (U.S.)

March 20, 1964—"Ready, Steady, Go" (U.K.)

March 25, 1964—"Top of the Pops" (U.K.)

April 18, 1964—"Morecambe and Wise Show" (U.K.)

May 6, 1964—"Around The Beatles" (U.K.)

May 24, 1964—"Ed Sullivan Show"—Film of Beatles on set of *A Hard Day's Night*. (U.S.)

July 8, 1964—"Top of the Pops" (U.K.)

July 11, 1964—"Thank Your Lucky Stars" (U.K.)

July 12, 1964—"Ed Sullivan Show" (U.S.)

July 15, 1964—"Road to Beatlemania" (U.K.)

July 25, 1964—"Juke Box Jury"—George on panel. (U.K.)

August 1, 1964—"Juke Box Jury"—Ringo on panel. (U.K.)

August 3, 1964—"Follow The Beatles—Beatles making *A Hard Day's Night.*" (U.K.)

September 20, 1964—"Ed Sullivan Show" (U.S.)

October 16, 1964—"Ready, Steady, Go"—Beatles appear live. (U.K.)

November 11, 1964—"Thank Your Lucky Stars" (U.K.)

November 27, 1964—"Ready, Steady, Go" (U.K.)

December 3, 1964—"Top of the Pops" (U.K.)

December 9, 1964—"Top of the Pops" (U.K.)

January 9, 1965—"Not Only . . . But Also"—John reads poetry. (U.K.)

January 20, 1965—"Shindig"—Beatles perform three songs. (U.S.)

April 3, 1965—"Thank Your Lucky Stars" (U.K.)

April 11, 1965—"Eamonn Andrews Show" (U.K.)

April 15, 1965—"Top of the Pops" (U.K.)

April 16, 1965—"Ready Steady Goes Live"—John and George interviewed. (U.K.)

April 18, 1965—"New Musical Express Poll Winners Concert" (U.K.)

June 18, 1965—"Tonight"—John appears to promote *A Spaniard in the Works.* (U.K.)

June 24, 1965—"Today"—John plugs his book. (U.S.)

July 3, 1965—"World of Books"—John promotes book. (U.K.)

July 17, 1965—"Thank Your Lucky Stars" (U.K.)

August 1, 1965—"Blackpool Night Out" (U.K.)

September 12, 1965—"Ed Sullivan Show" (U.S.)

December 2, 1965—"Top of the Pops" (U.K.)

December 4, 1965—"Thank Your Lucky Stars" (U.K.)

December 17, 1965—"The Music of Lennon and McCartney" (U.K.)

March 1, 1966—"The Beatles at Shea Stadium" (U.K.)

June 9, 1966—"Top of the Pops" (U.K.)

June 16, 1966—"Top of the Pops"—Beatles make surprise live appearance. (U.K.)

June 18, 1966—"Thank Your Lucky Stars" (U.K.)

December 26, 1966—"Not Only . . . But Also"—John appears in a skit. (U.K.)

January 10, 1967—"The Beatles at Shea Stadium" (U.S.)

February 9, 1967—"Top of the Pops"—Promo clips for "Penny Lane"/"Strawberry Fields Forever." (U.K.)

February 25, 1967—"Hollywood Palace"—Promos for "Penny Lane"/"Strawberry Fields Forever." (U.S.)

June 25, 1967—"Our World"—International live broadcast of The Beatles recording "All You Need Is Love."

September 29, 1967—"The Frost Programme"—John and George discuss meditation. (U.K.)

December 26, 1967—*Magical Mystery Tour*—Shown in black and white. (U.K.)

December 27, 1967—"The Frost Programme"—Paul talks about *Magical Mystery Tour*. (U.K.)

January 5, 1968—*Magical Mystery Tour*—In color. (U.K.)

February 6, 1968—"Cilla"—Ringo guests. (U.K.)

March 30, 1968—"Hollywood Palace"—"Lady Madonna" promo film clip. (U.S.)

May 14, 1968—"Tonight Show"—John and Paul appear to talk about Apple. (U.S.)

May 15, 1968—"Newsfront"—John and Paul talk about Apple and politics. (U.S.)

May 22, 1968—"Newsfront"—Repeat of previous week's appearance. (U.S.)

June 22, 1968—"Release"—John interviewed. (U.K.)

September 8, 1968—"Frost on Sunday"—Beatles perform "Hey Jude" and "Revolution." (U.K.)

September 14, 1968—"All My Loving"—Documentary. (U.K.)

October 6, 1968—"Smothers Brothers Comedy Hour"—George makes a surprise appearance to introduce film for "Hey Jude." (U.S.)

October 13, 1968—"Smothers Brothers Comedy Hour"—"Revolution" film clip. (U.S.)

February 23, 1969—"David Frost Show"—Paul introduces Mary Hopkin. (U.S.)

February 23, 1970—"Laugh In"—Ringo appears in a few comedy skits. (U.S.)

April 9, 1970—"London Weekend"—Paul appears. (U.K.)

September 22, 1970—"Dick Cavett Show"—John and Yoko are guests. (U.S.)

November 23, 1971—"Dick Cavett Show"—George guests. (U.S.)

December 3, 1971—"David Frost Show"—George guests. (U.S.)

January 13, 1972—"David Frost Show"—John and Yoko guest. (U.S.)

February 21–25, 1972—"Mike Douglas Show"—John and Yoko act as cohosts. (U.S.)

April 4, 1972—"Dick Cavett Show"—John and Yoko are guests. (U.S.)

May 11, 1972—"Dick Cavett Show"—John and Yoko appear. (U.S.)

May 11, 1972—"John and Yoko in Syracuse, N.Y."—Taped from Yoko's art exhibit at the Everson Museum. (U.S.)

June 28, 1972—"Top of the Pops"—Wings' promo for "Mary Had a Little Lamb." (U.K.)

September 4, 1972—"Jerry Lewis Telethon for Muscular Dystrophy"—John and Yoko (with Elephant's Memory) perform live. (U.S.)

October 12, 1972—"Flip Wilson Show"—Promo for "Mary Had A Little Lamb." (U.S.)

December 15, 1972—"One to One Concert" (U.S.)

April 16, 1973—"James Paul McCartney" (U.S.)

May 10, 1973—"James Paul McCartney" (U.K.)

December 1973—"Wonderful World of Disney"—Paul and Linda are hosts of Christmas show. (U.K.)

November 21, 1974—"Top of the Pops"—Promo for "Junior's Farm," and Wings perform with David Essex. (U.K.)

March 1, 1975—"Grammy Awards"—John is a guest presenter. (U.S.)

March 26, 1975—"*Tommy* Movie Premiere"—David Frost talks with Paul and Linda. (U.S.)

April 28, 1975—"Smothers Brothers Comedy Hour"—Ringo guests. (U.S.)

April 28, 1975—"Tomorrow"—John is the only guest. (U.S.)

May 21, 1975—"Beatles Special with Host David Frost." (U.S.)

June 13, 1975—"Salute to Lew Grade"—John performs. (U.S.)

June 28, 1976—"Goodnight America"—Paul and Linda (and Wings) are guests. (U.S.)

November 20, 1976—"Saturday Night Live"—George performs and presents promo film clips. (U.S.)

February 19, 1977—"Grammy Awards"—Ringo (with Nilsson) is a guest presenter. (U.S.)

December 9, 1977—"Midnight Special"—Promo for "Mull of Kintyre." (U.S.)

December 25, 1977—"Mike Yarwood Show"—Paul guests and film for "Mull of Kintyre" is shown. (U.K.)

February 19, 1978—"All You Need Is Love"—TV special about The Beatles. (U.S.)

April 17, 1978—"Mike Douglas Show"—Ringo guests. (U.S.)

April 26, 1978—"Ringo"—Special for NBC TV. (U.S.)

April 1978—"Phil Donahue Show"—Ringo guests. (Syndicated) (U.S.)

October 6, 1978—"Everyday"—Ringo is interviewed. (U.S.)

March 16, 1978—"Wings Over the World" (U.S.)

April 6, 1979—"Midnight Special"—Promo for "Blow Away." (U.S.)

April 6, 1979—"Wings Over the World" (U.S.)

September 3, 1979—"Jerry Lewis Labor Day Telethon"—Ringo appears live and promo for "Getting Closer" is shown. (U.S.)

November 1, 1979—"20/20"—Paul interviewed. (U.S.)

November–December 1979—"Back to the Egg" (Syndicated) (U.S.)

December 20, 1979—"Tomorrow"—Paul and Linda are guests. (U.S.)

February 26, 1980—"British Rock and Pop Awards"—Paul appears. (U.K.)

Addresses

Able Label
17 Berkeley Street
London W1 England

Apple
29 St. James Street
London SW 1 England

Beatles Book Society
45 St. Mary's Road
Ealing, London W 5 5RQ England
Beatles Monthly Magazine

Beatlefan
Box 33515
Decatur, Georgia 30033
U.S.A.
(*Beatles fan magazine*)

Beatlefest National Headquarters
Box 436
Westwood, New Jersey
U.S.A.
(*Beatle fans' conventions*)

Capitol Records
1370 Ave. of the Americas
New York, N.Y. 10019
U.S.A.

Columbia Records/CBS Inc.
51 West 52nd Street
New York, N.Y. 10019
U.S.A.

Dark Horse Records
3300 Warner Blvd.
Burbank, California 91510
U.S.A.

EMI House
20 Manchester Square
London, England

EMI Recording Studios
3 Abbey Road, St. John's Wood
London, England

Lennon/Ono Music
Studio One
1 West 72nd Street
New York, N.Y. 10023

McCartney Productions Ltd.
1 Soho Square
London WIV 6QB England
(MPL Communications Ltd.)

McCartney Productions Ltd.
34 West 54th Street
New York, N.Y.
U.S.A.
(MPL Communications Inc.)

Portrait Records/CBS Inc
51 West 52nd Street
New York, N.Y. 10019
U.S.A.

Strawberry Fields Forever
c/o Joe Pope
310 Franklin Street #117
Boston, Massachusetts 02110
U.S.A.
(*Beatles fan magazine*)

Wings Fun Club–*Club Sandwich*
P.O. Box 4UP
London W1A 4UP England